P9-DCJ-640

Thomas D. Lynch

Florida Atlantic University

PUBLIC BUDGETING IN AMERICA

Second Edition

PRENTICE-HALL, INC., Englewood Cliffs, New Jersey 07632

Library of Congress Cataloging in Publication Data

Lynch, Thomas Dexter, 1942–
   Public budgeting in America.

   Bibliography: p.
   Includes index.
   1. Budget—United States. I. Title.
HJ2051.L93   1985   350.72′2′0973   84-11487
ISBN 0-13-737354-6

Editorial/production supervision: *Edith Riker*
Manufacturing buyer: *Ron Chapman*
Cover design: *Edsal Enterprises*

© 1985, 1979 by Prentice-Hall, Inc., Englewood Cliffs, New Jersey 07632

All rights reserved. No part of this book may be
reproduced, in any form or by any means,
without permission in writing from the publisher.

Printed in the United States of America

10 9 8 7 6 5 4 3 2 1

ISBN 0-13-737354-6   01

Prentice-Hall International, Inc., *London*
Prentice-Hall of Australia Pty. Limited, *Syndey*
Editora Prentice-Hall do Brasil, Ltda., *Rio de Janeiro*
Prentice-Hall Canada Inc., *Toronto*
Prentice-Hall of India Private Limited, *New Delhi*
Prentice-Hall of Japan, Inc., *Tokyo*
Prentice-Hall of Southeast Asia Pte. Ltd., *Singapore*
Whitehall Books Limited, *Wellington, New Zealand*

CONTENTS

350.72
L987p

PREFACE *vii*

CHAPTER ONE   **PUBLIC BUDGETING IN CONTEXT**   *1*

What is Public Budgeting? *2*
The Budget Cycle, *10*
Context of American Budgeting, *14*
Economic Influences on Budgeting, *22*
Monetary Policy, *25*
Fiscal Policy, *25*
Other Economic Topics, *32*

CHAPTER TWO   **TOWARD MODERN BUDGETING**   *35*

Prelude, *35*
Evolution, *38*
An Executive Focus, *46*
A Legislative Focus, *53*

CHAPTER THREE   **BUDGET BEHAVIOR**   *73*

Politics and Perspective, *73*
Strategies, *93*

CHAPTER FOUR   **BUDGET FORMATS AND PREPARATION**   *101*

Budget Format, *102*
Building the Budget, *105*
Budget Reviews, *110*
Legislative Adoption, *118*

CHAPTER FIVE   **ANALYSIS APPLIED TO**
                          BUDGETING   *131*

                          Theoretical Foundation, *132*
                          Application Difficulties, *135*
                          Data Measure Constraints, *137*
                          Elementary Analysis, *138*
                          Crosswalks, *141*
                          Revenue Forecasting, *143*
                          Expenditure Forecasting, *146*
                          Productivity Analysis, *149*
                          The Benefit-Cost Concept, *156*

CHAPTER SIX   **ANALYTICAL PROCESSES**   *163*

                          Program Analysis, *164*
                          Budget Examination, *172*
                          Process Analysis, *187*
                          Program Evaluation, *195*
                          Auditing, *196*

CHAPTER SEVEN   **OPERATING BUDGETS AND**
                          ACCOUNTING   *203*

                          Designing Control, *204*
                          Budget Concepts and Reports, *208*
                          Cash Management and Investments, *218*
                          Accounting Fundamentals, *224*
                          Financial Administration, *227*
                          Reports and Analyses, *229*

CHAPTER EIGHT   **CAPITAL BUDGETING AND DEBT**
                          ADMINISTRATION   *241*

                          State and Local Debt, *242*
                          Creative Capital Financing, *247*
                          Nontraditional, *249*
                          Capital Budgeting, *259*
                          Bonding, *261*

CHAPTER NINE   **REVENUE SYSTEMS**   *269*

Intergovernmental Revenue System, *270*
Property Tax and Controversy, *276*
Assessment and Taxation, *295*
Other Revenue Sources, *303*

CHAPTER TEN   **INTERNAL SERVICE FUNCTIONS**   *307*

Property Management, *308*
Risk Management, *316*
Pension Funds, *328*

                       GLOSSARY   *336*

                       INDEX   *355*

PREFACE

I have made significant changes in this edition, based upon the advice of my fellow teachers around the country, who offered suggestions; of students, who freely expressed their dissatisfaction or indirectly showed their confusion by responding poorly to the text; and of book reviewers, who usually were kind but sometimes were critical. I should include myself in the list of critics, because at some point the first edition seemed to take on an independent existence, allowing me to assess it more objectively.

In reflecting on the changes, I believe that most were prompted by remarkable developments in the profession but that some were prompted by my desire to communicate this complex body of knowledge in a more intelligible manner. Such areas as forecasting and capital budgeting have undergone remarkable changes since 1979. I am still amazed at the rate of change and the increasing sophistication of the subject matter as it evolves. I grouped some topics together and added new material. For example, I grouped all the history sections into one chapter and I added text on double-entry bookkeeping and pension funds.

I maintain the same optimism as I did in the first edition. I was pleased by the many adoptions of the first edition, and I do believe the text has served as a focus for the study of public budgeting. Obviously, not all readers appreciate my pragmatic, practitioner-oriented approach or my extremely terse writing style, which does not fully spell out the implications of the concepts discussed. Nevertheless, the text is appreciated by many, and more readers now share my perspective that public administration, and budgeting in particular, is an applied social science, with the focus appropriately on the public manager. For this, I am particularly pleased.

In this preface, I must also acknowledge my appreciation to so many. First, I thank my critics, who cared enough to let me hear their voices. I am grateful to the following people for their helpful reviews of the manuscript: Khi Van Thai, University of Miami; Brian Donnelly, Southern Illinois University; and Peter Colby, SUNY-Binghamton. Second, I thank Prentice-Hall and people like Stan Wakefield. One could not have a better publisher. They know how to combine marketing and production with the more human skills of dealing with writers as sensitive and intelligent human beings. Third, I thank my secretaries, Sylvia Silvers, Linda Rabin, and Delpha Heinold, who interpreted my script and cleaned up my English. Last, because they are most important, I thank my family for tolerating my urge to write and for their continuing education of me as a human being.

All sins of omission and commission are still mine. I am continually amazed that errors exist after so many reviews, edits, and checks of galleys and proofs.

Prentice-Hall has me check them all, and these errors are definitely my responsibility. I still recall the embarrassing omission of a source on a chart in the first printing of the first edition. I hope that any errors in this edition are not significant.

Again, I ask professors and students for comments. Your views are appreciated; and as this edition demonstrates, your comments are useful.

Thomas D. Lynch
Boca Raton, Florida

ONE
PUBLIC BUDGETING IN CONTEXT

Public budgeting is a mystery to most people—even to many professionals working in the government. People are aware that chief executives propose budgets to legislative bodies and that these groups in turn make decisions on taxes and what programs will receive financial support. If they work in government, they know that material is prepared to justify "the budget" and that detailed controls exist which often prohibit simple management decisions. In the personal lives of most people, the family budget is a source of tension because of the need to live within one's income. Most people assume that public budgeting must deal with similar matters but that it must involve much more complex accounting techniques.

This chapter examines what public budgeting is and the contextual factors necessary to understand public budgeting in the American context. Public budgeting is an activity and many people view that activity from their own perspectives. Thus, the meaning of "public budgeting" is very much dependent upon perspective. The primary contextual factors in American budgeting are the ideologies of democracy and capitalism, federalism, decision-making theory, and economics. Each helps define how we approach and understand the purpose of public budgeting. This chapter should help the reader understand:

1. the various significant perspectives on budgeting, including that of the public manager;
2. important budgetary and political realities;

3. the nature of the budget cycle (i.e., phases, cycle variations, overlapping of cycles) and the activities associated with each budget phase;
4. the significance of ideology in influencing how we approach public budgeting;
5. the role of federalism as a factor in budgeting;
6. the significance of normative decision-making theory to public budgeting;
7. the major tools of monetary policy, what aspects of the economy they primarily affect, and their significance to public budgeting;
8. the variety of ways in which the federal government can act to stimulate or depress the economy and the theory behind such actions; and
9. an explanation of how economic policy has and has not worked since the 1960s.

WHAT IS PUBLIC BUDGETING?

Perspectives on Budgeting

One can define a term by seeking out the common usages or one can create a definition for one's own intellectual and conceptual purposes. The former approach is particularly useful when one is trying to understand the various perspectives that people bring to a given activity. The latter approach is useful when an author is attempting to establish a reasonably uniform body of thought. Both approaches are used here.

Public budgeting can be viewed from many perspectives, as illustrated by Professor Sydney Duncombe in Exhibit 1-1. Reading the variety of statements helps one to appreciate the various academic and practical perspectives found in the practice of public budgeting. There are many such perspectives, of which none are exclusively "correct." The parable of the three blind men and the elephant helps us understand the significance of perspective. One of the blind men examined the tail and pronounced his description of the animal. Another felt a large foot and leg and then argued that the first man's description was inaccurate. The third man, after examining the beast's trunk, said that the other two were quite wrong in their descriptions. The storyteller was said to laugh at the foolish arguing among the blind men because the storyteller could see all of the elephant. The point of the parable is not the importance of "better" perspective but rather the foolishness of the storyteller for not recognizing that he himself was blinded by arrogance because he was sighted. Each person was correct and each was wrong because our individual perspectives always prevent us from easily understanding another's "truth."

When one works in the world of public budgeting, each perspective is used by various key actors in the budget process. The person trained as a lawyer sees the phenomenon called budgeting as a sort of legal process. The economist and politician describe the phenomenon differently based upon their perspectives. The public manager sees budgeting differently from the others. None are incorrect, because all of them define the phenomenon based upon their educational or professional perspectives. They become incorrect, like the storyteller, when their arrogance blinds

EXHIBIT 1-1   What are the Main Purposes of Budgeting?

I view the budget system as *a means of balancing revenues and expenditures*. Our constitution requires a balanced budget and in preparing our budget we first make careful estimates of revenues for the next year. We then reduce agency budget requests to our revenue estimates for the next year.

I look on the budget process as *a semi-judicial process* in which state agencies come to the Legislature to plead their case just as I plead the case of my clients in court. Our job as a legislative committee is to distribute the available funds equitably among state agencies.

The main purpose of the budget system is *accountability*. The people hold the Legislature accountable through the electoral process. The Legislature holds state agencies accountable by reviewing their budgets, setting the appropriation levels the people want, and letting state agencies know how the people want their money spent through statements of legislative intent.

The most important single reason for a budget system is *control*. State agencies would spend the state bankrupt in two years if there weren't an adequate means of controlling their spending. The appropriations are the first line of defense against overspending. Important second lines of defense lie in allotment systems, position controls, and controls over purchasing.

The executive budget document should be *an instrument of gubernatorial policy*. When a Governor comes into office there are certain programs and policies he would like to see accomplished during the term of office. Many of these program and policy changes cost money, and the Governor will have to either raise taxes or cut expenses to pay for these changes. The people expect the Governor to show accomplishments and the budget is a major means of showing these accomplishments.

Budgeting is *public relations*. I write my budget justifications in the way I think will best gain the appropriations I need. If the budget examiner likes workload statistics, we'll snow the examiner with statistics. If a key legislator would be influenced by how the budget will affect constituents, we put that in the request.

A budget is *an instrument of good management*. Careful use of workload statistics, performance accounting, and standards of performance will tend to insure that personnel are effectively utilized.

A budget is really *a work plan with a dollar sign attached*. As an agency official, I am committing myself to certain levels of program which I promise to attain if I receive my full budget request. When the Governor and the Legislature discuss cutting my budget, I describe as accurately as I can the reduction in program level that will result.

The budget is an instrument for *planning*. A good budget system requires agency officials to project costs and program levels at least several years ahead. Such a system requires agency officials to examine the costs and benefits of alternatives to present programs in order to plan changes in programs where necessary. In short, budgeting should be an annual means for agency heads to reexamine the objectives of their programs and the effectiveness of the means used to accomplish these objectives.

Budgeting is *the art of cutting* the most fat from an agency request with the least squawking.

Prepared by Sydney Duncombe, 1977.

them to the significance of perspective when defining and understanding the phenomenon of public budgeting.

For the purposes of this textbook, the more important perspectives are those of the politician, the economist, the accountant, and especially the public manager. Given a democratic society, budgets are the tool used to frame much public policy; thus the politician's perspective is important. Both economists and accountants have professional perspectives which greatly influence how we understand budgeting and how we believe we should practice it. Economists give us theories and techniques which help us define how we should budget, what factors should be weighed, and how to weigh these factors in making budget policy decisions. Accountants give us conceptual frameworks in which to execute and evaluate budgets. Public managers must understand each of the previous perspectives when managing the affairs of government through the budget process.

Political leaders are often painfully aware that many of the most important policy decisions are made during the budget process. Former New York City Mayor Abraham Beame was reported to have said that "the budget is everything" when that city was undergoing its fiscal crisis during the 1970s. Mayor Beame was quite sensitive to the financial crisis of his city and the resulting policy dilemmas confronting him. Henry Maier, the mayor of Milwaukee, once said, "The budget is the World Series of Government." This mayor in the early 1980s had to support a 20 percent increase in property taxes. Both mayors were aware that many—if not most—of the major political decisions are made when a chief executive proposes the government's budget and a legislative body (e.g., the city council) adopts it.

The budgetary process can be viewed as a political event conducted in the political arena for political advantage. Politics—being a reflection of human nature—has its best and worst sides. In some instances, politicians or individuals who influence politicians are seeking money for themselves. In other instances, the political advantage sought is to further some ethical position or to aid others selflessly. Motivations differ, but the seeking of political advantage is constant. Thus, one significant perspective on budgeting is political.

Economists view budgetary decisions with the assumptions that budget decisions are made within restricted financial conditions and that economic analysis can therefore help identify the best decision. Every budget decision involves potential benefits which may or may not be obtained; it also involves "opportunity cost." If the available money is spent for one program, then another program is not funded or is funded at a lower level. In other words, opportunities are lost in every budget decision and there never seems to be enough money for every program. When choices have to be made, economic analysis can help one to evaluate the comparative benefits and costs, including opportunity cost. This view of budgeting focuses upon decison-making and places a high premium upon the value of analysis in helping decision makers make ''better'' decisions.

Accountants stress the importance of capturing accurate financial information. To the accountant, the budget is the statement of desired policy, and information on actual expenditures is compared with the budget to judge whether policy has been followed, as well as to question the wisdom of the original policy. The accountant's view largely defines how public managers understand how they should execute the budget and how some of their evaluators will judge their actions.

None of these views—the politician's, the economist's, and the accountant's—is incorrect. Each perspective is valuable in getting a more comprehensive understanding of public budgeting. Interestingly, the perspective of the public manager most closely approximates that of the storyteller in the parable. Public managers must try to achieve a more comprehensive view, but they cannot fall into the trap of arrogantly believing that such a view is anything more than one valid perspective among others.

A Public Manager's Perspective

Viewed from a public manager's perspective, the budget is often the principal vehicle for developing government plans and policies. There can be a separate planning process, but often such a process develops vague statements without stressing relative priorities. The budget states specific dollar amounts relative to proposed government activities and these decisions reflect the government's plans and policies much more accurately than most planning documents.

The budget also represents the chief executive's legislative program. It states which programs are to be active, emphasized, or ignored given the limited resources available to the government. Other public statements may be made which discuss a mayor's or governor's legislative program, but the comprehensive and detailed presentation is presented in the budget.

There are several different ways to categorize the request for funds to finance a government, but they all outline planned functions, programs, and activities. Program and performance budgets more clearly explain the relationship of money requested and government activities. However, even line item budgets, which focus upon specific items to be purchased with the budget, provide the knowledgeable reader with a detailed outline of planned government activities.

Most budgets present the planned program for the year against a background of past experiences and future needs. Even zero base budgets normally cite past experience to demonstrate the type of activities likely to be funded in the planned year. In some instances, budgets project future needs beyond the planned budget year in order to suggest the future year implications of budget year decisions. This past and future information is highly useful to decision makers: The past gives them an impression of what the program can accomplish and the future gives them warning of the long-run implications of current budget year decisions.

Strictly speaking the budget is a request for funds to run the government. The request is normally made by the chief executive to the city council, legislature, or Congress. It also states the revenue and other sources of resources (e.g., debt financing) needed to balance the suggested expenditures. Once the budget is modified or approved, the executive branch develops operating budgets for the budget year. Traditionally, the document sent to the legislature by the chief executive is called *the budget*. In the federal government, Congress receives the budget but passes several appropriation bills which constitute the modified approved federal budget.

An Operational Definition

As can be noticed from the previous discussions, the term "budget" is used in a variety of ways. Each may be quite correct given the perspective of the user of the word. In public administration, the following definition is normally an excellent operational definition:

> "Budget" is a *plan* for the accomplishment of *programs* related to *objectives* and *goals* within a definite *time* period, including an estimate of *resources required*, together with an estimate of the *resources available,* usually compared with one or more *past periods* and showing *future requirements*.

The budget always represents what someone wishes to do or have someone else do. It is a tool to help us control our affairs. Once the money is spent, it can be contrasted to the plan but it no longer represents something called a budget; rather it represents actual obligations or expenditures. Prior to that time, the budget may change many times. The document sent to the legislature by a chief executive is normally considered to be "the budget," whereas the plan used by the bureaucrats during the budget year is normally called the "operating budget."

People writing budgets have programs and program accomplishments in mind. Admittedly, those people may have rather vague notions of the exact nature of each program and their desired goals and objectives. Dealing with and avoiding vagueness is one of the major challenges of public budgeting. But in spite of vagueness, people preparing budgets do believe that the requested funds will be used for some set of activities and that those activities will result in accomplishments.

Budgets are focused upon a specific time period called the budget year. In some instances, the year used corresponds to the calendar year, but normally an arbitrary year called fiscal year (e.g., October 1 to September 30) is defined. The money is planned to be spent or obligated in the budget year. Years prior to the budget year (BY) are called prior or past years (PY) and the current time period in which the government is operating is called the current year (CY). Future fiscal years beyond the budget year are referred to as budget year plus one (BY + 1), budget year plus two (BY + 2), and so on. For example, let us say we are preparing the budget for the fiscal year (FY) 1990 but we are actually in FY 1989. The BY is 1990. The CY is 1989. The PY is 1988. The BY + 1 is 1991.

Budgets are planned for a specific time period and an estimate is always made of the resources required during that time period. The estimates include the revenue as well as the expenditures. Estimating is another challenge of budgeting as one can never be certain that a specific dollar sum will be raised or that the government can live within its proposed expenditures. The latter is more easily controlled, but unexpected emergencies or problems do occur.

In order to facilitate a better understanding of the requested resources, the budget usually compares the BY requests against the PY and CY actual obligations or expenditures. This provides a basis for comparing and permits the decision maker to focus upon the difference or increment between the CY and the BY. This is called incremental budgeting. In zero base budgeting, one ignores the differences and demands that the whole BY amount be justified. As will be explained later in more depth, this distinction between incremental and zero base budgeting is overstated. Increasingly, budgets also go beyond the BY and show BY + 1, BY + 2, BY + 3, BY + 4, and BY + 5. This showing of future requirements helps the decision maker realize that BY decisions have an effect beyond one budget year. Thus, a policy maker may decide that a given set of decisions may be affordable for the budget year but not wise, given the likely future requirements. Unfortunately, policy makers often ignore future implications and this situation represents yet another challenge of public budgeting.

Budget Realities

If you examine a budget, there will be many tables and charts. If you work in government, there will be many forms that must be completed so that a budget can be prepared, executed, and evaluated. The details in the forms and tables are an essential part of budgeting, but you can never understand public budgeting by examining those forms and tables *per se*. The numbers and the formats used to present the numbers are merely some of the means and not the ends of public budgeting.

Budgeting is a good reflection of actual public policy and often a better reflection than formal speeches or written statements. Politicians must get elected to hold office, and clarity of expression may be dysfunctional because it makes needless enemies. Also, it is often difficult to verbalize policy. The budget states the planned priorities and the programs in a meaningful way to the people who must carry out the policy. This is not to say that all policy is reflected in the budget, because some important policy matters have no fiscal implications. Nor is it to say that all budgets clearly present policy. But an expert can read the message which will be operationalized by the bureaucracy.

A budget focuses upon a given year (the budget year), but its preparation, execution, and evaluation take place over a period of several years (the budget cycle). Going back to the FY 1990 example, the preparation and approval of the 1990 budget year should have been finished just prior to the beginning of the fiscal year

(October 1, 1989). In order to have an approved budget on time, the preparation and approval process must begin much earlier. Sometimes the preparation begins a full year or more before the beginning of the budgeted fiscal year. During FY 1990, the operating budget is used to guide obligations and expenditures, but after FY 1990 no more money can be obligated, though some money can be spent to fulfill the FY 1990 obligations. The period in which to fulfill obligations can be open-ended, but sound practices place a one- or two-year limit so that the books can be closed. The final stage in the budget cycle is auditing and evaluating the program resources obligated in the earlier budget year. This can take place one to several years after the completion of the fiscal year. In other words, the FY 1990 budget cycle can start as early as 1989 and end as late as 1993.

Budgeting is highly emotional, detailed, and a great deal of work. When policy makers decide to fund or not to fund programs, people are profoundly affected, lives are changed. Not surprisingly, budget decisions evoke strong emotions because the stakes are high and the consequences are important. Budgets are also detailed. The one cardinal sin for a budget officer is to make an arithmetic error because that is one mistake everyone can catch and criticize. The budgets are often hundreds and thousands of pages long, filled with tables. Each number is usually important to someone and mistakes are not treated lightly. The preparation of this mass of information requires much work. Deadlines drive the process and require intensive 50- to 60-hour-plus work weeks, especially prior to a major deadline such as submission of material to a legislative committee. The work is consuming and requires almost complete devotion. The work is also extremely interesting because of the interrelationship of budgeting and politics.

Students of public budgeting must use concepts developed in political science, economics, accounting, the behavioral sciences, finance, and other disciplines. Political science helps the budget person understand the political nature of government and the public policy-making process. Economics provides useful analytical tools and highly influential theories. Accounting provides the means to keep track properly of the complex array of dollars. The behavioral sciences help the budget person understand the human as a part of the budget process. Finance gives the practitioner some conceptual tools to use, especially relative to the revenue aspects of budgeting. Public administration helps bring this information together and adds some concepts of its own. Students of public budgeting should be able to draw upon a broad interdisciplinary background so that they can more easily deal with their challenging problems.

Public budgeting does require highly specialized knowledge, critical behavioral patterns, and important skills. These can be learned through experience and the learning process can be facilitated through formal education. This text sets out the primary knowledge useful to those involved in public budgeting as well as those wishing to better comprehend government by understanding public budgeting. Public budgeting requires more than knowledge. To be effective, certain important behavioral patterns should be mastered and that requires a learning laboratory or experience. Also, certain skills must be acquired, such as being able to translate possible policy positions into dollars and cents almost instantly in order to deal effectively in active political bargaining situations. Public budgeting is one of the most professionally challenging and often most emotionally rewarding activities in public administration.

Budgeting is a constantly changing field and some of the significant public administration reforms took place in the 1970s. In later sections of this chapter and in chapter 2, the history of budgeting will be explained in more depth. A major Congressional budget reform took place in 1974 and two years later another major reform was considered. In the federal executive branch, Presidents Johnson, Nixon, and Carter each have sought major budget reforms. Debates at the highest level continue to occupy public attention in spite of the complexity of the subject.

One last public budgeting reality should be stressed. Public budgeting is very big money. The 1982 federal budget outlay was over $250 billion. In 1981 the government sector was 20.3 percent of the $2.9 trillion Gross National Product. State and local government is also huge today. For example, in 1929, the combined federal, state, and local expenditure was $10.4 billion; in 1977, the New York State budget alone exceeded that combined 1929 amount. Bureaucrats often round off their working tables in the thousands, and they commonly prepare and execute budgets for billions of dollars.

Political Realities

Budgets are decided through politics; analysis is only ammunition in the decision-making process. Sometimes the politics are crude and unethical; sometimes reason and ethical views prevail. Often the decisions involve complex, conflicting values supported by minimal analysis, but they are decisions which must be made. The analyses used in public budgeting are only significant to the political actors if those actors use the analyses in their deliberations. Even when used and not ignored the analyses are merely some of the ammunition used to persuade other political actors. In some cases, an appeal, such as to the nation's pride, may be more significant than an elaborate analysis. In other situations, an analysis can be the key to persuading political actors how they should vote on a major policy matter.

Budgets are proposed plans. The budget presentations sometimes can make the difference for a program but in some instances the presentation will make no difference because the program is politically weak. In other instances, the program may be so politically strong that even a bad budget presentation will not defeat the program. Often the proposed plan or budget of the executive is a significant factor in the public decision-making, and the quality of the presentation is considered to be a reflection of the managerial competency of the program.

Political sacred cows do exist. An influential congressman or political executive can successfully demand a specific project or program. The appropriateness of the project or program is irrelevant, but the power of the political actor is very relevant. In public budgeting, the professional must learn to tolerate this unless a moral or legal question is involved. The nature of the American political system almost insures the existence of sacred cows. Some of them are prompted by campaign promises and some by less desirable motivations. The percentage of programs and projects that are sacred cows will vary, but normally they are the exception. If the program decisions are dominated by sacred cows, then public management will suffer as foolish programs or projects cannot be stopped except by highly political and time consuming debate.

Public budgeting is strongly influenced by the political causes of the day. The causes vary over time but some contemporary causes include national security, energy, environment, poverty, recession, and inflation. Policy makers, who decide on budgets, are keenly aware of the political causes because their positions on those causes influence people to vote for or against them. Therefore, politicians wish to know how budgets relate to those causes. Not surprisingly, budget justifications are often cast in terms of those causes or, at a minimum, the agency is prepared to answer questions involving the program and the politically sensitive topic. For example, in a time of recession, with large numbers of people unemployed, a major defense project will be justified first on the basis of providing jobs and secondly on the basis of national security.

THE BUDGET CYCLE

The Nature of the Cycle

The budget cycle takes place in four phases which can extend over several years. The first phase is *planning and analysis*. Here, the issues are explored and the agency budget is prepared. The second phase is *policy formulation,* which involves extensive executive and legislative reviews and decisions. The third phase is *policy execution* and *reinterpretation* when the budget becomes operational. The final stage involves *audit and evaluation.* The beginning of the third phase is a key date. On that date, the operating budget goes into effect, to end in one year. Prior to that date, enough time must be provided to consider the issues, conduct analysis, prepare the budget, and permit various executive and legislative groups to modify the evolved budget. After the end of the operating budget, time is needed to close accounts and to audit and evaluate the programs. This latter phase can take place in a few months, but often involves several years.

Cycles vary from one government to another and from one agency to another. If the government or agency is small, then the smaller numbers of people normally require a briefer budget cycle. In a large agency with many field units, coordination is difficult and more time is needed to prepare the document.

The federal budget cycle is particularly important because state and local governments sometimes use the federal government as a model and—more importantly—local and state governments are dependent upon federal transfer payments, such as revenue sharing and grant programs. If the federal government delays, many other groups are affected.

One confusing reality of public budgeting is that the budget person and agency must operate with overlapping budget cycles. On the same day, a budget person may have to review the evaluations covering last year's program, prepare readjustments on the current year or operating budget, and answer Congressional questions on the budget year covering the next fiscal year. This can be and is confusing. Not surprisingly, people working in budgeting learn to refer to their work by specific fiscal years to minimize confusion.

Budget Phases

Planning and analysis. The planning and analysis phase was popularized by PPB in the 1960s, but the phase was not original to PPB reforms. The New York Bureau of Municipal Research encouraged planning and analysis at the turn of the century. Almost all budget preparation did and does involve some analysis, but the amount and sophistication were greatly increased during the PPB reform era. Planning and analysis can take many forms, but most of the techniques were developed in the disciplines of economics, operations research, and systems analysis. Techniques including modeling, sensitivity analysis, and survey research are used, but are not covered in this text because they are not closely associated with budgeting. Other techniques, such as forecasting and cost-benefit, cost-effectiveness, and marginal utility analyses, are introduced in various sections of this text.

The planning and analysis phase takes place at the beginning of the budget cycle, but analysis does occur at other periods in the cycle. In the policy formulation stage, time is a key factor so there is not the luxury of being able to prepare elaborate analyses. Only quick original analysis or reapplication of earlier analyses can be used in this phase. There is little analysis, except for forecasting, done in the policy execution phase. A great deal of analysis is done in the audit and evaluation phase. The techniques, analytical problems, and focus of analysis do change somewhat when this budget phase occurs relative to other budget activities.

Policy formulation. In the policy formulation process, the budget is developed and approved. Policy positions become operationalized as the budget is prepared. The agency is the preparer and significant advocate of the budget. The agency's clientele group and elements in the legislative and the highest levels of the executive branch may also support the agency's budget or aspects of the budget, but the agency is the advocate. The reviewers and modifiers of the budget include the department, the chief executive and his or her staff, and the legislature. A variety of conflicting influences converge on the budget process from various levels in the executive branch, the legislature, clientele groups, the media, and even sometimes the judiciary branch.

The federal process is elaborate, but it does illustrate the complex steps in the policy formulation process. Prior to this phase, the agency has submitted quarterly program financial plans which give budget reviewers initial indications of likely fund requests five years beyond the budget year. At the beginning of the phase, the central executive branch budget office (i.e., Office of Management and Budget) issues guidelines to the departments and agencies for the development of the new budget. Then the various agencies issue their budget calls to agency personnel in order to compile the necessary information for the budget. The agency uses this information to prepare its budget.

The remaining portion of the policy formulation phase involves budget reviews and eventually decisions on the budget. The agency submits the budget to the department budget office. The format can vary in style from a line-item to a program budget to decision packages. The department budget office and the highest officials review the budget and decide upon the department's recommended budget. The agency makes the necessary changes and the revised budget is submitted to the Office of Management and Budget. Again the budget is revised, OMB arrives at its recommendations, and the president revises and eventually approves the budget. In some cases, the president permits an appeal from the department. In the federal government, a current services budget is submitted to Congress with the president's budget in January. The Congress then reviews the submission and passes appropriation bills prior to the beginning of the new fiscal year.

Policy execution.   In the policy execution phase, the budget is used as guidance for specific decisions by bureaucrats. This phase takes place during the current year, and all obligations must be made in this year if they are to be attributed to the fiscal year. The executive branch can sometimes reinterpret policy during this phase by not spending the planned resources or by shifting funds from one activity to another. As a general practice, the latter does not occur at the federal and state levels, but does occur sometimes at the local level. The executive policy not to spend appropriated funds is an impoundment. The nonspending can take the form of a delay in spending in the intended budget year or of a recession from the budget. On the state level, some executives have the power of line-item vetoes or impoundment, depending on the state constitution.

At the agency and department level, the rate of obligation and disbursement of resources can be controlled by allotment. This power is intended to assure that funds are available when needed for proper economic and managerial purposes. With the greater emphasis upon macroeconomics, the federal government is more carefully controlling the rates of both obligation and disbursement. Sometimes the allotment power is used for political purposes, such as insuring maximum and timely obligations on key programs at the correct moment in a political campaign. The allotment power might be abused and treated as an illegal impoundment, but no evidence of such abuse has been publicly raised yet. Normally, allotments are used entirely for economic and managerial purposes.

Authorizations and appropriations are often phrased in technical budget language. The technical wording can be significant to the operating budget. The normal appropriation is for the budget year only, but the language need not be so limiting. For example, the appropriations may be for no-year funds, thus permitting the agency to obligate the funds in subsequent fiscal years if the money is not entirely obligated in the current year. Other technical devices are contract and bond authority. The Congress can also place special conditions on appropriations. For example, the appropriation can read, "$150 million is appropriated under section 204 of XYZ legislation but none of this money can be used to build a flag pole in front of the Bureau of Standards building nor can any money be spent on the ABC project." Often such detailed conditions are not included in the appropriation language, but are included in the nonlegally binding report which accompanies the appropriation bill. Agencies are sensitive to such requests and normally will comply unless some very unusual circumstance exists. Another technical budget device is for the appropriations committee to negate yearly contract authority by saying that no more than a specific amount can be obligated during the budget year.

The federal and state government use of the authorization and appropriation distinction is extremely useful, given the complex budget decisions which are made. Many local governments do not make the authorization and appropriation distinction because a two-stage process is not as useful to them. There are normally fewer city councilors or county supervisors, so a more elaborate two-stage process is not neeced to coordinate decision-making.

Once the allotments have been made, the agency can prepare its operating budgets. Normally, the operating budget is not the desired sophisticated managerial tool which has proper linkages to accounting, management-by-objectives and progress reporting, and program evaluation. The operating budget should inform the agency's units how much and at what rate resources can be obligated and disbursed. The operating budget should reflect the decisions made in the MBO process. The recording of progress and accounting of actual obligations and disbursement should be used in a classification scheme so that management can verify that budget and MBO decisions were executed. Also, proper program evaluations can be done only if the program direction is understood and necessary cooperation exists among the evaluators, managers, and budget persons.

Audit and evaluation.   The final phase takes place after the current year is complete. Some audit and evaluation work can and should be started much earlier in the cycle, but the focus of the work and the preparation of the final reports take place in this final phase. Audit and evaluation activities are conducted by such groups as the agency, the department, the General Accounting Office, and the Congress itself through its oversight function. Audits are often addressed to checking if the agency properly recorded its transactions and obligated resources legally. Increasingly, auditing has been expanded to include program evaluation, especially by GAO. However, program evaluation is often done in separate agency and departmental program evaluation units. To a limited extent, legislative bodies conduct oversight hearings and investigations which can be considered program evaluation.

Laws are sometimes quite specific in requiring audits and evaluations. States have audit agencies, and states require auditing in and of local governments. States often require a local government to submit its annual audit to the state. The audit is often examined by the state itself. States sometimes have legislative review commissions which perform program evaluation. Often, audit agencies are staffed by accountants who are reluctant to perform program evaluations because they are not trained in that activity. However, the trend is for audit agencies to become more involved in program evaluation and for new evaluation groups to be established. In the federal government, many programs are now being required to set aside and use a portion of program funds for program evaluation.

Local Government Budget Cycles

There are some differences between federal and state government and local government budget cycles. Revenue estimation is very important in local as well as state government, particularly in the planning and analysis phase. The estimation is normally done by the finance or central budget office. Budget formulation practices vary in local government, but often there is a small central budget staff. Procedures are much more informal, but sometimes state law or local charters require more formal practices such as public hearings. Often the budget is prepared by a budget office receiving input from the city agencies and guidance from the city manager or mayor. The chief city executive sometimes serves as the person who resolves outstanding issues and as a court of appeals. The exact procedure depends upon each local government, with some having the agency heads reporting directly to the city council or county elected board of supervisors.

Local governments vary greatly in their review and power over the budget. Normally, budgets are detailed line-item documents which part-time nonexpert board members must review and approve in a short-time. Nor surprisingly, budgets are confusing and frustrating to board members. They usually focus their attention upon small comprehensible items or pet projects rather than conducting a comprehensive review of the submitted budget. Often, local governments conduct public hearings in connection with the legislative deliberations on the budget.

Once the budget is approved, the focus of the budget is upon control. In some local governments, almost every change in the line-item budget must be approved by the legislature. In other local governments, almost any change can be made by the city manager or department head. The money is controlled, but the ability to make changes in the budget during the operating year varies.

CONTEXT OF AMERICAN BUDGETING

Ideology

Public budgeting is best considered in the context of the ideological culture of a nation. Budgeting practices in Canada, the United States, France, Panama, Israel, Yemen, India, the USSR, Japan, and the People's Republic of China are not identical, because the budgeting process relates to the fundamental political and economic value schemes of each society. Techniques and concepts can be similar across societies, but how those techniques and concepts are meaningfully applied depends upon the society's culture.

Ideas are powerful, especially when shared by many people, because they can guide behavior by discouraging "bad" and encouraging "good" activities and actions. Ideas can be and often are used to place a value on people, things, activities, and even other ideas. Sometimes ideas can be logically consistent or nearly consistent and form belief systems. These systems in turn can be shared by many people and can guide entire civilizations. These belief systems are called ideologies and every culture has them.

In the United States, two important ideologies, both of which influence the way public budgeting is conducted, are democracy and capitalism. Other belief systems and subsystems are important, but are not central to this simplified sketch. "Democracy" is a term that can have many meanings, as illustrated by its use in American and many Communist societies. Democracy as defined in the United States evolved from a desire to have a limited representative government which respected the political rights of minorities. In the agriculture-oriented colonies, certain rights, such as freedom of the press, were considered essential and were built into the Constitution. These rights were viewed as a means to prevent tyranny and permit the peaceful change of government. In time, the definition of "voter" extended from white male adult landholder to an adult citizen of either sex and any racial or religious background.

The American democratic system of government evolved into a pattern partially explained by the Federalist Paper No. 10 of the 1780s. Parties and groups interact to influence government in a manner deliberately designed to decentralize and diffuse political power. People continually learn that they can best influence government by acting in groups and directing their political efforts at partisans in the political process. The partisans interact and adjust policy based upon the relative strengths of lobbying forces and varying influential ideologies. The strength of policy in some instances may be due to economic interests, but often that strength rests upon shared and effectively argued belief systems.

In America, the notions of partisan bargaining, minority and fundamental human rights, diffusion of power, and the influencing of partisans through collective action over time together constitute the meaning of *democracy*. The activity called public budgeting tends to reflect that ideological culture. Thus, budget decisions are made through partisan bargaining in a system of diffused political power. Decisions made by partisans are influenced over time by a process called lobbying. Public agency clientele groups (i.e., those affected directly by the agency's activities) can and do lobby the legislature and the executive. The agency's actions are thus largely determined by the complexly combined influence of executive, legislature, and clientele; and the mechanism of that influence is often the budget. Freedom of information and sunshine legislation, logical extensions of minority and fundamental human rights, are taken seriously; and discussion of these issues opens up much budget detail to the media and the general public. In America, budget decisions require a melding of executive and legislative will to achieve the necessary policy mandates as prescribed in the Constitution. Often the influence of democratic ideas has even extended to requiring public hearings on budget decisions. The belief system called *democracy* does greatly influence the way Americans think public budgeting should be conducted.

The second major American ideology is *capitalism,* which does not exist in the strictest sense of the term. Unlike democracy, capitalism is subject to active ideological challenge, which has led to a blending of logically conflicting belief systems. Strict capitalism evolved from a reaction against the extensive English-government-dominated mercantilism of the 1760s and was reinforced by the Social Darwinism of the late 1880s to the 1930s. The desire was to limit the role of government in the economic activities of society. The capitalist ideology does have a role for government, but it is limited to "public goods" like national defense, and possibly could be extended to include:

1. coping with public allocations for the general good, like public education and pollution control;
2. avoiding inconvenient private monopolies on such things as highways, bridges, and water systems.

Advocates of capitalism raise severe protests when subjects such as redistribution of wealth and the use of government control to achieve economic stabilization and growth are raised.

From the 1890s to the present, a contrary belief system—called socialism—arose to challenge capitalism. Its proponents advocated a total role for government in society. The government would run society and curb the economic abuses of the wealthy elites. The most visionary advocates of the belief system expected that a classless society would eventually evolve, eliminating the need for government to act as the people's trustee. In over a third of the world, this belief system is now dominant. In the United States, the belief system has served to raise the social conscience of the nation, and earlier aspects of capitalism (e.g., child labor and long work weeks) have been greatly modified. Especially after 1932, the federal government has come to play an active role in society in such matters as consumerism, protection of the environment, inflation, recession, and worker and product safety.

The correct mix of capitalism and socialism in the United States continues to be the major issue dividing partisans in many major political battles. For purposes of public budgeting, the important point to understand is that this ongoing ideological debate is taken very seriously and affects budgeting. The very size and scope of government is at issue; thus the question of what is and should be budgeted is also at issue. Attitudes about how government can and should influence the overall national or regional economy are critical to the way budgeting is conducted. The stress on economy, efficiency, and productivity arises out of capitalism and its economic doctrines. The use of enterprise funds and government corporations also evolved from the ideological debate. A later unit in this chapter will discuss current economic thinking and its influence on budgeting.

Federalism

The United States is a federated government and budgeting differs on each level. The scope, size, and different nature of programs lead to the differences in budgeting. In public budgeting, the similarities are more striking than the dissimilarities. However, the differences are important and are discussed here.

In the national government, more effort is focused on the expenditure as opposed to the revenue aspects of budgeting. Taxes are important, but more effort is channeled into controlling, managing, and planning expenditures. The state of the economy and the role of the budget in stimulating the economy are actively debated and are very significant in shaping both presidential and Congressional budgets. The revenue side of the budget is considered in terms of its influence on the economy. The typical agency budget officer does not consider the revenue aspects of the budget. At the highest levels in OMB and Congress, attention is addressed to macroeconomics and the analysis of proposed expenditures. There is a strong desire to improve the analysis associated with public budgeting; productivity is considered important.

The national government manages many of its programs in cooperation with state and local governments. Sometimes the federal government interacts directly with citizens, as in the case with veterans' programs. In many programs, categorical and block grants are provided to state and local governments, which manage the programs. The government also has a significant revenue-sharing program with local governments. The result is that many federal activities are really intergovernmental in nature, with the actual services being provided by local government.

Unlike the federal government, state and local governments must balance their budgets. Sometimes that legal requirement is not met, but it does exist. Revenue and expenditure forecasts are thus important for state and local governments in developing balanced budgets.

State governments have a great deal of potential power over local governments. States commonly focus their efforts upon highways and education, with increasing interest being addressed to health, environmental control, and welfare. Like the federal government, state governments provide assistance to local governments, often acting as pass-through agents for the federal government. Unlike the federal government, state governments can directly control local governments. Many local budgeting requirements are established by state law.

The form of local government varies from large cities to small villages and townships. Each unit of government has a budget process. Each is concerned with balancing revenue and expenditure. Local governments provide direct services, including public safety, education, and sanitation. Many local government activities require large expenditures for capital items like schools and roads; thus debt administration is an important aspect of local government. Transfer payments in the form of grants and revenue sharing are an important source of revenue.

The complex overlapping jurisdictions, economy of scale, and the growth of suburban areas and decline of cities are important to local government budgeting.

The overlapping of jurisdictions means that tax collection is more complex and coordination of services is difficult. The existence of small governments means that many services are provided without the advantage of economy of scale. The declining tax base for cities is putting extreme pressure on city budgets. The increased population of suburban areas has strained the expertise and capability of the suburban governments to cope with the challenge. They must develop budgeting expertise while dealing with massive program growth. Each problem is significant and helps explain the challenge of local budgeting.

Decision-Making Models

Public budgeting is a decision-making process. Not surprisingly, there are several theories as to the way public policy decisions should be made. These theories or conceptual models are important because many people take them seriously and try to reform public budgeting using one of the theories as their guide. To better understand contemporary public budgeting reforms, these theories must be understood. But first, a criterion must be developed to judge the conceptual models, and the concept of conceptual models itself must be explained.

A conceptual model can be viewed as a tool which enables the user to understand and deal with complex phenomena. A tool can be judged "good" or "bad" in terms of the user's purpose. A hammer, for example, may be a good tool for building a shed, but it is bad for chopping wood. Professionals should judge conceptual models or theories in terms of the model's usefulness in helping them accomplish their tasks. Those tasks must be accomplished within a decision-making context largely induced by the ideologies of the culture.

Public budgeting in the United States must be conducted in a political, human, and often practical environment. The democratic ideology has helped to define the political environment. Consensus and partisan adjustments best explain the political context. Public budgeting is conducted by humans and it affects humans; thus emotional drama, error, pride, and other human characteristics help define the context of budgeting. In public budgeting, the practical is often a significant factor because decisions must be made. Even a so-called nondecision often represents an allocation of resources in budgeting. If the data or analyses are not available, then the decision maker must make do with conventional wisdom or personal biased judgment. Thus the "do-able" or practical is significant.

Decision-making models can be judged in terms of their applicability to the decision-making environment of the public budget person. If the model is not in harmony with the decision-making environment (which is unlikely to be changed) then the model is "bad." That is, the model is not appropriate to the user's purposes. This value judgment must be limited to the decision maker discussed here.

Some major and commonly noted decision-making models are the incremental change model, the satisficing model, and the ideal-rational model. To this list, a provocative but little-cited model called the "stages of problem solving" can be added. The incremental model is used for descriptive and normative purposes, but just because something exists in a certain way does not mean that it should continue to exist. The focus in this and subsequent paragraphs shall be on the normative use of the model. In the incremental model, major public policies evolve through cautious incremental steps; political forces mutually adjust their positions and, over time, public policy changes. This is an inherently conservative approach and it biases the decision makers against more radical innovative alternatives.

An agency develops a budget which it advocates to its department, to the Office of Management and Budget, and to Congress. In the major phases of the budget approval process, the agency takes the role of an advocate; the reviewer (e.g., Office of Management and Budget) questions the wisdom of the proposal; and the reviewer makes a tentative decision, which is often appealed to the secretary, the president, or the Senate. This model is consistent with the incremental change model in that policies are mutually adjusted because someone advocates and someone accommodates. Wildavsky merely points out the roles taken by the various actors in the incremental change process.

The satisficing model points out that decision makers develop a criterion to judge acceptable policy alternatives for a given problem. They then search the alternatives and select the first acceptable alternative they discover. Time is significant in the satisficing model. Alternatives are considered but the ideal is not sought. The acceptable is the standard for judgment. Like the incremental change model, the satisficing model is used for both descriptive and normative purposes; but the consideration here is only on the normative use. The reasons for the limited search are the lack of time for an exhaustive search and the opportunity costs of such a search.

The rational model is most commonly cited as the ideal way to reach decisions, especially major public policy decisions such as those in public budgeting. Its assumptions are deeply rooted in modern civilization and culture. The model systematically breaks decision making down into six phases:

1. establish a complete set of operational goals, with relative weights allocated to the different degrees to which each may be achieved;
2. establish a complete inventory of other values and resources with relative weights;
3. prepare a complete set of the alternative policies open to the policy maker;
4. prepare a complete set of valid predictions of the cost and benefits of each alternative, including the extent to which each alternative will achieve the various operational goals, consume resources, and realize or impair other values;
5. calculate the net expectations for each alternative by multiplying the probability of each benefit and cost for each alternative by the utility of each, and calculate the net benefit (or cost) in utility units; and
6. compare the net expectations and identify the alternative (or alternatives, if two or more are equally good) with the highest net expectations.

In fewer words, using the rational model is merely defining one's goals, analyzing the available alternatives, and selecting the alternative that best meets the goals.

Although similar to the rational model, the "stages of problem solving" model is amenable to observation and analysis, but it too can be a normative model.

EXHIBIT 1-2 **Stages of Problem Solving** (*Source:* Richard Wallen in Edgar H. Schein, *Process Consultation: Its Role in Organization Development.* Reading, Mass.: Addison-Wesley Publishing Co., Inc., 1964, p. 46.)

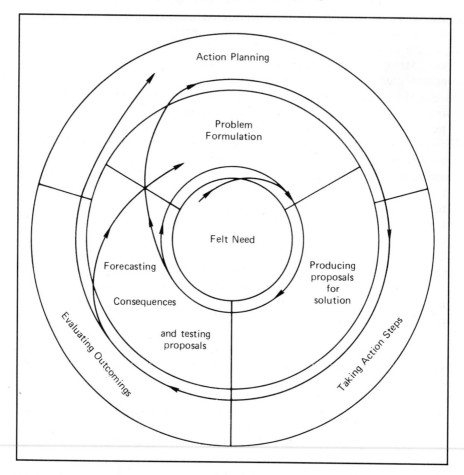

Exhibit 1-2 presents the model visually. The starting point is the perception that a problem exists—not the formulation of goals. Perception permits the possibility of multiple value perspectives, whereas in formulating goals one tends to ignore the possibility of multiple or conflicting values. Either formally or informally, the decision maker defines the problem, considers the solutions, and analyzes the alternatives in a manner similar to someone using the rational model. A key decision is then made either to reconsider the nature of the problem or to plan to resolve the problem. (This reconsideration step is not a part of the rational model.) If the decision is to proceed, the necessary action steps are taken and outcomes are evaluated. (This second reconsideration is also absent from the rational model.) From evaluation, the decision maker may either start over by reconsidering the problem or replan his or her action steps.

The incremental change model and the Wildavsky model are excellent tools for understanding the political environment of public policy making, but they are not useful for explaining the more technical difficulties associated with analysis. On the other hand, the rational model helps us comprehend the technical difficulties of analysis, but is relatively useless in explaining the highly important political environment.

With the incremental change and Wildavsky models, the public budget person can better understand how the budget process is dominated by the strategies employed by and the conflicts that arise among the participants (clientele groups, agencies, departments, the Office of Management and Budget). Definable strategies exist that require such practices as agency cultivation of an active clientele, the development of confidence among other reviewing government officers such as budget examiners, and skill in following tactics that exploit temporary opportunities. Analysis in the budget process must serve to aid the key actors involved in making public policy. Reasoning from the incremental change model, program and budget analysis must be timely, must be able to be used to seize political opportunities, and must be comprehensible to those who must use the analysis in partisan bargaining situations.

The satisficing and ideal-rational models are useful for understanding the difficulties associated with decision making. The satisficing model dramatically emphasizes that decisions are made under pressure, and severe limitations make achieving even a satisfactory alternative a significant accomplishment. The problem with the model is that one is often not satisfied that the best alternative has been selected. On the other hand, the desire for deciding on the best alternative is reflected in the ideal-rational model. The problem with that model is that the best alternative often cannot be achieved because of practical concerns such as a lack of time. We seem to be trapped between our desire for quality and the necessity to cope with our daily pressures.

The stages-of-problem-solving model can be contrasted to the ideal-rational model. In the problem-solving model, the starting point is the perception that a problem exists, thus permitting one to consider the significance of culture, time, and perspective. By contrast, in the rational model the starting point is the definition of one's goals. Next in the problem-solving model, the person formulates the problem, defines alternatives, gathers information, and tests proposals. In the rational model, the next steps cited are defining alternatives and gathering information. In the problem-solving model, the last steps are planning action, taking action steps, and evaluating outcomes. Again in contrast, the rational model is limited to deciding a given matter with the intention of maximizing goals. The rational model does not extend to taking action steps and evaluating outcomes. Another distinction is that the rational model does not have reconsideration as a factor, whereas the problem-solving model does.

The problem-solving model can help people working in public budgeting understand the nature of analysis. The rational model serves as the primary theoretical explanation of how analysis should be conducted, but the rational model cannot be attained. The problem-solving model serves as an alternative theoretical explanation of how analysis should be conducted in the budget process. The problem-solving model permits cycles of defining one's problem, producing alternatives, and testing alternatives. It implicitly recognizes that any given analysis will depend upon the ingenuity of the analysts, the kind of data available to them, the amount of resources at their command in undertaking the analysis, and other factors. Also the problem-solving model helps the public budgeting person relate budgeting, management-by-objectives, progress reporting, accounting, auditing, and program evaluation.

None of the models by themselves is adequate. The problem-solving, the incremental change, and the Wildavsky models help the bureaucrat to understand the role of program and budget analysis in the budget-making process. They can be significant, but there are some constraints in using them. The problem-solving model helps the bureaucrat to understand the context in which intelligence, knowledge, and analytical techniques must be used. Together, the models meet the criteria.

The rational model, the theoretical basis for some budget reforms, can lead individuals to make false and naive expectations. That model ignores the political context and demands the impossible in terms of analysis. This can encourage some individuals in the budget process to neglect timeliness, seek needlessly expensive data, search for needless alternatives, and quest for clarity in objectives which will not be forthcoming. The rational model can be useful, but not in the manner commonly assumed. The usefulness is more to point out the impossible rather than serve as an ideal for the possible.

ECONOMIC INFLUENCES ON BUDGETING

Twin Evils

As noted earlier in this chapter, capitalism as modified by socialism provides the ideological economic climate for the United States. The dispute between capitalism and socialism centers on the role of government in society and thus on the appropriateness of what should be included in a public budget. Today there is a belief that government can make a difference in the overall economy, but disagreement exists on the question of what government should and should not do to help the economy achieve the desired condition of minimum unemployment with minimum inflation.

The agreed-upon twin evils are *severe unemployment* (mild unemployment is called a recession and a severe recession is called a depression) and a *sustained increase in price without an equal increase in value* (a mild increase is called inflation and a radical increase is called hyperinflation). Both result in significant hardships for the people of the world. Unemployment means that many people in the economy who want jobs cannot find them. Usually, during a recession, the economy is not growing or is growing very slowly; as a result, families do not receive adequate money for a decent existence. Inflation often means that people can buy fewer goods and services with the same amount of money. People on fixed incomes or slow-rising incomes are more likely to be hurt by inflation.

Exhibit 1-3 shows the U.S. employment rates from 1929 to 1982. The reader can easily understand why the 1930s are called "The Great Depression" since more than 5 percent unemployment is normally considered unacceptable and the unemployment rate in that era reached a high of 24.9 percent. Some inflation is common, but the rate of inflation can rise to hyperinflation levels. Prices can rise so fast that no one is willing to receive or hold money. In Germany in 1923, the rate of hyperinflation was so high that paper currency became almost worthless and was used as wallpaper; barter reasserted itself as the principal method of trade. However, Western civilization has evolved to the point where it cannot sustain itself with a barter economy. Hyperinflation exists when a government enormously expands the money supply to finance large-scale expenditures. Mild inflation exists for reasons which will be discussed later.

Recession and inflation have been with us throughout modern society. Economic theory largely addresses these twin problems: How do they occur? What can

EXHIBIT 1-3   Unemployment Rates for Selected Years 1929-82 (% of Civilian Work Force)
(*Source*: U.S. Department of Labor, *Economic Report of the President*; U.S. Department of Commerce, *Statistical Abstract of the United States*. (Washington, D.C.: Bureau of the Census, 1983).

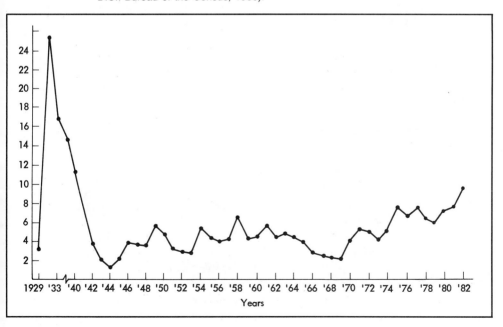

EXHIBIT 1-4 (*Source*: Lloyd G. Reynolds, *Economics*, 4th ed. Homewood, Ill.: Richard D. Irwin, Inc., 1973, p. 174.)

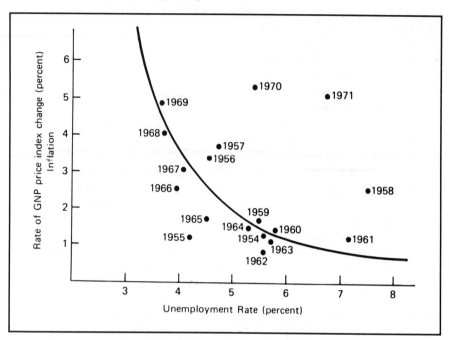

be done to avoid them? In the last quarter of the twentieth century, our tools to deal with these problems are monetary and fiscal policy. Both involve public budgeting.

Exhibit 1-4 is a Phillips curve which helps describe the relationship between the unemployment rate and the rate of inflation. Note that there is an inverse relationship. In the exhibit, as unemployment goes down, inflation goes up. Also note the odd locations of the points for 1970 and 1971, which reflect a different pattern than those for the 1960s.

Influence of Economics

When Franklin D. Roosevelt became president of the United States, the country was in the Great Depression. He advocated and the Congress strongly agreed that action was necessary and that jobs had to be created. FDR was not motivated or influenced by economic theory. He was influenced by the large number of unemployed people, as cited in Exhibit 1-3.

The Great Depression was a political turning point for the United States. Before that time, social and economic thinking called for minimum or laissez faire government. The works of Adam Smith, Herbert Spencer, and Charles Darwin were highly influential prior to 1929. The least government was considered the best government. Nature and business should take their courses without interference as if they were guided by invisible forces or laws which would enable society to evolve into a higher, improved state. The Great Depression was a harsh awakening. In 1933, 24.9 percent were unemployed. This was not an improved state. Voters and many intellectual leaders felt the old theories were unacceptable.

The idea that government could and should be used as a positive instrument in society gained widespread approval. No longer was the least government the best government. FDR launched massive public works programs for the times. Today, most economists agree that he was not bold enough. The spending for World War II is probably what got the United States and the world out of the depression. FDR's New Deal programs convinced many Americans that a strong, active federal government was "a good thing." World War II and the subsequent Cold War convinced even more Americans that the United States must remain a strong military power. Thus, the public's view of the role of government in American society has been greatly altered since 1929.

In the mid-1960s and 1970s, economic theory guided some of our most significant government decisions, and a variety of government units have arisen as the institutional means to consider and implement economic policy. Especially at the national level, economic theory has become the context in which major decisions are made.

The institutional mechanism is complex. In the executive branch, there is the Council of Economic Advisors, the Office of Management and Budget (OMB), and the Department of the Treasury. Each helps consider economic policy, and the OMB is the major implementer of fiscal policy once decisions are made by Congress and the President. In the legislative branch, the Congressional Budget Office (CBO), the Joint Economic Committee, the House and Senate Budget and Appropriations Committees, the House Ways and Means Committee, and the Senate Finance Committee all play important roles. The CBO and the Budget Committees are particularly important in setting overall fiscal policy. Partly independent of both Congress and the president, the Federal Reserve System largely establishes the nation's monetary policy. The detailed workings of each group are beyond the scope of this text, and readers are encouraged to take economics courses to pursue these subjects.

For both the legislative and executive branches, the primary device to establish fiscal policy is the federal budget. The primary device to establish monetary policy is the Federal Reserve System.

MONETARY POLICY

Central Bank

The Federal Reserve System is the central bank for the United States. It attempts to control the economy's supply of money and credit. This supply in turn affects unemployment and inflation. The Federal Reserve tries to expand money and credit to foster greater employment and to contract money and credit to combat inflation. The Federal Reserve banks have tools which influence member banks, and they in turn influence business and the public. These tools are based on the facts that banks maintain a reserve-to-loan ratio and borrow money from the Federal Reserve System banks. The three main Federal Reserve tools are as follows:

1. open-market operations;
2. discount-rate policy; and
3. changes in the legal reserve requirement of the member banks.

Two other less significant tools are (4) moral suasion and (5) selective controls over "margin requirements" for loans made to buy stocks.

The most frequently used tool is open-market operations. The Federal Reserve's Open Market Committee frequently meets to decide to buy or sell government bonds or bills. Selling results in tightening, and buying results in expanding, the money supply. For example, selling $10 million in government bonds depresses the overall money supply. The buyers of the bonds will draw checks at a member bank, and the Federal Reserve will present the checks to the member bank for payment. That bank will then lose an equivalent amount of its reserve balance. This will contract the money supply, often by $50 million. This anti-inflationary tactic results in decreasing the total money supply.

Another tool is the discount rate, which is the interest the Federal Reserve (Fed) charges member banks for short-term loans. An increase in the discount rate increases interest rates, which makes money more expensive, thus discouraging people from borrowing. This contracts the economy. The reverse Fed action will stimulate the economy.

The third tool, changing the reserve requirement, is the most powerful, but most clumsy, tool. In a previous example, a 20 percent reserve requirement was assumed. The Federal Reserve Board has the limited power to raise or lower that required legal ratio within Congressionally established limits. The Fed can tighten the money supply by requiring a greater reserve to be maintained, thus shrinking the loan amount available. The converse increases the money supply. Changing reserve requirements is the most powerful tool, but it is used infrequently because of its clumsy nature.

The minor tools are also useful. Moral suasion (e.g., "jawboning") might mean merely appealing directly to key banks. The appeal alone may be sufficient. Selected credit controls are another important tool, as they involve stock marginal requirements. The Federal Reserve establishes how much credit a person is allowed to use in the buying of common and preferred stocks. This selective control acts in the same manner as the reserve requirement.

Effectiveness

The major advantages of monetary policy are as follows:

1. decisions can be reached and applied rapidly due to the less political nature of the Federal Reserve; and

2. monetary policy does work if the proper vigorous action is taken, especially in combating some types of inflation.

The advantages are significant, but the use of monetary policy should be understood in terms of its effect on society. Federal Reserve policy severely affects companies in industries such as housing which depend heavily upon external credit. When banks are forced to restrict loans, the higher credit groups will have preference; thus smaller and newer businesses will suffer. Therefore, tight monetary policy will affect certain sectors of our economy more than others and certain groups (e.g., the young and the minorities) more than others. The events of fall of 1966 illustrate the dangers of restrictive monetary policy. At that time, the policy:

1. brought the capital market to the brink of crisis;
2. caused a radical decline in home construction;
3. threatened the solvency of intermediaries, e.g., banks; and
4. left banks reluctant to make long-term loans.

Monetary Policy and Public Budgeting

Monetary policy is significant to public budgeting in at least two important ways. First, all levels of government borrow and invest. Monetary policy affects available credit and especially interest rates. The interest paid and earned is important to any government. This shall become more apparent in subsequent chapters. Second, many government programs (e.g., housing, environment) are heavily influenced by monetary policy. Budget justifications and intelligent budget reviews would not be possible without a thorough understanding of the effects of monetary policy on those programs.

FISCAL POLICY

Policy Goals

The principal macroeconomic or fiscal policy goals are:

1. *Full employment:* Practically, this means about a four percent unemployment rate in the United States. At this rate, there are about as many people looking for jobs as there are jobs available.
2. *Maintenance of price stability:* Inflation increases prices. This brings a shift in the distribution of real income from those whose dollar incomes are relatively inflexible to those whose dollar incomes are relatively flexible. Thus, those on fixed incomes such as the elderly are hurt by inflation.
3. *Steady constant economic growth:* As the population increases, economic growth is essential, not only to maintain the past standard of living but to improve that standard.
4. *An adequate supply of collectively consumed goods:* Some activities are public in nature and involve services for the good of the society. These include police protection, national defense, highways, schools, and so on.

In macroeconomics, there is an assumed relationship between the total spending level in the economy and the existence of either unemployment or inflation. Total spending can be thought of in terms of the gross national production of the society. The gross national product (GNP) equals personal consumption plus gross private domestic investment plus government purchases of goods and services plus net exports of goods and services. The GNP is the total productive activity in a country during a certain period of time.[1] If GNP is at the target level, then the unemployment rate and the inflation rate are at acceptable levels. In Exhibit 1-4, the reader will notice the inverse relationship between the unemployment rate and inflation. The best possible rates in the United States are debatable but many consider them to be about 4 percent unemployment and about 3 percent inflation. These optimal rates occurred in 1966 and 1967. All the macroeconomic or fiscal policy goals were being achieved. In the other years, the goals were not met.

Role of Government

How does a society reach these goals each year? This is the challenge of macroeconomics. Examine again the definition of GNP. Notice the key ingredients are both private and public. Exhibit 1-5 defines the ingredients of the GNP in billions of current dollars.

Today, the GNP is well over $1 trillion, but the key relationships are the same. The private sector is the most significant (about 67 percent), but the public sector is large (33 percent). The key is total GNP. If the private sector is inadequate, then the government can act positively by changing its level of spending or influencing the private sector. If the level is too high, the economy will probably suffer inflation; and if the level is too low, the economy may suffer unemployment. The fiscal powers can be viewed as operating in pairs.

GOVERNMENT POWERS	EXAMPLES
1. Buy or sell	1. Purchase of goods or sale of stockpiles
2. Take or give	2. Taxes or rebates
3. Lend or borrow	3. Surplus or deficits in the budget

The economy can be influenced by government action. Buying as a consumer stimulates the economy. Selling depresses prices. Increasing taxes depresses the income because consumers and corporations have less to spend. Giving tax rebates stimulates the economy. A budget surplus will depress the economy and deficit spending will stimulate it. Fiscal powers exist through government action because the federal government is a major actor in the economy.

---

[1]Paul A. Samuelson defines GNP as ''the sum of final products such as consumption goods and gross investment (which is the increase in inventories plus gross births or productions of buildings and equipment)''.

EXHIBIT 1-5

1981 Gross National Product		
Personal consumption expenditure		$1,843
Durable goods	$235	
Nondurable goods	735	
Services	874	
Government purchases of goods and services		597
Net private domestic investment		240
Net foreign investment (net export of goods and services)		26
Net national product		$2,608
Depreciation		230
Gross National Product		$2,938

Source: *Statistical Abstract of the United States* U.S. Department of Commerce (Washington, D.C.: Bureau of Census, September 1983).

There is no one fiscal policy solution to an economic problem. An examination of the paired powers of government listed above implies that policy makers reasoning from macroeconomic theory can disagree on the appropriate fiscal solution. This does not imply that all methods or techniques will give the same results. For example, if faster consumer stimulation is desired, then rebates are probably better than deficit spending because the latter takes much longer to be felt in the economy. On the other hand, if the problem is chronic, then deficit spending may be the best solution. Possibly the economic problem is temporary and concentrated in one major product such as steel. Then the solution may be to stockpile the goods to stimulate jobs or to sell the stockpile to depress inflationary price increases.

Macroeconomic theory does not necessarily condemn the existence of a public debt or a national budget deficit. If the debt can be easily serviced, then there is no difficulty in having a public debt (as pointed out in a later chapter). Having a chronic national debt may lead to serious difficulties. The debt payments may interfere with the government's ability to finance other useful projects. Large interest payments can mean an equitable or nonprogressive redistribution of income. Note that these problems are manageable and do not speak against a deficit in one or more particular years. Also, there are beneficial aspects of a large national public debt:

1. the public debt provides the means for the Federal Reserve to increase or decrease the money supply in connection with reserve requirements;
2. it provides needed liquidity for all the financial and nonfinancial businesses; and
3. it provides a safe investment for the unsophisticated and unwary investor.

There are built-in fiscal stabilizers in the U.S. economy. Several fall outside the scope of this text, but one that is important for public budgeting is transfer payments. These payments rise substantially during periods of recession and fall during prosperity. When people are unemployed, they receive unemployment compensation and eventually they may receive welfare and food stamps. Farm prices are likely to fall so agriculture price supports programs automatically start working. Today, emergency public works programs also begin automatically. During prosperity, these transfer payments shrink. These are commonly referred to as entitlement programs, and they constitute a large share of the national budget.

Using Fiscal Policy

In the early 1960s, the unemployment in the nation was excessive. In fiscal terms, the actual GNP was less than the desirable GNP level but prices were stable. The fiscal policy adopted was a tax cut. The Investment Tax Credit of 1962 and later the Revenue Act of 1964 were passed. The former stimulated the private sector to increase investment, thus stimulating income, employment, and the economic growth rate. The latter reduced tax liabilities, thus stimulating consumption. The policy was successful. In 1965, further tax reductions were enacted and the fiscal policy seemed sound.

By early 1966 unemployment fell below 4 percent, and predictably (see Exhibit 1-4), the price level (inflation) was rising. Only modest steps were taken to increase taxes, but government purchases rose sharply. This was a period of guns and butter—a war in Vietnam and a war on poverty. In 1967 President Johnson did ask for a temporary tax surcharge, but Congress took no action. The Fed acted as noted earlier. The excessive use of monetary policy tools caused a credit crunch with high interest rates and a recession in the home building industry. In early 1968 the situation was getting worse. President Johnson requested another "war tax," but the Congress refused to enact this politically unpopular tax. Finally, in June 1968, a compromise tax surcharge was passed, but it proved ineffective.

President Nixon inherited an economic problem. Monetary policy continued to be quite restrictive. The U.S. role in the Vietnam war began to diminish and government purchases were cut. The Vietnam war boom ended by late 1969, and a recession started by 1970.

The 1960s experience with using fiscal policy indicates that it is not a flexible policy easily applied. Quick action might be desired, but Congress is slow to act, especially on unpopular tax increases. Thus, a significant lag occurs.

Look again at Exhibit 1-4 and notice 1970 and 1971. Unlike the other years, they are not on the Phillips curve. We experienced both relatively high unemployment and inflation. The Phillips curve seems to have shifted to the right. In other words, we experienced a time in which both unemployment and inflation were at unacceptable levels at the same time. Economists call this stagflation—stagnation accompanied by price inflation.

Economists and political leaders are arguing about this phenomenon. In August 1977, a Treasury Department official was quoted as saying of President Carter: "I don't think that he understands why there's high inflation and high unemployment at the same time. But, then neither does anyone else."[2]

[2]Robert J. Samuelson, "The Enemy Among Us," *National Journal*, 9, 42(October 15, 1977), 1619.

Some facts can help us to understand the phenomenon, but confusion on this subject continues. The recession fell disproportionately on narrow groups—particularly the young and blacks. Monetary policy curbed economic activity in the sectors of the economy dependent on borrowing, but the nation has evolved into a service economy which is not as affected by monetary policy. Inflation originated most in food and oil price increases which rippled throughout the economy. The new labor and industry custom of applying automatic cost-of-living increases prevents the traditional groups from absorbing the inflation loss, thus lengthening the inflation effects. In other words, the American economy after 1975 is more complex than before, and the aggregate monetary and fiscal policy actions of the 1960s were apparently not as effective as they once were.

President Reagan approached the stagflation economy with a new economic theory largely developed by Professor Arthur B. Laffer of the University of Southern California. The heart of this theory is the relationship between tax rates and tax revenues. The Laffer curve is presented in Exhibit 1-6.

In this exhibit, the vertical line represents tax rates and the horizontal line represents tax revenues. The two extremes of zero tax rate and 100 percent tax rate produce no tax revenue. In between, the curve demonstrates that at some point an increase in tax rates actually reduces tax revenue. This is because at the higher rates individuals reduce their taxable work effort, spend more time seeking ways to reduce tax liabilities, and engage in more nontaxed activities. The implication for budgeting is that if marginal tax rates have exceeded that key point, then, ironically, a reduction in tax rates will actually lead to an increase in tax revenues.

President Reagan and his economic advisors felt that the way to get the American economy out of stagflation was to cut the tax rates. Because such a cut would result in higher budget deficits, they advocated cutting government expenditures (with the exception of military expenditures, which they increased). The immediate

EXHIBIT 1-6   Laffer Curve (Based on: Dom Bonafede, "Reagan's Supply-Side Policies Push Economics Writers into the Spotlight," *National Journal*, 9/26/81, pp. 1723.)

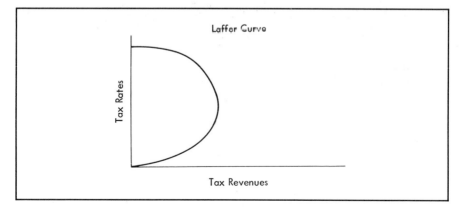

result was lower inflation, higher unemployment, and a larger federal debt. Given the automatic fiscal stabilizers built into the government programs, the federal budget expenditures grew to offset rising unemployment and revenues fell because there were fewer taxpayers. The larger federal debt, coupled with a monetary policy of high interest rates and with other factors, resulted in high interest rates which retarded economic growth and recovery.

Fiscal Policy and Public Budgeting

At the national level, fiscal policy largely influences federal budgets. Once policy is determined, using macroeconomics, then those policies influence the following budget concerns:

1. the overall size of the budget, including revenue and expenditure totals;
2. the types of spending, such as capital investment versus direct payments;
3. the timing of spending programs;
4. the balance of activities—federal programs do work at cross purposes, and it must be decided which to emphasize and which to deemphasize;
5. the size of entitlement programs, and the amount available for the controlled programs;
6. the building or selling of stockpiles;
7. jawboning big labor or big corporations; and
8. tax policy.

A federal budget professional and most state and local budget officers must understand fiscal policy. Macroeconomics is the theory used to make many key budget decisions. Budget justifications and reviews are often done using macroeconomics. With the CBO and budget committees, Congress is likely to be more effective in using fiscal policy than it was in the 1960s, but political forces will still discourage the use of tax increases.

OTHER ECONOMIC TOPICS

In a text of this nature, all aspects of economics important to public budgeting cannot be covered in a single chapter. Subsequent chapters use various economic concepts, but the important contribution of economics to public budgeting is still not stated fully. Students are encouraged to read various economics texts, especially public finance books. The following subjects are worth investigating at greater length:

1. multiplier effect;
2. economic growth;
3. balance of payments;
4. regional economics;
5. public interest, including Rawl's "justice is fairness" implication to economics;

6. pareto-optimum;
7. welfare economics;
8. labor economics;
9. public goods theory; and
10. public choice theory.

REVIEW QUESTIONS

1. Explain the various perspectives one can have on public budgeting and how the definition of public budgeting can be affected by each perspective.
2. Assuming policy is defined as "a guide to action," explain how budgeting is policy. Why and in what way is this understandably significant?
3. What is the budget cycle? How does the local budget cycle differ from the federal one?
4. In what ways are American ideologies significant in shaping public budgeting?
5. Explain the federal context of American budgeting and the significance of that context.
6. What are the major normative decision-making theories and how do they affect public budgeting as a practice?
7. Explain why inflation and unemployment rates act in inverse relationship.
8. What happened in 1970 and 1971 which cast doubt upon macroeconomic theory?
9. Why does the shift in the American economy from an industrial to a service economy have significance to the effectiveness of monetary policy?
10. How can liberals and conservatives disagree on fiscal policy but still base their thinking on macroeconomic theory?
11. Why is public debt not bad *ipso facto*? Explain why entitlement programs are consistent with macroeconomic theory.
12. Explain the economic theories which Reagan relied upon in making his economic recommendations. Contrast them to the other, more accepted macroeconomic theories.

REFERENCES

BAKKER, OEGE. *The Budget Cycle in Public Finance in the United States*. The Hague: W. P. Van Stockum, 1953.
BARTIZAL, JOHN R. *Budget Principles and Procedures*. Englewood Cliffs, N.J.: Prentice-Hall, 1942.

BRUNDAGE, PERCIVAL FLACK. *The Bureau of the Budget*. New York: Holt, Rinehart & Winston, 1970.

BUCHANAN, JAMES M. *The Demand and Supply of Public Goods*. Chicago: Rand McNally, 1968.

BUCK, A. E. *Public Budgeting*. New York: Harper & Row, Pub., 1929.

BURKHEAD, JESSE. *Government Budgeting*. New York: John Wiley, 1965.

_____ and JERRY MINER. *Public Expenditure*. Chicago: Aldine, 1971.

CENTER FOR THE STUDY OF AMERICAN BUSINESS. *The Supply-Side Effects of Economic Policy*. St. Louis, Mo.: Washington University, 1981.

DAHL, ROBERT A. *A Preface to Democratic Theory*. Chicago: University of Chicago Press, 1956.

DAVID, JAMES E., JR. (ed.). *Politics, Programs and Budgets*. Englewood Cliffs, N.J.: Prentice-Hall, 1969.

DORFMAN, ROBERT. *Measuring the Benefits of Government Expenditures*. Washington, D.C.: Brookings Institution, 1965.

DUE, JOHN F. and ANN F. FRIEDLAENDER. *Government Finance*. 5th ed. Homewood, Ill.: Richard D. Irwin, 1973.

HAVENMAN, ROBERT H. and JULIUS MARGOLIS. *Public Expenditure and Policy Analysis*. 2nd ed. Chicago: Rand McNally, 1977.

LEE, ROBERT D. and RONALD W. JOHNSON. *Public Budgeting Systems*. Baltimore: University Park Press, 1973.

MILLER, RODGER L. E. *Economics Today*. 4th ed. New York: Harper & Row, Pub., 1982.

MOAK, LENNOX L. and ALBERT M. HILLHOUSE. *Local Government Finance*. Chicago: Municipal Finance Officers Association, 1975.

Municipal Performance Report, 1, 4 (August 1974).

MUSGRAVES, RICHARD A. and PEGGY B. MUSGRAVES. *Public Finance in Theory and Practice*. New York: McGraw-Hill, 1973.

NICHOLS, DOROTHY M. *Modern Money Mechanics*. Chicago: Federal Reserve Bank of Chicago, 1975.

RABIN, JACK and THOMAS D. LYNCH. *Handbook on Public Budgeting and Financial Management*. New York: Marcel Dekker, 1983.

REYNOLDS, LLOYD G. *Economics*. 4th ed. Homewood, Ill.: Richard D. Irwin, 1973.

SAMUELSON, PAUL A. *Economics*. 10th ed. New York: McGraw-Hill, 1976.

SWAN, WALLACE K. "Theoretical Debates Applicable to Budgeting" in *Handbook on Public Budgeting and Financial Management*. Jack Robin and Thomas D. Lynch (eds.). New York: Marcel Dekker, 1983.

TRUMAN, DAVID. *The Governmental Process*. New York: Knopf, 1951.

TWO
TOWARD MODERN BUDGETING

This chapter examines public budgeting, reflects upon how it has evolved into its present condition, and reflects upon its significance in the larger context of public administration. Some attention is given to explaining what knowledgeable people define or characterize as public budgeting. Particular attention is focused on the critical issues which shaped the evolution of public budgeting. This chapter should help the reader understand:

1. the major historical reforms which have shaped public budgeting in America, and how the issues implicit in those reforms are still influencing what we perceive to be the "proper" role of budgeting in our government;
2. the executive focus on contemporary budget reforms;
3. the legislative focus on contemporary budget reforms; and
4. the state of modern budgeting in America.

PRELUDE

Parliament versus the King

Public budgeting in the United States is very much influenced by early English history. The word "budget" seems to have originated in the Middle English *bouget,* meaning bag or wallet. A great leather bag was used by the king's treasurer—later called the exchequer—to carry the documents explaining the king's fiscal needs. That bag was called the budget. Over time the document came to be called the budget, and the system used to prepare and execute the document came to be called budgeting. The bag was used primarily when the king's treasurer went to Parliament seeking funds for the king.

English history is largely a struggle between the king and the Parliament over control of the nation. Not surprisingly, the budget was central to that struggle. In 1215, King John signed Magna Carta; the twelfth article of that document stated that no taxes could be imposed "unless by the common council of the realm." The council of the realm was made up of the elite nobles and it evolved into the Parliament. In 1688, the English Bill of Rights established that no man could be compelled to pay a gift, loan, or tax "without common consent by Act of Parliament." The king was losing the struggle to unilaterally control the budget and by 1760 the king agreed to an annual specified grant controlled by the Parliament.

This struggle or tension between the legislature (the Parliament) and the executive (the king) is also one of the most important characteristics of public budgeting in the United States. At the time of the American Revolution in 1776 and the drafting of the Constitution in 1789, the English experience influenced American leaders. The tension was considered good. Power, they thought, should be separated, especially between the legislative and executive branches. The separation helped prevent executive abuse of power but still enabled strong leadership to exist. Almost every American budget reform tends to address or affect this intended tension.

Colonial America

In colonial America, the revenue was generated within the colonies and the various state houses had a great deal of control over revenues and expenditures. The king's representatives administered the government. The legislatures became the place where the leading colonists gathered. They became accustomed to exercising power with a separate group actually administering the government programs. The separation from England, abetted by the primitive means of transoceanic transportation, fostered independence. But the need to live within their own resources and to decide how to apply their own resources using a locally elected legislative body were the important factors leading to self-reliance.

Many of the causes of the American Revolution relate directly to public budgeting issues. England decided to impose taxes (e.g., the Stamp Act) on the colonies largely because of the expensive French-Indian War. This unilateral act seemed unfair given the legislative authority over tax matters and the reasoning of such documents as Magna Carta and the Bill of Rights. Of course, many other reasons as well explain the emotions leading to the American Revolution, but issues concerning public budgeting were some of the most emotionally charged subjects of that era.

Not surprisingly, those strong feelings helped shape the U.S. Constitution. For example, Article I, Section 9 of the Constitution requires that all matters dealing with revenue must originate in the House of Representatives. The founders of the United States were not content to say that Congress had to act on revenue matters, as the English Bill of Rights had said of Parliament a century earlier. Rather they stated that this matter had to start with the chamber of Congress which was to be *the* representative of the people. Today, the president presents his budget somewhat as the king's treasurer did. The House passes the appropriation bills first. The Senate often acts as an appealing body and eventually the two chambers agree upon the appropriations. However, the House is still considered the leading chamber on matters concerning revenue and appropriations.

Budgeting in the 1800s

For the first few years of the federal government, Alexander Hamilton was the influential secretary of the Treasury. He viewed his role as being much like that of the English exchequer, and his department was the most significant nonmilitary department. The national government's revenue source was customs duties, and the Coast Guard was an important force in ensuring their proper collection. Hamilton also effectively had the very large Revolutionary War debt retired.

Thomas Jefferson came to be the leader of the anti-Federalist faction which opposed Hamilton. The Federalist view was influenced by contemporary England, where the ministers dominated the Parliament and the executive activities. Jefferson thought separation of powers critical, and his and later administrations stressed that budgetary decisions were largely the dominion of the Congress. Executive leadership on comprehensive budget matters was considered improper by some presidents, but, interestingly, Jefferson's administration was characterized by strong leadership by Secretary of the Treasury Albert Gallatin.

Congress started with a unified and comprehensive approach to public budgeting. The Ways and Means Committee was extremely powerful, as it made decisions on revenues and appropriations. With few exceptions, the executive branch did not have a unified approach. The Treasury department did compile the expenditure estimates from all the agencies, but it did not edit or analyze the estimates. Such activities were considered to be legislative in nature.

As the century evolved, the Congress eroded its unified approach to the budget. By 1865, a separate House Appropriations Committee was established, so that revenue and expenditures were considered separately. By 1885, there were eight separate committees which recommended appropriations. This disunity lessened the budgetary focus of power; but except for periods of war or depression, the federal government was not concerned about tight budgets. In this era, there was a constrained view of what government should do in society, so budgets tended to be small. Also the major revenue source—the customs—was providing more revenue than there were demands for expenditure, so that Congress had the unusual problem of dealing with large surpluses.

Municipal Budget Reform

The modern reforms in budgeting started with reactions against corruption and not with concerns for government efficiency. The reforms were addressed more to the municipal level, largely due to the efforts of popular newspaper and book writers called "muckrakers." They reported noted examples of municipal corruption and called for government reform. The most effective municipal reformers were the National Municipal League (founded in 1899) and the New York Bureau of Municipal Research (1906).

The latter group is one of the most remarkable in American history. One of the leaders was Charles Beard, who was a noted historian and founder of the academic discipline of political science. Luther Gulick and other members of that Bureau were also instrumental in founding public administration as a study and practice. The research arm of the Bureau moved to Washington, D.C., and evolved into today's Brookings Institution. The training arm was moved to Syracuse University in 1925 and became the Maxwell School of Syracuse University. The Bureau served as a model and "mother house" for many other bureaus throughout the country. The members of the bureau led and staffed almost every major governmental reform committee between 1910 and 1950.

Not surprisingly, the New York Bureau of Municipal Research was highly influential in budget reforms. One year after its creation, it prepared the first detailed report demonstrating the need for adopting a municipal budget system. In that same year, the Bureau produced an object classification budget for the New York City Department of Health. By 1912, the reforms of the bureau were reflected in the Taft Commission report, which called for object (line-item) classification budgeting in all federal departments and agencies. By the 1920s, most of the budgets of major American cities were reformed. In 1929, A. E. Buck, a staff person of the bureau, wrote the first (and very influential) text on public budgeting.

Budget reform was stimulated by "social contract" political thought. Influential reformers believed that democracy could be strengthened if citizens could vote for candidates who had the power to carry out their promises. Therefore, the chief executive should be strong and budget reform was one of the best ways to strengthen the executive. They also argued that a political-administrative dichotomy existed, permitting the professionalization of the administrative class while still permitting popularly elected leaders. This dichotomy has been discredited, but it served an important conceptual function for most of the personnel and budget reforms from the 1890s to today.

EVOLUTION

Prior to 1921

In the early 1900s, the federal government started to experience large federal expenditures and budget deficits. The customs revenue was not adequate and a federal income tax was passed. This new tax solved the fundamental revenue problem, since the tax rate could be increased to provide the necessary revenue. This tax also attracted the keen attention of the business community, as they now had a vested interest in minimizing the money that the government took from them as corporations and individuals. Business interests dominated the times. Business and many citizens stressed the importance of economy, efficiency, and government retrenchment. Many felt that the least government was the best government.

President Taft issued a report prepared by the Commission on Economy and Efficiency Goals titled "Need for a National Budget." The report stressed that the president should be responsible for preparing a unified executive budget. The rationale was motivated by two themes: (1) economy and efficiency, and (2) strengthening democracy. A budget would better enable the president to plan government activities so that maximum economy and efficiency were achieved. A president's budget would also strengthen the president's power—thus citizens could vote for or against a person who had the power to fulfill campaign promises. President Taft was not successful in his reforms and Woodrow Wilson's income tax temporarily took the pressure off.

Prior to 1921, agencies still followed the Jeffersonian tradition of preparing their estimates and transmitting them to the Treasury department, which passed them on to Congress. Treasury conducted no analyses. The various Congressional committees considered the estimates with minimum coordination among themselves. The agencies did sometimes overspend the appropriations and Congress felt obligated to appropriate the overspent amount. The president did not participate in the budget process and there was no overall Executive Branch Plan.

Budgeting and Accounting Act of 1921

President Taft's reforms were largely enacted in 1921. Pressures for budget reform continued, especially with the expense of World War I. The Budget and Accounting Act of 1921 provided for a national budget and an independent audit of government accounts. The law specifically required the president to submit a budget, including estimates of expenditures, appropriations, and receipts for the ensuing fiscal year. The new legislation created the Bureau of the Budget (BOB) in the Treasury department. Section 209 of the legislation states:

> The Bureau, when directed by the President, shall make a detailed study of the departments and establishments for the purpose of enabling the President to determine what changes (with a view of securing greater economy and efficiency in the conduct of the public service) should be made in (1) the existing organization, activities, and methods of business of such departments or establishments, (2) the appropriations, (3) the assignment of particular activities to particular services, or (4) the regrouping of services. The results of such study shall be embodied in a report or reports to the President, who may transmit to Congress such report or reports or any part thereof with his recommendation on the matter covered thereby.

This landmark legislation greatly strengthened the president and created the powerful BOB as an arm of the president. The agencies were required to submit their estimates and supporting information to BOB. Agencies were not allowed to initiate contacts with Congress. Also legislation established that all recommended legislation from agencies had to be sent to BOB for review and clearance. This clearance function greatly increased presidential power because it allowed the president to insure the executive branch was in step with presidential policy. The Bureau could and did prepare the president's budget, which was the executive branch (president's) proposal to the Congress. The agencies and departments in the executive branch were and are required to support the president's budget.

Budgeting is largely a story of relative legislative-executive strength. With Hamilton, executive strength was asserted but short-lived. After Jefferson, legislative strength in the budget area dominated but was diminished by the nonunified approach which evolved in the Congress. With the passage of the 1921 legislation, executive branch strength started to grow in spite of the fact that the Congress largely initiated the legislation. The power of the Congress was not diminished, but the 1921 Act did increase the power of the president.

The Budget and Accounting Act of 1921 also created a Congressional agency called the General Accounting Office (GAO) to audit independently the government accounts. This agency is headed by the comptroller general, who is appointed to a 15-year term by the president. The purpose of the audits is to verify that government funds are being used for legal purposes. The independence of the agency prevents improper pressure being exerted upon it by members of the executive branch.

The president's 1937 Committee on Administration Management (Brownlow Committee) recommended the strengthening of BOB's management activities. The 1921 legislation had given the bureau certain managerial responsibilities, but they were not exerted. The Brownlow Committee's report eventually led to the Reorganization Act of 1939. This in turn led to the establishment of the Executive Office of the President and the transfer of BOB to that new office. President Roosevelt defined the duties of the Bureau as follows:

1. to assist the president in the preparation of the budget and the formulation of the fiscal program of the government;
2. to supervise and control the administration of the budget;
3. to conduct research in the development of improved plans of administrative management, and to advise the executive departments and agencies of the government with respect to improved administrative organizations and practice;
4. to aid the president in bringing about more efficient and economical conduct of the government services;
5. to assist the president by clearing and coordinating departmental advice on proposed legislation and by making recommendations as to presidential action on legislative enactment, in accordance with past practices;
6. to assist in the consideration and clearance and, where necessary, in the preparation of proposed executive orders and proclamations;
7. to plan and promote the improvement, development, and coordination of federal and other statistical services; and
8. to keep the president informed of the progress of activities by agencies of the government with respect to work proposed, work actually initiated, and work completed, together with the relative timing of work between the several agencies of the government, all to the end that the work programs of the several agencies of the executive branch of the government may be coordinated and that the monies appropriated by the Congress may be expended in the most economical manner possible with the least possible overlapping and duplication of effort.

The Bureau became the right arm of a strong president.

Post-1940 Reforms

During World War II, the Bureau became even more important with all activities directed toward the war. Taxes were increased and record deficits were incurred. The Bureau assumed added duties, including supervision of government financial reports and establishing personnel ceilings. In 1945, the Bureau's budget function was extended to include the government corporations. Also accounts had to be maintained on a program basis and full cost information was required. The Government Corporations Act of 1945 also directed the GAO to appraise the corporations in terms of their performance rather than merely in terms of the legality and propriety of their expenditures. This provision was eventually extended to all GAO reviews.

The Full Employment Act of 1946 called for economic planning and a budget policy directed toward achieving maximum national employment and production. The late 1940s saw the addition of more duties to BOB. The Classification Act of 1949 required the director to issue and administer regulations involving agency reviews of their operations. The Travel Expense Act of 1949 assigned the director regulatory functions on travel allowances.

President Truman appointed the Hoover Commission in 1947 and a report was submitted in 1949. The Commission recommended that

1. a budget based on functions, activities, and projects, called a "performance budget," be adopted;
2. the appropriation structure be surveyed and improved;
3. the budget estimates of all departments and agencies be separated between current operating and capital outlays; and
4. the president's authority to reduce expenditures under appropriations "if the purposes intended by the Congress are still carried out" be clearly established.

Several reforms resulted from the Hoover Commission, but the Budget and Accounting and Procedures Act of 1950 was particularly important. It recognized the need for reliable accounting systems and the president was given the authority to prescribe the contents and budget arrangements, simplify the presentations, broaden the appropriations, and make progress toward performance budgeting.

The Second Hoover Commission (1955) led to more technical but equally important budget reforms. Agency accounts were to be maintained on an accrual basis. Cost-based budgets were encouraged. Synchronization between agency structure and budget classifications were encouraged. The President's Commission on Budget Concepts in 1967 did not address any fundamental budget reforms but concerned itself with smaller technical issues. In summary, the post-1940 period saw many reforms which continued to strengthen the executive budget process.

Approaches to Budgeting

By the 1950s, there were three accepted formats for budgeting—line-item, program, and performance—with two underlying philosophic perspectives on budgeting—incremental and rational. In line-item budgeting (Exhibit 2-1), the

EXHIBIT 2-1 Hennepin County Line-Item Budget

| | | PROGRAM ACTIVITY BY LINE ITEM | | BUDGET YEAR 1980 | |
| | | DEPARTMENT COMM. SERVICES | | PROGRAM CODE 8831 | |

MAJOR PROGRAM: COMM. SERV. & ECON. ASST.
PROGRAM: COMMUNITY SERVICES
SUBPROGRAM: MANAGEMENT & PLANNING
ACTIVITY:

ACCOUNT NO.	DESCRIPTION	1979 BUDGET	1979 ACTUAL & ESTIMATED	1980 DEPARTMENT REQUEST
	Personal Services (8000)			
8002	Salaries & Wages-Reg	$1,586,573	$1,673,696	$1,763,765
8004	Salaries & Wages-Temp	14,137	25,000	24,000
8006	Overtime	11,117	12,000	13,000
8008	Intern Stipend	—	—	—
8014	On Call	—	—	—
8016	Emergency	—	—	—
8020	Shift Differential	—	—	—
8022	Sunday Differential	—	—	—
8048	Long Term Disability Insurance	14,694	15,308	11,789
8052	Life Insurance	1,456	1,422	1,489
8054	Health Insurance	70,401	80,619	77,388
8060	FICA	82,649	91,050	102,421
8062	PERA	106,810	111,275	104,828

Code		Col 1	Col 2	Col 3
8064	MERA	—	2,658	2,951
8066	Severance	—	—	—
8068	Stability	37,242	37,242	40,330
8070	Supplemental Retirement	13,236	13,789	11,851
8072	Unemployment Compensation	6,915	3,400	3,600
8074	Worker's Compensation	4,872	4,872	5,424
8080	Other Personal Services	10,000	10,000	10,700
8099	Personal Services-Contra	—	—	—
	Subtotal	$1,960,102	$2,082,331	$2,173,536
	Commodities (8100)			
8012	Office Supplies	$ 38,557	$ 43,000	$ 49,000
8103	Photocopying	22,181	15,000	16,500
8104	Film & Photographic	33,900	25,000	27,500
8110	General Supplies	6,000	2,000	2,200
8120	Food & Beverages	—	500	500
8130	Clothing & Linens	—	—	—
8134	Kitchen & Dining	—	—	—
8140	Surgical & Medical	—	—	—
8142	Drugs & Medicine	—	—	—
8150	Laboratory	—	—	—
	Subtotal	$ 100,638	$ 85,500	$ 95,700

Source: Hennepin County, Minnesota Budget.

items necessary to run a government process (e.g., salaries, supplies) are identified for each government unit, and the sum of money required for each item is identified by year. Program and performance budgeting are more sophisticated approaches. In the former, a logical grouping of government activities is defined and money is allocated to these activities. Performance budgeting goes one step further, identifying specific program outputs which are associated with specific program money requests. Exhibit 2-2 illustrates performance budgeting.

Those working in budgeting in the 1950s tended to follow either the incremental or the rational philosophic perspective. The former stressed that budget deci-

EXHIBIT 2-2   Hoover Commission Performance Budget Model

MEDICAL CARE

Summary: This appropriation request in the amount of $43,648,008 is to provide for the care of a daily average of 18,696 sick and injured, maintenance and operation of 34 hospitals, 2 medical supply depots, 2 medical storehouses, 6 medical department schools, 11 research facilities, operation of 432 other medical activities ashore, instruction of personnel in non-naval institutions, and care of an estimated 1,859 dead; and for Island Government—6 hospitals, 80 dispensary beds, and instruction of native practitioners. Specific programs are as follows:

1.	Medical and Dental Care Afloat—to provide technical medical and dental equipment, supplies, and services for an average of 232,485 personnel at sea, and initial outfits for 4 new naval vessels to be commissioned in 1948	$ 2,822,923
2.	Medical and Dental Care Ashore	48,419,168
3.	Care of the Dead—to provide services, supplies, and transportation for an estimated 1,859 deaths in 1948	502,700
4.	Instruction of Medical Department Personnel	2,645,347
5.	Medical and Dental Research—to provide civilian employment of 328 and supplies and equipment to operate and maintain 6 research facilities and 5 field research units in 1948	2,519,742
6.	Medical and Dental Supply System	2,936,396
7.	Island Government	1,910,463
8.	Departmental Administration—to provide civilian employment of 550, travel, telephone, telegraph, supplies, and equipment for the departmental administration of the responsibilities of the Bureau of Medicine and Surgery in 1948	1,432,100
	Appropriation Request, 1948	$43,648,008

Source: Hoover, 1949.

sions should be viewed as essentially incremental, with the last fiscal year serving as the base upon which the new year is judged. This is why budget formats often show the PY, CY, and BY (and, normally, BY-CY)—so that the incremental difference can be examined. The latter perspective, popularized by economists, stresses that rational decision-making requires examining budget decisions for a set of objectives, using analytical techniques to help discern the best decision possible.

Critics of incrementalism stress that the CY numbers may remain the same in the BY, but that significant policy shift can occur even if the numbers remain constant. Agencies may focus their arguments on the BY-CY difference, but their success rate on such requests is low. Incrementalists agree that this is true, but insist that it does no harm to their original arguments, because decisions still focus upon the current services in the CY and the proposed difference in the BY. Critics of the rational philosophic perspective argue that it is a logical absurdity and is inconsistent with a pluralist political system which accepts a multiple-value culture. A counterargument used by rationalists is to stress that the analytical techniques associated with the perspective do help executive branch decision makers.

There are three common purposes behind the budget activity: control, management, and planning. If control is the main purpose then budget formats are designed to insure that the money is spent according to established policy and that no resources are used for illegal purposes. If management is the purpose, then budget process stresses directing people in the bureaucracy and achieving efficiency and economy in those programs. If planning is the purpose, then the process emphasizes improvements in the political decision-making process. These three stresses are not mutually exclusive. All of them exist in most budget processes, but the three-purpose distinction is conceptually useful. Reformers in various eras tended to emphasize one budget purpose over the others, but the other purposes did not cease to exist.

If reformers are stressing control, they wish to guarantee fiscal accountability. They are fearful of corruption and of leaving the decisions of public employees unchecked. Those arguing for greater control are supported by arguments to increase the strength of the chief executive (which will also achieve greater economy and efficiency in government). Strong chief executives can enhance their strength through improved budget control mechanisms. Strong control can also mean that inefficient and uneconomical activities are increased because not enough management flexibility is permitted to deal with changing situations. The added procedural requirements can result in more workers and less productivity.

Early American public budget literature stressed the control function. Given the well-publicized political corruption of the era, the stress on control is certainly understandable. The reforms included such well-known budget features as the following:

Annual budget: revenues and expenditures presented for one fiscal year period;
Comprehensive budget: all revenues and expenditures included in the budget;
Detailed line items: presenting the exact amount planned to be spent for every separate thing or service to be purchased;

Identification of all transactions: recording every obligation and transfer of money and liquidation of obligation;

Apportionments and allotments: an executive branch mechanism to regulate the rate and actual spending of authorized funds.

Stress on budget control comes with a price tag. Extreme control limits management flexibility, which might be essential in many situations. Interestingly, the reform for efficiency can lead to inefficiency because management cannot easily adapt to more efficient procedures. Budget control is a high administrative cost activity. Recording all transactions and every line item requires many people even in this era of the computer. Another cost of budget control is more subtle in its effect upon government. By stressing control, the emphasis is upon detail and the big policy decisions tend to be ignored. Thus government becomes less responsive to the problems of society.

If reformers are stressing management, they view the budget as a tool of the executive to achieve effective operational direction with greatest efficiency. The budget can be used as a mechanism to guide the massive bureaucracy. Reforms like performance budgeting (i.e., categorizing the planned activities to stress the relationship of money to achievement) and productivity improvements (i.e., getting greater results for relatively fewer resources) are stressed. Often reformers decentralize the details to the agency level while stressing means to achieve greater centralized direction. Normally those reforms are more conservative and business-oriented, and, not surprisingly, these reforms were stressed more in the 1920s, early 1930s, 1970s, and 1980s, when conservative Republicans were president.

If reformers are stressing planning, they view the budget as a way to bring greater rationality into the public policy-making process. These reformers are appalled at the poor decision-making situation of top policy makers and the noncoordinated nature of many decision-making processes. They believe that coordinated and rational decision-making is important and that more planning and greater use of analysis will improve the decision-making process. Those reformers stress the importance of analysis, data, and categorizing the budget to facilitate analysis. In the 1960s, PPB (planning-programming-budgeting) and the use of analysis was stressed in public budgeting. In the 1970s, ZBB (zero base budgeting) also stressed analysis.

AN EXECUTIVE FOCUS

Planning and Analysis

Planning-programming-budgeting (PPB) was an attempt in the federal government—continuing today in some state and local governments—to institutionalize analysis in the executive branch decision-making process. The advocates of PPB believed public budgeting was the key to most of the important decisions made in government and that public policy-making lacked enough analysis for top level decision makers. They believed that procedural reforms could insert essential analysis into the public budgeting process, thus improving public policy-making.

PPB was not a new creation in the 1960s. In 1907, the New York Bureau of Municipal Research developed the first Program Memorandum. The Hoover Commission advocated performance budgeting and budgets were organized into programs in the 1940s. In the 1930s, welfare economics developed many of the same techniques later associated with PPB. In the 1950s, operations research and systems analysis also developed techniques later associated with PPB.

PPB was popularized in the 1960s by Secretary of Defense Robert McNamara and spread by President Johnson to the whole federal government. Secretary McNamara had a strong analytical background and asked Charles Hitch to apply the concepts developed at Rand Corporation to the Defense Department. Most people, and especially President Johnson, were impressed with the McNamara management of the Department of Defense. In 1965, President Johnson ordered that PPB be used in every federal department and agency. In time, PPB also spread to many state and local governments as well as to governments around the world.

The era of PPB was one of guns and butter. The United States was fighting a war on poverty and a war in Vietnam. There were strong, intelligent people (then called the "best and the brightest") running the country, but the goals outmatched the available talent and resources. This was true with PPB because the goals were visionary, but the resources, including talented people, were inadequate for the challenge.

PPB was an attempt to embody the rational model of decision-making into the executive branch's policy-making process. The attempt and PPB were declared dead in the Nixon administration, but the verdict was too harsh. PPB was officially deleted from the U.S. Office of Management and Budget (the renamed Bureau of the Budget) official guidelines, but federal agencies continued to use it. In some federal agencies PPB worked, in many others it was never really tried, and in some agencies it just didn't work. PPB does continue to exist in some state and local governments.

A common misunderstanding of novices about budgeting is to equate PPB and analysis. PPB was and is an attempt to institutionalize analysis into the public budgeting process. PPB is not analysis or a form of analysis. It does encourage the application of marginal utility analysis, cost-benefit studies, cost-effectiveness analysis, sensitivity analysis, pay-off matrix, present values, and other techniques.

Analysis can be characterized as various art forms—many would argue sciences—which examine alternatives, view them in terms of basic assumptions and objectives, and test as well as compare alternatives. All this is done with a purpose of finding "useful" information or conclusions concerning policy questions. The techniques vary and were developed in several different disciplines.

PPB was operationalized through the use of several mechanisms. The use of analysis was stressed, particularly in the early stages of the budget cycle. A categorization of government programs called a "program structure" was required to facilitate analytical comparisons. The greater use of data associated with the programs was encouraged. Output measures and five-year projections beyond the budget were considered essential. Analysis was further encouraged by the use of mandated special studies and analyses addressed to specific major program issues.

What are the lessons which can be learned from the PPB experience? They can be summarized as follows:

Theoretical and Conceptual Issues

1. Program budgeting, policy analysis, and other related concepts are vague, and thus present a difficult challenge to the practitioner who wishes to apply the concepts. A great deal of effort and creative talent is necessary to tailor and operationalize these concepts.

2. The rational model, as an ideal for practitioners, can result in serious mistakes.

3. The use of one program structure does not strengthen but rather limits policy analysis. Subjects of analysis vary and one categorization greatly limits the necessary range of analysis.

4. Government programs often do not have and may never have logical, consistent operational objectives. Policy makers recognize the value of vagueness in achieving necessary political consensus and know that vagueness often hides conflicting views on the proper direction of a program. Public administrators inherit this confusion and must deal with it even though most analytical techniques cannot work with such ambiguity.

5. Analysis normally is helpful only for relatively narrow but often important policy questions. The use of analysis is constrained by such things as the ability of the analyst and the nature of the subject being examined. Analysis is often most useful on technical questions.

Implementation

1. A significantly large amount of money and many talented people must be devoted to making a reform like PPB work.

2. A phased implementation plan should be adopted so that agencies and portions of agencies most likely to accept the change can be introduced to the innovation first, and resisting agencies can be introduced to the change last. As a matter of realistic strategy, one can expect resistance from some top management which will effectively prevent successful implementation. Training and hiring policies can minimize the problem, but such effective resistance cannot be avoided entirely.

3. The key person for insuring effective policy analysis is the agency head. A desire and ability to use policy analysis effectively should be one criterion for hiring a person for this position. Then a tailor-made brief orientation course could be given new agency heads which could include the use of policy analysis in public policy making.

4. One particularly difficult problem is to achieve coordination of policy among the policy analysts and planners, the budget officer, the accountants, the lawyers, the public affairs officer, the analysts preparing the agency's progress reports, and the program managers within an agency.

Political Factors

1. The use of plans covering five years does not appear to limit the political options available.

2. Policy analysis rarely addresses the political costs and benefits of a program to specific key individuals such as legislators, but good analyses do address analytical questions which set out political costs and benefits in general.

3. The political advantages of not using analysis with explicit objectives may be critical to reaching some decisions in some specific political situations, but there is no reason to believe there is a common circumstance.

Human Factors[1]

1. People in an agency must believe that the reform is a significant and legitimate undertaking. The real test for them will be how seriously key people (like the agency head) and key agencies (such as the Office of Management and Budget) treat the reform. If these people and groups continually demand and use the products of this reform, then significance and legitimacy will be established.

2. Positive and politically practical recommendations must be the products of the reform. If they are not generated, the people directly responsible for operationalizing the reform in the agency will lose effectiveness both among organizational peers and also among the key decision makers who use the products.

Management

1. Systematic attempts to institutionalize policy analysis do tend to centralize governmental decision-making.

2. Reforms like PPB do not greatly influence government reorganization.

Management by Objectives

At the beginning of the second term of the Nixon administration, the White House and the Office of Management and Budget strongly encouraged the federal departments and agencies to use management-by-objectives (MBO). The technique called MBO is the setting out of specific objectives for agencies and requiring regular high level periodic reports on the progress toward achieving those objectives. The Nixon administration's use of MBO varied from the conventional MBO, especially by not stressing lower level participation in the formulation of objectives. Also the adoption of MBO was not done through OMB regulations, as PPB had been, but was required through the use of the informal memorandum from OMB to the various departments and agencies requesting information to a specific MBO format.

Serious government-wide presidential use of MBO was short-lived and died with the Nixon administration. The reform did have a significant influence on many federal departments and agencies as the technique was integrated into their standard operating procedures.

In a few agencies, there was an attempt to link MBO and public budgeting. Such a linkage is theoretically possible but is rarely done. The linkage is accomplished by using a matrix table with MBO objectives and budget activities. The matrix table squares contain the amount of money needed to carry out the objective

---

[1]Some items were covered under "Implementation."

during the budget year. A given program may have multiple objectives; therefore the money cited would not be placed in mutually exclusive categories. Also, not all program activities would be covered by the objectives used in MBO. The advantage of the linkage is to insure that resources are available to meet the high-priority objectives of the government.

Zero Base Budgeting

Zero base budgeting is an approach to public budgeting in which each budget year's activities are judged in a self-contained fashion, with little or no reference given to the policy precedents of past years. ZBB is contrasted to incremental budgeting, in which the budget justification is focused upon the difference between the current year (CY) and the budget year (BY). In making the distinction between ZBB and incremental budgeting, a false impression can be given of both concepts as they are practiced. In ZBB, the analysts normally will want information on past funding levels and past accomplishments, but the analysts could also ignore such data. In incremental budgeting, the analysts normally will want information on all activities being planned in the budget year but their focus will be upon the program changes from the current year. The analysts already know much of the program information from reviewing last year's budget.

In 1964, the U.S. Department of Agriculture used a ZBB approach to prepare its budget. It was an additional exercise on top of the normal budget process. ZBB required voluminous documentation and a great deal of departmental time and energy. Critical evaluators of the approach concluded that, except for a few small decisions, the department reached the same conclusions as it would have reached with the less expensive incremental approach. The higher level officials did feel that they gained a much fuller understanding of their organization because of the ZBB experience. However, ZBB was abandoned.

Peter A. Pyhrr used ZBB in the private sector and popularized its wider use. Mr. Pyhrr used it successfully in Texas Instruments and wrote a book titled *Zero-Base Budgeting,* and also authored an extremely influential 1973 article in *Harvard Business Review*. The then governor of Georgia—Jimmy Carter—read about ZBB and invited Mr. Pyhrr to help him apply the approach to the state of Georgia. Presidential candidate Carter talked a great deal about the virtues of ZBB and President Carter required its adoption by the federal government.

The use of ZBB in the private sector has been confined primarily to overhead activities (i.e., expenses needed to maintain the organization versus expenses needed to produce the product). There is a great deal of difference between public and private budgeting, but they are the most similar in the area of overhead. In private budgeting, revenue comes from sales, which can fluctuate due to a variety of factors. If sales are up and unit costs are constant or lower, then the company has more money to spend or give back to the investors. In public budgeting, revenue comes from taxes, which normally are intended to buy certain services. The focus is upon the services which are sometimes difficult to define, such as national defense preparedness. In the private sector, overhead is meant to be a service to the organization, much as government is a service to the society. Not surprisingly, the private sector has had little difficulty budgeting for its major functions, but has had greater difficulty budgeting for its overhead functions. ZBB has proved to be a useful budgetary approach for the private sector's overhead activities.

The use of ZBB in the public sector is a recent development, with the exception of the Department of Agriculture experience. ZBB was adopted by a few cities and several states (including Georgia, New Jersey, Idaho, Montana, and Illinois). The assessment of its success and failure is unclear, but its initial advocates were enthusiastic. Problems have arisen similar to the ones experienced with PPB but conclusions are unclear, with the few empirical studies generally negative.

There are several different ZBB approaches. This is appropriate, as ZBB should be tailored to each government's unique circumstances. Normally, the ZBB consists of preparing budget proposals and alternative levels of spending grouped into "decision packages." Program and higher level managers then rank those decision packages in the order of priority. The lowest levels don't get funded.

Decision packages are self-contained units for budget choice containing input and output data (i.e., resources needed to operate the program and the products of the program) as well as the expected levels of performance for each defined level of expenditure. These packages are prepared by the manager responsible for each discrete activity at the lowest level of an organization capable of formulating a budget request. Alternative decision packages are prepared and ranked, thus allowing marginal utility and comparative analyses. Often the guidelines stipulate that a package should be prepared for the minimum cost essential to carry out the activity effectively, but some guidelines recognize the extreme latitude given the manager using that type of guidance. Some states have selected arbitrary percentages to insure that an amount smaller than last year's request is considered. They do this by stipulating that one alternative must be 50 or 80 or 90 percent of last year's request.

Decision packages are then ranked by managers and executives by priority. Other, lower cost packages within each activity are necessarily given higher priority over the more costly packages. The packages are ranked by the managers preparing the packages and by executives at each level above the manager. A chief executive can and does establish a cutoff point for the government as a whole, as well as for each agency. Only the packages above the cutoff are included in the executive branch budget submitted to the legislature.

There are some serious problems in using ZBB. The most obvious is that ZBB can be a paper monster which buries executives in an avalanche of documents. ZBB necessarily means thousands of decision packages. For example, in Georgia there were 10,000 decision packages, and no chief executive can review each one. Mechanisms must be created to manage the paperwork, limiting it to only the critical decisions. Another problem is dealing with programs which are effectively uncontrollable in the budget, such as veterans' benefits, social security, interest on the debt, retirement, and food stamps. ZBB cannot address them, yet they represent over 75 percent of the federal budget and are significant in many state and local budgets as well. The technique does not help judge priorities between budget activities such as defense, welfare, and environments. Also the technique does not lend itself to demanding responsive grant programs (e.g., grant-in-aid programs), which are designed to let communities largely define objectives and priorities. Marginal analysis of the budget packages cannot be used in those programs because the granting agency cannot accurately forecast benefit. The agency does not know who will qualify or what the funds will be used for and therefore what benefits should result. Also a very serious question still exists: Are government decisions different from private-sector decisions or is there something to which government decisions are being compared?

There are some apparent advantages to ZBB. In programs involving clear operational missions, such as highways, recreation, and public works, the technique is analytically relevant to the program analysts and decision makers. The approach shifts budget attention away from adding to the current year program and focuses consideration upon increases to the minimum level of operational support. The approach is successful in educating higher level executives and their staffs on the nature of government programs. Also the approach may stimulate redirection of resources within budgets and programs into more productive activities.

TBB and Envelope Budgeting

There is a nonrational approach to budgeting which rejects PPB and its foundations; it is called target base budgeting (TBB) in Cincinnati and Tampa and envelope budgeting in Canada. In sharp contrast to PPB, envelope budgeting is a top-down rationing process which is concerned with establishing priorities and limits at the top as a means to force choice among alternatives at the bottom. It does not stress economic rationality but rather political rationality by:

1. permitting the Canadian Committee on Priorities and Planning to establish ceilings—priorities and envelope expenditure levels—for each ministry;
2. delegating authority to Policy Committees to fund new proposals from established envelope resources; and
3. permitting additional funding for new proposals through a limited policy reserve.

TBB is quite similar to envelope budgeting. Both rely heavily upon BY revenue forecasting, with most of the projected revenue assigned to city agencies or national departments according to their proportion of current year budget allocations. In envelope budgeting that linkage is not stressed as heavily as in TBB. The remainder is put in a "discretionary reserve" in Cincinnati and Tampa; in Canada it is put in a "policy reserve." In both situations, the major government units are required to submit their budgets within the targets or envelope ceilings. Requests upon the discretionary reserve or policy reserve are considered.

Reagan

President Reagan advanced and strengthened the executive in terms of the budget process by adding a third important executive power. The first power was the pulling together of the agency budget requests and their organization into the

EXHIBIT 2-3   Executive Legislative Clearance Process

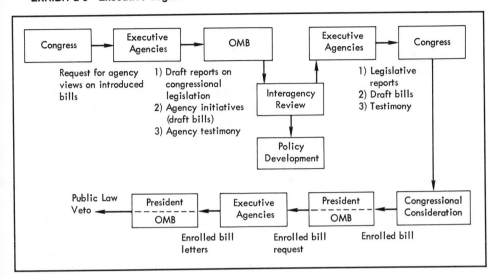

President's budget recommendation. The second was the OMB legislative clearance process (see Exhibit 2-3), which covers agency legislative proposals, agency reports and testimony on pending legislation, and enrolled bills. OMB insures that proposals, reports, and testimony conform to presidential policy and coordinates agency recommendations on presidential vetoing of enrolled bills. The third power was added in 1981 by Executive Order 12291. All federal agencies which have proposed regulatory changes must send them to OMB for its clearance on regulatory budget and economic implications. This greatly strengthens OMB's influence, especially over entitlement programs.

A LEGISLATIVE FOCUS

The 1974 Budget Reform Motivations

The Congressional Budget and Impoundment Control Act of 1974 is one of the landmark pieces of budget reform legislation in this century. The law's passage is dramatically related to the events surrounding President Nixon's resignation. The 1974 legislation created a unified congressional budget reform and it made the Congress a coequal branch with the executive on budgetary matters.

President Nixon and the Democrat-controlled Congress were constantly in battle. Nixon wished to decrease the role of government in society and Congress passed legislation seeking government action to redress various societal problems. Nixon had the advantage because it is much easier to defeat programs than it is to initiate them. One tactic employed by President Nixon was to use the disputed presidential impoundment powers on a wide range of programs, including those he had vetoed with the veto being overriden. Another tactic was to stress that the Congress was acting in an irresponsible manner because of its piecemeal and uncoordinated approach to appropriations. As Herbert Jasper—an important actor in developing the legislation—pointed out, the Congress was most upset at Nixon's charge of reckless Congressional spending.

The Watergate crisis weakened President Nixon and strengthened the Congress. The 1974 Act was one of several reforms directed toward strengthening the legislative branch. The Congressional Research Service and the General Accounting Office were expanded. Various reforms were passed to improve the Congressional oversight activities. The important legislation was to achieve a unified Congressional budget approach and neutralize the presidential impoundment powers. There was a great deal of difficulty in drafting the Act because it affected the strength of some of the most powerful legislators in both the House and Senate. Congress was able to overcome its internal struggles and passed the legislation in 1974 so that it could deal more effectively with President Nixon.

The 1974 legislation should be viewed in the context of the historical tension between the executive and legislative branches built intentionally into our system of government. After the Jefferson administration, the purse strings were clearly controlled by Congress, but Congress itself fractionalized the power over the years. This was not particularly significant as the executive did not attempt to exercise leadership in this area. With the passage of the 1921 legislation and a series of strong presidents, the power of the executive greatly increased against a fractionalized Congress. With the 1974 legislation, Congress once again focused its purse string powers and could deal with a strong executive.

Unified Congressional Budget Reforms

The 1974 legislation made several changes. It created the new Senate and House Budget Committees, created a new Congressional Budget Office, required a current services budget, and required various reforms addressed to the presidential budget. The new Congressional committees' duties included drafting overall budget targets. They could prepare reconciliation bills between budget resolutions and appropriation bills. Also the new committees were intended to, and have, put pressure on Congress to meet established budget deadlines.

Linda Smith, a former House Budget Committee staffer, pointed out in *The Bureaucrat* that the committees were challenged but the process worked. In one House vote, the margin of victory for the Budget Committee was thin. But both chambers have supported the reforms on every challenge and have voted to support a unified budgetary approach in spite of powerful legislators seeking exceptions to the approach. The reform will work only if the Congress has the desire to make it work, but the initial tests were passed. The Budget Committees have strongly urged the Congress to meet its deadlines, and Congress has succeeded in spite of extreme reservations from most observers.

The Congressional Budget Office (CBO) is a source of nonpartisan budget expertise for both chambers of Congress. The office is charged with presenting the Congress with respectable and viable alternatives on aggregate levels of spending and revenue. The office must also make cost estimates for proposed legislation reported to the floor and provide cost projections for all existing legislation. The Act requires CBO to prepare an annual report covering "national budget priorities" and "alternative ways of allocating budget authority and budget outlays." One last important duty is to keep score on administration and Congressional actions related to the budget. See Exhibit 2-4 for a complete list of responsibilities.

EXHIBIT 2-4   CBO Responsibilities. CBO's analyses usually take the form of published studies comparing present policies and programs with alternative approaches. The responsibilities of CBO are (1) budgetary estimates and (2) fiscal and programmatic analysis.

Budgetary Estimates

Scorekeeping.   Each spring, the Congress formulates and adopts a concurrent resolution on the budget, setting expenditure and revenue targets for the fiscal year to begin on the coming October 1. In September, the Congress reviews the detailed spending and taxing decisions it had made during the summer in the form of individual bills. It then arrives at and adopts a second concurrent resolution, reconfirming or changing the totals in the spring resolution. While the first resolution sets targets, the second establishes an actual ceiling for spending and a floor for revenues. CBO keeps score of Congressional action on individual bills, comparing them against targets or ceilings in the concurrent resolutions. The Office issues periodic reports showing the status of Congressional action.

Cost Estimates.   Four types of cost estimates are required of CBO by the Budget Act.

CBO prepares, to the extent practicable, a five-year estimate for what it would cost to carry out any public bill or resolution reported by Congressional committees (except the two appropriating committees).

CBO furnishes to a reporting committee a report on each committee bill providing new budget authority. Each report shows: (a) a comparison of the bill with the most recent concurrent resolution, (b) a five-year projection of outlays associated with the bill, and (c) the amount of new budget authority and resulting outlays provided for state and local governments.

CBO also furnishes to a reporting committee an analysis of each bill providing new or increased tax expenditures. The reports cover: (a) an assessment of how the bill will affect levels of tax expenditures most recently detailed in a concurrent resolution, and (b) a five-year projection of the tax expenditures resulting from the bill.

As soon as practicable after the beginning of each fiscal year, CBO prepares a report that analyzes the five-year costs of continuing current federal spending and taxing policies as set forth in the second concurrent resolution. The purpose of these projections is to provide a neutral baseline against which the Congress can consider potential changes as it examines the budget for the upcoming fiscal years.

Fiscal and Programmatic Analysis

Fiscal Analysis.   The federal budget both affects and is affected by the national economy. The Congress thus must consider the Federal budget in the context of the current and projected state of the economy. To provide a framework for such considerations, CBO prepares periodic analyses and forecasts of economic trends. It also prepares analyses of alternative fiscal policies.

Inflation Analysis.   Beginning in 1979, CBO prepared estimates of the inflationary effect of major legislative proposals and, more generally, identifies and analyzes the causes of inflation. These estimates are intended to provide the Congress with guidelines, as it undertakes new programs, of the cost in terms of inflation that these programs might entail.

Program and Policy Analysis.   CBO undertakes analyses of programmatic or policy issues that affect the federal budget. These reports include an examination of alternative approaches to current policy; all reports are nonpartisan in nature. These reports are undertaken at the request of: (1) the chairman of the committee or subcommittee of jurisdiction of either the House or the Senate; (2) the ranking minority member of a committee of jurisdiction of either the House or the Senate; or (3) the chairman of a Task Force of the House Budget Committee.

Annual Report on Budget Options.   By April 1 of each year, CBO furnishes to the House and Senate Committees on the Budget a report that combines many aspects of the functions outlined above. The annual report presents a discussion of alternative spending and revenue levels, levels of tax expenditures under existing law, and alternative allocations among major programs and functional categories.

Source: 21.S. Congressional Budget Office, 1982.

Thus far, the CBO has been successful. The Congress was slow to appoint the first CBO director and there were some beginning controversies. However, most concur that the CBO is making useful contributions, especially in the scorekeeping area. CBO is not the Congressional counterpart to the executive branch OMB. That type of power rests with the budget and appropriations committees. CBO provides essential information so that the Congress knows the fiscal implications of various proposals and can act in a deliberate manner on fiscal policy matters.

Another innovation of the 1974 legislation was to require a "current services budget." In judging budget requests, normally reference is made to how much money was requested or spent for the same item in last year's budget. This is useful information, but it is still difficult to assert what exactly is the change in the budget. Last year's expenditures do not reflect accurately how much the program will cost in the budget year, given a maintenance of current services. To get that information, Congress has required the executive branch to prepare a current services budget. Some argue that the effort involved is not justified, given the small analytical advantage over merely using last year's expenditures. This still remains an open question.

The 1974 Act changed some of the previous requirements in the presidential budget development. The president's budget is still due in mid-January but the detailed backup information supplied by the agencies is due with the presidential budget. Given the president's normal habit of delaying decision until the budget is distributed, and given the time needed to prepare the agency backup material, this requirement is unrealistic, but it does accelerate the agency submissions by several weeks. This earlier information is made available to CBO, the Budget Committees, and the Appropriations Committees, thus providing them with more time to conduct essential analyses. The Act also stipulates that the following data is required:

1. a list of existing tax expenditures, including revenue lost through preferential tax treatment and proposed changes;
2. funding projections on all *new* legislative proposals of the president;
3. budget figures presented in terms of national needs, agency missions, and basic federal programs;
4. five-year projections of expected spending; and
5. requested authorizations (procedures for obligation including ceilings) for legislation a year in advance of appropriation (budget year specific guidance on obligations and expenditures) legislation.

The required data in the 1974 legislation reflected a thorough knowledge of the budget process. By requiring a list of tax expenditures and projecting funding of new added legislation, presidential surprises can be minimized. The requirement that budget figures must be presented by national need, agency mission, and basic federal programs permits the Congressional analysts to conduct program analyses. The timing for authorization is essential to prevent preferential treatment of new presidential legislation rather than the desired Congressional comprehensive and unified approach to the budget.

The drafters of the legislation carefully designed budget procedures and timing to insure a unified appropriations consideration (see Exhibit 2-5). The final action on appropriations is prohibited until after the budget committee action. Not one of the thirteen appropriations bills can be considered until all have been marked up in committee. A deadline is established on final action for the appropriation bills. The deadlines and other requirements establish clear Congressional standards for responsible committee action, and the budget committee chairpersons have not been reluctant to use that standard in prodding Congressmen and Senators. There is a two-stage budget reconciliation: The first stage sets initial targets by resolution; the

EXHIBIT 2-5   Budget Timetable

Late January: President submits budget (15 days after Congress convenes).

March 15: All legislative committees submit program estimates and reviews to Budget committees.

April 15: Budget committees report first resolution.

May 15: Committees must report authorization bills by this date.

May 15: Congress completes action on first resolution. Before adoption of the first resolution, neither house may consider new budget authority or spending authority bills, revenue changes, or debt limit changes.

May 15 through the seventh day after Labor Day: Congress completes action on all budget and spending authority bills.

Sept. 15: Congress completes action on second resolution. Thereafter, neither house may consider any bill, amendment, or conference report that results in an increase over outlay or budget authority figures, or a reduction in revenues, beyond the amounts in the second resolution.

Sept. 25: Congress completes action on reconciliation bill or another resolution. Congress may not adjourn until it completes action on the second resolution and reconciliation measure, if any.

Oct. 1: Fiscal year begins.

Source: 21.S. Congressional Budget Office, 1982.

second stage permits reconsiderations and face saving. The use of House and Senate resolutions places a heavy burden on both the Appropriations and Ways and Means Committees to act within the consolidated-unified approach or appear irresponsible. In the House, the Budget Committee uses an interlocking directorate with the other key powerful committees in order to facilitate consensus. Finally, the 1974 legislation guarantees a unified approach by calling for a reconciliation bill on all spending and revenue measures with the second concurrent resolution.

The Congressional budget reform also changed the federal fiscal year from July 1 through June 30 to October 1 through September 30. This was realistic. The Congress always had difficulty approving a budget by the beginning of the July 1 fiscal year and the new reforms anticipated even more Congressional deliberation. Everyone agreed that public management would be improved if Congress were timely in its passage of appropriations, so the fiscal year had to change. Exhibit 2-6 is a summary of the federal budget process.

Backdoor Spending

One of the concerns of the advocates of the 1974 reform was the use of back-door spending (the commitment of federal funds outside the effective control of the appropriation process). Reformers argued that backdoor spending is contrary to the concept of a unified consolidated Congressional budget because some activities can-

EXHIBIT 2-6

THE FEDERAL BUDGET PROCESS

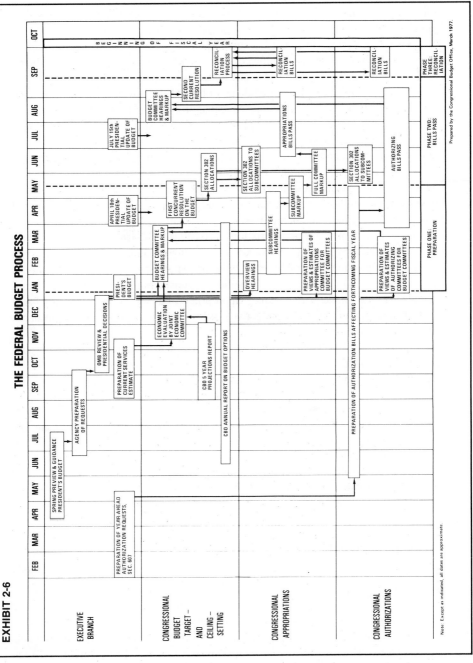

Note: Except as indicated, all dates are approximate.

Prepared by the Congressional Budget Office, March 1977.

not be balanced against the competing claims of other activities. The 1974 legislation outlaws or tries to control backdoor spending, with some major exceptions. The major exceptions were necessary or the legislation would not have passed.

There are various forms of backdoor spending. One is permanent appropriations, by which the program is allowed to spend whatever is necessary. This blank check is theoretically possible but is not found in practice. Another is contract authority, by which government officials can obligate the government through legal contracts and Congress must pass subsequent appropriations to fulfill the obligation. Borrowing authority is similar except the government official can borrow money and the Congress must pass subsequent appropriations to liquidate the debt. Yet another method is mandatory for entitlement spending, such as unemployment compensation, welfare, food stamps, payment on the national debt, veterans' benefits, and so on. The payment levels are established by programmatic rules set down in legislation and administrative regulation. If there is a recession, the government will *automatically* pay more in unemployment compensation, welfare, and food stamps, and the Congress must pay appropriations to fulfill the obligation. Earmarked revenue is considered by some to be backdoor spending because funds from a specific source (e.g., gasoline tax) can be spent only for a specific activity (e.g., highways). This earmarking prevents a unified consolidated consideration of the budget. Use of the unexpended balance (i.e., money appropriated but not spent in the last fiscal year) by carrying it over to the budget year is also contrary to the unified approach, but it is allowed in many programs.

The backdoor spending exceptions cover about 75 percent of each year's budget. The 1974 prohibition applies only to *new* contract authority, budget authority, and entitlement programs. Other major exceptions are as follows:

1. all Social Security trust fund programs;
2. all trust funds that receive 90 percent or more from designated taxes rather than from the general revenue (e.g., highways);
3. general revenue sharing;
4. insured or guaranteed loans;
5. federal or independent public corporations; and
6. gifts to the government.

Impoundment

As was pointed out earlier, the extensive use of impoundment by President Nixon was quite upsetting to the Congress. Nixon impounded large sums of money because he did not favor the programs which Congress had enacted and funded. The impoundment was not used because the executive branch found it could accomplish the Congressionally mandated purpose with less money. It was used because it was a type of veto which could not be overriden by Congress. Interestingly, in some cases the Nixon administration impounded funds for programs which had been preserved by the Congress only by overriding a presidential veto. Congress felt that Nixon violated the spirit if not the letter of the Constitution.

The judicial branch concurred with the majority of Congress. In every instance that someone took the expense and time to battle the Nixon administration on impoundment, the president lost and was forced to spend the money. Court challenges take months and often years, so the delay tended to *de facto* establish the impoundment. The program administration was crippled by this executive-judicial decision-making process because of the extreme delays.

The 1974 legislation redefined the impoundment powers. The Congress and the courts pointed out that neither the Constitution nor the law granted the president the impoundment power. The executive branch argued that ample precedent existed over the many years of the nation's history. Congress recognized the best solution was to redefine the impoundment powers so that the president could not cripple a program regardless of the true validity of the impoundment powers. Congress pragmatically wanted to prevent a president from overruling the will of Congress on government spending issues.

Today there are two types of impoundments, each handled somewhat differently. If the impoundment is to defer the spending appropriated by Congress, then *either* the House *or* the Senate can force the release of funds by passing a resolution calling for their expenditure. If the impoundment is to cut or rescind the appropriations, then *both* House *and* Senate must pass recession resolutions within 45 days of the recession or it is not valid.

One technical problem for Congress was how to deal with a president who might not inform the Congress of an impoundment. The threshold of trust between the Congress and the president was at a low ebb in 1974. The legislation required the president to send a message to Congress requesting impoundment and setting forth the rationale for it. The legislation then stated that if the president did not comply with the law, then the comptroller general (a Congressional branch employee) would report the impoundment to the Congress. If the president did not comply, the comptroller general was directed to go to the courts to get a court order forcing compliance.

The ultimate strategy involved is complex. The Constitution provides for a means to impeach the president and requires the president to execute faithfully the laws of the nation. If the courts rule against the president after the new procedure has been applied faithfully, then the president has an extremely weak defense against the argument that he refuses to execute the law faithfully. Under the procedure, both the Congress and judicial branch would have said he must comply. The Congress would be in an excellent position to impeach the president under such circumstances.

There has been only one minor test of the new impoundment process. President Nixon resigned about the same time the law became effective. President Ford did send the required impoundment messages to Congress and did comply with the will of Congress except for one situation. On April 15, 1975, the comptroller general of the United States filed a lawsuit in U.S. District Court for the District of Columbia. Named as defendants in the suit were Gerald Ford, president of the United States, James T. Lynn, director of the Office of Management and Budget, and Carla A. Hills, secretary of Housing and Urban Development.

The new legislation was being tested. On October 4, 1974, President Ford transmitted his impoundment messages, including the deferment of approximately $264 million in contract authority for the section 235 housing program, but the legislation was due to lapse on August 22, 1975. The comptroller general reasoned that this would permit only 52 days to obligate the money, thus it was a *de facto* recession, and under the law the comptroller general reported the error in a formal message to Congress. This meant that Congress had 45 days to act or the money had to be spent; it did not act, nor did the president release the funds. The comptroller general then notified Congress of his intention to bring a lawsuit and the Senate passed a resolution in support of the comptroller general. The Ford administration challenged the 1974 legislation on the grounds that (1) the comptroller general was improperly carrying out an executive function by instituting the lawsuit, and (2) the Constitution provided means other than the courts for resolving disputes between the branches of government. The legal arguments continued, but the case came to an abrupt end without a court resolution. On October 17, 1975, Carla Hills announced that the section 235 program would be reactivated and there was no longer a need for the suit. The Congress had won.

Reconciliation

The major architect of the 1974 Budget Act, Richard Bolling, was surprised by the ploy that was tried in the Congress by the Republicans and the conservative Democrats (called "Boll Weevils") soon after President Reagan took office. Although the reconciliation provision of the 1974 Act clearly says that a concurrent resolution on the budget may "determine and recommend changes in laws, bills, and resolutions . . . ," the Democratic Congressional leadership had carefully avoided serious confrontation with their powerful committee chairmen. With Ronald Reagan's election in 1980, the Republicans not only captured control of the White House and the Senate, but also gained a working majority in the House of Representatives by joining forces with Democratic conservatives. President Reagan and his aides worked with their Congressional allies to use effectively the reconciliation power stated in the 1974 Act but not previously used.

The confrontation and its success were a surprise to the House leadership, as illustrated in Exhibit 2-7. The Republican-controlled Senate concurred with President Reagan's budget suggestions (e.g., increased national defense, reduced taxes, and a huge cut in domestic spending). It passed the necessary instructions to other committees in its first concurrent budget resolution. The real confrontation occurred in the House, where the Democratic budget resolution was dramatically overturned on the House floor by a Republican/Boll Weevil coalition which supported the pres-

EXHIBIT 2-7 House Speaker Thomas P. O'Neill, June 25, 1981

I have never seen anything like this in my life, to be perfectly truthful. What is the authority for this? Does this mean that any time the President of the United States is interested in a piece of legislation, he merely sends it over? You do not have any regard for the process, for open hearings, discussions as to who it affects, or what it does to the economy? But because a man, who does not understand or know how our process, sends it over, are we to take it in bulk? . . . Do we have the right to legislate? Do we have the right to meet our target or can he in one package deregulate, delegislate, the things that have taken years to do?

Source: Congressional Record, June 25, 1981, #3383–85.

ident's views. This monumental budget resolution, called Gramm-Latta I, contained instructions for budget reductions in fifteen House committees and fourteen Senate committees, required very large outlay reductions (i.e., of $56 billion), and provided reconciliation saving of discretionary and entitlement programs. The Congressional committees responded as called for by the 1974 Act, but the result was unacceptable. The next ploy was a quickly fashioned, massive reconciliation bill called Gramm-Latta II. This extraordinary law (see Exhibit 2-8) changed eligibility rules for entitlement programs (e.g., food stamps), limited programs earlier authorized, and rewrote major parts of substantive law. No hearings were held on the law; amendment possibilities were strictly limited; debate lasted only two days; and the law was passed in a single vote rather than a section-by-section vote. Speaker O'Neill's reactions are not surprising. Reconciliation was clearly demonstrated to be a powerful budget tool.

The future effective use of the reconciliation process is open to question. President Reagan's total mastery over budgeting eroded because of stiffened opposition from the appropriations committees, less effective political maneuvering on his part, and a subsequent election which gave House Democratic leadership more loyal Democratic representatives. The helter-skelter enactment of the reconciliation bill and later tax bills was antithetical to the traditional process of slow deliberation by the committees and fostered greater long-term opposition to President Reagan's legislative liaison. In addition, Reagan's next offensive was not well received, with the result that few appropriation acts were passed on time and the president even vetoed a continuing resolution. Finally, the off-year election of 1982 gave Speaker O'Neill more loyal Democrats, thus making a repeat of the 1981 situation unlikely. The Democrats may choose to use the reconciliation process, but their past leadership style has emphasized more coordination and tolerance for various committee decisions.

EXHIBIT 2-8 Final Reconciliation Savings

The final version of the reconciliation package (HR 3982) altered existing programs to achieve the following budget savings (by House committee jurisdiction, in millions of dollars).

Committee	FISCAL 1982 BUDGET AUTHORITY CUTS	FISCAL 1982 OUTLAY CUTS	FISCAL 1983 BUDGET AUTHORITY CUTS	FISCAL 1983 OUTLAY CUTS	FISCAL 1984 BUDGET AUTHORITY CUTS	FISCAL 1984 OUTLAY CUTS
Agriculture	$ 2,449	$ 3,264	$ 3,042	$ 3,878	$ 3930	$ 4,661
Armed Services	846	882	767	731	374	374
Banking, Finance and Urban Affairs	13,566	481	15,954	1,154	18,402	2,115
District of Columbia	39	40	56	58	72	69
Education and Labor	10,088	7,297	12,414	10,749	14,261	13,881
Energy and Commerce	7,955	7,115	7,457	7,710	6,686	6,961
Foreign Affairs	376	286	524	463	538	515
Interior and Insular Affairs	820	736	+236[1]	111	68	5
Judiciary	72	30	70	71	59	66
Merchant Marine and Fisheries	242	106	242	212	265	253
Post Office and Civil Service	4,706	5,163	6,253	6,690	7,214	7,555
Public Works and Transportation	6,606	1,411	5,070	3,136	6,371	5,418
Science and Technology	1,395	828	961	1,016	1,209	1,065
Small Business	504	823	540	517	527	506
Veterans' Affairs	110	116	122	127	124	128
Ways and Means	4,140	8,981	4,455	9,822	4,763	10,803
Total Cuts[2]	$51,900	$35,190	$55,734	$44,033	$61,721	$51,353

[1]Increase in budget authority attributable to an increase in the cap on Interior Department funding; conferees' elimination of a provision to increase the price of government uranium enrichment services; and increased funding for the Naval Petroleum Reserve, requested by the administration.
[2]Adjusted for jurisdictional overlap.

Sunset Legislation

In many states and in the federal government, sunset legislation is being considered and implemented. The sunset concept is that government programs should automatically expire unless positive action is taken to renew them every few years. The form of the legislation varies. In most instances, the sunset provisions permit the program to remain on the law books but the authorization for funds expires. In other words, the program technically exists but no money can be spent on the program unless the legislature reenacts the authorization section of the law. The cycle for renewal varies, but often a staggered five-year cycle is used.

The states of Colorado and Florida have taken the lead in sunset legislation. Colorado was the first state to enact major sunset legislation, but it is limited to the state's regulatory agencies. In June 1976, Florida also passed sunset legislation directed toward regulatory agencies, but it set termination dates for both the agencies and substantive laws.

The federal government is considering enacting sunset legislation. Sunset provisions exist on many federal government programs, but comprehensive sunset legislation has not existed. The proposed federal legislation calls for the automatic termination of statutory authorization over a five-year period. The termination schedule is staggered so that programs within a budget function can be reviewed at the same time. Some programs are exempt, such as interest payments on the national debt, retirement, health care, and disability programs. The review process is controlled on a day to day basis so that Congress can decide the form, scope, and time allotted for each review appropriate for the subject.

Sunset legislation is misleading. The title and the first explanation lead people to believe that there will be wholesale terminations of government programs. This is unlikely. If there is a strong enough reason to create and fund a program, then there is strong enough reason to reenact the authorization section of the legislation. Some programs will expire, but not on a wholesale basis. The legislation will mean a great deal more paperwork addressed to justifying programs, and, potentially, to a situation in which Congress may not be able to handle the generated volume of justifications.

Federal Budgetary Madness

Clearly, the current federal budget process is widely considered to be inadequate. In a 1983 article, this author questioned the process and made specific recommendations for significant change.[2] Naomi Caiden called for reform and described the current process as "preventing consistent policy making, and encouraging deadblocks, blackmail, and symbolic voting."[3] Thirty states have called for a constitutional convention to address an amendment that would mandate

[2]Thomas D. Lynch, "Federal Budgetary Madness," *Society,* 20, 4 (May/June 1983), 27–32.
[3]Naomi Caiden, "The Myth of the Annual Budget," *Public Administration Review,* 42, 6 (November/December 1982), 516–523.

a balanced budget. The Congress's General Accounting Office has published a report, "Federal Budget Concepts and Procedures Can Be Further Strengthened,"[4] which calls for reform. Civil servants have called for reform (see Exhibit 2-8) and the National Capital Area Chapter of the American Society for Public Administration has called for reform (see Exhibit 2-9).

The mid- and late 1980s should see greater attention to these responsible voices seeking reform because the fundamental problems with the federal budget process will not improve without serious attention. The large and growing national debt will remain a major concern. The inability to pass timely appropriations, compounded by a cumbersome, repetitive process, will continue to plague the federal government.

Federal budget decision-making, as it is currently practiced, can be said to have the following characteristics: (1) it is concerned more with many special political interests to the disadvantage of the larger public interest; (2) it is fragmented, with little appreciation shown for the connection between programs and money; (3) key officials do not take the necessary time to familiarize themselves with budgets; (4) key officials are willing to accept less than the best from the process; and (5) key decision-making takes place in unreasonably and unrealistically short time frames.[5]

Surprisingly, the debate on these issues prior to 1982 was not particularly enlightening, but the quality and number of voices improved as concerned professional groups and individuals began to articulate more the various dimensions of the problem. Federal budget reform shall remain on the agenda for the mid- and late 1980s.

State and Local Challenges

The situation at the state and local level is best described as "challenging." Many local governments do not have professional budget staffs at a time when forecasting, capital financing, financial management of enterprise funds, and computers are requiring advanced professional talent. Few governments have progressed beyond line-item budgeting and very few are able to use performance measures to judge program effectiveness and efficiency. Very few professional budget staffs can conduct and are routinely conducting sophisticated budget and program analysis.

The professional challenges of budgeting and financial management are significant, as demonstrated by the illustrations in this book. However, budgeting is an activity which can be done with a minimum of professionalism. Thus, governments can "get by" with yearly balanced budgets. Unfortunately, the loser is government, the image of government, and the taxpayer, who receives fewer and poorer services for the tax dollar. A good budget and finance office will not solve all of government's problems, but more services and a higher quality of performance should be

[4]"Federal Budget Concepts and Procedures Can Be Further Strengthened" (PAD 81–36) (Washington, D.C.: U.S. General Accounting Office, 1981).

[5]Carl Grafton and Anne Permaloff, "Budgeting Reforms in Perspective," in *Handbook on Public Budgeting and Financial Management*, ed. Jack Rabin and Thomas D. Lynch (New York: Marcel Dekker, Inc., 1983), pp. 89–124.

EXHIBIT 2-9 Agenda for the Budget

1. Observations
   a. The budget is the primary management system, partly because it is the only action-forcing process. It can be expected to remain the chief arena for policy debate, program planning, and execution.
   b. Its six phases are often confused. They are: long-range planning based on analysis of program/policy issues; setting out concrete objectives and short-term goals; costing out resource allocation decisions; winning support of OMB, Congress, and the public; budget execution/monitoring effectiveness and controlling the pace; and program evaluation (which completes the circle and links to planning).
   c. Certain factors affect the current atmosphere: breakdown in trust and confidence between executive and legislative branches, sometimes for good reason; growth of congressional staff and consequent interstaff competition; growing influence of single issue interest groups; more congressional control; and too much yielding by executive agencies.
   d. The budget process is overextended, dysfunctional. It serves too many purposes; focuses on detail at the expense of thinking; takes too much time; frustrates and exhausts managers and political leadership. All recognize the need for a better way.
   e. The overcontrol and inflexibility in budget execution promotes waste through rigidities. The execution process often does not track plans well.
   f. Recommendations should: shift the focus to front-end analysis and planning; make room for time and energy for concentrating on the most important issues; stabilize the system and allow more certainty on the part of managers; and simplify the process and reduce workload while allowing the appropriate degree of control.

2. Major Recommendations
   a. Reemphasize the planning and analysis function at the presidential level.
      (1) One way of establishing a focus on planning is to change the name of OMB to the Office of Planning and Budgeting (which would be symbolic).
      (2) If focused on the future, OMB can be a valuable resource to any president as a source of dispassionate analysis and by virtue of its cross-cutting, interagency responsibilities.
      (3) OMB is now deteriorating. It has too many jobs to do, some inconsequential; too little staff; good people overwhelmed and burned out; is politically top-heavy; and seems to be in competiton with, rather than complementary to, the White House staff.
      (4) Access to the president is the key, which might also be achieved by securing more management strength in OMB or by the establishment of a separate office in the executive establishment.
      (5) Establish a president's management agenda to function as a driving force.
   b. Allow more opportunity for analysis and planning by shifting to a two-year budget and appropriations cycle. It would allow:
      (1) more front-end loading (e.g., planning, learning about programs, opening up the process to affected groups before going into the budget stage, tying evaluation to planning);
      (2) more time for OMB and congressional staff to think about programs, interact with agencies, and operate in a more relaxed manner;
      (3) more stability and certainty for the executive and managerial staff;

(4) cutting down the problems in budget execution; and

(5) emphasizing the need for flexibilities and adjustments because of lead time in making estimates.

3. Other Recommendations

a. Find better techniques for dealing with program cuts than the arbitrary, unthinking approaches so often used.

b. Find better ways to work things out with congressional staff, as an alternative to earmarking funds.

c. Reestablish programming flexibility.

(1) The president should push for some governmentwide tolerance, such as five percent programming authority.

(2) Give executives the leeway to move dollars to where they can be better used, as a means of reducing potential spending waste.

Source: The Bureaucrat, Fall 1981, p. 81.

EXHIBIT 2-10 NCAC Position on Budget Reform

I. Problems With the Current Budget System. The current Federal budget and financial management systems contain a number of problems which are having increasingly serious effects on Congress, Federal managers, recipients of Federal funds (including State and local governments and private sector contractors), and private financial markets. As a result, these problems are affecting not only the internal workings of the Federal government, but also the national economy and the general public. These problems can be described as follows:

A. The detailed, iterative Congressional budget process has produced a cumbersome, repetitive process which results in heavy workloads for both Congress and the Federal agencies. This process is based in current law, which requires Congress to go through an authorization and appropriation process, with statutory deadlines and requirements, every year. The resulting workload, in turn, produces:

1. a tremendous waste of Federal labor hours in the formulation, presentation, and implementation of sometimes three budgets a year;

2. inadequate time for Congressional policy setting and oversight;

3. delays in action on appropriations bills.

B. The frequently delayed action on appropriation bills results either in continuing resolutions or a shutdown of the Federal government. Both result in:

1. Uncertainty for program managers, causing program delays, disruptions and other inefficiencies, and reduced cost-effectiveness.

2. Funding disruptions cause instability and incoherence for recipients of Federal funds. These disruptions are especially harmful for capital outlays (such as highways and defense items), R & D and the planning processes of State and local governments.

C. Both the workload and disruption problems increase the costs of operating the government. Manpower costs are high and funding stretch-outs usually increase the total costs of contracts and grants. Relatedly, costs are increased by iterative annual authorizations, without overall funding commitments, for multiyear programs (e.g., capital outlays).

    D. The overwhelming amount of detail to be prepared by the agencies and reviewed by Congress prevents officials of both from concentrating on the larger policy issues. This situation results in:

        1. an inadequate link at all levels between planning and budget formulation;

        2. lack of adequate Congressional supervision.

    E. The vast number of Executive Branch financial management and other information tracking systems (planning, budget formulation, budget execution, accounting, auditing, evaluation, MIS, etc.) increase the difficulty of program management by:

        1. increasing managers' information overload;

        2. being unable to provide adequate feedback to managers about decisions made by others, causing them to be "in the dark" about their own programs;

        3. producing program-specific rather than policy-oriented information;

        4. segmenting rather than integrating useful facets of information.

II. NCAC Objectives for Budget Reform

    A. To reduce the time and paperwork required in the budget process.

        1. To allow more time for policy making and planning and less time for detailed microbudgeting;

        2. To allow more time for Congressional oversight and evaluation;

        3. To minimize delays on appropriations bills.

    B. To increase the stability of Federal activities and funding.

        1. To improve the efficiency of government procurement and program management;

        2. To provide consistency for projects and entities being funded.

    C. To reduce unnecessary Federal operating and funding expenses.

    D. To increase the policy and planning role and capability of Congress and of agency officials.

        1. By improving the link between policy and budget formulation;

        2. By moving from specific manpower planning to general workforce planning.

    E. To streamline and integrate the Federal financial management and related information tracking systems.

        1. To provide better feedback to managers;

        2. To enhance oversight and program review.

Source: National Capital Area Chapter, American Society for Public Administration. *Newsletter.* February, 1983.

---

the results of such an office. If forecasting is improved, then idle cash will produce more revenue and disruptive financial emergency controls need not be used. If capital financing practices are good, then less interest will be paid on the government debt and more capital improvements will be possible for the same tax dollar. If creative financial management of enterprise funds is used, governments will have more revenue available at a time when taxpayers are hostile to tax increases. If budget and financial offices can make more effective use of the rapidly improving computer, then time-consuming, routine "numbers crunching" can be replaced with more sophisticated analyses designed to improve the quality of government management. The professional challenges are exciting, but they will not easily be confronted and conquered. The highest levels of professionalism will be required.

REVIEW QUESTIONS

1. The roots of the executive/legislative struggle go back as far as 1215, but the struggle greatly influences how budgeting is done in the United States today. Explain those roots and how that struggle helps us understand modern budgeting. In what ways do we see that struggle taking place in modern budgeting?

2. Compare and contrast the rationalist approaches to budgeting (e.g., PPB, MBO, and ZBB) with the incrementalist approaches. Explain how the role of analysis varies—if it does—in each approach.

3. Compare and contrast line-item budgeting, program budgeting, and performance budgeting.

4. Explain the 1974 Congressional budget reforms. What was meant to be accomplished and what means were devised to accomplish those ends?

5. The current federal budget process is said to be inadequate. Why? What reforms could help resolve the identified problems?

6. The professional challenges of state and local budgeting are significant. What are those challenges? What should be done by professionals to meet those challenges?

REFERENCES

Advisory Commission on Intergovernmental Relations. *ACIR State Legislative Program.* Vol. 4. *Fiscal and Personnel Management.* Washington, D.C.: Government Printing Office, November 1975.

ALYANDARY-ALEXANDER, MAND (ed.). *Analysis for Planning, Programming and Budgeting,: Proceedings of the Social Cost-Effectiveness Symposium.* Washington, D.C.: Washington Operation Research Council, 1968.

ASPIN, LES. "The Defense Budget and Foreign Policy: The Role of Congress," *Daedalus* (Summer 1975), pp. 155–74.

BAKKER, OEGE. *The Budget Cycle in Public Finance in the United States.* The Hague: W. P. Van Stockum, 1953.

BARTIZAL, JOHN R. *Budget Principle and Procedure.* Englewood Cliffs, N.J.: Prentice-Hall, 1942.

BEAUMONT, ENID. "The New York Case from a Public Administration Perspective," *The Bureaucrat,* 5, 1 (April 1976), 101–12.

BEKER, JEROME. "Measuring Cost Effectiveness in Human Services," *Canadian Welfare,* 51, 1 (January/February, 1975), 5–6.

BENSON, GEORGE et al. (eds.). *The American Property Tax: Its History, Administration and Economic Impact.* Clairmont, Calif.: Institute for Studies in Federalism, Clairmont Men's College, 1965.

BLACK, GUY. "Externalities and Structure in PPB," *Public Administration Review,* 31, 6 (November/December 1971), 637–43.

BREAK, GEORGE F. *Agenda for Local Tax Reform.* Berkeley: Institute of Government Studies, University of California, 1970.

BRUNDAGE, PERCIVAL HACK. *The Bureau of the Budget.* New York: Holt, Rinehart and Winston, 1970.

BUCK, A. E. "Performance Budgeting for the Federal Government," *Tax Review* (July 1949).

GOOD, DAVID. "Envelope Budgeting: The Canadian Experience." Paper prepared for the 1983 Annual American Society for Public Administration Conference, New York City.

HARTMAN, ROBERT W. "Congress and Budget-Making," *Political Science Quarterly* 97, 3 (Fall 1982), 381–402.

LELOUP, LANCE T. "After the Blitz: Reagan and the Congressional Budget Process." Paper presented at the Southern Political Science Association Meeting, Memphis, Tennessee, November 5–7, 1981.

RABIN, JACK and THOMAS D. LYNCH (eds.). *Handbook on Budgeting And Financial Management.* New York: Marcel Dekker, 1983.

WENZ, THOMAS W. and ANN P. NOLAN. "Budeting for the Future: Target Base Budgeting," *Public Budgeting And Finance,* 2, 2 (Summer 1982), 88–91.

THREE
BUDGET BEHAVIOR

Public budgeting is done by human beings and one can understand a great deal about budgeting by examining the factors which influence human behavior within this special context. This chapter first examines how the key actors in the budget process interact. The next major topic is an in-depth examination of the agency budget office and the perspectives associated with the office. The final major topic is a careful examination of the strategies associated with the game of budgeting. This chapter examines:

1. the political influence patterns among the key actors in the budget process;
2. means commonly used to cultivate an active clientele;
3. the duties of an agency budget office;
4. the perspective of a budget officer and typical behavioral patterns;
5. four common philosophic attitudes of budget officers toward the budget process;
6. explanation of how confidence in the budget officer is developed;
7. the significance of program results in budgeting;
8. the preparation process for hearings;
9. the review setting;
10. spender's strategies;
11. cutter's strategies;
12. strategies to support new programs; and
13. some important cautions in public budgeting.

POLITICS AND PERSPECTIVE

Four Institutional Roles

Public budgeting can be understood in terms of four institutional roles. Each has a definable behavior. Exhibit 3-1 shows the interrelationship among the groups.

The four institutional roles are the agency, the executive, the legislature, and the clientele. Two other groups, the courts and the media, are significant, but are not discussed here because their influence patterns are unusual. Discussion of their influence is outside the scope of this text. The agency is the institution with the responsibility for managing the programs and preparing the initial budget. The executive is loosely defined here to mean the chief executive, his or her staff, and the central budget office. (The department, of which the agency is a part, plays an odd role, sometimes acting as an extension of the executive but often acting as superagency, depending on the stage of the budget process.) The legislature is the legislative branch of government, such as the Congress in the federal government. The clientele is a group affected by the agency's programs and it takes an active interest in the agency's policy.

The double lines in Exhibit 3-1 represent several two-way influence patterns. The agency influences the executive through its budget request and the executive's budget decision is one form of executive influence on the agency. The executive influences the legislature through its executive budget requests, and the passage of laws is one form of influence upon the executive. The agency's programs by definition affect its clientele. Clientele groups are well known for their lobbying (influencing) activity on legislators, but they also lobby and influence the chief executive and the agency. Less well known is that legislatures and executives can influence clientele groups directly. To make matters more complex, an influence pattern may involve more than two groups. For example, a clientele group influences Congress on appropriation legislation which ultimately becomes law and then the agency is influenced by the language of that appropriation legislation.

A case study involving the U.S. Maritime Administration illustrates the influence patterns. In the Nixon Administration, there was a strong desire at the highest levels in the U.S. Office of Management and Budget to phase out the operating and ship building subsidies at an accelerated rate. OMB required the Maritime Adminis-

EXHIBIT 3-1

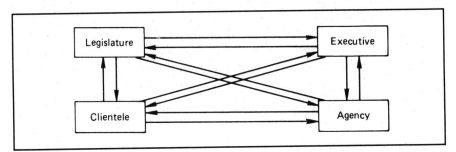

tration to launch an analytical study of exactly how this was to be accomplished. Somehow, Mrs. Sullivan, who headed the House Appropriation subcommittee, discovered the OMB study. She was extremely upset that OMB wished to change policy clearly established in the law and phoned OMB Director Mayo. The substance of that conversation was not recorded, but the director withdrew the request for the study. This series of events illustrates the influence of the central budget office on an agency as well as the strength of a single legislator on a central budget office.

Clientele influence on agencies is not fully appreciated. In *Policy Analysis for Public Policymaking,* this author presented several case studies involving the budget process in the U.S. Department of Transportation. In February 1970, the Office of Management and Budget called for a special analytical study by the Urban Mass Transportation Administration of that agency's policy guidance for capital grants reflected in the published *Information to Applicants.* In time, the study and a revised *Information to Applicants* was prepared. Before it became official, a letter was formally sent (as required by OMB Circular A-85) to inform state and local government associations of the proposed new guidelines. The Circular A-85 standard OMB guidance requires an agency-to-clientele interrelationship prior to the time that the final government policy becomes effective.

In this instance, representatives of the transit industry and the cities were taken by surprise. They took strong exception to the "unrealistic data demands and planning analyses" that would be imposed. They felt that DOT committed a breach of faith because there was no informal consultation prior to sending the official notification. They reacted by developing a counterstrategy—they met with agency officials and tried to soften the most undesirable aspects of the new selection criteria. The agency officials felt that they came close to the clientele's feeling while keeping within the strict OMB policy prescriptives. This case illustrates the infrequently documented influence of a clientele group on an agency.

Legislative groups and chief executives can directly influence clientele groups. The most noticed such influence is at the large conventions of these groups when high-ranking legislators or executives address the members. Less publicized meetings occur when legislative and executive officials request cooperation or seek lobbying support for key legislation.

End runs and finesses do occur in this complex four-way relationship. For example, an agency can influence its clientele group by pointing out the implications of existing proposed policy. The clientele group can then go to either the legislature or the executive to kill the proposed policy. A more complex situation would be when the agency has to proceed with some action (e.g., conserve energy) which its clientele group may find distasteful. The agency might be able to counter likely pressure by having the chief executive lobby the clientele group and the legislature. This would strengthen the chances of success for the agency by minimizing clientele resistance.

In the budget process, the agency-to-clientele-to-legislature triangular relationship is a common pattern. The more sophisticated clientele groups recognize that the size of the budget and the individual programs are significant. In many cases, an informal communication network exists between the agency and the clientele group. Any formal, publicly available information is monitored, analyzed, and communicated to clientele members. Sometimes active campaigns are launched to build a strong lobbying presence for particular budget issues of importance to the clientele.

State and local patterns normally are not as complex as those found on the federal level. However, large state and local governments have patterns more similar to the federal level. The seriousness of lobbying and clientele groups not surprisingly relates to the money or potential money involved; thus large governments with large programs tend to have the active clientele groups. In medium and small governments, clientele groups can and do act less formally. Clientele interests are handled as nonpaid part-time activities via simple phone calls and meetings. Often, on-the-record views are expressed in public hearings, or possibly even a demonstration or media event might be organized. Highly emotional confrontations are rare on budget issues, but they do occur.

The agency, executive, legislature, and clientele each has a separate institutional role. Each perceives itself as a separate group although individual exceptions can be cited—for example, an agency political appointee may identify solely with the chief executive. Also, each group can be further subdivided, and subdivisions may come into conflict and threaten to harm the larger group. For example, the Maritime Administration is composed of maritime unions and operators. When they work together they are surprisingly powerful for their respective sizes, but the alliance can and does break down on specific issues. In the Congress, the substantive and appropriation committees sometimes are in conflict. In the executive, two staff agencies such as the White House staff and the Office of Management and Budget can also be in conflict on issues, but in the executive branch the chief executives can more easily arbitrate internal disputes than in the legislative branch.

Role Objectives and Enemies

The agency and its leadership almost always have pride or a sense that its programs are worthwhile. The career employee recognizes that his or her job and income are associated with the agency's objectives. In some instances, an almost missionary zeal and self-identification with the agency can exist among the top agency leadership. In other instances, the zeal may be only a belief that what the agency does is a worthwhile function. Rarely do top agency leaders disagree with the mission or the fundamental value of the agency and its programs.

Another factor to consider is the budget process itself. The agency is always placed in the position of requesting and defending. Reviewers are always doubting the agency and demanding facts and better arguments. Not surprisingly, agency executives often find themselves defending the agency when it comes under attack. President, governors, and mayors sometimes act surprised when their agency appointees argue the agency position. Given the dual elements of self-worth and role demands, chief executives should be more surprised if their appointees don't speak for their agencies.

Given those circumstances, issues are viewed from the perspective of the agency's mission and the people in the organization. Does a change further or detract from the agency's mission? Will the people in the organization benefit or lose from a change? Programs are justified with these questions well in mind.

The chief executive plays a different role. The executive wishes to economize, cut requests, and coordinate programs. There is an arm's length relationship between the executive and the agency leadership in spite of the fact that agency political appointees serve at the pleasure of the executive. The executive must maintain the option of saying "no" to an agency request. Requests must be reviewed carefully and cuts are necessary for purposes of economy and better allocation of resources around the executive branch. When the executive decision is reached, the chief executive expects that the agency will formally support the executive decision even though the agency may not perceive the decision to be in its own best interest. Discipline is maintained in several ways: formal statements are cleared by the executive's staff, budget requests must follow the executive's budget and allowance letter, the political influence of the chief executive is significant, and the agency head can be fired.

Another factor for state and local government agency heads to consider is that their chief executives can sometimes veto or reallocate items in line-item budgets. These powers vary greatly from one government to the next, but some chief executives can unilaterally reconstruct the council-approved budget using the line-item veto. The only limit on the power is the likely political resistance the chief executive would receive from the legislature or city council. When chief executives wield this type of power, agency officials would be hesitant to challenge or to try to circumvent them.

The legislature (sometimes called council, board, or commission) plays an entirely different role. It is the people's elected deliberative body, normally composed of well-intended, intelligent individuals. However, on budget matters the legislature is often confronted with confusing information and little time to make decisions. At the federal level and in some large state and local governments the legislatures may even dominate the policy-making process, but this is not often the situation. Normally, legislatures are not the initiators, but rather play a more reactive role. Attention is given more to pet projects and issues of local popular concern rather to than a unified, comprehensive approach to the budget.

The clientele members are interested in how an agency's program affects them. They meet and discuss in conferences the significance of existing legislation, the chief executive's attitudes toward programs, and the policies of the agency. Sometimes the clientele works as a whole, but often various subgroups act, with some coordination among the groups. Clientele groups vary, with success often depending on clientele leadership, the stakes involved, the organizational network, the dedication of the members to the issue, and the strategies and tactics employed.

The paths of clientele influence vary. Often a special agency-clientele relationship occurs because an unofficial policy of job rotation exists. For example, a former lobbyist or key member of a client group can be and often is appointed to a high level government position which is important to the client group. Sometimes clientele groups support the winning president or congressman. This also can lead to a cordial climate. Lobbying is the standard path of influence. Also formal and informal relationships can exist between the agency and the clientele, as illustrated in the UMTA and Maritime case examples cited earlier.

Agencies and clientele groups can have anticlientele groups. For example, consumer groups can oppose the manufacturing interests and government regulating bodies. In recent years, more groups from right-to-left political spectrum—Nader, environment, antinuclear, and so on—have become active. These groups are often significant.

Who the "good and bad guys" are depends on values, issues, and perspectives. For some agencies, there is a pattern in which various actors tend to be allies on most issues. This need not be the situation. From the agency's point of view, the executive may be the stumbling block on an issue and the essential ally on yet another issue. From the clientele's viewpoint, the agency may be an enemy causing useless red tape or a vital agency necessary for the survival of the clientele members. Each situation must be examined separately. Rarely does a uniform and consistent pattern exist over time, with one set of actors who are always friends and another set who are always enemies. The patterns evolve and change; thus the actors must adapt to a dynamic environment.

Cultivation of an Active Clientele

For most government agencies, there is no problem identifying a clientele group. Highway departments are well aware of their clientele. The Veterans' Administration hears from its clientele. However, some agencies cannot easily identify clientele groups. For example, the United States Information Agency does not serve people in this country. What group is its clientele? The U.S. Bureau of Prisons does not have an active clientele group. In such cases, the nature of the organization or its mission precludes a clientele group; thus the agency is handicapped in the pluralist style of American government.

The most obvious way to cultivate a clientele is to carry out the agency's programs, but some strategy is involved in building a supportive clientele. In the first place, the clientele members should understand and appreciate the full extent of the benefits they receive from the agency's programs. In the second place, most legislatures represent the whole population, so a breadth of clientele members across the nation, state, or city is best if the clientele wishes to lobby the legislature. Thirdly, some clientele members may be in a better position to aid the agency, such as a group in the House Appropriation Committee chairperson's home district. Lastly, mute clientele members are not that useful so they must be encouraged to be active politically.

Strategies of both expanding and concentrating the clientele are used. An agency can take care to provide grants or assistance across the country or build a balanced set of programs which appeal to several specific sectors of society. Agencies have their public information officers explain the programs, and attendance at clientele conferences is considered very important. Some clientele members can be acquired by changing or adding attractive services for that group. For example, in an area where senior citizens are well organized, the parks department is wise to have programs for the elderly. Often the intensity of support is important, so the program may be altered to be sure to benefit a particularly influential group.

The clientele must be heard by the legislature and the executive. In some instances, the clientele members are poorly organized or not adept in dealing with American democratic institutions. Congressmen, senators, and legislators often assume that if they do not hear from supporters, no one cares. Given the need to cut, the tendency is to cut where no one cares enough to complain. Legislators do consider themselves to be guardians of the treasury, but they do not like the uncomfortable feeling they get when cuts return to haunt them at the next election. Even saying "no" to an impassioned plea is not pleasant. An agency rarely advocates lobbying the legislature, but its officers can explain the significance of lobbying and stress that the small budget is a problem which can be corrected by the legislature.

Sometimes agencies structure subunits to attract clientele. For example, the agency is broad-based but effective lobbying is done by narrow focus groups. The agency can appeal to those narrow groups. For example, the National Institute of Health uses subunits focused upon specific diseases which correspond to the active health clientele groups. The result is a strong set of clientele groups. The hazard in this approach is that a glamorous subunit can lessen support for the other units.

Another approach is the creation of an advisory committee. Even the most conservative group of advisors tends to advocate the desirability of the agency's program. This can lead to increased and more effective clientele support.

Agency Budget Office

The place for developing and orchestrating the budget process is the agency budget office. The duties of such offices vary, as they sometimes include the accounting function and an analytical/planning unit. There are some common duties which describe what an agency budget office does. The following is an excellent list of duties from one agency budget office—the Budget Division of ACTION in the federal government:[1]

1. In conjunction with the appropriate operating officials, develops budget estimates for programs and offices, conducts budget reviews, and recommends budget allocations.
2. In conjunction with appropriate operating officials, develops, presents, and justifies ACTION's budget submission to the Office of Management and Budget and to the Congress, including financial and personnel exhibits, budget narrative material, and

[1]Budget Execution Responsibilities, ACTION, 1975.

budget back-up data. Prepares Agency witnesses for hearings before the Office of Management and Budget and the Congress.

3. Recommends budget priorities as the result of Office of Management and Budget and Congressional budget guidance for use within the Agency.

4. Prepares apportionments, allotments, and maintains overall control of Agency financial resources and position allocations.

5. Issues operating budgets with position and average grade allocations to all offices, regions, and posts and insures budget execution with legislative authority and limitations.

6. Conducts budget reviews and analyses during the fiscal year and recommends reprogramming actions and other funding adjustments.

7. Recommends and implements budgetary procedures, budget controls, and reporting systems and makes recommendations regarding the financial aspects of the management information system to improve financial management within the Agency.

8. Works with appropriate operating officials to coordinate the budget with Agency plans, objectives, and programs.

9. Acts as the Agency's primary point of contact with other governmental agencies on budget matters.

Exhibits 3-2 and 3-3 illustrate the variety of activities of budget execution responsibilities and the complex interrelationships which commonly exist among people performing budget responsibilities.

Perspective of the Budget Officer

Much of the work of the budget officer is repetitive. Exhibits 3-2 and 3-3 point out the yearly routine. The budget process has an established pattern and after a few years the substantive issues of the agency also take on a familiar pattern. Budgeting is largely repetitive and the filling out of reports tends to make the work mechanical.

The budget officer sees the world in terms of dollars, accuracy, and legality. The agency and its activities must always be translated into money. Budget officers will discuss new and old ideas, but eventually they ask, "What does this mean in terms of money?" Accuracy is essential. As will be discussed later, having the confidence of others is quite useful to the budget officer and confidence is not increased by making mistakes, especially in simple math. Care must be taken to establish procedures which double-check tables, insure final typing is error free, and verify the accuracy of stated facts. Legality is also a concern. If money is spent for reasons not permitted by law, then the budget officer may go to jail. There are few agency level decisions which the budget officer does not know about and often the law fixes responsibility for agency action on the agency head and budget officer. Wisdom dictates that the budget officer must be sure of the legality of questionable matters in order to avoid later problems.

Deadlines are the guiding force for a budget officer. Sometimes they seem impossible and often they are crucial. A common situation is to see a budget officer working late at night or on the weekends in order to meet some deadline. If a dead-

EXHIBIT 3-2

FUNCTIONS	OFFICIALS: DIRECTOR/ DEPUTY	ASSISTANT DIRECTOR FOR OPP	BUDGET DIRECTOR	ASSISTANT DIRECTOR FOR A&F	ALLOTMENT HOLDER	INTERMEDIATE BUDGET HOLDER (10 REGIONS; OFFICE)	OPERATING BUDGET MANAGER
Apportionment request	Responsibility delegated to OPP	Submits request to GMB	Prepares request from sum of allotments; monitors	Receive info copy of apportionment; monitor for pos. viol.			
Continuing resolution	Concur with GC interpretation		Coordinates activity; issues instructions				
Treasury warrant request			Prepares request	Request to Treasury			
Allotment issuance	Reviews, approves	Issues allotments	Prepares allotment from sum of operating budgets	Receive info. copy of allot.; monitor for pos. violation	Receive allotment; monitor		
Operating budget issuance			Directs; issues jointly; monitors		Review and approve budgets; jointly issue	Review and approve subordinate budget request	Recommend operating budget totals
Reapportionment	Request to the OMB	Concurs in request	Prepares request with backup				
Allotment reprogramming	Final approval in cases of question	Approves reprogramming	Recommends; prepares documents		Request reprogramming		
Operating budget reprogramming			Reviews requests; con-	Insures account reporting com-	Review request;	Review; approve if operating group	Request reprogramming

Activity			curs in all decisions	patible with format	approve if operating group budgets change	budget totals unchanged	Manage within budget totals and restrictions
Estimation of receipts/reimbursements			Prepares; estimates; monitors				
Allotment management	Concurs		Monitors				
Operating budget management			Monitors		Manage within budget totals and restrict		Manage within budget totals and restrictions
Quarterly review	Approves new budget allocations		Directs review; recommends new allocation		Prepare data; recommend new levels	Recommend new levels for operating group	Recommend change in operating budget
Year end review	Approves new budget allocation		Directs review; recommends changes	Complete review of open obligations	Recommend changes	Recommend changes	Recommend changes
Violation reports	Receive report; report to president and Congress			Instigate report to director with evidence			
Personnel and average grade ceiling	Reviews and approves allocation to 10 major offices	Develops/reviews allocation to 10 major offices	Recommends allocations to operating units		Recommend intermediate level totals	Recommend allocations to operating units within operating groups	
Review of past year performance			Analyzes; prepares report				
Preparation of status of funds report			Provides budget input to reports	Generate reports and distribute			

Source: Budget Execution Responsibilities, ACTION, 1975.

EXHIBIT 3-3

President's Budget Request to Congress

Presentation of ACTION Budget Justification to Congress

Internal ACTION Planning process to allocate expected appropriation

Enactment of Appropriation or "Continuing Resolution"

Request from OMB and apportionment (s), authorizing obligational authority for a specific period

Receive from OMB an apportionment granting obligational authority

Request from Dept. of Treasury a Treasury authorizing disbursement of funds for period of "Continuing Resolution"

Receive from Dept. of Treasury a Treasury Warrant allowing disbursement of government funds

Issue allotments to each allottee. Within each allotment, issue operating budgets to each operating unit.

Monthly Review

Review Status of Funds. Update key indicators. Revise operating budgets, allotments and apportionments as required.

Quarterly Review

Request budget needs in detail for remainder of year from each operating unit. Receive status of past quarter funds from

Evaluate budget requests at operating unit level, operating group level, allottee level, apportionment level.

Reallocate available funds, personnel and average grade ceiling on the basis of program changes.

Issue new operating budgets, allotments, and apportionments, as required.

Year End Review

Request final budget projections program estimates for fiscal year. Revise open obligations and make adjustments as required.

Issue summary operating budget adjustments, as required. Revise allotments or apportionments, as required.

At Any Time

Reprogramming Request – Accept request from operating unit and/or allottee; evaluation request; find source of funds for increase; reallocate funds; issue joint memo of agreement; update operating budgets and allotments, as appropriate.

ACTION on new funding authority (i.e. new appropriation of continuing resolution): follow flow chart from beginning.

After end of year, review last year performance, issue report to allottees, operating and Deputy Director.

line is missed, then someone—usually the agency head—will be upset. More significantly, the agency may have lost an important opportunity or handicapped itself in a decision-making situation. Timeliness can mean even the survival of the agency's program. On the other hand, some deadlines are foolish and the wiser person will take the extra time to do a better job because timeliness is not significant. The decision to ignore a deadline should be based upon a knowledge of how and when the information will be utilized.

The budget can be used to minimize or surface disagreements. The budget officer is an artist who realizes that a budget can be presented in many ways in spite of the requirements of format. For political or internal management reasons, specific issues may best be hidden or minimized. This can be done by placing the issue within a larger, more dominant subject. In many situations, surfacing disagreement is a much better strategy. An issue can be surfaced by presenting it with some prominence in the budget document. This forces decision makers to deal with the problem and try to resolve it. In many instances, minimizing or surfacing a disagreement is mandated by outside forces, such as a major media story on the subject, which cannot be ignored. In some instances, these decisions are made by the budget officer; thus his or her political and management judgment is important.

Deadlines and other pressures force the budget officer to use the satisficing approach to many decision-making situations. When someone is demanding a budget submission, and the timeliness of that submission is important, then the budget officer may be pleased to find even a satisfactory answer. Budgeting is done under pressure and the budget officer must do the best that he or she can in the time available. Searching for ideal answers on all occasions is not compatible with budgeting.

Agency Budget Behavior

As explained earlier in this chapter, loyalty to an agency is a common behavioral phenomenon. This loyalty is similar to that found in professional athletes. When they work for a team, loyalty to the team is given. Budget officers believe in their agency's mission and feel that their role is important for the well-being of the agency. Blind loyalty does not exist because program weaknesses are well-known A more balanced loyalty prevails which recognizes faults but believes the program is or can be essentially sound.

Individuals working in a public agency take pride in their work. This can lead to the desire to expand the projects and programs. Budget reviewers are often frustrated by agency desires to expand programs, but such expansion tendencies are positive indicators of the health of the program's management. Agencies should not be criticized for being enthusiastic. Reviewers should applaud positive attitudes while recognizing the reviewers' role may call for them to disapprove expansion.

Budgeting's political context often supersedes apparent rationality. What might appear to be the best solution is not necessarily the best position for the agency to take. Recall that agencies exist in a context of powerful interacting forces. When a person is sailing, the best sailing course may not be directly toward the ultimate objective. Sometimes tacking into the wind is necessary owing to the force of the opposing wind. In public administration, the budget game strategy may not be to advocate or oppose a position directly but rather to wait for the clientele or legislature to react to circumstances. Judgment is essential.

There often is some flexibility in budgeting as a result of what some call gimmicks. How to employ those gimmicks is another important talent. For example, the timing of obligation and disbursements can be significant and this timing can be controlled by the budget officer. Another trick is that a given expense item can be assigned to one of two programs. This choice permits some often needed flexibility. Gimmicks exist because some discretion exists and a budget officer can use that discretion to ease the burden of managing the program. Skillful budget officers are aware of the available discretionary decisions and use them to ease the problems of public management.

Public budgeting requires decision makers. Even decisions not to act represent policy choices. If a budget reviewer delays a program or project for another year, that is a decision which often has important implications. Decisions may be based on sound reasoning, but they do affect people. Decision makers must be able to live with criticism because budget decisions often generate strong arguments. Also, decisions are often made on meager information, thus contributing to the possibility of self-doubt in the minds of public budget officers. If the budget officer cannot emotionally deal with criticism and doubt, then he or she should consider a different type of work. Doubt and criticism are a part of public budgeting.

Public budgeting requires the highest professional characteristics. Later in this chapter, the importance of confidence in the budget officer will be explained. Confidence is established through professionalism. Honesty and integrity are essential professional characteristics. This does not mean that the budget officer does not prepare the *strongest case possible* for a program, but it does mean that "possible" includes avoiding lies and misrepresentations. No one faults a budget officer for being sensitive to shifting political causes (e.g., environment, energy, inflation, unemployment) and framing budget justifications to take advantage of those shifting but temporarily persuasive rationales. This political sensitivity comes together with accuracy, legality, honesty, integrity, and other factors to constitute a professional.

One unfortunate characteristic of some budget officers is arrogance. This characteristic exists more in budget reviewers found in units like the department budget offices and the U.S. Office of Management and Budget (OMB). Lord Acton once stated that power corrupts and absolute power corrupts absolutely. Even budget officers and budget analysts possess some power because of the nature of their job; a few are corrupted but many more become intoxicated. They know they have power and they let others know it with their arrogance. For example, young OMB budget examiners may be mild-mannered before they start working for OMB, but once on the job they can visit the "field" and act in a cavalier, flippant, or even bossy manner to people with much higher civil service rank and longer experience. Such behavior is not professionally wise because it often leads to a needless lack of cooperation from the agency, thus making the examiner's job that much more difficult.

Budget officers are almost always career civil servants who work quite closely with politically appointed agency or department heads. This close rapport is sometimes influenced by the unusual position agency heads must face. Often they are expected to give their allegiance exclusively to the chief executive but the role of agency head strongly induces a loyalty to the agency. In some instances, these two loyalties are in conflict, thus presenting an agency head with an extremely difficult emotional dilemma. When such situations arise, the budget officer will become quite aware of the dilemma because the agency head's handling of that dilemma will influence the budget process. Understanding the dilemma is helpful, but there are no easy answers to this type of situation.

Public budgeting is an activity which requires responsible people. In the federal government, this responsibility is dramatized. If a budget officer over-obligates or permits to be spent an amount in excess of that apportioned by OMB, then a legal violation has occurred which can result in his or her being fired, fined, or sentenced to jail. Exhibit 3-4 is the quote from the Anti-deficiency Act which details the action required when violations occur. A fine or jail sentence results from willful violations. Such violations are rare.

One last important observation should be made about agency budget behavior. Good professionals love the game. They find it challenging and exciting. They love being important and having responsibility. They love the need to work under pressure and yet deliver quality work. They love knowing all the complexities of

EXHIBIT 3-4   Anti-deficiency Act (Section 3527 of Revised Statutes, as amended)

Actions required when violations occur.

1. *Administrative discipline; fines; or imprisonment.* In addition to any penalty of liability under other law, any officer or employee of the United States who shall violate subsections (a), (b), or (h) of this section shall be subjected to appropriate administrative discipline, including, when circumstances warrant, suspension from duty without pay or removal from office; and any officer or employee of the United States who shall knowingly and willfully violate subsections (a), (b), or (h) of this section shall, upon conviction, be fined not more than $5,000 or imprisoned for not more than two years, or both.

2. *Reports to President or Congress.* In the case of a violation of subsections (a), (b), or (h) of this section by an officer or employee of an agency, or of the District of Columbia, the head of the agency concerned or the Commissioner of the District of Columbia, shall immediately report to the President, through the Director of the Office of Management and Budget, and to the Congress all pertinent facts together with a statement of the action taken thereon.

budgeting and being able to use their skills. They love the intrigue and excitement of both politics and public management.

Four Views

In chapter 1, decision-making models and their importance were explained. People working in budgeting are often influenced by these normative theories, and four ideal types can be used to describe typical reactions to those normative theories. The four ideal types are the true rational believer, the pure reactive person, the budget-wise person (the cynic), and the wise budget person.

The true rational believer. With the influence of PPB, there are people working in public budgeting who strongly believe that decision-making related to public budgeting should use the rational approach. If decisions don't follow that approach, then they consider the decision highly questionable and in error due to lack of professionalism or the unfortunate intrusion of politics into proper decision-making. They try to insure that as many decisions as possible, especially significant decisions, should follow the rational approach: (1) set goals and objectives; (2) define alternatives; (3) analyze alternatives; (4) select the best decision or make the recommendation.

Such faith in the normative decision-making theory called the rational approach leads to unfortunate consequences in public budgeting. Many public organizations have vague multiple and sometimes mutually conflicting goals and objectives. Articulating specific goals and objectives may be impossible, but analysis may still be useful for decision-making. If analysis is limited to the rational approach, then analysis cannot be conducted. This is an unnecessary constraint applied to circumstances in which analysis could be useful. Thus the decision maker is unnecessarily handicapped. Another problem with the rational model is that it implies no limits exist to the defining of alternatives and the analysis of alternatives. As is pointed out in this author's book *Policy Analysis in Public Policymaking,* some individuals will proceed to spend large sums of money on analysis when the end results will be as useful as a much more limited analytical effort. Those individuals are motivated by the rational model to pursue the alternatives and exhaustively examine those alternatives. Another problem with the rational model is that its believers don't appreciate the importance of feedback in analysis; thus helpful feedback can be ignored.

A more subtle problem of the rational model is the inherent assumption that there is one overall perspective. Recall the earlier cited fable involving several blind men and an elephant. The storyteller stresses how each blind man examines a different segment of the elephant and proceeds to argue with the other blind men over the nature of the beast. The ironical thrust to the story is that all parties including the storyteller were inherently limited by their perspective. Any object or series of events can be described in an infinite number of ways and there is no one description, contrary to what the storyteller assumed. The rational model leads us to make the same mistake as the storyteller. One is wiser to recognize that there are only shared perceptions of felt needs which can be translated into formulations of problems and objectives. Unfortunately, the common use of the rational model does not encourage such sophistication.

The pure reactive person.   In contrast to the true rational believer is the pure reactive budget person. This type of person acts in a stimulus-response pattern. The budget calendar and the requests govern this type of person. Little thought is given to shaping events or somehow making a difference through the reactor's product. The job is merely a task to be done as defined in the job description or by the demands of the job. Decision-making models mean little to this type of person. However, the political-administrative dichotomy is used as the justification for his or her mechanical response. Such a person believes that political decisions should be left to the political appointee and that civil servants should merely respond to the wishes of the political appointees.

The hazard of this approach is that mindless or potentially foolish mistakes are not avoided. The budget person has a unique vantage point and can often understand both the political actors' viewpoints as well as the workings of government. By merely reacting, the government loses the important insight of the budget expert; thus more errors are likely to occur. An aggressive, outspoken budget staff can greatly improve government, but a reactive staff will permit policy makers to make unnecessary—often significant—errors. Most policy makers recognize the value of an aggressive and outspoken rather than a reactive budget staff.

The budget-wise person.   These people are aware of all the forms and tables, but discount them almost completely because the government's decisions are all political. They are often cynical about life in general and stress the public nature of ''public administration.'' They can sometimes cite dramatic examples of gross politically inspired decision-making, sometimes involving corruption and often involving vote trading. Such decision-making often does preclude effective public management. This type of person stresses that such decision-making is inevitable and that all that a budget staff can do is react and watch events unfold. In some government settings, the cynic is right; but in many others, the political actors in the political process are influenced by well-prepared budget justifications, and professional budgeting does translate into effective public management. If a cynical view dominates where professional budgeting could make a difference, then a valuable opportunity for more effective government is lost.

The wise budget person.   People of this type recognize that politics is sometimes of overriding importance. They also believe that analysis has its limitations but can often greatly help in decision-making situations. Professional public budgeting can be extremely significant to the way government is managed. We hope that this text will help more people be wise budget persons.

Develop Confidence

Having the confidence of the budget reviewers, especially the appropriations committees, is extremely important to the budget officer. If confidence doesn't exist, any reviewer can ask hard questions and force the agency to justify every detail. If the appropriations committees lack confidence, they can write into the appropriation bill or committee report very specific special conditions, thus tying the hands of the agency and making program administration a nightmare. If confidence is established, the budget reviews are less difficult and greater administrative latitude is provided for public management discretion.

There is a natural tendency on the part of the reviewers to place confidence in budget officers because some facts and management judgment must be accepted on faith. The sheer complexity of the budget plus the lack of time to review budgets means that not everything can be reviewed in depth. Priorities of reviewers' efforts in examining are decided upon with the more questionable or politically sensitive topics receiving the greatest attention. Budget reviewers would like to trust the expertise of the best budget officer because valuable budget reviewer time can be saved. Thus, a budget officer is wise to establish a reputation as being highly professional.

The ideal model of a highly professional budget person is used by reviewers to "rate" budget officers. The criteria vary but a fairly accurate picture can be painted of the type of person most likely to be trusted. Such a person is

1. a master of detail;
2. hard working;
3. concise;
4. frank;
5. self-effacing and devoted to the work;
6. tight with the taxpayer's money;
7. capable of recognizing a political necessity when it is present; and
8. conscientious about keeping key reviewers (e.g., congressmen) informed of sensitive changes in policy or important developments.

Budget officers find that a reputation of playing it straight is wise. Lying, covering up, and being tricky are highly undesirable characteristics for the career civil servant. Memories can be long among top reviewing staffs. If reviewers, especially appropriations committees, feel that they have been misled, then strong punitive actions can be taken, such as tying the agency into administrative knots with special appropriation language. On the other hand, a positive reputation can even mean securing emergency or supplemental funds on the basis of skimpy hearings: that is, getting funds almost entirely on the integrity of the budget officer.

Reputations are enhanced with professional friendship. A close personal relationship with budget reviewers, such as the agency's Congressional subcommittee staff, can ease tensions. Years of outstanding service are even more significant than friendships because such experience often builds a sense of integrity and trust which constitutes "professional friendships." In many cases, these professional friendships are built upon shared work experiences and service together in professional associations.

One of the characteristics associated with building confidence is being capable of recognizing political "necessity." However, judgment can differ on the question of "necessity." Some accommodation to favors and pet projects does occur, but such practices can move from the unusual to the expected. When this occurs, effective public management cannot be carried out. Part of building confidence is being able to turn down political actors so that requests are not considered a "political necessity." Techniques for pleasant turn-downs include:

1. "My hands are tied"—other factors may exist, such as an executive mandate which precludes the favor.
2. "Maybe in the future"—the favor may be granted but the timing is simply not wise then.
3. "But look at the other positive actions we have taken"—stress that other decisions were in their favor or to their liking and appeal to the notion that one should only expect to win a "fair share" of the time.
4. "It cannot be done"—economic, technical, or other reasons can be cited why the request is either impossible or extremely unwise to fulfill.

Other strategies can be employed to minimize granting favors. Action on the favor can be delayed. If they are truly serious, the political actors will pursue. Delay thus acts as a filter for the true "necessities." A parallel strategy is to give in on the most intensely sought favors and pet projects. Intensity can also be measured by means used to bring pressure upon the agency. Regardless of how intensity is shown, the strategy is to give in on the intense favors and resist on the less intense favors and pet projects.

Strategies and techniques can help, but in a few cases the consequences must be faced. Sometimes budget officers must face a no-win situation due to their professional or personal ethics or the need to support other persons in the bureaucracy such as the agency head. In some instances, the situation can be mitigated by allowing one political actor (e.g., a congressman) to do battle with another political actor (e.g., a political appointee or the media); but such a ploy can result in making two enemies and losing rather than gaining their confidence. In other situations, the budget officer may merely have to use time to heal relationships or hope that key actors don't blame the budget officer but blame the deed. The consequence may be severe, but sometimes one's professional integrity requires action which ironically can harm one's professional reputation.

There is no developed method for establishing confidence. All that can be done is to be aware of the techniques and strategies available, to observe successful budget officers, and to use careful judgment. No one approach is useful for all budget reviewers or all situations. Each set of circumstances must be considered separately before action is taken.

Results

Confidence in a government program often rests upon demonstrated results. Results are significant because the public and political leaders anticipate that some benefits will be evident from government programs.

There is an important distinction between an activity accomplishing its purpose and people feeling that they are being served. Politically, the latter is more significant. Often the distinction is only theoretical because accomplishment translates to people's realizing their lives have enhanced, but this need not be the case. The people—the agency's potential clientele—may be unaware of the importance of the program, may have come to take it for granted, or may not feel that the program is important. Earlier in this chapter, the significance of the clientele in the political process was noted. If the potential clientele members are not active supporters of the program, then the program may very well fail, given the normal political competition for funding support.

For an agency, serving an appreciative clientele is ideal. The best kind of result is one that provides services to a large and strategically placed appreciative clientele. The best type of clientele is one which brings its satisfaction to the attention of decision makers, such as the appropriation committees and the president. Not all agencies are blessed with such a happy harmony of circumstances, so attempts must be made to develop alternative means to build and maintain the essential support of key decision makers.

If an agency doesn't enjoy overwhelming public support, a persuasive case can be made with tangible accomplishments. In the budget justification process, emphasis is placed on the accomplishments of the program. The criteria used to judge success are sometimes the subject of debate and sometimes semantic confusion is used to rationalize odd criteria for success. In such circumstances, the merits of the accomplishments are less persuasive. Nevertheless, the citation of accomplishment is normally highly useful in any budget justification.

If the listing of results is not sufficiently impressive, the agency can extend an invitation to the decision makers or anyone likely to influence the decision makers (e.g., the media) to visit the agency. Budget reviewers and other influential people are shown the need (e.g., the poor being helped), the activity (e.g., the production of a missile), or heroic efforts by an overworked staff (e.g., emergency room care at a hospital). Often this technique is extremely useful. The U.S. space program used this approach quite successfully to maintain high public interest in its efforts. However, there are significant risks. The reviewers may not be impressed and this can translate into lower budgets rather than increased or sustained budget support.

A hazard of visits and other attempts to explain highy complex programs is the problem of explanation. Most political decision makers are not experts, so explanations and visits must be simplified to communicate the essential message without technical verbiage. If they are too simple, then the complex nature of the challenge is not understood and the level of funding seems unwarranted. If they are too complex, then the reviewer questions the clarity of the management direction and again the level of funding is reduced or the program is cut entirely. Selecting the exact visit format and explanation for complex programs can indeed be a challenge.

A hazard of demonstrating tangible accomplishment is that the program may be praised and then cut because the program objectives have been met. Government programs are designed to meet a problem and success may mean the problem ceases to exist. If that occurs, the program should cease to exist. The irony is that losing one's job seems like a punishment rather than a reward.

Some government programs are disadvantaged by not having tangible accomplishments which they can demonstrate. For example, unless the civil defense program is called on in an emergency, the civil defense agency cannot point to any tangible accomplishment. Another example is the International Communications Agency, which broadcasts propaganda overseas. How does one deal with such programs when tangible results cannot be shown? There are several ploys that can be used:

1. "Our program is priceless"—argue that results are not evident but what if the program did not exist? If we did not have civil defense, what cost would there be in human lives if disaster occurred?

2. "Results of our program cannot be measured"—argue that a demonstration of results is simply not possible given the nature of the program. This may be a truthful argument, but it will not be very persuasive.

3. "Results will be evident in the future"—argue that results are not evident now because the program is new or the program's results are only evident when an emergency occurs. This is a more appealing argument, but skeptics can say that an emergency is the wrong time to find out that the program does not work.

4. "Figures show"—argue facts and figures show results in spite of the fact that they really are not relevant. This is a foolish ploy, given the potential loss of confidence that could result.

5. "In this complex situation, the figures confirm . . . "—argue by ignoring the questionable cause-effect relationships within a multiple causal situation. This is a reasonable ploy, but care must be taken in the wording so that the statements are positive but not false. Extreme claims which cannot be tested should be avoided.

6. "Please notice that we reviewed more than a thousand applicants"—argue by focusing not on results but on the procedures and process measures of the organization. The critical observant reviewer can always ask, "So what?" but making a display of facts and figures is better than saying nothing because the information does demonstrate some activity did take place.

7. "You must appreciate that we cannot prove the relationship of this education to later achievement, but we know such a relationship exists"—argue that faith establishes the relationship between the program and the desired benefits in society. If the subject is something that is taken for granted, then such an argument might be successful.

Preparing for Hearings

Hearings often are important in building confidence in a program and program officials. In some situations, hearings only serve to brief decision makers or to create a record to be used to convince others. However, hearings can and often do affect decision makers, given the competing pressures on their time and the inadequate preparation they give to the review of budget material. Hearings are particularly important in establishing confidence. Program officials who cannot answer or who poorly answer questions create an impression that those running the organization don't really understand what they are doing.

Rehearsals for budget hearings are essential. The number of hearings vary by agency and government, but four hearings on the budget alone are the minimum number in the federal government. As noted in an earlier chapter, rehearsing, or holding mock hearings, is a standard practice. Agency administrators play the role of key reviewers such as the appropriations committee chairperson. Tough questions are anticipated and answered before the hearing in order to avoid later difficulties. Mock hearings are an excellent device to expose weak justifications, to build effective agency coordination in handling questions, and to appreciate the perspective of the reviewer. Mock hearings also help the budget officer decide what subjects should be discussed and stressed in the traditional opening statement.

The key to preparing for budgeting hearings is to do sufficient research to avoid or minimize surprises in the hearing. A surprise usually makes the administrator appear to be ignorant and can rattle him or her to the point of answering all the remaining questions poorly. A diligent search of past hearings and statements often indicates what the reviewers consider important. Also a review of the program itself and reactions to the program are essential in framing the tough questions. Often the rapport of the budget officer with others, such as people in the central budget office, can be a vital resource for intelligence.

Briefing books for hearings are useful. Normally, they include only the tough or standard questions and answers which are anticipated. They may include a brief discussion on the perspectives of each reviewer, but such information is often common knowledge. Also such descriptions can fall into the wrong hands, leading to unneccessary embarrassment.

Questions in a hearing come from a variety of sources, including the reviewer (e.g., senator), staff, clientele, and even the agency itself. Questions are sometimes planted, with entire lists of questions supplied by the agency. Sometimes the planted questions are the most difficult, so that the agency can go on record on a subject in the best possible manner. Planted questions rarely occur at the department and OMB hearings, but they are common in the Congress, where friendly legislators wish to aid a program. In some instances, the rapport between staffs is so close that the effect is the same as planted questions.

Presentations at hearings tend to create a portrait of the agency leadership in the minds of the reviewers. Hearings are an opportunity to paint a self-portrait of credibility and generate a favorable mood toward the agency. The leadership can take on such mantles as protector-of-the-public-safety, man-of-science, statesman, guardian-of-the-environment, and so on. Effective hearing presentations tend to ward off unpleasant and time-consuming probes of an agency.

The best way to make a positive impression at a hearing is to know the budget. There is no adequate substitute for being knowledgeable, but knowledge can be coupled with a good organized presentation. Normally, presentations and answers which are brief and to the point but which offer an opportunity to go into more depth on follow-up questions are most effective. Care can be taken not to give the impression that important subjects are being slighted. An administrator can be forgiven for not knowing a detail and in fact such data are often supplied for the record after the hearing. Administrators are sometimes not forgiven for not knowing the answers to questions involving management direction. Questions—even on detail—often can be anticipated and answered or transmitted at the time of the hearing. Such action is extremely impressive and builds confidence.

Hearings are a game with certain taboos. Agency officials recognize that they have two masters—the legislature and the executive—but agency officials cannot challenge the chief executive's budget even though they may wish for more support, but everyone present can tell if the officials mean otherwise. This communication is achieved by:

1. exhibiting a marked lack of enthusiasm;
2. being too enthusiastic to be credible;
3. refusing to answer questions by protesting loyalty to the chief executive; and
4. yielding to sharp-pointed questioning.

This taboo is significant. If the central budget office or the department feels the agency is not adhering to the established executive branch policy, then the agency head and other political appointees can be fired. "Speaking against the administration" can be taken extremely seriously; but in a few instances the central budget office or department may not wish the agency to resist legislative desires to increase the budget over executive branch requests as a political strategy. Each situation must be judged separately.

Another taboo is that the agency should not admit yielding to clientele pressure. The agency is accountable to all the people; thus yielding to one clientele is an admission of favoritism. It also admits that pressure can be successful. Instead, language is carefully phrased to indicate the agency wishes to receive advice from citizens and does act upon suggestions which have intrinsic value; the agency does respond to sound advice but the decision is made only on the merits of the advice. Pressure is not influential according to this taboo and should not be admitted to openly.

STRATEGIES

Reviewers versus Reviewed

The budget game requires advocates and reviewers. The agency is the advocate, but clientele groups and sometimes even legislators can also be called advocates. The reviewers are the department officials, the central budget office (e.g., OMB), the House appropriations subcommittee, and the Senate appropriations subcommittee. As the budget moves through the budget cycle, reviewers change roles and become advocates. For example, after the central budget office has reviewed the budget requests and final executive branch decisions are made, then that former reviewer is an advocate to the legislative appropriations subcommittees. The primary advocate, however, always is the agency. If the game is played well, there always exists an arm's length relationship between advocate and reviewer. Each plays the role with caution, care, and an awareness of the natural tendencies associated with each role. A requirement for a good game is that each party know the rules and strategy. Ideally the game should be played by professionals. An uneven game results in unreasonable cuts or unreasonably high budgets. Both results are undesirable.

One budget strategy failure illustrates the gamesmanship. Occasionally, an agency will resubmit the previous year's budget with the only change being the fiscal years mentioned in the text. When this occurs, the reviewers question the budget request because intervening variables since last year must cause some program changes. The possibility of an *identical* budget request approaches zero because administrative environments always change. A distinct likelihood exists that another reviewer may have ordered the agency to use the same budget level as the previous year's budget, but to use the *identical* budget request seems to imply lack of adaptability to changing conditions. Part of the game is to at least give the appearance of managing the program, and this is not done by using last year's budget.

Budget requests are rarely approved intact and reviewers normally reduce (cut) the request. There are several common rationales given for cutting budgets:

1. a climate of opinion existed which was against spending;
2. strong views by influential decision makers necessitated the cut;
3. spending on your program became a political football; and
4. there was an overriding need to balance the budget.

The reason cited may address the management capability or fundamental objectives of the agency's program. However, such statements are more difficult to rationalize against the superior expertise of the agency on those topics. The reasons cited above are less subject to dispute and appeal, thus they are more likely to be cited.

Some ironies can exist with budget cutting. An agency may wish to have a certain program cut or may even cut its own program. For example, maybe the agency leadership lost faith in a program, internal discipline called for cuts, or higher priorities in some programs meant cuts in other programs. Interestingly, cuts can stimulate mobilization of the agency clientele, thus eventually resulting in even higher budgets than would have occurred without those earlier cuts.

Another phenomenon which can occur is intra-legislative conflict. One obvious area of conflict is between the two chambers (House and Senate). Conference committees are intended to resolve such disputes, but strategies can be used so that one chamber's position dominates. For example, the Senate may raise the amount in order to achieve the desired amount through compromise. Another tactic is to have a chamber pass a resolution supporting its conferees, thus permitting them to cite the solidarity and intensity of feelings in their arguments. Conference committees are often unpredictable and most agencies would prefer to avoid this uncertainty unless one chamber cuts their requests significantly. A less obvious area of conflict is between the substantive committee and the appropriations committee. In some instances, the agency can be the innocent victim of such disputes.

Spenders' Strategies

There are game strategies that an agency can apply in seeking to get its budget requests approved. This section explains the various strategies which are commonly used, but does not attempt to comment in depth upon how, when, and in what way the strategies should be applied to maximize their effectiveness. Such matters require judgment based upon each separate budget situation.

There are some fairly common safety strategies which are employed. Budget requests are often padded because the agency wishes to be able to meet unanticipated contingencies and to compensate for the fact that reviewers often almost automatically cut requests. Obvious or nondefensible "padding" can lead to an important loss of confidence, but "extras" can normally be easily defended. A related strategy is always to ask for more. This demonstrates an aggressive agency which has a strong belief in its mission. The increase may not be merited, but the reviewers are forced to address the increase and may forget to argue the possibility of a program level decrease. In connection with this strategy, the agency is careful to spend or obligate all the current year's funds. If there is any surplus, the reviewer may argue that the agency's current funding is more than adequate and there is no need for additional money. Another safe strategy is to alter the written or oral budget presentations as much as possible to highlight the best aspects of the agency's program and minimize the worst aspects.

Budgeting is a complex activity. "Sleight-of-hand" tricks do exist and they can be part of a budget strategy. For example, numbers in budgets are rounded often to the nearest hundred thousand or even million. For some small but politically important budget items, the practice of rounding can be an advantage. Another "trick" is to recast the budget into different categories than those used in the previous year. The redone categories can be utilized to focus attention upon or away from programs, depending upon the budget's strategic purposes. Also, redone categories inhibit longitudinal analysis and this may be an advantage to the agency. In addition, there are a variety of back-door spending devices; one of them is no-year funds. One sleight-of-hand technique is to use unobligated appropriations or disobligated appropriations (i.e., funds previously obligated but for which obligation was subsequently withdrawn, often because of nonuse by grantees) to finance projects beyond the apparent level of budget year appropriations. For example, let us say that an agency has $15 million left over from last year's budget and also has $20 million disobligated from previous years. This $35 million technically should be deducted from the budget request, but normally the subtraction is not cited or is poorly cited by the agency.

Another sleight-of-hand trick is the fund transfer. An agency can often transfer money from one account to another. By using several transfers among several funds, illusions can be created about the money that was obligated. This unprofessional trick can be used also to defraud the government or mislead reviewing groups such as prospective bond buyers. Careful accounting can uncover such abuses, but such work is detailed and time consuming.

Most spender strategies are direct and simple. The agency merely points out that the tasks it performs have expanded and more money is needed to fund the program. Another strategy is to point out the backlog of requests or tasks. The argument is then made that an increase is needed to eliminate the backlog and that a cut would increase the size of the backlog. A third strategy or argument is to appeal to a national standard by showing that the agency can meet the standard with a given level of budget support. This strategy is used often by highly professional groups (e.g., medical and educational).

Sometimes the strategy is to argue with economic concepts. A program activity may involve a fee, such as an entrance fee or license. The agency argues that a given budget level would attract more people to the activity, thus increasing the revenue from the activity. The increased revenue might be larger than the expenses in the budget. A more complex argument is that an increased budget for a program like a subsidy would increase the operation and payroll size. The argument is made that because of the multiplier effect of the subsidy the government would recover more in additional taxes (e.g., income tax) than was paid out for the subsidy. Another argument is that an increased budget would permit greater productivity owing to a better cost average per unit or the use of the extra money to purchase labor-saving devices.

Other arguments are predicated more on emotion. The agency argues that the revenue of the government has grown and that the agency should receive a fair share of the growth. A bolder strategy is to argue that a high-level commitment exists on the project and there is no option but to fund the program. A less bold but equally emotional strategy is to plead that the program is "squeezed to the bone" and a certain funding level is essential for meaningful program operation.

In many situations, the agency wishes to start a new program but the newness must be masked. Once funded, a "foot-in-the-door wedge" or "camel's nose under the tent" has been established. This precedent greatly helps the agency convince reviewers because the standard for new programs tends to be harsher than the standard for existing programs. The agency will often argue that the money does not represent a new initiative but rather a continuation of old programs. This may be quite true literally, but the new dimension may constitute an entire new major emphasis which logically should be considered a new program. However, such treatment would bias the reviewers against the effort.

Spenders' strategies can constitute a high political risk for the agency and agency officials. One strategy is to react to a request or cuts by suggesting cuts be taken first on projects which enjoy strong political support. By cutting the "sacred cows'' or popular programs, the cutter is placed in a politically difficult position and may withdraw the request to cut the program. The risk for the agency head is that the chief executive may be offended by the use of this strategy and fire the political appointee. A second strategy is to shift the blame. The agency points out that if the full requested amount is not funded, then certain specific activities will not be undertaken. The agency makes it clear to the reviewer that the responsibility for not funding the activity will be placed on the reviewer. In some situations, reviewers are sobered by such responsibility and the related political implications; thus they act favorably on the budget request. A third strategy is to argue that a cut is irresponsible and that the project must be funded at the requested level or not funded at all. This is a sound argument for many projects because there is a lower limit at which the project cannot be sustained as viable. The risk in such an argument is that the reviewer may indeed decide to cut the whole project.

Another high-risk strategy is to spend fast to be short. The agency deliberately spends the money at a fast rate and then goes back to the reviewers for supplemental appropriations. This strategy is employed infrequently but does occur, especially when the agency is asked to absorb large cuts. This is an extremely high-risk strategy because of the likelihood that the top agency officials will be considered to be irresponsible and poor managers. Firing of top officials is often a result of the use of such strategies.

Cutters' Strategies

Just as there are game strategies for an agency, there are strategies for the reviewing groups. Some strategies are safe and are fairly standard. Other strategies are essentially counterstrategies to be used against spenders' arguments and ploys. The discussion here, like the previous spenders' section, is addressed to explaining the strategies and not to an in-depth treatment of their application in a variety of contingencies.

The safe approaches include reducing increases, questioning hidden ''revenues,'' cutting less visible items, and employing delay. The political support for existing programs can be quite strong and the pressure for increases may be strong also. However, the exact size of the increase is almost always open to discussion and cuts in the increases are easier to sustain. Another safe approach is to investigate and try to isolate ''hidden'' revenue, such as the use of the previous fiscal year's appropriations or the use of existing government property rather than the purchase of new property. Normally, some savings can be found with this approach and few can fault the results. A third approach is to cut the less visible or less politically supported items. This approach should be employed with some discretion because such ''saving'' may be false economy. For example, the replacement program for a city water pipe system can be deferred but the wiser policy is probably a yearly systematic program. Delay is a particularly easily applied strategy. Whenever another study is conducted or delays are caused for other reasons, the result is that the item is not included in the budget. This is one of the most successful cutter's strategies because all that need be done to justify a delaying study is to raise a question.

Several fairly standard arguments and ploys exist. One is always to cut something. If no cuts are made, the credible power of the reviewer is questioned. Also, the reviewers are aware that the spenders have a natural tendency to include items that they could do without. Thus cuts will eliminate those "frills." A second approach is to argue that initial allocations are unnecessary. If nothing starts, then budget expansion is diminished. A third approach is to defer or record projects on the grounds that initial dollars cannot be spent correctly by the end of the fiscal year. New programs normally experience difficulty in staffing themselves; thus they rarely can do a decent job in the first year. By arguing that a program will not do a decent job in the first year, the cutter can each year prevent the program from coming into existence. A fourth approach is never to allow a precedent to be established. Precedents lead to continued budget requests. An effective ploy is to argue that there is only so much money and that some is available for program increases. The question is then asked: Whose turn is it? This focuses the debate away from the amount and gets the various units to argue against each other. A sophisticated ploy to be used in a few circumstances is to eliminate interagency competition, which tends to be more expensive due to the expansive nature of competition itself in the public sector.

The cutter need not accept or live with strategies employed by the spender. Counterstrategies do exist. If the agency says the increase is "so small," the counter is to argue that no item is too small to eliminate or to suggest that such small items can be absorbed without a budget increase. If the agency argues that they should have a fair share of the growth, the cutter can ask what is "fair" and never accept any definition. Another counterstrategy is to challenge work load data. Often such data are collected poorly and can be easily challenged on methodological grounds. The cutter can normally argue that productivity increases—for a number of reasons, such as a worker's becoming more experienced at a new job (i.e., learning curve)—should mean that increases or even decreases are appropriate in a given program.

One spender's strategy is to place the blame on the cutter for the cuts, but that blame need not be accepted. The cutter can force the agency officials to say what they believe should be cut first. If the spender is likely to put forth political "sacred cows" for cutting, the cutter can anticipate and neutralize the strategy by insisting that the agency must suggest items to be cut but stipulating which items cannot be considered as candidates for cutting.

Cutters normally have the advantage because they need only question and the spender has the burden of proof. The strongest asset the spender has is expertise, and care must be taken to maintain the expert's credibility. Spenders can employ strategies but most of them must be executed with an aura of expertise.

New Programs

The previous strategies are for normal day-to-day budget situations. New programs require extraordinary efforts on the part of the spenders. Often new programs are established in reaction to a crisis or what some consider to be a crisis. Such crises rarely are manufactured, but groups do take advantage of crises to establish new programs or radically increase existing programs. The political climate in a crisis is such that political forces concur that the need is obvious and the debate centers on the "solutions." But even that debate is different in that the political climate calls for a solution, and delay is an unacceptable condition. Standards are lowered and the key is effectiveness. Efficiency becomes a less significant topic. In such an environment, agencies have a much greater opportunity to get viable ideas accepted and new or radical increases in programs do occur.

Agency or clientele advertising and salesmanship can sometimes result in the creation of new programs. Dramatic names or labels such as *Mission 66* or *Headstart* can be significant in capturing enough popular attention. Good presentations are necessary. A well-organized effort can start new programs, but the presence of anticlientele groups (even small groups) can be fatal to such efforts. Rarely are advertising and salesmanship adequate by themselves. Normally they must be linked to a cause of the day (e.g., environment, pollution, national defense, inflation, unemployment). Ironically, overselling sometimes can be dysfunctional because the new program can become so popular that the agency's other programs suffer. Advertising and salesmanship should not be underrated, but the times and places are more significant in the beginning of most new programs.

Cautions

Unlike a parlor game, the budget game has serious consequences. Spenders' and cutters' strategies are used and sometimes one side or the other plays the game poorly. This is unfortunate because the budget process is usually best served when both sides play the game well. One particularly serious game fault is when the agency leadership forgets that the agency is a *public* agency designed to serve *all* the people. True, the clientele is only part of the public and most of the agency's dealings need only concern the clientele, but circumstances do exist where the public nature of an agency prohibits continuous harmonious relations with the clientele group (e.g., a coal company dealing with the Interior Department on a strip mining question). Public agencies can be captured by their clientele.

The mood of the times often is much more important than given strategies of spenders or cutters. Such moods change and they create a significant climate which favors, disfavors, or is neutral to specific programs. Government officials are sensitive to current events and recognize that those events are much like the weather for the farmer. The weather is very important and the farmer can do some things to mitigate the bad effects of weather, but it is still a largely uncontrolled governing force. Some political storms must be accepted as either a favorable or unfavorable reality by government officials.

One last caution is noted. If the mood of the times becomes favorable to a program and the reviewers become converts to the mission of an agency, the agency will discover that its new role expectation according to the reviewers is to think and act very big. The meaning of "big" depends on the size of the government and the dimensions of the problem. If the agency doesn't think in expansive terms, then criticisms, such as being overly concerned about "petty economies," are likely to occur. Such role expectations are sometimes difficult to comprehend given the normal budget process, but the agency must accommodate to the role expectation or be subject to remarkably unpleasant political pressure.

REVIEW QUESTIONS

1. What political influence patterns exist in the federal government in terms of budgeting? Why are they important to understand?
2. Why is it important for an agency to cultivate a clientele? How is that done? What problems and cautions are important to understand?
3. What are the typical duties of an agency budget office? What views and behaviors should be anticipated?
4. What is the agency budget officer's perspective? Contrast that to the executive and legislative perspective.
5. Why are confidence, results, and hearings important? Explain how confidence can be enhanced. How can one prepare for hearings?
6. What strategies can be used by advocates of spending and by reviewers critical of spending?

REFERENCES

ANTHONY, ROBERT. "Closing the Loop Between Planning and Performance," *Public Administration Review* (May/June 1971).

ANTON, THOMAS J. *The Politics of State Expenditure in Illinois.* Urbana: University of Illinois Press, 1966.

AXELROD, DONALD. "Post-Burkhead: The State of the Art or Science of Budgeting," *Public Administration Review* (November/December 1973).

PARKER, STEVE. "Budgeting as an Expression of Power," in Jack Rabin and Thomas D. Lynch (eds.), *Handbook on Public Budgeting And Financial Management.* New York: Marcel Dekker, 1983.

WILDAVSKY, AARON. *The Politics of the Budgeting Process.* Boston: Little, Brown, 1964.

FOUR
BUDGET FORMATS
AND PREPARATION

This chapter addresses the topics of budget formats, building the budget, budget reviews, and legislative adoption. It covers:

1. why budget formats are significant;
2. the various budget formats and how they apply to general policy, budget balancing, and the improvement of government management;
3. the role and work of the central budget office in initiating the process of building the budget;
4. the central role and tasks of the agency in preparing the budget;
5. the importance of the steps associated with executive and legislative reviews of the budget;
6. the use of executive budget hearings in the review process;
7. the ingredients and preparation of the executive budget document;
8. the Congressional budget timetable;
9. the legislature's deliberative process on the budget; and
10. the formats used in legislative adoptions of budgets.

BUDGET FORMAT

The Important Means

Formats are important and procedures are not neutral. The *means* of budgeting affect the *ends* of budgeting. How? Decision makers tend to think about what is put in front of them. Thus, budget classifications tend to define reality for budget makers and reviewers by channeling their attention and thought to specific areas. To illustrate this point, Edward A. Lehan in *Simplified Governmental Budgeting* asked his readers to examine two exhibits similar to Exhibit 4-1 and Exhibit 4-2 and to prepare simple follow-up questions.

The line-item format focuses thinking and discussion on things to be bought and tempts officials to alter expenditure patterns in ways largely unrelated to policy issues on service levels.

A third format—performance budgeting—is illustrated in Exhibit 4-3. Note how the reader's mind tends to be directed toward questions of efficiency.

In summary, each format channels thought differently. Line-item budgeting tends to take decision makers away from policy issues and focus attention on expenditure savings. Program budgeting tends to focus attention on policy differences and on choices among policy options. Performance budgeting places the focus on questions of efficiency rather than of effectiveness.

Ends Defining Means

Which budget format (line-item, program, performance, PPB, ZBB, TBB) is the best? Given that the format does influence the decision-making focus, then the selection of a format depends on the desired decision-making environment. What

EXHIBIT 4-1 A Line-Item Format

CODE ENFORCEMENT	BUDGET
Personal Service	$60,238
Contractual Service	7,863
Supplies	1,376
Total	$69,477

EXHIBIT 4-2 A Program Format

CODE ENFORCEMENT	BUDGET
Plain examination	$12,331
Inspection	40,339
Education	15,529
Total	$68,199

EXHIBIT 4-3 A Program Format

CODE ENFORCEMENT	ITEMS	BUDGET	UNIT COST
Plan examinations	744	$12,331	$16.57
Inspections	19,371	40,339	2.08
Education (graduates or trainees)	12,333	15,526	1.26
Total		$68,196	

Typical questions:

1. Are there any inefficiencies?
2. Can we lower unit cost? How?
3. Why is the unit cost of plan examination so high?

mind-set do you wish to create? The three major concerns of a budget officer are (1) to raise the level of debate, (2) to insure that policy control is maintained, and (3) to improve the quality of management in the government. Given these objectives, the choice of format can still vary substantially, depending on the political and managerial context. Fortunately, the three objectives of a budget office can be met not only by the recommended budget but also by the operating budget, the capital budget, other budget office documents, and meetings. Thus, some flexibility exists in the means to accomplish the objectives. However, in this chapter, only the format of the recommended budget will be addressed. In an excellent book (*Effective Budgetary Presentations: The Cutting Edge,* compiled by Girard Miller), the Government Finance Officers Association presented examples of the common components of local government budgets. These components are the budget cover, table of contents, organization charts, transmittal letter, financial summaries, goals and objectives, divider pages, revenues, departmental and activity budgets, program budget summaries, performance measurements, enterprise and internal service funds, capital outlay, special analyses, accompanying documents, reader's guides, budgetary procedures, budget preparation instructions, and legislative adoption. Students are encouraged to review this unique collection of samples to understand some of the format possibilities available to a budget office.

From a format design perspective, the desired ends should influence what format or formats should be used. A tendency of budget presenters is to use a standard approach for all programs, and this is desirable because it permits comparisons. Nevertheless, various programs do deserve individual presentations in order to highlight the most useful information for decision-making purposes. Format designers should decide first on the general format and then on extra information useful for specific programs.

Three common concerns should be weighed when deciding on format:

1. How to help decision makers deal with *general policy* matters?
2. How should the *budget* be *balanced*?
3. How can decisions of policy makers be used to *improve* the *quality* of *government management*?

Four common difficulties associated with helping elected decision makers formulate policy are (1) trying to get elected officials to focus upon the major policy issues rather than insignificant and time-consuming issues which make relatively little difference to the future of the community; (2) fostering a decision-making environment in which counterproductive political tensions are reduced so that important and timely policy can be made; (3) sensitizing decision makers to the future year implications of their decisions; and (4) achieving an awareness that budget decisions do relate to specific government actions which affect individuals and society. The first difficulty is commonly handled with program budgeting and formalized budget approaches like PPB and ZBB. The latter is especially useful as a means to inform novice political executives of the policy implications of budget decisions. The second situation, according to one noted author, Aaron Wildavsky, can be handled well by line-item budgeting, which permits more face-saving because it focuses attention on relatively unemotional subjects such as salaries, travel, and supplies. The third difficulty is handled by requiring revenue and expenditure forecasts to be made possibly five or more years beyond the BY. Requiring a financial program schedule is also an appropriate procedural way to meet this concern. The fourth difficulty is resolved by having program budgets include performance measures which show the products or services produced by government programs as well as their impact on individuals and society.

Dealing with the challenge of balanced budgets commonly requires (1) getting both policy makers and government agencies to accept the existence of resource constraints; (2) helping policy makers justify to the public the need for more government resources (i.e., higher property taxes); and (3) shifting political pressure from the more controversial revenue sources to the more acceptable revenue sources. The first type of situation is best suited for a TBB approach, which assumes a given revenue level and works from that assumption. Ideally, with TBB, budget decisions beyond the arbitrarily established limit simply should not be considered. The limitation of such an approach is that government problems are not limited by arbitrarily established revenue limits. The second situation occurs when policy makers decide that more taxes are needed, but the public is not yet supportive of that policy position. Budgets can be constructed to stress the need, how government action can resolve that need, and the necessity for more money if that need is to be resolved. Program budgeting is particularly useful if it is combined with appropriate measures of program services and social needs. The third situation is more complex. Governments receive their revenues from various sources, of which some are more politically sensitive at various times than others. One way to help deal with that political reality is to minimize pressure on the politically sensitive revenue sources by shifting as much cost as possible to less sensitive revenue sources. For example, if property tax is a hot political issue, then user free revenues can be increased as much as possible to cover expenses. The budget format can show, for each expense item, the source of revenue. This would permit the probing inquiry which would seek to shift the burden to the least politically sensitive revenue source.

Striving to improve government management usually includes (1) stressing efficiency and productivity in government management, (2) establishing top level control procedures in order to ensure that policy is carried out and that fraud and abuse are minimized, (3) establishing proper review practices to minimize overhead costs, (4) stopping unnecessary end-of-the-year purchases, and (5) improving management through better use of new technology and development of professionals and other employees. The first concern is normally addressed with performance budgeting or, more commonly, separate ad hoc productivity studies, internal audits, and the hiring of more program reviewers. Edward A. Lehan advocates a format (see chapter 5) which includes marginal analysis and allows decision makers to consider the optimum funding level which will result in the greatest productivity. The second concern can be addressed in the operating budget by using a line-item format which assigns dollars to specific units. Another strategy often employed is to increase audit and inspector general staffs. The third concern is associated with a greater organizational sophistication. Formats which include overhead comparative and longitudinal cost data focus attention on that concern and are helpful. The fourth concern can be addressed by good accounting practices. Accounting data illustrating the problem can be included in the budget or in a special analysis accompanying the budget. The fifth concern can be spotlighted in the budget by a narrative which discusses plans for the use of new technology and how staff will be developed. First-priority use of new funds can be singled out for upgrading technology, which should result in productivity improvements. Professional development (i.e., training) can be included as one of the fringe benefits of employment and made less vulnerable to normal line-item budget cuts.

In summary, one can choose among budget formats in order to better highlight particular concerns. Such highlighting will not necessarily guarantee specific decisions, but it will channel thought.

BUILDING THE BUDGET

Program Financial Schedule

On a quarterly basis, each department and agency can be required to transmit a program financial schedule to the central budget office. This now fairly common budget requirement provides useful information to the budget office. On a quarterly basis, the central budget office can better forecast expenditure needs. The schedule categorizes the program by activity, method of finance, and fiscal year. Schedules commonly forecast five years beyond the budget year and include output measures associated with the desirable appropriation levels. The schedules are also divided into obligations and expenditures, thus providing useful information to economists and analysts concerned with the government's cash flow. Thus, the data can be used to estimate likely expenditure demands. This is useful data in preparing the budget call and issuing executive guidance on budget preparation.

These forecasts should not be viewed as extremely accurate, but merely as an indication of likely financial patterns given existing policy. In each quarter, policy can change and other factors can evolve, making periodic updating essential. The program financial schedule is particularly significant prior to the development of the central budget office's budget call. The total of the schedules equals a reasonably high estimate of what all the departments and agencies will request. This intelligence is useful in framing budget office guidance for building the budget.

Budget Call

Budget coordination.   Exhibit 4-4 presents a slightly modified budget calendar used by the city of Los Angeles. The calendar is important to the building of the budget because it establishes essential deadlines. Preparing a budget is a complex undertaking involving the whole government. Coordination is achieved by first deciding who must do what when. This is decided in the calendar. The budget calendar milestones of a local government include:

1. distribution of instructions and forms;
2. preparation of revenue estimates;
3. return of completed budget request forms;
4. completion of review and preliminary preparation work assigned to the central budget agency;
5. completion of executive review and executive determination of final budget content;
6. submission of the budget to the legislative body;
7. completion of public hearings;
8. preliminary legislative determination of the content of the appropriation ordinance or budget to be approved;
9. final action by the legislative body;
10. executive approval or veto of the adopted budget and legislative action;
11. completion of administrative actions, if any, needed to finalize budget appropriations; and
12. beginning of fiscal year.

Once the preliminary estimates of expenditures and budget calendar have been prepared, the central budget office can proceed with preparing for the budget call. The call gives guidance to all the departments and agencies on how to go about preparing the budget. In many governments, including the federal government, much of the guidance is standardized and established in official bulletins and circulars such as OMB Circular A-11. Agency budget officials need only refer to the established procedures and report forms. In addition to the standard operating procedures, each year special guidance is issued in the form of a "policy" letter, "allowance" letter, an executive policy message, or a statement on the budget. The "policy" letter is used in the federal government to convey executive guidance and budget ceilings. The "allowance" letter comes later to inform federal agencies and departments of presidential or OMB decisions after the executive review process.

EXHIBIT 4-4 Budget Calendar, Los Angeles

Date	Action to be Completed
January 2	Mayor's Budget Policy letter requesting Department heads to submit proposed work programs and budget estimates for ensuing fiscal year. Necessary forms and revisions to budget manual are transmitted with that letter.
February 1	City Administrative Officer approves staff budget assignments which are thereafter distributed to the staff.
February 15	Current level work programs and budget estimates received from department heads.
March 1	Service betterment budget estimates, if any, received from department heads.
April 10	City Administrative Officer reviews tentative Capital Improvement Expenditure Program and, upon approval, transmits it to the Public Works Priority Committee by April 10.
April 10	City Administrative Officer submits annual salary recommendations to City Council by April 10.
April 10-30	Hearings conducted by the Public Works Priority Committee to determine final priority of capital projects to be included in Capital Improvement Expenditure Program for ensuing year.
April 10-17	Preliminary budget hearings held by City Administrative Officer and Budget Coordinator with the Assistant Budget Coordinator and staff analyst for each department.
April 18-28	City Administrative Officer assisted by Budget Coordinator conducts departmental budget hearings with each department head at which time the staff analysts' recommendations for that departmental budget are presented and department head is given an opportunity to express his viewpoint.
May 1[1]	Final date for submission by City Controller of the official estimates of revenue from all sources (other than general property taxes).
May 1[1]	City Administrative Officer submits his official estimate of revenue from general property taxes.
May 1-5	Mayor, assisted by City Administrative Officer, conducts budget conferences with each department head. Attended by Council members, press and taxpayer groups.
May 5-12	Final budget decisions made by Mayor assisted by City Administrative Officer.
May 12-31	Budget printed under supervision of City Administrative Officer.
June 1[1]	Mayor submits proposed budget to City Council.
June 1-20	Council considers Mayor's veto of any item and may override Mayor's veto by two-thirds vote.
June 20-25[1]	Mayor considers any modifications made by City Council and may veto such changes.
June 25-28[1]	Council considers Mayor's veto of any item and may override Mayor's veto by two-thirds vote.
July 1[1]	Beginning of fiscal year—Budget takes effect.

[1]Charter requirement.

Budget guidance. The executive policy message or statement on the budget at the state and local level requests budget information and establishes guidance. For example, the policy may be one of "hold-the-line," retrenchment, or expansion. Also, programs and activities to be emphasized or deemphasized are announced. Common subjects discussed in municipal statements include:

1. mandated increases, such as pension payments, salary increments, and debt service;
2. raise or change in taxes;
3. request to hold the line or identify inadequate services requiring expanded effort;
4. plea for economy;
5. explanation of local economic trends influencing the budget; and
6. explanation of who must provide what information and when it is due (the budget calendar).

The detailed explanation call may be in the form of a budget instructions booklet which provides guidance to the agencies and departments. The booklet contains:

1. the preliminary statement of executive budget policy;
2. the table of contents, including listing of forms;
3. the budget calendar;
4. general instructions; and
5. specific instructions for each form, including a sample form.

Budget office follow-through is essential. The instructions must be sent to the chief departmental officials. Each level of government will repackage the instructions and reissue them to lower levels. Eventually, the program managers receive the information requests. Meetings are useful at all levels to clarify and avoid possible confusion. Special care should be taken to explain any changes in the procedures. Every official involved should understand the current financial status and likely trends, including personnel pay trends. Emphasis must always be given to the need for accurate, prompt, uniform replies. The types of forms required are explained in Municipal Finance Officers Association publications cited in this chapter's references.

The budget call always asks for a statement of government functions, activities, and work programs, or some narrative explaining what services are to be received for the tax dollar. The general instructions asking for this budget explanation normally stress the desirability of brevity, clarity, and comprehensiveness. The explanation should reflect any program changes and even emphasize those changes. Each level in the executive branch uses the information, with the central budget and department levels focusing upon having a complete inventory of government activities keyed to specific units assigned to functions and activities. The descriptive detail is greater at the unit and agency level.

Agency call. Exhibit 4-5 is a sample agency call for estimates used in past federal budget training manuals. The call draws attention to the executive policy

August 1, 19PY

MEMORANDUM TO ASSIST DIRECTORS AND DIVISION HEADS

Subject: *Instructions for Preparation of the Budget Estimates for FY 19BY*

The 19BY budget submission to the Office of Management and Budget (OMB) will conform generally to the program and activity structure used for the 19CY budget estimate. The overall budget estimate will be prepared to reflect policy and program decisions which resulted from budget meetings held by the Director on the 19BY budget.

For purposes of the presentation to OMB, descriptive materials for the various programs should be brief statements covering the points outlined in the following format. It is expected that the submission to the Congress will be a more detailed budget.

Since no appropriation has been approved for the Agency for 19CY, the program estimates for that fiscal year will be the same as in the 19CY Budget to the Congress. Under item "C." of the instructions, supplenentary data is being requested for the preparation of staff salary estimates and travel and other administrative expenses that are spread among the activities shown in the Salaries and Expenses appropriation.

Estimates and drafts of the justification material must be received by the Budget Office by August 20.

Comptroller

and the required format to be used in the agency. The call points out that the agency is still operating under a continuing resolution for the current year. Reference is made to instructions which are particularly sensitive. The call states who should prepare the information (i.e., assistant directors and division heads) and when the information is due (e.g., August 20). Note that only 20 days are allowed to compile the information. Tight deadlines do occur in budgeting. If zero base budgeting were used, the instructions would require alternative decision packages and priority rankings.

Preparing a budget at the agency level is a difficult task. The material must be assembled from the units and the budget figures in particular must conform to agency policy set down by the agency head. Personnel statistics and cost information is normally calculated by the budget office to compute the salaries and expense portion of the budget. If the agency has field units, the process is more complex because more groups are involved. Extreme accuracy and consistency are important because their absence denotes sloppy preparation and poor management.

The format of the agency budget requests varies greatly depending upon which budget reform happens to be in vogue. The format can be a detailed line-item presentation that permits greater control over the bureaucracy, a program budget that stresses policy issues and their budget implications, a performance budget that relates input to program accomplishments, a zero base budget that focuses on marginal value and prioritization, or an incremental budget that stresses changes from past policy decisions. The format selected is important, but a more important factor is the quality of professionalism devoted to preparing and reviewing the budget. Good professionalism calls for in-depth understanding of the agency and the related budget implications. How this is done is explained in chapter 6. Too often the format is established by some budget reform movement instead of being tailored to the type of programs administered by the agency as well as to the needs of the central budget office.

BUDGET REVIEWS

Once the agency prepares the budget, the review process begins in the executive and legislative branches. The agency first meets with the department officials. They conduct a complete examination of the budget request, often including budget hearings. Departmental budget decisions are made and the agency budget request is revised based on department level decisions. Normally, the department recommends cuts but is a more friendly reviewer than the central budget office. The latter unit next reviews the agency or compiled departmental budget. Recommendations are made by the central budget office to the chief executive and sometimes departmental officials make direct last-minute appeals to the chief executive. Finally, the chief executive's budget is released.

Executive Budget Hearings

Normally, the agency submits its budget to the reviewing party, who carefully analyzes the submission. Chapter 5 describes how program and budget analyses can be conducted. After the initial analysis of the submission and any other available material, the reviewing party, such as the department budget office, is prepared to seek additional information. Often this is done by formal written questions to the agency on specific inquiries and sometimes more informal inquiries are made. The reviewers—budget examiners—prepare an analysis of the material and prepare background material for a hearing. Hearings need not be held but they enable the budget officer and the executive to obtain a better understanding of an agency's request and reasons supporting that request.

Agencies also prepare for hearings. The depth of preparation varies but the agency is wise to prepare carefully. Anticipated questions from the reviewers can be developed, and responses can be written and studied by the agency's representatives. A plan of action or strategy can be prepared, keeping in mind the factors discussed in the next chapter on budget behavior.

The hearing itself is semi-formal, with testimony rarely transcribed. The chief executive of the department should chair the meeting to ask questions and understand the budget request. The principal budget officer is present and plays an active role. Often questions are prepared for the chief executive to facilitate the process. The agency presents a statement and questions follow or the review is handled entirely with questions and answers. Regardless of the style used, the agency should explain its program, especially any program changes. The questioners should probe for elaborations on vague points as well as potential political or management problems. The hearing is only for information purposes and this forum is inappropriate for tentative or final decisions because more deliberation is necessary.

After the hearing is completed, the budget analysts carefully review their notes and reconsider the submission and other material. Guidance from the departmental chief executive is also reviewed. Often the reviewers may ask some additional questions by phone or in writing. The departmental budget office then prepares its final analysis and recommendations.

The departmental chief executive is then briefed on the budget. The briefing depends upon the management style of the chief executives. Some delegate the entire responsibility to the budget office and others review the requests in detail. Normally, the pressure of time on the chief executive prevents long, detailed reviews of requests. A set of briefing information usually includes:

1. summary of agency requests;
2. recommendations of budget office;
3. summary of the past year's chief executive's ideas relative to the budget;
4. added suggestions by the budget office;
5. preliminary budget (balanced for state and local government); and
6. summary of policy issues.

A similar process exists at the gubernatorial or presidential level of government. This review takes place after the departmental reviews.

Executive Budget Document

Budget message.   Budgets sent to legislatures and city councils are almost always accompanied by a budget message. The contents vary depending upon the political situation. Normally, the message includes a discussion of the financial condition of the government and a commentary on the current year operating budget, such as "the current budget is and will continue to be balanced." Revenue highlights are mentioned, including revenue estimates, new revenue sources, and prospects on increased or new taxes. The government is usually put into perspective by citing major trends in finance, population changes, income level shifts, and so on. The principal elements of the proposed expenditures are explained, including the rationale for any major program changes. Sensitive topics like "mandatory" increases as well as pay and fringe benefit policy are mentioned. Problem areas not addressed by the proposed budget are cited, often with an explanation for that omission. At the local level, the message could also explain the relationship between the operating and capital budgeting. The message summarizes the highlights of the budget and blunts political criticism if possible.

Budget summary.   A summary of the budget is essential. It should present consolidated summaries of revenues and appropriations. At the federal level, various economics-related information is presented. At the local level, the comparative statement of resources includes:

1. cash surplus at the end of the first prior year;
2. estimated receipts for the current year;
3. anticipated expenditures during the current year;
4. estimated cash surplus at the end of the current year;
5. anticipated income during the budget year;
6. proposed expenditures during the budget year; and
7. projected cash surplus at the end of the budget year.

Additional information can be included in the local level budget summary. A statement on the tax rate and the assessed valuation of the property, including amount of land, improvements, and exemptions, is often included. A statement on other revenue sources is useful. The statement of appropriations by organization unit can be included. Finally, a summary of appropriation to various activities can be mentioned.

Budget detail.   After the summary material, the detailed revenue and expenditure estimates are presented. The revenue estimates are grouped by funds and presented by comparing the budget year estimates with the prior year and current year. Appropriate footnotes are added to explain tax rates, tax base, and nonrecurring humps or valleys in the estimates. All assumptions used in preparing the revenue estimates are explained. The detailed expenditure estimates often include:

1. a narrative explanation of the functions of each department, suborganization unit, and activity, as well as a separate section for comments on the major changes proposed in each activity;
2. a listing by department and suborganization unit of the objects of expenditure and by activity with an identification of proposed resource changes;
3. a listing by position title for each unit and activity as well as any proposed changes; and
4. an identification of the work load volume being undertaken in conjunction with each activity.

The executive budget document is often considered to be the budget even though the legislature may make some changes. In some jurisdictions, the budget is the final document passed and approved by the legislature. Regardless of the stress given the executive budget document, it is extremely influential in the decision-making process. The document is the chief executive's plan. Any modification must be done with the awareness that any changes cannot be simply additions or deletions. Even in the federal government, additions to the budget raise the question of either "Where is the extra money going to come from?" or "What programs are going to be cut?" If deletions are suggested, the easier but still difficult question raised is either "Where is the extra money going to be spent?" or "What taxes should be cut?" These are not simple questions and the executive budget becomes the point of departure for legislative consideration of the budget.

Congressional Budget Timetable

Budget milestones.   In the earlier discussion of the budget calendar there are target dates set for legislative action on the budget. For many governments, the executive may be considered presumptuous to state target dates for the legislatures because of the separation of powers concept. In spite of that attitude, most budget people can estimate fairly accurately what the target dates are in the legislative budget process. Often the legislative body will state its own targets in its rules. The one forcing deadline is the beginning of the new fiscal year, by which, everyone agrees, the budget should be adopted. The other deadlines fall between the time when the legislature receives the chief executive's budget and the beginning of the fiscal year.

In the federal government, the Congressional deadlines were set by the 1974 Budget Act. These critical targets, coupled with serious prodding by the budget committees, encourage the Congress to pass timely appropriation legislation, avoiding the pre-1974 practice of passing appropriation legislation three to six months into the current year. Both the targets and the active pushing of the budget committees are essential. The targets set a standard. Budget committees use social and political pressure to achieve responsible Congressional action.

The seriousness of not passing timely appropriations is often overlooked. If no appropriation legislation is passed, then the government cannot pay its employees or anyone else. Government operations cease to exist because no one has the authority to spend money. If a decision has not been reached on appropriations prior to the beginning of the new fiscal year, then a legislative body passes a continuing resolution which normally says that the government can continue to obligate and spend at last year's budget levels. The wording of the continuing resolution could also say the government can proceed at the lower of either last year's budget or the approved version of the House or Senate bill. The wording is normally framed to permit spending at the lowest amount the legislature is likely to pass. Managing a program under a continuing resolution is no significant problem unless the final legislation provides the manager with significantly less or more money than the continuing resolution. If less money is provided, the entire program may have to stop. If more money is provided, the program may have to obligate money recklessly in order to use it during the remainder of the fiscal year. Either situation is bad public management which can be compounded by repeated yearly use of the continuing resolution, as happened with Congress prior to 1974.

Congressional budget timetable. The Congressional budget deliberative process starts with the presidential submission of the Current Services Budget. This budget alerts the Congress, especially the Congressional Budget Office, the budget committees, and the appropriation committees, that they should be anticipating specific revenue, expenditure, and debt levels unless current policy is changed. The Current Services Budget also provides a baseline of comparison to the later presidential budget.

The presidential budget, with the Current Services Budget, is sent to the Congress 15 days after Congress convenes in the new calendar year (e.g., January 20). The budget normally follows the State of the Union Address to Congress by about one week. Presidents usually address Congress with a specific budget message which is more detailed and specific than the earlier State of the Union speech. The budget messages vary in content with a president's style, but the earlier discussion follows a common pattern, with the exception that more emphasis is often placed on the national economy.

By February 1, the Congressional Budget Office must send its annual report to the budget committees. This report analyzes the economy, the Current Services Budget, and the president's budget. Alternative levels of spending are suggested. Interestingly, the original legislation called for an April 1 submission, but the CBO realized this did not give the budget committees sufficient time to digest the CBO report so the date was changed by mutual consent.

By March 15, the various committees, like appropriation, must submit their respective reports to the budget committees. This is a tentative financial guess by the committees on revenue, expenditure, and debt. The committees use the CBO report, the president's budget, and the detailed backup information supplied by the agencies to help them arrive at reasonable budget estimates.

One month later, on April 15, each budget committee reports its recommended budget resolution. This resolution represents the difficult compromise on the entire budget: the revenues, expenditures, and debt, as well as targets for each committee important to the budget process. One month later, on May 15, each chamber votes on its own resolution. An inability to reach a decision would destroy the process. Opposition can come from the conservatives for spending too much money and from the liberals for spending too little money. The resolutions need not be the same in each chamber. May 15 is also the deadline for reporting all authorization bills. The Congress doesn't want unanticipated expenses resulting from authorization legislation, so this deadline is essential.

Seven days after Labor Day in September final action on appropriation bills is required. This gives the appropriation committees several months to hold their hearings and make their difficult decisions.

By September 15, final action on the second budget resolution is required. This permits last-minute changes possibly due to intervening circumstances since the first resolution was passed. Often, there may be no difference between the first and second resolution, but an opportunity for flexibility has been provided. By September 25, all final actions on budget reconciliation should be passed, thus providing a uniform consolidated Congressional budget in each chamber.

The remaining days in September are used to resolve differences between chambers, pass the legislation, permit a presidential veto, and reconcile or override the veto. All this can be done if there is perfect cooperation among the chambers and the president. If not, then delays will result and a continuing resolution may be necessary because the federal fiscal year begins on October 1.

Legislative Considerations

At all levels of government, legislative bodies consider budgets and budget supporting material. This information is the key to proper legislative understanding of government operations. The considerations and the subsequent legislation permit the legislative oversight activity to exist. The purse strings are important. If weaknesses are identified, legislators can re-tailor policy often with their redrafted budget. The budget consideration in legislatures is a much more open process than the executive review. Thus legislative budget hearings serve as a forum for better community understanding of government as well as a device to permit citizens to express their views on budget matters.

The time needed for legislative consideration of the budget varies with the size of government. Committees must have time to study the budget and related information, conduct hearings with public officials and possibly with interested citizens, discuss policy internally, and finally enact the legislation. Normally, 60 days is a reasonable time for smaller local governments.

Legislative organization to deal with the budgets also depends largely on the size of government. Larger governments should have standing committees with highly competent professional staff support. Committees and staffs can be organized on a partisan or a nonpartisan basis. Given the complexity of government and budgeting, more of the smaller states and local governments should hire professionally trained and experienced public administrators. Exhibit 4-6 presents an illustrative page from a legislative analyst's review of a budget request. The reader will notice how a good analyst can focus attention upon the items which should concern the legislator.

The hearing is the standard method used to gather information and focus upon potential problems of concern to the legislature. Often these problems are isolated through careful staff program and budget analysis. The legislative hearing is conducted differently from the executive hearing. With legislative hearings, a transcript is often maintained and there are more co-equal questioners of the agency personnel. Some legislators are friendly and others are hostile. Just as in the executive hearings, the agency is wise to prepare for the hearings with briefing books, to plan strategies and tactics, and to have rehearsals. The hearings are usually scheduled more at the convenience of the legislative committee than of the agency. Follow-up questions are common, as in executive hearings. Decisions are not made at hearings, but rather at closed door "mark-up" sessions.

If public participation is part of the hearing, then the committee normally takes care to give due notice of the time and place of the meeting. Failure to give due notice or to notify all the likely interested "publics" can result in heated public criticism.

EXHIBIT 4-6 Legislative Analyst's Review Sheet, Department of Hospitals and Institutions, 1963 Budget Request

Newark City Hospital

The 1963 Budget request of $6,469,185.00 for the Newark City Hospital shows an increase of $229,131.67 over 1962 Operations as follows:

1963 Budget Appropriations	$6,453,424.00	1963 Request	$6,469,185.00
1962 Emergencies	115,149.96		
	$6,568,573.96		
Less Cancellations	328,520.63		
Net 1962 Operations	$6,240,053.33	1962 Operations	6,240,053.33
		Increase	$ 229,131.67

The request for 1,270 employees is 25 less than the 1,295 in 1962.

Page No.	Line No.	
4		There were 29,669 less patient days in 1962 than in 1961 resulting from a drop in admissions from 18,760 in 1961 to 15,460 in 1962, a net drop of 3,300.
5		The average day's stay per patient dropped from 9.5 to 9.1. The average daily admissions dropped from 60.9 in 1961 to 56.4 in 1962, a net drop of 4.5 admissions. The average daily census of patients in the hospital dropped from 575.6 in 1961 to 549.9 in 1962, a drop of 25.7 in 1962.
6	1 & 2	What is the status of the Medical Director and the Assistant Medical Director?
6	3	Will the Comptroller's position be filled? Is the present incumbent Joseph Rubino to remain on the hospital payroll?
10	12A	Has this position been filled?
19	37	Is this position going to remain in the hospital?
25		New employee, Director of Surgery. In accordance with policy followed in similar cases the appropriation for this employee will be deleted because there is no valid ordinance supporting it. The appropriation will be made after adoption of the ordinance and before final adoption of the budget by amending the approved budget.
41	103A	Bernice Lippe replaced the Director of Nurses on January 14, 1963 at the minimum salary of $7,500.00. Her salary as Assistant Director of Nursing Education on Page 112 was $6,460. One pay should be deleted from the Director of Nurses' appropriation and one pay remaining in the Assistant Director of Nursing Education's line on Page 112.

The legislatures normally have the power to modify the executive's budget, but that is not always the case in local government. Even if the power exists, modifications are difficult because all components of the budget are interdependent. If one figure is adjusted upward, another figure must be cut if the budget is to balance. Exhibit 4-7 illustrates one city council's modifications.

EXHIBIT 4-7   Schedule Setting Forth Changes Made by City Council in City Manager's Original Estimate of 1990–91 Budget

	Manager's Estimate	Revised Amount
Office of City Manager	$ 146,135	$ 138,246
Reason for Change—Reduced cost of annual report, reduction of .5 man year administrative analyst. Add cost of salary increase.		
Secretary-Treasurer	166,844	169,484
Reason for change—Add cost of salary increase.		
Accounting	77,686	74,751
Reason for change—Delete one accountant position. Add cost of salary increase.		
Data Processing	179,470	181,303
Reason for change—Add cost of salary increase.		
Purchasing	30,867	31,539
Reason for change—Add cost of salary increase.		
Tax	400,390	408,861
Reason for change—Add cost of salary increase.		
Legal	99,472	101,636
Reason for change—Add cost of salary increase.		
Retirement Administrator	22,731	23,043
Reason for change—Add cost of salary increase.		
Personnel and Civil Service	29,703	50,349
Reason for change—Add cost of salary increase. Add cost of salary and wage survey.		

The adoption of the budget can vary in terms of detail. Appropriations should be itemized by department in order to fix responsibility. Some argue that they should be itemized by major object classification and others by program or activity. There is no one correct way. Object classification is good for greater control, especially when there is a low threshold of trust afforded the government's middle and lower level managers. Program classifications are good for situations which need management flexibility to operate effectively and efficiently. Detailed line-item budgets are extremely inflexible. Necessary taxes and a formal resolution on the final official revenue estimate accompany or are passed at the same time as the budget.

LEGISLATIVE ADOPTION[1]

The ultimate budget is the legislative adoption version, which can be several appropriation laws (the federal government's approach), one massive, complex appropriation law (used by many states), or a relatively brief text (used by some local governments). Sometimes the budget submitted to the legislative body includes the recommended act or ordinance. Exhibit 4-8 is the simple, streamlined budget legislation used by Abilene, Texas. Note that the resolution approves revisions to the current year's budget estimates, authorizes current year appropriations transfers, and adopts the city manager's proposed budget. All fiscal details are incorporated by reference.

Often budget ordinances are complex because of state legal requirements. In some jurisdictions, the resolution includes tax rates, purchasing authority, personnel action authorizations, and transfer procedures. Some use broad legislative grants of authority and others have extensive line-item detail for each government unit. Exhibit 4-9 is a more complex ordinance used by Durham County, North Carolina. Note that enterprise fund budget items are included; some people argue that such items do not belong in the appropriation document.

The ordinance:

1. acknowledges receipt of an executive budget from the county manager;
2. recounts earlier publication and a public hearing;
3. summarizes appropriation by fund and category;
4. estimates revenue;
5. levies property taxes;
6. authorizes administrative transfers of appropriations within a fund; and
7. approves and reappropriates funds for ongoing capital improvements

---

[1]Much of the material in this section comes from Girard Miller, Compiler, *Effective Budgetary Presentations: The Cutting Edge* (Chicago: Government Officers Finance Association, 1982).

EXHIBIT 4-8 Abilene, Texas, Fiscal Year 1982, Budget Adoption Ordinace

ORDINANCE NO. 89-1981

AN ORDINANCE APPROVING REVISED BUDGET FIGURES FOR FISCAL YEAR 1980-1981; APPROVING AND ADOPTING BUDGET FOR THE FISCAL YEAR OCTOBER 1, 1981, THROUGH SEPTEMBER 30, 1982, FOR THE CITY OF ABILENE; APPROPRIATING FUNDS; AND CALLING A PUBLIC HEARING.

WHEREAS, the City Manager has prepared a revision of certain figures in the 1980-1981 budget and submitted same to the City Council; and,

WHEREAS, the City Manager on August 10, 1981, filed a proposed budget with the City Secretary for the fiscal year commencing October 1, 1981; and,

WHEREAS, the City Council has reviewed and considered said proposed budget and made revisions of same; and,

WHEREAS, said proposed budget, as revised by the City Council, was duly set for a public hearing ordered to be called by the City Council and held on September 10, 1981, after due notice, as required by the Charter of the City of Abilene and laws of the State of Texas; now, therefore,

BE IT ORDAINED BY THE CITY COUNCIL OF THE CITY OF ABILENE, TEXAS:

PART 1: That the revised figures, prepared and submitted by the City Manager for the 1980-1981 budget, be, and the same are hereby, in all things, approved and appropriated, and any necessary transfers between accounts and departments are hereby authorized, approved and appropriated.

PART 2: That the budget proposed by the City Manager for the fiscal year commencing October 1, 1981, as revised by the City Council, be, and the same is hereby approved, adopted and appropriated.

PART 3: That upon passage of this ordinance on first reading, the City Secretary be, and she is hereby authorized and directed to have published in the Abilene Reporter News, a daily newspaper of general circulation in the City of Abilene, a notice that a public hearing will be held in the Council Chambers of the City Hall in Abilene, Texas, at 9:00 A.M., on the 10th day of September, 1981, to permit the public to be heard prior to consideration of this ordinance for second and final reading, said publication to be made more than ten (10) days prior to the time designated for such public hearing.

Girald Miller (Compiler). *Effective Budgeting Presentations: The Cutting Edge.* Chicago: Government Finance Officers Association, 1982.

EXHIBIT 4-9   Durham County, North Carolina 1981–82 Budget Ordinance

WHEREAS, the budget estimate for the fiscal year 1981–82 for Durham County, North Carolina was, on June 15, 1981, submitted to the Board of Commissioners by the County Manager (Budget Officer) and filed in the Office of the County Manager at least ten (10) days prior to the adoption of this ordinance; and

WHEREAS, on June 15, 1981, the Board of Commissioners of Durham County, North Carolina adopted a preliminary budget ordinance for the General Fund and established the tax rate for general and bond indebtedness and the tax rates for the school and fire districts as indicated in Section 4 of this ordinance; and

WHEREAS, on June 15, 1981, the Board of Commissioners of Durham County, North Carolina held a public hearing on the budget; now therefore, pursuant to North Carolina General Statute 159-13.

BE IT ORDAINED BY THE BOARD OF COMMISSIONERS OF DURHAM COUNTY:

Section 1. That for the purpose of financing Durham County, North Carolina, for the fiscal year 1981–82 beginning July 1, 1981, and ending June 30, 1982, there is appropriated from the taxes and other revenues collectible for the use of the various funds, departments and subdivisions of the County, including salaries and wages hereby affixed in accordance with the pay plan adopted by the Board of Commissioners, and for the payment of its bonded indebtedness, the following amounts:

COUNTY GENERAL FUND:

General Government	$ 1,805,601
Community Services	2,738,162
Public Protection	2,908,093
General Services	1,152,560
Education	14,178,500
Human Services	39,665,584
Nondepartmental	451,000
Transfers	3,720,000
TOTAL APPROPRIATIONS	**$66,619,500**

SPECIAL REVENUE FUNDS:

General Revenue Sharing Fund	$ 2,750,000
City Schools Supplemental Tax Fund	3,043,000
County Schools Supplemental Tax Fund	5,518,340
Bethesda Fire District Fund	168,000
Lebanon Fire District Fund	95,467
Parkwood Fire District Fund	90,000
Redwood Fire District Fund	30,193
Tax Reappraisal Fund	175,000
TOTAL APPROPRIATIONS	**$11,870,000**

DEBT SERVICE FUND $ 3,030,000

ENTERPRISE FUND

Sanitary Sewer	$ 739,000

Section 2. Appropriations made for purposes other than those authorized by North Carolina General Statute 153A-149 are hereby made and authorized from revenues derived from sources other than the levy of property taxes.

Section 3. It is estimated that revenues will be available during the fiscal year beginning on July 1, 1981, and ending on June 30, 1982, to meet the foregoing appropriations, according to the following sources.

TOTAL	TOTAL	GENERAL COUNTY FUND	SPECIAL REVENUE FUND	DEBT SERVICE FUND	ENTERPRISE FUND
Property Taxes					
Current year levy	$30,550,611	$22,407,720	$8,142,891	$ —	$ —
Prior years' collections	1,222,530	1,000,000	222,530	—	—
Interest and penalties on taxes	156,280	156,280	—	—	—
Total Property Taxes	31,929,421	23,564,000	8,365,421	—	—
Other Local Taxes					
Local option sales taxes	3,800,000	3,800,000	—	—	—
Intangible property taxes	790,000	790,000	—	—	—
ABC taxes	150,000	150,000	—	—	—
Animal control	24,000	24,000	—	—	—
Total other local taxes	4,764,000	4,764,000	—	—	—
Licenses and Permits	92,721	92,721	—	—	—
Intergovernmental Revenues	33,044,467	31,467,023	1,577,444	—	—
Investment and Rental Income	2,171,556	2,002,000	169,556	—	—
Charges for Current Services	1,727,000	1,727,000	—	—	—
Operating Revenues	239,000	—	—	—	239,000
Other Revenues	71,000	71,000	—	—	—
Total Revenues	74,039,165	63,687,744	10,112,421	—	239,000
Transfers From Other Funds	3,705,000	—	175,000	3,030,000	500,000
Total Revenues and Transfers	77,744,165	63,687,744	10,287,421	3,030,000	739,000
Fund Balances Appropriated	4,514,335	2,931,756	1,582,579	—	—
Subtotal	82,258,500	66,619,500	11,870,000	3,030,000	739,000
Less: Interfund Transfers	(3,705,000)	—	(175,000)	(3,030,000)	(500,000)
Total Budget	$78,553,500	$66,619,500	$11,695,000	$—	$239,000

Section 4. For the purpose of raising the revenues to finance the appropriations for the proper government of Durham County, the payment of bonds and interest thereon, to supplement school expenditures for the Durham County School Administrative Unit and the Durham City School Administrative Unit, and to finance the appropriations for special fire districts for the fiscal year 1981–82, the following Ad Valorem Taxes (all as shown in the Revenue Section of this ordinance as General Property Taxes) are hereby levied on all real and personal property subject to Ad Valorem taxes within Durham County, North Carolina on the first day of January, 1981, to wit:

(a) A tax rate of eighty-seven cents ($.87) on each one hundred dollars ($100.00) of assessed valuation of property for general and bond indebtedness purposes.
(b) A tax rate of twenty-seven cents ($.27) on each one hundred dollars ($100.000) of assessed valuation of property located within the Durham County School Administrative Unit.
(c) A tax rate of thirty-eight cents ($.38) on each one hundred dollars ($100.00)of assessed valuation of property located within the Durham City School Administrative Unit.
(d) A tax rate of four cents ($.04) for the Lebanon Fire District; six cents ($.06) for the Parkwood Fire District; three cents ($.03) for the Bethesda Fire District, and five cents ($.05) for the Red-wood Fire District on each one hundred dollars ($100.00) of the assessed valuation of property located within the respective special fire districts.

Section 5. That the taxes hereby levied shall be due and collectible on September 1, 1981.

Section 6. The Budget Officer is hereby authorized to transfer appropriations within a fund as contained herein under the following conditions:

(a) The transfer of amounts between objects of expenditure within a program without limitations and without a report being requested.
(b) The transfer of amounts up to $2,500.00 between programs of the same fund with an official report on such transfers at the next regular meeting of the Board of Commissioners.

Section 7. In accordance with North Carolina general Statute 115D-51, Durham County shall provide; based upon the appropriations herein, funds to Durham Technical Institute (DTI) as needed to meet the D. T. I. County Current Fund and Plant Fund expenditures. All accumulated unexpended and unencumbered amounts at the end of the fiscal year shall be returned to Durham County wihin thirty days after the close of the fiscal year. Reserves for future capital projects shall remain with Durham County to the credit of Durham Technical Institute until requested for payment of duly appropriated obligations.

Section 8. That capital projects, water and sewer construction projects and special assessment projects are hereby authorized in accordance with the Local Government Budget and Fiscal Control Act (North Carolina General Statute 159-13.2). The following schedules summarize (1) those projects previously authorized, under which expenditures may be made during the 1981–82 budget year, (2) those authorizations added during the 1980–81 fiscal year, under which expenditures may be made during the 1981–82 budget year, and (3) those authorized for the 1981–82 budget year.

	TOTAL AT JUNE 30, 1980	ADDITIONAL 1980–81	RECOMMENDED 1981–82
CAPITAL PROJECTS FUND:			
Durham County General Hospital	$23,177,599	$ —	$ —
Health Services Building	1,850,258	—	—
Judicial Building	10,195,807	—	—
Durham County Library	3,031,148	—	—
Ambulance Maintenance Center	250,000	—	—
County Memorial Stadium	50,000	—	—
Lincoln Community Health Center	—	1,100,000	500,000
Parking Lot—Peabody Street Realignment	—	70,000	—
County Courthouse Building	—	—	1,500,000
Durham Technical Institute Cooper Street Building	—	—	750,000
WATER AND SEWER CONSTRUCTION FUND:			
Water and Sewer Construction-1982	$	$ —	$ 500,000
Water and Sewer Construction-1981	—	500,000	—
Water and Sewer Construction-1980	2,000,000	—	—
Water and Sewer Construction-1979	1,150,000	—	—
Water and Sewer Construction-1978	1,200,000	—	—
Sewer System Construction-1977	900,764	—	—
SPECIAL ASSESSMENT (STREET PAVING) FUND			
Street Improvement Assistance-1982	$ —	$ —	$15,000
Street Improvement Assistance-1981	—	15,000	—
Street Improvement Assistance-1980	15,000	—	—
Street Improvement Assistance-1979	15,000	—	—
Street Improvement Assistance-1978	12,500	—	—
Street Improvement Assistance-1977	10,037	—	—

Section 9. A copy of this ordinance shall be furnished to the Budget Officer, the Finance Officer, and the Tax Supervisor for direction in performing their respective duties.

Section 10. This ordinance shall be in full force and effect from and after its adoption.

Girald Miller (compiler). *Effective Budgeting Presentations: The Cutting Edge.* Chicago: Government Finance Officers Association, 1982.

EXHIBIT 4-10a The Federal Budget Cycle. Phase one: Executive preparation and submission.

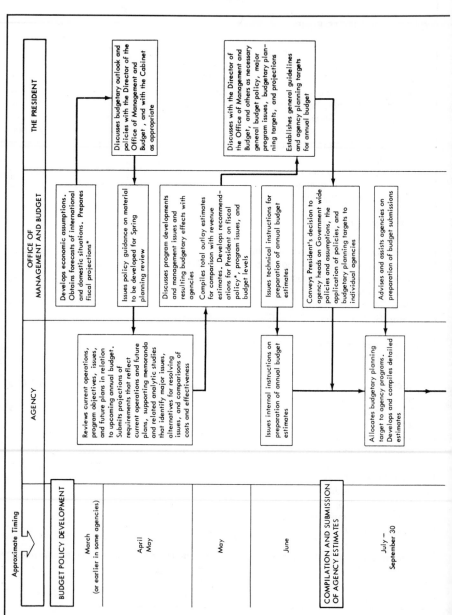

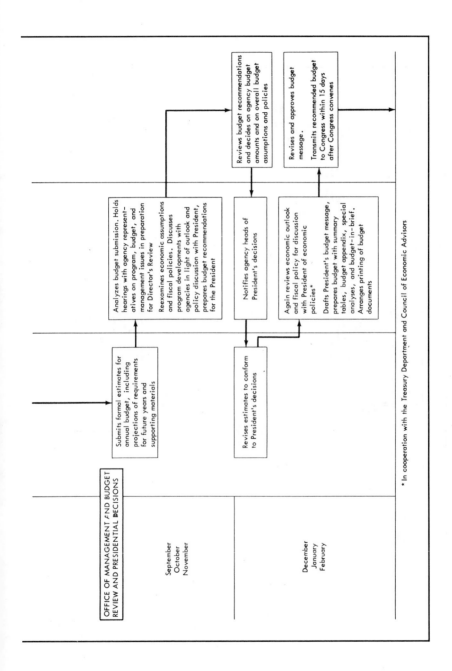

OFFICE OF MANAGEMENT AND BUDGET
REVIEW AND PRESIDENTIAL DECISIONS

September
October
November

Submits formal estimates for annual budget, including projections of requirements for future years and supporting materials

Analyzes budget submission. Holds hearings with agency representatives on program, budget, and management issues in preparation for Director's Review

Reexamines economic assumptions and fiscal policies. Discusses program developments with agencies in light of outlook and policy discussion with President, prepares budget recommendations for the President

Reviews budget recommendations and decides on agency budget amounts and on overall budget assumptions and policies

December
January
February

Revises estimates to conform to President's decisions

Notifies agency heads of President's decisions

Again reviews economic outlook and fiscal policy for discussion with President of economic policies*

Drafts President's budget message, prepares budget with summary tables, budget appendix, special analyses, and budget-in-brief. Arranges printing of budget documents

Revises and approves budget message.

Transmits recommended budget to Congress within 15 days after Congress convenes

* In cooperation with the Treasury Department and Council of Economic Advisors

125

EXHIBIT 4-10b   The Federal Budget Cycle. Phase two: Congressional budget process.

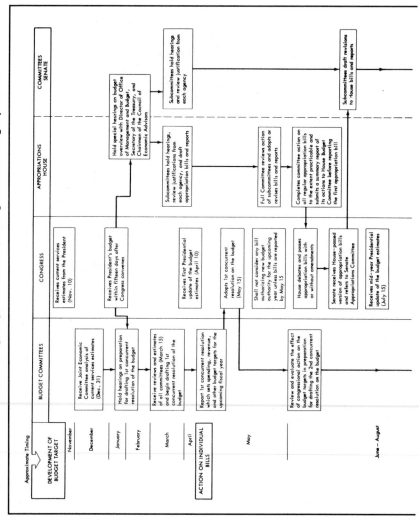

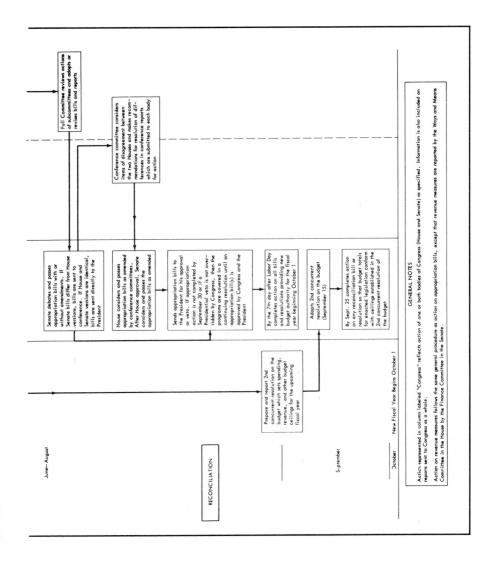

June—August

Full Committee reviews actions of subcommittees and adopts or revises bills and reports

Senate debates and passes appropriation bills with or without amendments. If Senate bills differ from House versions, bills are sent to conference. If House and Senate versions are identical, bills are sent directly to the President

Conference committee considers items of disagreement between the two Houses and makes recommendations for resolution of differences in conference reports which are submitted to each body for action

House considers and passes appropriation bills as amended by conference committee. After House approval, Senate considers and passes the appropriation bills as amended

Sends appropriation bills to the President for his approval or veto. If appropriation action is not completed by September 30 or if a Presidential veto is not over-ridden by Congress, then the programs are covered in a continuing resolution until an appropriation bill(s) is approved by Congress and the President

By the 7th day after Labor Day completes action on all bills and resolutions providing new budget authority for the fiscal year beginning October 1

RECONCILIATION

Prepare and report 2nd concurrent resolution on the budget which sets spending, revenue, and other budget ceilings for the upcoming fiscal year

September

Adopts 2nd concurrent resolution on the budget (September 15)

By Sept. 25 completes action on any reconciliation bill or resolution so that budget totals for enacted legislation conform with ceilings established in the 2nd concurrent resolution of the budget

October | New Fiscal Year Begins October 1

GENERAL NOTES

Action represented in column labeled "Congress" reflects action of one or both bodies of Congress (House and Senate) as specified. Information is also included on reports sent to Congress as a whole.

Action on revenue measures follows the same general procedure as action on appropriation bills, except that revenue measures are reported by the Ways and Means Committee in the House by the Finance Committee in the Senate.

127

EXHIBIT 4-10c The Federal Budget Cycle. Phase three: Implementation and control of enacted budget.

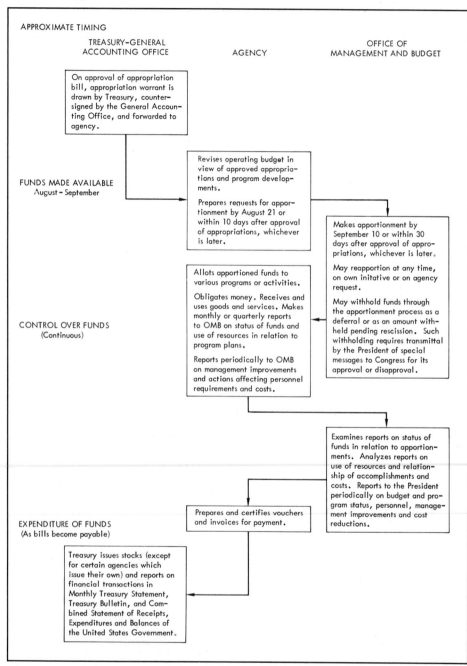

APPROXIMATE TIMING

| TREASURY–GENERAL ACCOUNTING OFFICE | AGENCY | OFFICE OF MANAGEMENT AND BUDGET |

On approval of appropriation bill, appropriation warrant is drawn by Treasury, counter-signed by the General Accounting Office, and forwarded to agency.

FUNDS MADE AVAILABLE
August – September

Revises operating budget in view of approved appropriations and program developments.

Prepares requests for apportionment by August 21 or within 10 days after approval of appropriations, whichever is later.

Makes apportionment by September 10 or within 30 days after approval of appropriations, whichever is later.

May reapportion at any time, on own initative or on agency request.

May withhold funds through the apportionment process as a deferral or as an amount withheld pending rescission. Such withholding requires transmittal by the President of special messages to Congress for its approval or disapproval.

CONTROL OVER FUNDS
(Continuous)

Allots apportioned funds to various programs or activities.

Obligates money. Receives and uses goods and services. Makes monthly or quarterly reports to OMB on status of funds and use of resources in relation to program plans.

Reports periodically to OMB on management improvements and actions affecting personnel requirements and costs.

Examines reports on status of funds in relation to apportionments. Analyzes reports on use of resources and relationship of accomplishments and costs. Reports to the President periodically on budget and program status, personnel, management improvements and cost reductions.

EXPENDITURE OF FUNDS
(As bills become payable)

Prepares and certifies vouchers and invoices for payment.

Treasury issues stocks (except for certain agencies which issue their own) and reports on financial transactions in Monthly Treasury Statement, Treasury Bulletin, and Combined Statement of Receipts, Expenditures and Balances of the United States Government.

EXHIBIT 4-10d   The Federal Budget Cycle. Phase four: Review and audit.

APPROXIMATE TIMING

TREASURY–GENERAL ACCOUNTING OFFICE	AGENCY	OFFICE OF MANAGEMENT AND BUDGET
PROGRAM EVALUATION, MANAGEMENT APPRAISAL, AND INDEPENDENT AUDIT		
Periodic		
General Accounting Office performs independent audit of financial records, transactions, and financial management generally. "Settles" accounts of certifying and disbursing officers. Makes reports to Congress including reports on special messages on deferrals and proposed rescissions.	Reviews compliance with established policies, procedures, and requirements. Evaluates accomplishment of program plans and effectiveness of management and operations.	Reviews agency operations and evaluates programs and performance. Conducts or guides agencies in organization and management studies. Assists President in improving management and organization of the executive branch.

Source: Office of Management and Budget, Jan. 1977.

REVIEW QUESTIONS

1. Explain how budget formats channel thought. Explain how formats can direct thought to and highlight general policy matters, budget balancing issues, and improvement of the quality of government management.
2. Why are the program financial schedule and budget calendar important preliminary steps to the budget call?
3. What budget instructions are important in building a budget? Why?
4. Contrast executive and legislative hearings.
5. Why is the central budget office "powerful"?
6. What information should be in an executive budget? Why?
7. Explain the significance of the Congressional budget timetable.
8. Contrast the virtues of a simple versus a comprehensive budget ordinance or law.

REFERENCES

ARONSON, J. RICHARD and ELI SCHWARTZ (eds.). *Management Policies in Local Government Finance.* Washington, D.C.: International City Management Association, 1975.

BURKHEAD, JESSE. *Government Budgeting.* New York: John Wiley, 1956.

FISHER, LOUIS. *Presidential Spending Power.* Princeton, N.J.: Princeton University Press, 1975.

JASPER, HERERT N. "A Congressional Budget: Will It Work This Time?," *The Bureaucrat,* 3, 4 (January 1975), 429–43.

LEHAN, EDWARD A. *Simplified Governmental Budgeting.* Chicago: Municipal Finance Officers Association, 1982.

MILLER, GIRARD (compiler). *Effective Budgetary Presentations: The Cutting Edge.* Chicago: Municipal Finance Officers Association, 1982.

MOAK, LENNOX L. and KATHRYN W. KILLIAN. *Operating Budget Manual.* Chicago: Municipal Finance Officers Association, 1963.

MUNICIPAL PERFORMANCE REPORT, 1, 4 (August 1974).

SMITH, LINDA L. "The Congressional Budget Process—Why It Worked This Time," *The Bureaucrat,* 6, 1 (1977), 88–111.

U.S. Civil Service Commission, Bureau of Training, The Management Science Training Center. *Budget Formulation,* 1976.

FIVE
ANALYSIS APPLIED
TO BUDGETING

Budgeting requires analysis, and this chapter introduces a wide variety of analytical techniques useful in public budgeting. It is not a how-to-do-it chapter, rather it shows how significant types of analysis relate to budgeting. The first section focuses on the theoretical foundation on which analysis can be applied in the public sector. The following sections describe the difficulties associated with applying the theory, describe useful elementary analysis, explain the important analytical tool called *crosswalk*, focus on revenue and expenditure forecasting, explain productivity analysis, and explain benefit-cost analysis. At the completion of this chapter, the reader should know:

1. a theoretically useful model that is consistent with the context of a democratic society;
2. application difficulties associated with the model;
3. simple analytical techniques that help us understand key relationships;
4. the three common approaches to revenue forecasting as well as the basics of econometrics;
5. expenditure forecasting approaches including bargaining, unit cost, and time series methods;
6. how an econometric model can be useful in expenditure forecasting and simulation;
7. the basics of productivity analysis, underlying productivity through regression analysis, and how to strengthen budget requests;
8. the difference between benefit-cost and cost-effectiveness analysis;

9.   the fundamental concepts associated with benefit-cost analysis; and
10. the analytical limitations to the benefit-cost technique.

THEORETICAL FOUNDATION

Accountability and a Systems Model

This budget system model, based upon an operational concept of accountability in the public sector, assumes a chain of cause and effect within the system, from input (money, expertise, policy direction) to process (the performance of administrative activities) to outputs (the products and services produced by the unit) and finally to outcomes (the impacts on individuals and society). Between the beginning of the chain and the end—and especially between outputs and outcomes—intervening variables from the environment are likely to exist. Nevertheless, this model assumes that the input eventually and necessarily causes the outcomes, even though that cause may not be sufficient to produce the effect itself. If that is not the case, then the reason for having the input is lost and funding cannot be supported in the budget process. Thus, the model helps decision makers address the first critical question of budget analysis—program effectiveness. The model also helps them address the second critical question of budget analysis—program efficiency. By examining the ratio of input to output and then focusing upon the process, decision makers can gain insight into how to do the same or similar work with fewer resources.

Accountability within government can be facilitated by budget analysis. Policy makers tend to address accountability implicitly when they create programs because they intend to induce certain desired social and economic effects as a result of government action (e.g., improved traffic flows in a city). Accountability is achieved merely by monitoring these programs to see that the input requested is leading to the desired or acceptable levels of outputs and outcomes. Accountability is fostered in the budget process when decision makers are helped to understand the interrelationship between budget requests (input) and program accomplishments (outputs and outcomes). The role of the budget analyst in the budget office is not to make policy but to raise the level of debate among the policy makers so that they can focus upon the truly significant policy questions. Thus, the budget office should facilitate accountability and encourage more intelligent decisions about the allocation of government resources.

The model assumes that decisions are made in a democratic society in which the elected leaders and the people do not necessarily share values. Actual and desired program outcomes must be appreciated and considered in a political context in which diverse social values compete in an ongoing (and, one hopes, nonviolent) conflict over community policy. The model does not assume that there is one correct government solution or best set of values. The model does assume that the conflict in political values does not give consistent and clear guidance to government program managers and that logically consistent government policy will not necessarily be selected. Given that democratic reality, the model calls upon the budget office to communicate salient information which permits policy makers to confront and deal more intelligently with their multiple-valued electorate. Although policy recommendations can and should be made by budget offices, the offices must appreciate that the data collected, especially program outcome measures, should first and foremost facilitate the policy makers' ability to make more intelligent decisions in their political environment. Outcomes are to be understood and defined in the political context of the government and the larger society it serves.

Program Impact Theory

The focus in budget examination is upon understanding existing and planned management strategy as well as upon program effectiveness. Regardless of the approach (e.g., PPB, ZBB, or TBB) to budget preparation, a common theoretical framework exists which assumes a cause-and-effect interrelation between the program's inputs and its ultimate impacts on the society or environment. The examiner (also called the budget analyst) assumes that such a relationship can and should exist, and then attempts to discover if the actual or intended approach to managing the program can and is likely to lead to the intended program outputs and outcomes. Also, the examiner wants those results accomplished with the greatest program effectiveness consistent with the political values of the policy makers.

Almost all government programs are intended to affect society or individuals in some way or the necessary legislation would not have been passed. Often, the desired impacts on society are vague and even internally contradictory, but there almost always is some purpose behind each law and government program. There is an assumed cause-and-effect relationship: The government program is intended to produce an effect on society. This assumption is central to much of the analysis useful in budgeting. Often budget analysts try to determine if a resource request and even the program itself is worthwhile given the results of that program.

The burden of proving the worth of a program and a specific resource request is placed on the agency. The agency must justify the budget to the department, the executive, and the legislative body. Often those involved act as if absolute proof exists that a given program is worthwhile. Unfortunately, those holding such a view are not sensitive to the philosopher Descartes, who held that absolute proof for any subject other than one's own existence (*cogito ergo sum*) is not possible; therefore, we must use other criteria in evaluating it.

In public administration, the criterion of "necessary but not sufficient cause" is normally the best. For example, if the ultimate desired effect is to reduce the crime rate, holding the police force responsible for that effect may seem reasonable until one realizes that poor police work is not the only reason for the existence of crime. Good police work may be necessary, but it alone is not sufficient to reach a low crime rate. Too often analysts and decision makers apply the harsher "necessary and sufficient" criterion in judging the worth of government programs. This unfortunate conceptual mistake merely leads to false expectations and frustrated administrators and citizens.

Conceptually, an analyst should be able to develop a program impact theory.

Given a set of resources and the conditions in society, a government program can produce outputs which in turn will lead to outcomes. The resources, in part, are reflected in the budget request. The outputs are the achieved objectives of management. Those objectives provide guidance to the lower officials and administrators in the bureaucracy. The outcomes are the achieved objectives one cites in program evaluations. Those impacts or outcomes are what higher level decision makers should view in judging the government program.

The program impact theory is the heart of any good budget justification. The person justifying the budget should be arguing that the agency will achieve the legally stated desired effects (i.e., the law's purpose) on society or individuals if the agency is given the requested resources. The program impact theory should be the conceptual means to relate the resource requests to the stated end results caused in society.

If the desired end results do not occur, then two types of failure are possible: (1) the agency did not do its job correctly or (2) the theory was incorrect. If the agency conceptually separated outputs and outcomes correctly and gathered the necessary data, then the type of failure can be determined. If the objectives of management were met, then one type of failure can be eliminated. This permits proper focus upon theoretical failure, which is the responsibility of the highest level decision makers for using poor theory or the academic community for not developing adequate theories. Once the failure is identified, then attention can be focused upon discarding faulty theories and developing more useful theoretical understandings. This identification of failure is particularly significant and helps us understand the relationship of social science research and the needs of higher level administrators.

Date measures are critical because the assumption is made that each key portion of the model (e.g., input, process, output, and outcome) can be accurately described. Data measures for input tend to be easy to define because line-item budget detail or aggregate numbers representing money and positions almost always exist. Data measures for process normally are not difficult to acquire and not critically needed for most budget analyses. Output data measures are obtained by asking what the unit produces in terms of products or services. For most units and programs, isolating data measures is not difficult, but the information may not be collected on a routine basis. Outcome data measures are often very difficult to obtain, as government units normally do not routinely record the individual and societal impacts of their programs.

Deciding what data measures to use is not an easy task. Normally, the best process to follow is to reason backward while focusing upon a specific unit and program. The question "What impact does this particular program have upon the organization (if the program is administered by a service unit to an organization) or upon society (if the program directly affects society)?" should be asked. Then the analyst should seek specific means to measure that impact. Next, the analyst should identify the program outputs by seeking to understand exactly what the unit does or produces which causes those previously identified program outcomes. Data measures of output should give an accurate picture of what takes place. Outputs are defined and are relevant only in the context of program outcomes. The process stage can be omitted, but it does permit a more in-depth analysis which helps postulate recommended efficiency improvements. The last stage in reasoning backwards is the input. What input contributes to and affects the process, output, and outcome? Input which does not contribute to output and outcome, is not needed.

APPLICATION DIFFICULTIES

The application of a theoretical model in public administration can be difficult, but the difficulties can be anticipated. Commonly, analysts and line officials using the model will (1) mixup outputs, outcomes, and process data measures, (2) confuse the types of appropriate output measures, (3) not understand how to apply the concept to staff and service units, and (4) not fully appreciate that an inability to determine outcome and output measures may indicate program nonperformance.

Mix-Up

The most common mistake, when applying this model, is to mix up the model elements and measures. For example, an agency may insist upon using descriptive measures which explain its administrative process. Those measures often indicate work effort (e.g., ten hours to write the report) or ratio of staff to clients (e.g., student/teacher ratio of 30 to 1). There is nothing wrong with such measures *per se*, but program output and outcome measures must also be determined, and each measure should be correctly defined. Questions addressed to program effectiveness cannot be answered with process data alone.

Another mix-up is confusing outcomes and outputs. In fact, the two are often used interchangeably. This is an unfortunate mistake as it leads to improper use of analysis. Proper identification of model components makes it possible to determine program effectiveness and efficiency. The best approach to avoiding such confusion is to address program outcome first and reason backward to program outputs.

Types of Output Measures

Public administrators are sometimes unaware that program outputs, especially services, consist of two types which should be treated differently. The first type is the result of a project with a defined end product or service. Constructing a building or writing a report are examples of that output type. The second type reflects a desire to provide ongoing services or products within some defined limits of acceptability. As long as the service is done correctly within those limits, then the output is judged satisfactory. Failure or less than satisfactory service is defined by the number of occasions that the level of service falls outside the ideal limits.

A common mistake is to be unaware of how best to define the second type of output. Administrators will judge a license bureau by the number of licenses issued rather than the percent of licenses issued within an acceptable waiting time. The quality of output is not considered, and important managerial considerations are ignored. End products or services are counted, but the program output quality is overlooked.

Staff and Service Units

When first introduced to the model, individuals tend to focus upon units which are the primary service producers within the government. As they start to apply the model, they discover staff units (e.g., budget offices) and service units even within line departments (e.g., bus maintenance). They become confused about how to apply the concept in situations in which staff and service units do not have a direct impact upon citizens and society.

The best approach is to work backward from outcomes. If the analyst or manager is focusing upon a bus maintenance unit in public transit, the first point to understand is that the overall unit outcome is to improve the movement of people along traffic routes and permit the mobility of the transportation disadvantage. How does the maintenance unit contribute to that overall transit outcome? The answer is the unit's outcome—for example, keeping a percentage of the bus fleet in operation at all times. Since public transit program output is measured in terms of ridership, the next question should focus upon how the actual work or work products of the bus maintenance unit contribute to ridership. For example, the unit preventatively maintains 10 buses each week. That would be one of the unit's program outputs.

For many professionals, the question of how to handle a staff unit like a budget office is confusing. The first point to understand is that the role of a staff unit is to service the government so that it can work effectively. For example, a budget unit should (1) help raise the level of debate for policy makers so that they are more likely to make better decisions, (2) monitor budget execution so that the policy of the duly constituted decision makers is followed unless a conscious decision is made not to follow that policy, and (3) promote and foster better public management within the government. Specific data measures can be developed for each program outcome. The second point is that outcomes should be understood as a function of the program outputs. For example, program outputs such as the annual budget document and various reports are not sufficient program outcome measures *per se*. The outputs should be judged in terms of their contribution to program outcome, such as raising the level of policy debate. The budget execution system should be judged in terms of its success in getting government units to follow policy. Various *ad hoc* reports and studies should be judged in terms of their impact on improving public management or raising the level of policy debate. Thus, budget office output must be understood in terms of its positive contribution to the office's outcomes.

Nonperformance Option

Sometimes program outputs and outcomes are unsuccessfully defined. The potential reasons for failure include the professional inadequacy of the budget analyst and insufficient cooperation from an agency which refuses to define necessary data measures. Perfect measures are often inappropriate for use, owing to the time it takes to collect those measures or to high costs in collecting the data. Therefore, trading off the quality of the measure against the effort to collect it is a common professional challenge. An unacceptable situation occurs when top agency personnel fail to make a reasonable attempt to resolve trade-off problems. In such cases, budget office leadership must be apprised of the situation and must decide whether to attempt to force the agency to develop the desired output and outcome measures. Not all such battles can be won; the budget office must decide if that particular battle should be fought and when it should be fought. Normally, government executive leadership is willing to support the budget office leadership on such matters, as it is in the best interest of executive leadership to have such information.

A possible reason why program outcomes and outputs cannot be defined is that the agency may not be performing any useful service. Often when an agency is particularly uncooperative in defining outcomes and outputs the behavior is simply a defensive attempt to cover up poor management. That possibility must always be appreciated by the budget office and top management. Care must be taken that other explanations are eliminated because charges of agency cover-up are likely to evoke attacks upon the professional competency of the budget analyst by the program manager. If problems of this type are possible, budget office leadership should involve top management assistance as soon as possible so that an intelligent approach can be taken to deal with this type of defensive behavior.

DATA MEASURE CONSTRAINTS

The application of this model is always dependent upon the constraints associated with the use of data measures. To use this model properly, an understanding of quantitative techniques and research methods is necessary. For example, some measures used will apply only to an ordinal data scale, and the uninformed will misapply analytical techniques meant to be used for only ratio data scales. For the most sophisticated use of analysis, the best scale is ratio, but that is often impractical or impossible given the character of the problem and data.

The best measures to use are uniform in nature and contain a high number of units of output for which one assumes the same level of quality in each unit of output. For example, the water and sewer systems measure their output in gallons of water or sewerage processed at an acceptable level of quality. Measures of this type permit the use of the most powerful analytical techniques. Unfortunately, not all program outputs are susceptible to this ideal type of measure. For example, a planning unit's outputs are not useful for budget analytical purposes if these outputs are merely considered to be updated comprehensive plans. The usefulness of those plans must be judged using some type of ordinal or even interval scale.

A common ploy by agency officials is to use measures which are ratios between ideal and actual performance. For example, animal control agencies might compare the number of strays to actual captured dogs. Normally, the ratio shows that the program is doing reasonably well, but the impression is given that more resources (input) would improve the ratio. The problem with such ratios is that the ideal is often a highly questionable figure, and the ratio may not be measuring the true outcomes and outputs. If the stray dog problem is defined as the existence of stray dogs, then the measure of dogs captured may be quite correct. If the dog problem is more accurately described as strays in inappropriate areas, then outcomes should be defined differently. Maybe the dog problem is capturing strays within a given time after a complaint has been registered. If so, again the animal control unit outputs should be restated to indicate how many dogs are not captured within acceptable time constraints. Notice that occasionally the outcome and output can be identical or almost identical for operational purposes.

Although perfect program outcomes and outputs may be found, there is the problem of selecting one or more data measures. In some circumstances, the data measures selected could be more expensive to acquire than the cost of the programs they are to measure. Obviously, practical trade-offs must be made in deciding if added clarity in the budget decision-making process is worth the added cost of the data measure.

Another problem with data measures is that they can react with and influence negatively the workings of a program. For example, the knowledge that data is used by decision makers can encourage some managers to distort the data or engage in defensive behavior which avoids facing up to and resolving managerial problems. The negative energy which can be created by data measures must be understood and countered to the extent possible.

One tactic is to use nonreactive measures. For example, worn tile in front of a museum exhibit indicates popularity. Normally, nonreactive measures are easily available and often inexpensive to acquire. Another advantage is that their apparent lack of connection with key program events means that monitoring them will not affect the measurement instrument itself. The problems with nonreactive measures are that they can be isolated only by a creative imagination and that their positive relationship with program outcomes and outputs is not often perfect. Nevertheless, good nonreactive measures should be used when practical.

ELEMENTARY ANALYSIS

Defining Relationships

Most analysis used in budgeting is not complex. Trend charts, scatter diagrams, and simple regression analysis, marginal cost analysis, discounting to present value, and Kraemer's Chi Square are all relatively simple analytical techniques. Often relationships involving budget requests, final budgets, year-end estimates of current expenses, and actual performance are important. If relationships can be established, then the budget analyst's job is made easier. Normally, relationships are best described using a conventional scale, but sometimes a logarithmic scale or index numbers can be employed to better highlight the significance of the data. One common relationship is to show a given variable as it changes over time. If a trend is apparent, then long-term forecasting is made easier and future consequences become more predictable.

In many situations the relationship between two variables is more difficult to determine. One approach is to place the two variables on two axes, as illustrated in Exhibit 5-1. The analyst then places dots representing each simultaneous occurrence of the two variables. This results in a scatter diagram which may indicate a relationship between the two variables. Exhibit 6-1 shows such a relationship for a car between maintenance cost and miles driven. The line is a simple regression analysis defining that relationship.

Marginal Cost and Discounting

Another useful technique is marginal cost. The initial cost of a government program is often expensive, while further effort leads to less unit costs. This means that in many circumstances the analyst should understand that marginal costs are lower. This might prove to be highly significant. For example, if an agency is asking for a proportionate increase in funding, the analyst might question this request because marginal costs should not increase proportionately.

In order to perform marginal cost analysis, the data must be separated into one-time fixed costs and recurring costs. Common one-time fixed costs include research, project planning, engineering, tests, evaluations, land purchases, facility construction, equipment, and initial training. Common recurring costs include personnel expenses, employee benefits, maintenance, direct contributions to people, payments for services, and overall and replacement training. The fixed costs remain

EXHIBIT 5-1   Illustration of Statistical Analysis

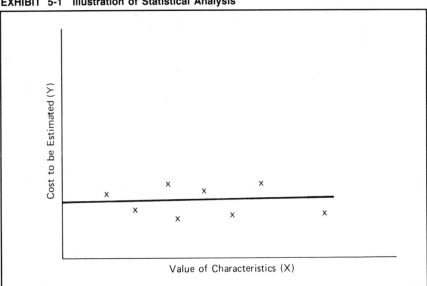

the same, but the recurring costs increase with added units. Thus, as the units increase the unit cost decreases. These data can be plotted on a simple chart or described in simple statistical expressions.

Another technique is discounting to present value. A dollar received or spent in the future is not equivalent to a dollar received or spent today. Therefore, adjustments should be made if comparisons are to be made. The technique is similar to the statistical concept used to compute compound interest at the bank. This technique is useful when comparisons must be made, but the two subjects must not occur during the same time period or involve different financing methods.

Fred A. Kramer has cited a simple but common situation to illustrate the use of this analytical technique.[1] A city must choose between contracting with a private garbage collector for $65,000 per year or having city employees do it. The latter option would require a $40,000 truck and a $55,000 yearly operating expense. Without discounting, the best option is to have city employees collect the garbage, because $10,000 can be saved by that approach. With discounting, the best option is the contract. The following shows the arithmetic:

YEAR	SAVINGS IN THE YEAR	× 8% DISCOUNT FACTOR =	PRESENT VALUE
1	$10,000	.926	$ 9,260
2	10,000	.857	8,570
3	10,000	.794	7,940
4	10,000	.735	7,350
5	10,000	.681	6,810
Total Present Value of Annual Savings =			$39,930

In the example, the private contract is the best buy because the total present value of annual savings is less than the capital investment.

Caution must be stressed in using the discount technique. Numbers have a way of seeming so final and clear. Realistically, the ingredients in the question should be carefully weighed in terms of their sensitive character. An output of a program is sensitive when the results can be altered by minor changes in a variable. If the analysis is highly sensitive, then any recommendations made on the basis of the analysis should be questioned because the technique does not warrant the implied certitude. This technique can be abused by changing the annual returns or savings, the life of the asset, the amount of the investment, the discount rate, or the annual returns in the earlier years. This does not mean the technique should not be used, but it should be used with a complete understanding of the possible distortions.

[1]Fred A. Kramer, "The Discounting to Present Value Technique as a Decision Tool," *Special Bulletin* 1976E (Municipal Finance Officers Association, November 24, 1976).

CROSSWALKS

Conceptual Bridge

One of the most useful analytical tools for the budget examiner is the crosswalk. It is a simple matrix table relating different categories. It serves as a conceptual bridge between two organizational means to describe and control agency activities. By constructing several bridges, the examiner can explore various organizational perspectives on what should be done and what is done as well as check important interrelations. Some of the more common categories which can be crosswalked are:

1. programs, projects, activities, tasks;
2. uniform object classifications;
3. appropriation structure;
4. major organizational units;
5. objectives used in connection with management-by-objectives or program evaluations; and
6. funds (including grants-in-aid) used in government accounting.

A few simple examples can illustrate the use of the crosswalk. A common crosswalk is between the so-called program structure (e.g., a given set of mutually exclusive programs, projects, activities, and tasks) and the appropriation structure. The program structure is used by the executive to make major decisions on program direction. The appropriation structure is the language used by the legislature to make its decisions. Both decision makers are significant so the agency and the budget examiners must be able to translate from one language to the other—the crosswalk is the device which permits translation.

Another common crosswalk is between the program structure or appropriation structure and the major organizational units in the agency. This permits the examiner to pin down who is responsible and judge management capability to carry out the budget. Without such a crosswalk, lower level management responsibility and judgments about capability cannot be made by the examiner.

Two other useful crosswalks for accountants and budget examiners are (1) appropriation structure—uniform object classification, and (2) funds—uniform item object classification. The budget examiner uses these crosswalks when a line-item budget is used to control the government. Also these crosswalks are useful to achieve a better understanding of exactly what does take place under various labels.

An unused but potentially significant crosswalk is between the MBO objectives and the program structure or appropriation structure. MBO can be an extremely useful public management technique, but often it is applied without reference to the budget. This is foolish because how can one reasonably expect objectives to be met without also establishing that necessary resources are available to conduct the program? The two should not be treated in isolation, but they are by many agencies. If they are treated separately this strongly indicates a lack of coordination of management direction with the agency because both MBO and the budget are tools to achieve management direction.

If the agency has activities which fulfill more than one objective at a time, then a program evaluation objective—program structure crosswalk is treated somewhat differently from the other crosswalks. Normally, each matrix square states dollar amounts representing mutually exclusive activities. This permits the crosswalk to be validated for internal consistency by merely checking if the horizontal and vertical summary columns are equal. In the case of evaluation objectives, dollar amounts can be counted more than once if they fulfill more than one purpose. For example, a given activity may increase safety and reduce energy consumption (e.g., enforcing the 55-mile-per-hour speed limit). Thus, the crosswalk matrix squares would show the dollar amount (maybe even the name of the activity) under two different vertical categories. This type of double counting can also exist with a crosswalk using MBO objectives.

Determining Consistency

The budget examiner can ask to see various crosswalks for the reasons suggested above. Essentially, crosswalks help the examiner determine if the agency has internally consistent management direction and control capability to insure the integrity of that direction. If the agency does not act with one management direction, the crosswalks expose that problem. If the agency cannot provide crosswalks, this suggests poor management. It is possible for the agency to manage its affairs well without using crosswalks, but it should be able to construct them if there is a consistent management direction. If crosswalks cannot be constructed or if the ones provided show inconsistent management policy, then the budget examiner can probe further to isolate the exact nature and reasons for the internal management inconsistency.

Crosswalks can also be used to check for external consistency of management direction with past publicly announced positions and orders of higher authorities. A set of crosswalks is among the best evidence of the exact management policies of an agency. Those policies may not be consistent with the agency's past policies or positions articulated to the public or policy directives from higher authorities. If the budget examiner happens to have the crosswalks from past budgets, then they can be compared with the most recent crosswalks. In this manner, policy shifts can be isolated. Budget examiners can also determine if the policy direction from the crosswalks matches public positions and policy established by higher authorities. If there is inconsistency, then further probing may be warranted to determine the reason for the inconsistency.

REVENUE FORECASTING

Three Approaches

Revenue forecasting calls for a separate treatment of each revenue source. The standard approach is, first, to determine the patterns associated with each revenue source. Next, the base must be determined and then the forecast is made based on assumptions and the determined pattern. Forecasting is merely a sophisticated form of guessing which depends on good data and good judgment, often refined through experience. The techniques of forecasting range from the simple to the complex, but all should be used with the principle of conservatism (i.e., underestimating revenue and overestimating expenditures) in mind.

Information is important to revenue forecasting, and certain background information should be retained. This includes copies of legislation, legal history, administration factors concerning the tax, or any change in the tax; charts showing changes in the tax rate over time and the monthly yield, with an explanation of any abnormal change in the trend line; and data on any significant variables which affect the revenue yield.

The three revenue forecasting approaches are qualitative, time series, and causal analysis. Qualitative (also called judgmental) approaches are, in essence, based solely or primarily upon human judgment, but math can be involved. William Earle Klay of Florida State University surveyed the revenue forecasting practices of all fifty states and found that thirty used panels, interagency work committees, or conferences in their revenue forecasts. Normally, economists constituted these "expert" groups of forecasters, but occasionally politicians were included. Expert judgment is best used when key revenue elements are highly variable, no history exists, or revenues are strongly influenced by political considerations (e.g., intergovernmental transfers).

Time series (e.g., trend analysis) is based upon data which has been collected over time and can be shown chronologically on graphs. One such approach involves using the last completed year as a basis for the revenue estimate (in France, this method is called "rule of penultimate year"), assuming that there is growth in the economy and related revenue sources. Another simple technique—the method of averages—is to average the revenue generated over the last three to five years. Again, the assumption is made that there is a growth trend in the tax source, rather than a decline or an uneven tax yield. A more sophisticated method involves using moving averages and attributing greater weight to more recent revenue yields. A still more sophisticated method is the Box-Jenkins method, which will be described later in the expenditure estimates section. Normally, the trends are shown on arithmetic graphs, but some analysts prefer semilogarithmic graphs because they reveal rates of change in tax yields more clearly.

When using time series techniques, the forecaster is especially interested in the nature of seasonal fluctuations which occur within a year, the nature of multiyear cycles, and the nature of any possible long-run trends which might underlie the seasonal and cyclical fluctuations. The major weakness of this approach is that economic turning points are not easily identified. Trend analysis should be used to forecast revenue items which arc not highly variable and which (1) amount to minor percentages of the budget or (2) are not dependent upon economic or political considerations.

Causal methods deal, not with the history of a single variable, but with the historical interrelationship between two or more variables. One or more predictor variables forecast tax yield directly or indirectly by first forecasting the future tax base. For example, multiplying the estimate of the average tax to be collected per taxpayer by an estimate of the number of taxpayers results in a forecast of income tax revenue. Various survey techniques can be used to determine these two predictor variable estimates. Some communities use a payroll tax. To forecast the revenue, they estimate the area payroll and tax rate and multiply them. A variation is to calculate the tax rate by occupational groups. A third method is first to determine the interrelationship between personal income and leading economic indicators and then to use the leading indicators to determine personal income. The tax yield is determined from the personal income. For sales taxes, the area or state sales are forecasted, and the tax yield is calculated from that level of sales.

These causal forecasting methods are predicated upon selecting the correct predictor variables, defining their interrelationship to tax yield correctly and, finally, collecting accurate data. An added advantage to these methods is that they can help policy makers reflect upon various "what if" options for taxes and other policies so that they can better gauge the implications of their policy choices. Drawbacks to these methods include the need to collect extensive accurate data, the cost of developing causal models, and high computer costs. Fortunately, computer costs are decreasing. If revenues are strongly influenced by changing economic conditions, causal models (e.g., econometrics) are especially useful.

Accuracy in revenue forecasting is important, especially when the forecast predicts more money than is actually received by a government which must have a balanced budget. The results are painful government midyear adjustments which result in frozen positions, elimination of travel and other easily cut costs and, finally, payless "paydays." If forecasts embarrassingly result in unpredicted surpluses, then the government faces the politically difficult task of explaining tax rates which appear to be unnecessarily high. Measuring historic accuracy of revenue forecasts within a jurisdiction is simply a matter of contrasting forecasts with actual receipts. Once these comparisons are made, it is possible to determine where forecasting improvements are needed. Normally, large inaccuracy in small revenue items is not significant because often such inaccuracies tend to cancel each other out in the aggregate. Serious problems occur when there are modest errors in large revenue items because they can mean significant revenue shortfalls. Normally, the further away the forecast from the forecasted event, the more likely it is that there will be forecasting errors; thus, forecasters prefer late forecasts whenever possible.

Econometric Forecasts

Econometric forecasts are complex causal analyses which have many causal variables and are often computer-dependent. The age of econometrics began in the 1930s with Jan Tinbergen, a Dutch economist. He developed a number of equations to represent the workings of his nation's economy. In America, the use of econometrics by state governments has mostly occurred since 1978, with few local governments using the technique today (some exceptions are New Orleans, Dallas, Winston-Salem, and Mobile). The basic equation is $Y = f(X)$, with Y, the dependent variable, affected by the independent, explanatory, predictor variable X. The statement merely says that Y is somehow dependent on (is a function of) the value of X. To develop a revenue forecasting model, the following are essential:

- to develop a data history or time series for all variables;
- to develop a set of mathematical expressions which best explains the past relationships among the variables; and
- to devise a means of identifying the future values which one or more of the explanatory variables will assume.

Causal models may consist of a single regression equation or several regression equations. Semoon Chang used a single regression equation for his econometric model for Mobile's sales tax receipts. At the other extreme, Florida's state estimates make use of 123 regression equations. Many analysts rely upon popular national econometric models such as those provided by Chase Econometrics, Data Resources, Inc., and Wharton Econometric Forecasting Associates. Worthy of note is an observation by John Peterson of the Govermnent Finance Officers Association: "As a general rule, sophisticated models have been ignored by practitioners in the past. After their construction and initial operation by consultants, they have sometimes ended up gathering dust on the shelf."[2] This method involves statistics, and unless staff can explain statistical concepts so that officials can understand them, informed official judgment may be impossible. To use this technique, the following statistical concepts should be understood:

1. R squared coefficient of determination, which shows the proportion of variation in the dependent variable attributable to variation in the independent variables;
2. the T test of relationship with a particular independent variable;
3. the F test concerning the significance of the equation as a whole;
4. the Durbin-Watson statistic, which is an indicator of whether serial correlation exists, thereby suggesting that important information has been omitted;
5. the standard error of estimate; and
6. the mean absolute percentage of error.

[2]J. E. Peterson, "State and Local Fiscal Forecasting," *Resources in Review* (Chicago: Government Finance Officers Association, 1979), p. 16.

EXPENDITURE FORECASTING

Bargaining and Unit Cost Approaches

The burden for estimating expenditures normally rests upon the agency, but the techniques are often similar to those of revenue forecasting. In some situations, a bargaining approach is used in which the agency's estimate of its optimum program is tempered by the economic and political climate, including budget call instructions. (Agency estimates can be based upon detailed work plans involving months of preparation or upon quick judgments involving a few minutes.) The central budget office reviews the request, refining, cutting, and adding to the judgment of the agency, with the possible participation of political executive and legislative officials. The final adopted expenditures represent the collective judgment of dozens of officials and staff.

Another set of expenditure forecasting techniques is based on accounting information which uses unit cost data. This method is similar to "fiscal impact analysis," which calculates the municipal costs of proposed local real estate developments by using per capita cost multipliers, the average cost of providing a certain level or standard of service, and other simple calculations. The three major steps in the unit cost approach are: (1) choosing a level of analysis, (2) analyzing units and unit costs, and (3) making necessary assumptions and calculations.

In selecting the level of analysis, budget analysts will often use the object code level, but subcode or function levels can be used. An example of subcode level use is found in Arlington County, Virginia, which records each employee's anniversary date, wage rate, grade, longevity increase (if any), fringe benefit costs, and other data. Using this information, the computer does an annual projection of the wages and fringe costs for each employee, and aggregates these costs into the desired object codes, divisional units, departments, and funds. An example of function-department level use is found in Syracuse, New York, where expenditures by department are broken down into labor, nonlabor, fringe, and miscellaneous expenditures. These relatively gross aggregates are aggregated for a jurisdiction forecast.

The second step of analysis of units and unit costs is done by examining past and current units and unit costs, such as the gallons of heating fuel charged to object code 306 of the Building Management Department. A more sophisticated version would be to multiply the unit cost by the price index when one is calculating specific future year forecasts.

The third step is to include assumptions for future years and then simply to multiply. For example, in the heating fuel situation, assume that 50,000 gallons are to be consumed in the BY at a cost of $2 per gallon; 50,000 multiplied by $2 equals $100,000, to be budgeted in object code 306 of the Building Management Department. The result is an annual or multiyear forecast for a particular expenditure which can be aggregated to arrive at a total expenditure forecast.

Time Series Methods

Many agencies use an incremental or trend line approach in expenditure forecasting. Historical data defines the trend line, which shows the expenditure pattern over time. The slope of the line is the rate of change. The formula for a line is $Y = a + bX$ where Y is the dependent variable, X is the independent variable, and b is the slope of the line. The trend line establishes a historical pattern, and the forecaster need only take the next time period (e.g., BY) and read up to the trend line and over to the expenditure level. In Exhibit 5-2, this approach shows that the expenditure forecast for the BY is $50,000. Judgment is used to determine any appropriate deviation from the trend based upon factors likely to cause unusual change.

Two other time series methods are moving averages and exponential smoothing. In moving averages, one adds up the expenditures in past time periods and averages them. The assumption is that averaging the values will minimize data randomness and seasonality. Thus, the more data points used, the smoother the forecast. The limitations of the method are as follows: (1) it depends on sufficient data observations, thus it is not useful for new programs; (2) it is only useful for short-term forecasts involving one to three time periods; and (3) it is unable to forecast a change in the basic trend. In exponential smoothing, one uses the last forecast value and the estimated "alpha factor weight" of any value between 0 to 1 (e.g., 0.1, 0.5, 0.9) and takes the difference between the forecast value for the most recent time period and the actual value realized. For example, $5000 was spent in the PY=1 and $4500 in PY. To calculate the BY with a 0.3 alpha factor, we calculate $5000 + 0.3($4500 − $5000), which yields a BY forecast of $4850. If the forecaster expects little data randomness, then a small alpha factor would be used; conversely, much data randomness would make a high alpha factor appropriate. The

EXHIBIT 5-2 Trend Line Forecast

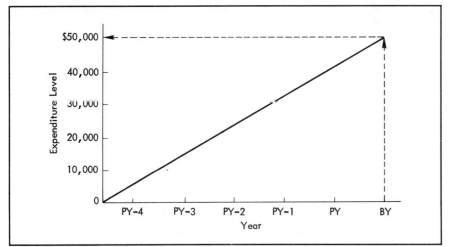

major value of this technique over moving averages is that fewer data points are needed and recent rapid trend changes are better reflected. The inherent disadvantage of the technique is the necessity for arbitrary assignment of an alpha factor.

A third time series technique is adaptive filtering. The four steps of the technique are as follows: (1) a forecast is developed by taking a weighted average of the previous observations; (2) the forecast and actual value realized are compared and errors calculated; (3) the weights in the weighted average are adjusted to minimize calculated error; and (4) the new set of weights is applied to forecast the subsequent period. The process is repeated as new actual data become known. This technique requires many calculations and is normally done with a computer. The technique is particularly useful when a great deal of historical data is available and those data exhibit considerable randomness.

A fourth, emerging technique is autoregressive moving averages (ARMA), of which there are two types: autoregressive models and moving average models. Autoregressive models (AR) assume that future values are linear combinations of past values. Moving average models (MA) assume that future values are linear combinations of past errors. Autoregressive models use past data on the dependent variable at various time intervals to develop the forecast. Moving average models seek to eliminate the randomness of data by dropping a past observation as a new one becomes available. Box-Jenkins techniques are used to select and test ARMA models. ARMA techniques tend to produce very good one- to three-year forecasts. The techniques are very complex, but advances in computer software have eliminated many time and cost problems.

The Box-Jenkins method is a systematic elimination procedure to identify the most appropriate ARMA model and determine the appropriate forecasting model. First, the model is identified by means of various statistical tests and judgmental evaluations. Second, a trial-and-error approach using statistical estimation techniques is employed to determine the data array with the smallest mean square error. Third, after an adequate model is constructed, a forecasting equation is derived which reflects the data through the current period. A bonus of this technique is that it not only forecasts, but it does so with delineated limits of reliability.

Expenditure Econometric Model

Various expenditures are largely predicated on factors which lend themselves to econometric models. For example, at the state level, social service expenditures are directly related to the state economy, and education and criminal justice expenditures are related to state demographics and economic factors. Models can be used which not only predict likely expenditures but also help policy makers understand the most sensitive factors which influence each functional activity.

One such example is the Massachusetts Welfare Model developed by Data Resources, Inc. That model is used for short-term forecasts and sensitivity analyses of eligibles, case load, and expenditures in various welfare assistance categories. The model contains: (1) earnings distribution of the state and individuals; (2) an estimation routine for calculating Aid to Families with Dependent Children (AFDC) and General Relief (GR) eligibles from a combination of welfare policy standards and state demographic parameters applied to the earnings distributions for families and unrelated individuals; (3) econometric equations explaining eligibles' rate of participation in AFDC and GR, by sex and family status; (4) econometric equations explaining average expenditures per case in AFDC and GR; (5) identities deriving AFDC and GR case loads by a combination of items 2 and 3; and (6) identities deriving AFDC and GR total expenditures by a combination of items 4 and 5. The model uses 77 variables, including economic, welfare policy, and endogenous variables, as well as welfare eligibles definitions, rates of participation, miscellaneous inputs, and numerous simultaneous econometric equations.

The model is used both for forecasting and simulation ("what if" analysis). It forecasts welfare eligibles, case load, and expenditures by program. It forecasts the earnings distributions of families and individuals. It simulates the impact on eligibles, case load, and expenditures of alternative U.S. and state economic scenarios. It simulates the impact on welfare case load of changes in the unemployment compensation program. And finally, it simulates the impact on eligibles, case load, and expenditures of alternative welfare policies such as (1) cost-of-living increases, (2) a change in the income deduction for work-related expenses, (3) a change in the assistance tables reflecting new budget levels by family size and living arrangements, and (4) a change in federal statutes.

In forecasting, the model works in several steps. First, the U.S. and state economic data are used to derive family earnings distributions and to determine persons eligible for welfare. Next, welfare participation rates are calculated, using such factors as work availability and wage opportunities (normally, if the economy has worsened, welfare benefits and participation are higher). Welfare case load and total projected welfare expenditures are calculated. Finally, administrative costs are determined.

In simulations, the model works with "what if" scenarios. For example, "What if 5 percent federal eligibility regulations are changed to exclude persons with any income?" The model calculates the changes and predicts the mean monthly case load and other factors.

PRODUCTIVITY ANALYSIS

Productivity

Productivity is a measure of efficiency usually expressed as the ratio of the quantity of output to the quantity of input used in the production of that output. Commonly, productivity focuses upon output per man hour of change or changes in cost per unit of output. It does not measure the work completed versus the work needed to be completed.

The concept of productivity is often misunderstood. It is falsely tied to harder physical work, when it is in fact tied to doing the work with less effort but still increasing output. This is normally done by better work procedures, better use of machines, or better worker attitude toward the job. In quantifying productivity, the mistake is made of using outcomes (benefits to individuals and society) instead of outputs (products of the program). There are normally too many intervening variables between outcomes and outputs to permit a meaningful usage of outcomes. Another conceptual confusion is that an increase in productivity may reflect a cost reduction, but a cost reduction is not always a result of an increase in productivity. Other reasons for cost reduction can exist, such as a simple budget cut. However, too often we do equate productivity with cost reduction.

A study on productivity in the federal government was conducted in the mid-1970s, and its findings on the reasons for increases in productivity are enlightening. A commonly cited reason for a productivity increase was an increase in the work load, thus allowing the agency to lower its unit cost. Fixed and variable costs explain how productive advantages can result from increased work loads. In other cases, productivity increased because of improved training, increased and better use of job evaluations, greater upward mobility, or the use of a career ladder to develop the work force. In some instances, greater productivity was due to automation and the use of new labor-saving equipment.

Although productivity is a simple concept, there are not simple uniform answers for increasing productivity. Each situation must be examined separately. The federal study illustrates this point by saying the greater productivity resulted from (1) improved morale resulting from job redesign and enrichment, and (2) reorganization and work simplification. The study seems to say that making a job more complex and making a job simpler both result in greater productivity. This apparent contradiction can be resolved by understanding the human factor related to the job situation. For some people, the job is too complex and beyond their abilities. The answer is work simplification. For some people, the job is too simple and their boredom leads to poor work habits. The answer is job enrichment, such as rotation or a larger range of responsibilities. Sound increased productivity recommendations must be based on a knowledge of management science as well as human behavior. Exhibit 5-3 is a useful checklist developed by the National Center for Productivity and Quality of Work Life.

EXHIBIT 5-3   What Do You Know About Your Productivity?

The following set of questions can be used as a self-audit to determine what your organization is doing and what your organization may need to do to make programs more productive.

1.   IS THE EFFICIENCY OF STAFF PERSONNEL MEASURED?
     Are critical outputs identified for each program?
     Are work counts and time utilization records maintained for these critical outputs?
     Are unit times developed for the outputs?

Are trend data available for the unit times?

Is unit cost information available?

Are efficiency data reported periodically to management?

Are unit times compared among regions? Are they compared with other organizations doing similar work in or out of government?

2. ARE PERFORMANCE STANDARDS SET FOR CRITICAL PROGRAM OUTPUTS?

Are time standards used?

What percentage of the work is covered by standards?

Are performance reports regularly prepared and distributed to persons responsible for performance?

Are standards used by supervisors of day-to-day operations to plan and schedule work?

Are the standards used in planning and budgeting?

3. IS PROGRAM EFFECTIVENESS MEASURED?

Are performance indicators available that address program effectiveness?

Do performance indicators include the target population, the level of service, and the desired impact?

Are measurable goals tied to indicators of program effectiveness?

4. IS THE QUALITY OF WORK PROPERLY CONTROLLED?

Are error and timeliness data maintained and reported on a regular basis?

Are quality standards used?

Is quality of performance measured and reported on a regular basis?

5. IS OVERALL PRODUCTIVITY PERFORMANCE MEASURED?

Are measures used that combine effectiveness and efficiency by relating to results?

Are cost-effectiveness measures used?

Are the major cost elements identified for each program and are costs determined?

6. ARE METHODS AND PROCEDURES ANALYZED FREQUENTLY?

Are your managers currently aware of what others are doing in operations similar to yours?

Are mechanization and new technology continually reviewed for possible application to your operation?

Are staff specialists asked to make improvement studies?

Do supervisors and employees make suggestions on improving operational details?

7. ARE EMPLOYEES MOTIVATED TO PERFORM AT A SATISFACTORY LEVEL?

Are employees told how well they perform?

Are merit increases and awards tied to performance?

Are "quality of working life" motivational techniques used?

Source: Improving Productivity: A Self Audit and Guide, National Center for Productivity and Quality of Working Life, Washington, D.C. Fall 1978, pp. 10-11, 13.

The same federal study also cited some common reasons for declines in productivity. Increased product complexity cannot always be factored out of the measurements, and that complexity can mean less productivity. For example, increased environmental, safety, and legal requirements mean added work steps, equipment, or additional features. This may be in the public interest, but one of the disadvantages is increased production costs, thus a loss in productivity. Another reason for loss is a steady and sharp decline in work load which is not matched by staff reductions. Either human compassion or labor agreements can mean lower productivity, but again other practical reasons supersede the desire for efficiency. A third common reason for a decline is, ironically, the installation of a new or automated system. For a period of time during the installation, both the automated and old system must be operated, thus decreasing productivity until the old system is phased out. These reasons are significant and suggest the complex issues which prevent us from always achieving increased productivity.

Simple Regression Analysis

The basic assumption of regression analysis is that change in the dependent variable Y is related to change in the independent variable X, either positively or negatively. In regression analysis the independent variable need not necessarily cause the dependent variable, but a relationship does exist which may be causal in nature. Simple regression analysis uses a straight line $Y = a + bX$ to describe the relationship. The slope b is the regression coefficient and measures the change in Y given one unit of change in X. The constant a represents the distance between the point where the regression line intercepts the Y axis and the origin. In order to draw the regression line, the method of least squares is used. This type of analysis assumes a normal probability distribution for the observations and assumes that the error values are independent of each other (i.e., no autocorrelation exists).

Exhibits 5-4, 5, and 6 are used in a simple linear regression for neighborhood libraries in an urban county. The independent variable X is the full-time-equivalent circulation staff working at each library unit. There is an assumed relationship between circulation staff size and actual books in circulation during the CY. Exhibit 5-5,6 states the input and output data and show how the least square method is used to determine the line on Exhibit 5-4. Note that the line fits or explains the various actual data observations which are coded library names.

How does this type of analysis assist in the budget process? Essentially, the regression line is the CY average productivity curve for the library system. Libraries to the left and above the line are more productive; hence an examination can be undertaken to see what they are doing right. Of course, an examination can also be addressed to the least productive units. Another useful feature of this analysis is that any requested additional FTE circulation staff of a unit should generate, ideally, the normal productivity output. Budget analysts can query, "Will the library indeed

EXHIBIT 5-4   Book Circulation

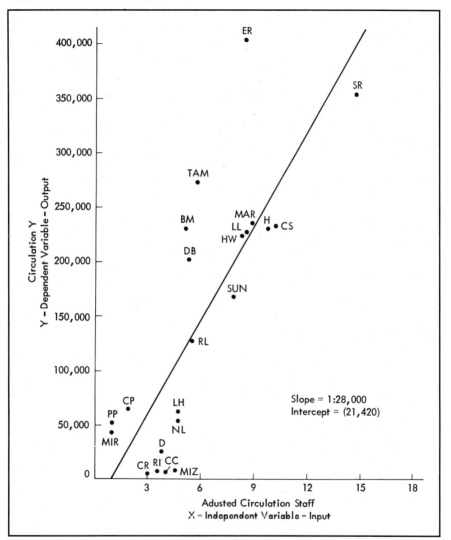

generate the desired circulation or will productivity be lowered if that additional staff is added?'' Regression analysis can be useful in determining and fostering greater productivity.

Multiple regression is considered more useful than simple regression analysis because more independent variables can be used. Thus, it should yield a more accurate fit when compared to actual data. Normally, however, the number of variables should be kept to a minimum (e.g., four).

EXHIBIT 5-5,6   Productivity for Libraries—Circulation Staff (Input): Circulation (Output)

LIBRARY OUTLETS	INPUT	OUTPUT	$(x-\bar{x})$	$(y-\bar{y})$	$(x-\bar{x})(y-\bar{y})$	$(x-\bar{x})^2$
BM	4.5	233170	−1.54	85750.68	−132134.01	2.37
CP	2	62222	−4.04	−85197.32	344274.62	16.33
CR	3	2939	−3.04	−144480.32	439351.51	9.25
CC	4	4929	−2.04	−142490.32	290809.79	4.17
CS	10.7	238127	4.66	90707.68	422615.34	21.71
D	3.6	25615	−2.44	−121804.32	297313.27	5.96
D/CC	0	0	0.00	0.00	0.00	0.00
DR	5.6	203404	−0.44	55984.68	−24684.16	0.19
ER	8.3	406135	2.26	258715.68	584462.24	5.10
H	9.7	236389	3.66	88969.68	325548.15	13.39
HW	8.6	2048727	2.56	57307.68	146655.57	6.55
LL	8.7	227368	2.66	79948.68	212590.81	7.07
LH	4.8	63214	−1.24	−84205.32	104491.14	1.54
M	8.8	234892	2.76	87472.68	241345.08	7.61
MR	1	45184	−5.04	−102235.32	515358.94	25.41
MZ	4.5	7449	−1.54	−139970.32	215681.54	2.37
NL	4.7	55722	−1.34	−91697.32	122957.77	1.80
PP	1	50406	−5.04	−97013.32	489035.32	25.41
RL	5.7	137722	−0.34	−9697.32	3305.90	0.12
RI	5.5	5129	−0.54	−142290.32	76966.13	0.29
SR	14.7	355862	8.66	208442.68	1804924.13	74.98
SI	7.8	165386	1.76	17966.68	31605.03	3.09
TM	5.7	277234	−0.34	129814.68	−44255.01	0.12
Total	132.9	3243225	0.00	0.00	6468219.11	234.83
Averages	6.04	147419.32				
Slope	27543.89					
Intercept	−18970.81					

$$b = \frac{\Sigma(x-\bar{x})(y-\bar{y})}{\Sigma(x-\bar{y})^2}$$

$$b = \frac{}{234.85} = 27{,}543.89 \text{ slope}$$

$y = bx + c$
$c = y - bx$
$c = 147419.32 - ((27543.89)(6.04))$
$c = -18970.81$ intercept at y

NOTE: Due to computer rounding, this number is 25.04 higher than these summary numbers indicate.

Productivity and Budgeting

Agencies can strengthen their budget requests by citing productivity measures. Reviewing authorities normally more readily accept cost estimates based upon data involving productivity. Those requests are more impressive and help establish agency creditability. Exhibit 5-7 is extracted from the 1975 U.S. Budget Appendix. It illustrates how hard facts strengthen the agency's justification of its budget even

EXHIBIT 5-7   Selected Illustration of a Presentation of Output Data in the 1975 Budget Appendix; *Federal Mediation and Conciliation Service Salaries and Expenses.*

The Service, under title II of the Labor Management Relations Act of 1947, assists labor and management in mediation and prevention of disputes affecting industries engaged in interstate commerce and defense production, other than rail and air transportation, whenever in its judgment such disputes threaten to cause a substantial interruption of commerce. Under the authority of Executive Order 11491 of October 29, 1969, as amended by Executive Order 11616, dated August 26, 1971, the Service also makes its mediation and conciliation facilities available to Federal agencies and organizations representing Federal employees in the resolution of negotiation disputes.

1. *Mediation Service.* During 1973, dispute notices and other notifications affecting 117,884 employers were received by the Service. Cases totaling 21,745 were assigned for mediation, and 21,032 mediation assignments were closed during the year. About 89% of the mediation assignments closed which required the services of mediators were settled without work stoppages. A total of 26,973 mediation conferences were conducted by mediators during 1973. The workload shown above includes assignments closed in both the private and public sectors. Cases in process at the end of 1973 totaled 5,449; this is the normal carryover of open cases from month to month, with seasonal fluctuations. The following chart shows a 5-year comparison of workload data:

DISPUTE WORKLOAD DATA

	1969	1970	1971	1972	1973
Cases in process at the beginning of the year	5,260	5,113	5,020	4,889	4,736
Mediation assignments	21,839	19,769	21,727	19,308	21,745
Mediation assignments closed	21,986	19,862	21,858	19,461	21,032
Cases in process at end of year	5,113	5,020	4,889	4,736	5,449
Mediation conferences conducted	31,605	30,334	32,293	29,223	26,973

Source: Extracted from p. 878 of the 1975 Budget Appendix

in an agency such as the Mediation and Conciliation Service. Exhibit 5-8 illustrates how productivity measures can be melded into a budget justification document. The most helpful data and measures are:

1. productivity indices which relate end products produced to manpower or cost measures;
2. unit cost ratios which relate work performed to all or a part of the cost of performing the work;
3. work measuring ratios which relate work performed to manpower needs in carrying out the work;
4. program or work load data which show trends in the program work; and
5. statistical data, such as regression analysis, which relate experience data to manpower.

Since the activation of DSA, constant management attention to the basic goal of maximum efficiency has produced significant operating economies. In the early years of DSA, 1962-1966, increased productivity was realized through manpower reductions as numerous organizational and procedural improvements were effected. However, it was not until FY 1967 that a formal output and productivity evaluation system was installed. Since that time, overall output per man-year has increased almost 30 percent.

Chart 1 depicts the composite productivity trend for the agency from FY 1967 through FY 1973. The index shown was derived from the basic data which constituted DSA's input to the Government-wide productivity project. Improvement has averaged about 5 percent per year for the past six years. DSA currently employs about 52,000 military and civilian personnel in performing its assigned mission. Had the increase in productivity reflected on this chart not been realized, today's job would require about 10,000 more personnel than are currently employed.

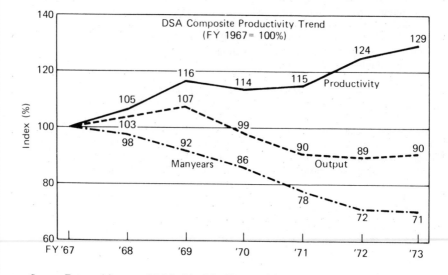

Source: Extracted from pp. 35–36 of the Joint Financial Management Improvement Program "Report on Federal Productivity, Volume II, Productivity Case Studies" (June 1974).

THE BENEFIT-COST CONCEPT

Concept: What and Why

Benefit-cost analysis is based on the rather simple belief that projects should be judged on the basis of project cost versus project benefits. At best, benefit-cost analysis is a guide for investment decision. It can help decision makers decide if specific expenditures should be undertaken, if the scale of the project is appropriate, and what the optimum project size should be. Some treat benefit-cost as a framework for a general theory of government investment.

Cost-effectiveness is sometimes confused with benefit-cost analysis, but there are advantages to maintaining the distinction. Cost-effectiveness assumes benefits and does not compare them with cost as in benefit-cost analysis. In cost-effectiveness analysis, the analyst wishes to determine the least costly means to achieve the objective. Frequently, all methods of analysis using inputs, alternatives, and outputs mean cost-effectiveness analysis including benefit-cost. However, cost-effectiveness can often be the more effective analytical technique, and blurring the distinction between the techniques tends to blind practitioners to the comparative advantages of the two techniques. Both have their advantages, but often cost-effectiveness can be used where benefit-cost is a meaningless technique.

The sophisticated benefit-cost analysis is useful. It can establish a framework for reasonably consistent and uniform project evaluations at the staff level. This can lead to added discipline in the political process because weak projects will appear inferior, thus making their funding difficult in an open political setting. The technique is most useful when the choice set is narrow and the decision involves economic alternative investments. The technique draws increasing criticism when intangibles and complex social values are present in the analysis. Value perspectives such as reallocation of wealth are not addressed well with benefit-cost analysis.

Benefit-cost analysis involves defining a choice set, analytical constraints, measurements, and a choice model. Analysis must be made manageable so that the work can be done within a reasonable time frame. Thus, parameters or range of projects must be established. Analytical constraints, e.g., legal, political distributional, financial, and physical, must be understood, stated, and either treated as side considerations of the analysis or included in the analytical objective functions. Benefit-cost analysis involves measurements; therefore, all the challenges and analytical limitations of data apply to benefit-cost analysis. Those challenges and limitations must be understood or serious analytical mistakes will be made and decision makers will be given misleading advice. A full treatment of this topic is beyond the scope of this text, but is covered in books concerning research methods. The choice model is the means used to relate the estimated costs and benefits. It is the formula. The model (formula) is used to decide how the measures will be incorporated into the overall analysis.

Procedures

The procedures of benefit-cost analysis involve defining the objective functions, benefits, and costs as well as calculating present value. The objective functions specify without weighing the ultimate values used in the analysis. Examples include increasing national income, aggregate consumption, supply of foreign exchange, and employment. The functions must be quantifiable, or they cannot be treated in the analysis. Benefits are defined normally as present value of the contributions in relationship to the objective function. Costs are sometimes defined in terms of reducing the objective function. They are also the present value of the resources that are employed and are valued as opportunity costs as a consequence of implementing the project.

The calculations in benefit-cost analysis are complex owing to several factors. Both benefits and costs must be measured over time in order to permit a broad view of project impacts, especially economic consequences. Benefits are measured by the market price of the project outputs or the price consumers are willing to pay. Costs are measured by the monetary outlays necessary to undertake the investment. Both occur over time. Unlike the private sector, externalities—i.e., project effects on others which occur because of the project's existence (such as down-stream pollution from a plant)—are calculated into public sector benefit-cost analysis. Also, opportunity costs are valued because full employment and scarce resources are assumed to exist. This means that some worthwhile choices are forgone once the decision is made to undertake the project, and this is a project cost. If the assumption is incorrect, e.g., full employment does not exist, then costs should be revised downward.

Alternative Choice Models

The decision on projects is often made by ranking alternative projects. The ranking depends on the choice model (formula) used. The various models do not give the analyst the same results. The four models are:

Benefit-cost	Based on discounted present value
Benefit/cost	Ratio of present value of benefits and costs
Rate of return or marginal investment efficiency	Discount rate which puts the benefits and costs at equilibrium
Payout period	Number of years of benefit needed so that the benefit equals the cost

Each model has its inherent bias. The benefit-cost model biases the decision in favor of large projects because of the manner in which the figures are calculated. Any deductions from benefits rather than adding to costs would affect ratios and thus would affect the benefit/cost model. If benefits or costs do not occur evenly over time, this may not be properly computed in mathematical models unless special provisions permit this unevenness.

Virtually all practitioners prefer the benefit-cost (discounted present value) model. It focuses on explicit treatment of budgetary and other constraints as well as project indivisibility and interdependencies. This model forces the separate treatment of those matters without confusing them with the determination of the proper discount rate. Also, calculation of present value is not a behind-the-scenes adjustment because it must be treated openly in the analysis.

Benefit-Cost Ingredients

A purpose of this chapter is not to explain how benefit-cost analysis is done but rather to stress the sophisticated analytical nature of the technique as well as the inherent limitations of the technique. Too many professionals advocate and even use the technique without understanding its true analytical sophistication. It is a worthwhile technique, and it should be studied by those interested in public budgeting. However, the first step is to recognize the complex nature of this type of analysis and to be especially sensitive to its limitations.

The remainder of this section examines key factors associated with benefit-cost analysis. Stress is placed on the limitations and cautions which should be associated with this technique. This stress is meant to sensitize the reader to the analytical problems associated with the technique. A full explanation of how to apply the technique is beyond the scope of this text, and readers are encouraged to learn more about this and other analytical techniques in further study.

Benefits and Estimation

Benefits are classified as primary, secondary, and intangible. Primary benefits are the values of goods or services resulting from project conditions. They are included in the analysis. Common examples are additional crops due to land irrigation and annual savings in flood damages. Associated costs, e.g., seed for irrigated land, are subtracted from primary benefits. Secondary benefits either stem from or are induced by the project, but do not directly result from the project. Their inclusion as benefits is subject to controversy. Intangibles are nondollar-value benefits, e.g., aesthetic quality of the landscape, which by definition cannot be included in the benefit-cost calculations.

What gets counted as ''benefits'' is important. Therefore, if the major benefits are intangibles, then the analysis often loses much of its worth. Also, if the major benefits are secondary, the inclusion of them is controversial and the resulting analytical conclusions would be subject to a complex debate involving the technique more than the project. The purpose of analysis is to aid decision makers, and the result of using controversial techniques is to confuse further the decision-making process.

Benefit-cost analysis is almost always used prior to the project's existence; therefore, costs and benefits are estimated over the projected life of the project. Cost estimates include construction engineering, relocation of households, erosion, and third-party effects. Benefits are harder to estimate, especially if they do not occur evenly over time. Decisions must be made on when to stop counting, what not to count, how to count, and how to aggregate benefits. These decisions may greatly affect the analysis; therefore, controversial decisions may lead to controversial analytical conclusions.

One commonly voiced concern is how to handle costs which have already been made, i.e., sunk costs. This is not a controversial subject because they are almost uniformly treated as not relevant to the project cost and are not calculated. Sunk costs may be of significant political concern, but they are not added into the project cost.

Discount Rate

The most controversial ingredient of benefit-cost analysis is the discount rate. The controversy centers not on its proper role in the analysis, but on how it should be determined. It is significant because a higher rate means that fewer projects will be justified, especially if they have costs accumulating over a long period of time. The rationale for a discount rate is that the resources used in a particular project could have been invested elsewhere to yield future resources larger than the amount invested; therefore, this should be taken into consideration in the analysis.

Several approaches to determining discount rates are advocated. One says that a discount rate should have a bias toward present goods over future goods, whereas another argues for giving higher value to future goods. Others argue opportunity cost should be based upon equivalent private investments, whereas still others say external effects should be added and subtracted from those private opportunity costs. The debate is endless and most analysts end up by using an arbitrary interest cost of federal funds in a certain period to select a rate.

If the projects analyzed are similar in size and duration, then the rate used is not significant as long as the same approach is used for all projects. If not, then the analytical results become controversial.

Externalities, Risk, and Other Considerations

Externalities are included in benefit-cost analysis, but they are difficult to determine. Technological externalities involve the physical input-output relationship of other producing units. Pecuniary externalities involve the influences of the project on the prices of other producing units. For example, a public recreation facility may affect demand on, and thus the price of, nearby private facilities. Measurement of externalities is treacherous. Ideally, only "important externalities" are included in the analysis. Interestingly, the influence on the local wage rate is normally not included as "important." Controversy can easily exist on the inclusion of externalities as well as the measurement of them.

Often benefits and costs involve risk and uncertainty. Risk can be described by a probability function normally based on experience. Uncertainty, in its purest meaning, is not subject to probability determination. This means that risk can be included in the analysis, but uncertainty cannot be included. Methods of calculating risk and uncertainty vary. Some methods establish a higher permissible rate than 1.0. Some use a higher rate of discount, and some rationalize the arbitrary benefit stream cutoff by referring to risk and uncertainty. An analyst can deal with risk by including a probability function in an already complex formula, but uncertainty by definition must be treated arbitrarily. Such treatment leads to controversy over the analytical results.

Two other considerations illustrate the complexity of this technique. As was pointed out, sometimes private opportunity costs are used to determine public project opportunity costs. The danger is that private market costs are higher owing to the different tax statuses and costs of financing. Another consideration is that user charges may not be independent of the benefit measures. User charges will restrict use, thus benefits will be reduced. Benefit-cost analysis requires a great deal of thought and care. If that professional treatment is not afforded, then embarrassing controversy can develop over the quality of the analysis.

Benefit-cost analysis is biased toward values associated with money. It does not work well with projects concerning social equality, and the poor tend to be discriminated against with this technique. For example, the value of life is often computed in terms of earning power, thus an airplane passenger is treated as worth more than a bus rider. Values such as equality of opportunity cannot be treated well with this technique. If the project involves such values, then the use of the benefit-cost technique itself will be controversial.

REVIEW QUESTIONS

1. Explain the budget system model, its consistency with democratic theory, and the importance of data measures.
2. Explain the various application difficulties associated with using the budget system model.
3. Compare and contrast a scatter diagram, marginal costs, and discounting. In what ways is each a useful analytical technique in budgeting?
4. Explain the significance of a crosswalk as an analytical tool. What would be crosswalked and why?
5. Compare and contrast qualitative, time series, and causal analysis approaches to revenue forecasting. Explain why good forecasting is important to government.
6. Compare and contrast the various approaches to expenditure forecasting.
7. Misunderstanding the productivity concept can lead to what types of difficulties? What are some of the most common reasons for government not to increase productivity? Why are there no simple uniform answers to the question of how to increase productivity?
8. Explain how regression analysis can help one achieve greater productivity.
9. Compare and contrast benefit-cost and cost-effectiveness analyses.
10. Explain why benefit-cost is a sophisticated and difficult technique to apply. Explain how benefit-cost analysis can be abused as a technique. How can benefit-cost analysis be counterproductive to decision-making?

REFERENCES

BURKHEAD, JESSE and JERRY MINER. *Public Expenditure*. Chicago: Aldine, 1971.

Committee for Economic Development. *Improving Productivity in State and Local Government*. New York: Committee for Economic Development, March 1976.

DAVIES, THOMAS R. and JAMES A. ZINGALE. "Advanced Software for Revenue Forecasting: What to Consider Before Investing in Technology." Paper prepared for the 1983 American Society for Public Administration National Conference, New York, April 17, 1983.

HATRY, HARRY P. "Overview of Modern Program Analysis Characteristics and Techniques: Modern Program Analysis—Hero or Villain?" Washington, D.C.: Urban Institute, 1969.

———, LOUIS BLAIR, DONALD FISK, and WAYNE KIMMEL. *Program Analysis for State and Local Governments*. Washington, D.C.: Urban Institute, 1976.

ISAAC, STEPHEN, in collaboration with William B. Michael. *Handbook in Research and Evaluation*. San Diego: Edits Publishers, 1971.

KLAY, WILLIAM EARLE. "Revenue Forecasting: An Administrative Perspective," in Jack Rabin and Thomas D. Lynch (eds.), *Handbook on Public Budgeting and Financial Management*. New York: Marcel Dekker, 1983.

KRAMER, FRED A. "The Discounting to Present Value Technique as a Decision Tool," *Special Bulletin* 1976E (November 24, 1976).

MOAK, LENNOX L. and KATHRYN W. KILLIAN. *Operating Budget Manual*. Chicago: Municipal Finance Officers Association, 1963.

ROSS, JOHN P. and JESSE BURKHEAD. *Productivity in the Local Government Sector*. Lexington, Mass.: Heath, 1974.

TOULMIN, LLEWELLYN M. and GLENDAL E. WRIGHT. "Expenditure Forecasting," in Jack Rabin and Thomas D. Lynch (eds.), *Handbook on Public Budgeting and Financial Management*. New York: Marcel Dekker, 1983.

U.S. Joint Financial Management Improvement Program. *Productivity Programs in the Federal Government*. Washington, D.C.: U.S. Joint Financial Management Improvement Program, July 1976.

Urban Institute and International City Management Association. *Measuring the Effectiveness of Basic Municipal Services*. Washington, D.C.: International City Management Association, February 1974.

WRIGHT, CHESTER and MICHAEL D. TATE. *Economics and Systems Analysis: Introduction for Public Managers*. Reading, Mass.: Addison-Wesley, 1973.

SIX
ANALYTICAL PROCESSES

In public budgeting, there are five analytical processes which are designed to help professionals deal more intelligently with their policy and administrative challenges. Each one—program analysis, budget examination, process analysis, program evaluation, and auditing—is briefly described here, but greater attention is given to budget examination and process analysis due to their central importance to public budgeting. The reports produced from each process should be viewed as normally useful input to better budgets. Program analysis looks *de novo* at the policy implications of major programmatic budget decisions. Budget examination is the primary analytical process which actually produces the budget. Process analysis is a careful focus upon the management process itself so that improvements can be identified. Program evaluation looks backward and helps the budget examiner decide if the program was effective or sufficiently effective to justify the requested money in the BY. Auditing is also reflective in character and helps the budget examiner focus on questions of both effectiveness and efficiency. The chapter will explain:

1. the approach essential for useful program analysis;
2. how budget examination can be undertaken using the various concepts and techniques explained in the text;
3. a useful approach to look closely at the process and identify process improvements;

4. the basics of program evaluation; and
5. the essentials of auditing, especially the types of information which can be forthcoming from a "good" program audit.

PROGRAM ANALYSIS

In program analysis—sometimes called policy analysis—the focus is on considering the new policy options which are implicit in the budget. Such analyses are often highly quantitative in character, but that need not be true. There are elements common to all program analyses, regardless of their character. A frequent complaint of high level executive officials is that they really could not get the agencies to provide the information necessary to judge budget requests. Often this is more an admission of professional incompetency than a commentary on the budget process. If a reasonable effort, as explained here, is put into budget examining by competent professionals, then the central review staff will be in a position to make reasoned judgments based upon agency requests and alternative policy options. Good program analysis should isolate sensitive policy questions and identify the likely implications of the various viable policy options within the limitations of the data and the analytical technique used.

Selecting Issues

Selection of potential issues can proceed systematically. What are the unsettled influential issues which determine program direction and emphasis? What issues are being raised by key influential people in the legislature, executive, clientele, media, and judicial settings? What are the apparent policy dilemmas facing the agency? The analysts can use these questions to develop a reasonable list of potential issues for analysis. Normally program issues are abundant. The usual problem is not to find issues but to select the best issues for program review purposes. The Urban Institute has developed the following criteria for selecting issues for analysis.

IMPORTANCE OF AN ISSUE

1. Is there a decision to be made by the government? Can the analysis significantly influence the adoption of various alternatives?
2. Does the issue involve large costs or major consequences for services?
3. Is there substantial room for improving program performance?

FEASIBILITY OF ANALYSIS

4. Can the problem be handled by program analysis?
5. Is there time for the analysis to be done before the key decisions must be made?
6. Are personnel and funds available to do the analysis?
7. Do sufficient data exist to undertake the analysis, and can needed data be gathered within the time available?

The first consideration is the importance of the issue. As suggested by the above criteria, the potential significance of an analysis of the issue, the consequence, and the potential for improvement should be considered. If no one will use an analysis of an issue, then proceeding with the analysis is certainly foolish. Given a lack of time to perform analysis, the analyst is normally wise to concentrate on the big issue, especially if notable improvements are possible.

The next consideration is the feasibility of analysis. Many problems do not lend themselves to program analysis or the time available is so brief that useful analysis cannot be conducted prior to the time the key decisions are made. Personnel, fund, or data limitations may exist which preclude analysis. Each of these factors must honestly be assessed before work on program analysis begins or the effort may be worthless.

Exhibit 6-1 presents some illustrations of the issues which might be subject to program analysis.

EXHIBIT 6-1   Illustrative Issues for Program Analysis

Law Enforcement

1. What is the most effective way of distributing limited police forces—by time of day, day of week, and geographical location?
2. What types of police units (foot patrolmen, one- or two-man police cars, special task forces, canine corps units, or others) should be used and in what mix?
3. What types of equipment (considering both current and new technologies) should be used for weaponry, for communications, and for transportation?
4. How can the judicial process be improved to provide more expeditious service, keep potentially dangerous persons from running loose, and at the same time protect the rights of the innocent?
5. How can criminal detection institutions be improved to maximize the probability of rehabilitation, while remaining a deterrent to further crime?

Fire Protection

1. Where should fire stations be located, and how many are needed?
2. How should firefighting units be deployed, and how large should units be?
3. What types of equipment should be used for communications, transportation, and firefighting?
4. Are there fire prevention activities, such as inspection of potential fire hazards or school educational programs, that can be used effectively?

Health and Social Services

1. What mix of treatment programs should do the most to meet the needs of the expected mix of clients?
2. What prevention programs are desirable for the groups that seem most likely to suffer particular ailments?

Housing

1. To what extent can housing code enforcement programs be used to decrease the number of families living in substandard housing? Will such programs have an adverse effect on the overall supply of low-income housing in the community?

2. What is the appropriate mix of code enforcement with other housing programs to make housing in the community adequate?

3. What is the best mix of housing rehabilitation, housing maintenance, and new construction to improve the quantity and quality of housing?

Employment

1. What relative support should be given to training and employment programs which serve different client groups?

2. What should be the mix among outreach programs, training programs, job-finding and matching programs, antidiscrimination programs, and post-employment follow-up programs?

Waste

1. How should waste be collected and disposed of, given alternative visual, air, water, and pollution standards?

2. What specific equipment and routings should be used?

Recreation and Leisure

1. What type, location, and size of recreation facilities should be provided for those desiring them?

2. How should recreation facilities be divided among summer and winter, daytime and nighttime, and indoor and outdoor activities?

3. What, and how many, special summer programs should be made available for out-of-school youths?

4. What charges, if any, should be made to users, considering such factors as differential usage and ability to pay?

Issue Assessment

Once the issues have been defined, then a preliminary assessment can be made before an in-depth analysis is conducted. In most situations, an agency suggests issues and the central budget office decides which issues to investigate. Those issues may or may not be the ones suggested by the agency. The involvement of the central budget office is wise as it helps to insure the significance of the report once it is written, but the lack of a preliminary assessment of the issues is not wise. In far too many analytical situations, reports have been commissioned without a proper appreciation of what was requested. The instructions requesting the study may have been too vague or misleading. Another possibility is that further thought will reveal that there is no real need for an analysis, thus saving thousands or even millions of dollars. Preliminary assessments are extremely useful.

The issue assessment is a written presentation which identifies and describes the major features of a significant issue facing the government. The assessment is only a few pages long, but it clearly sets out the ingredients which would be considered in a major issue study. According to Harry P. Hatry of the Urban Institute, the outline or major subjects in an issue assessment are:

1. *The Problem.* What is the problem and its causes? Identify specific groups (e.g., the poor) affected. How are they affected? Identify characteristics of the group. How large and significant is the problem now? What are the likely future dimensions of the problem?

2. *Objectives and Evaluation Criteria.* Define the fundamental purposes and benefits of the program. Identify the evaluation criteria by which progress toward the program objectives should be judged.

3. *Current Activities and Agencies Involved.* Identify all relevant groups involved in attempting to deal with the problem. Identify what each group is doing, including costs and impacts. Activities, costs, and benefits should be projected into the future.

4. *Other Significant Factors.* Cite the other major factors, including political realities, that affect the problem. Identify unusual resources, timing limitations, or other factors of significance.

5. *Alternatives.* Describe alternative programs designed to meet the problem and the major characteristics of each.

6. *Recommendations for Follow-up.* Making choices among alternatives is inappropriate because, by definition, this work is only an assessment. Recommendations can be made on the next administrative step (e.g., full-scale analysis). What is the best timing for and scope of the needed follow-up analysis? Should the analysis be a quick response or an in-depth study? Frank descriptions of analytical difficulties should be cited. What major data problems exist? How should they be dealt with under the circumstances?

The assessment serves as the basis for deciding to request a special analytical study and for framing instructions for the study.

Commentary on Analysis

The conduct of analysis largely depends upon the subject to be analyzed, the context of the study, and the techniques used. Each of these subjects is outside the scope of this chapter and can properly be studied under the heading of microeconomics, operations research, systems analysis, and statistics. Chapter 6 discusses some elementary analytical concepts useful in budgeting as well as in explaining benefit-cost analysis.

There are ten factors—five technical and five bureaucratic—which particularly influence the results of analysis. Those factors are:

1. study size;
2. study timing;
3. methodological adequacy;
4. consideration of implementation;
5. nature of problem studied;
6. decision maker interest;

7.   implementor's participation;
8.   single-agency issue;
9.   proposed changes in funding; and
10.   immediate decision needed.

There are five factors which appear to be more significant than the others. The three most significant "technical" factors are study timing (i.e., studies were well timed so that study findings were available at key decision points); consideration of implementation (i.e., studies included an explicit consideration of political and administrative issues which might affect the implementation of study findings); and nature of problem studied (i.e., studies focused on well-defined problems rather than on broad or open-ended ones). The two most significant "bureaucratic" factors are immediate decision needed (i.e., issues which could not be deferred by policy makers); and decision maker interest (i.e., issues in which decision makers had shown clear interest).

In program analysis, care must be taken to avoid four common mistakes which occur as a result of an unrealistic desire to analyze for the sake of analysis. One mistake can be labeled "search under the lamp." A well-known story tells of the man who was searching at night for his lost watch under a street light. A friend comes by and offers to aid in the search. The friend asks where the man lost the watch and the man replies that the watch was lost half a block up the street. The friend then asks why the man is searching next to the street lamp. The man answers that the light is much better under the street light. In policy analysis situations, analysts often will concentrate their investigation on those aspects which are easy to measure and downplay the aspects difficult to measure. Thus they are looking under the street lamp instead of "up the street" where the watch was lost.

Another common mistake is to become fascinated by technique. An intellectual challenge for an analyst is to use and develop more sophisticated analytical—often mathematical—techniques. The normal desire is to select issues which require complex techniques or use more complex techniques when simpler ones would be adequate. Analysts should address the analytical problems and not techniques, otherwise there is means-ends confusion.

A third mistake is to delay reports and even policy decisions so that analyses can be performed for their own sake. Analysts can be consumed with interest in the analytical question, much as some people are consumed by crossword puzzles, mysteries, and good books. This consuming interest can overwhelm the original reason for the analysis. As was pointed out earlier, report timeliness is critical and sometimes analytical purity is sacrificed for timeliness.

The fourth mistake is to overanalyze. In some situations, a good analyst quietly thinking for a few hours may produce results equal to or better than an army of survey researchers. We automatically tend to use certain well-known approaches to analysis without appreciating their limitations and the tolerance for error implicit in the issue being studied. The advantage of the issue assessment mentioned earlier is to avoid such a mistake.

A final commentary of analysis is that there may be only "poor" solutions to problems. This commentary may seem obvious, but this realization is often difficult for decision makers to accept. If a program analysis is conducted and only "poor" solutions are cited, the decision maker can conclude either that solutions are indeed "poor" or that the analysis was bad. Thus, the analyst can be placed in an awkward position. The only professionally acceptable course of action is to be sure that no desirable answers exist and to explain this fact properly in the analyst's report.

Presentations of Results: Some Prescriptions

A common failure of program analysis is providing a poor presentation of study results. The work may be excellent, but the presentation is inadequate.

The first advice on presenting results is to review them carefully before they are distributed. The pressures of meeting a deadline and the distasteful chore of proofing combine to discourage proper review of papers before they are distributed. These final checks are essential if embarrassing mistakes or insensitive political statements are to be avoided.

Report findings should be in writing. Oral reports are useful but they should supplement or summarize written reports. Written reports provide the essential record which is often useful even years after a report was prepared.

Care must be taken to prepare compact, clear summaries. The summary is normally the first important portion of the report that is read—the other material may never be read. Long, vague summaries are counterproductive as they discourage use of the report.

In most program analysis reports, two or three options are discussed. If only one option were discussed, then the credibility of the report would be questioned. Many options only tend to confuse matters. Two or three options are adequate normally to illustrate the varieties of solutions. If the range of solutions is broad, the presentation of only two or three options is done to illustrate the types of solutions.

Studies must set out limitations and assumptions. Professional standards alone require such candor. On a more practical level, professional reputation and confidence are enhanced by frank, honest reports. A decision maker may not like the qualifications, but if something goes wrong the analyst is protected by that candor. Also, the decision makers are apprised fully of the risks inherent in their decisions.

Studies should discuss potential windfalls and pitfalls related to the issue. Windfalls are collateral benefits resulting from actions and decisions. Pitfalls are collateral hazards or disadvantages. Both can be easily overlooked in the analyses and by decision makers. The potential for oversight is the reason why this material should be in the report.

The studies should contain simple graphics where possible to communicate major findings and conclusions. Most readers will benefit from both written and graphic explanations. Graphics should not stand alone—reference should be made to them in the text. Complex graphics should be avoided because readers may not be able to understand them.

Clarity requires that jargon be avoided. If a special vocabulary is well known and used, then such jargon (e.g., piggyback containers, subsystem) can be used. Jargon is the shorthand means of communication. However, most program analysis reports are meant for managers and other decision makers unschooled in the jargon; thus it only makes the report difficult to read.

Reports and studies should be written for the decision makers. Authors of reports and studies should know who are the intended and likely users of their work. What are the backgrounds, knowledge, and biases of thè report and study users? If the users have extensive technical knowledge, then authors should use that fact in preparing the report. If the user has strong biases and the report finding runs counter to those biases, then greater care should be taken to explain and fully document the findings.

From the public budgeting perspective, one of the most obvious failures in the presentation of program analysis results is the omission of an explanation of how the recommendations should be translated to operational management direction. People working in budgeting are interested in policy debates and analysis, but their lives involve operational decisions. Study findings and recommendations must be translated to the operational before they can be treated as something more than a possibility. Exactly in what ways should the current program be changed? What specifically are the present and future budget implications? These questions should be addressed in the program analysis reports and studies if they are to be meaningful to the budget process.

Role of the Chief Executive

The product of program analysis is meant for decision makers, especially chief executives. If there is support from the chief executive and that person uses the products of program analysis, then there is a reasonable chance that program analysis will be significant in the government decision-making process. On the other hand, without top level support and use, program analysis as an activity is worthless. Detailed top level involvement is not needed, but the following types of involvement are essential. According to the Urban Institute, officials should:

1. participate actively in the selection of program and policy issues for analysis;
2. assign responsibility for the analysis to a unit of the organization which can conduct the study objectively;
3. ensure that participation and cooperation are obtained from relevent agencies;
4. provide adequate staff to meet a timely reporting schedule;
5. insist that the objectives, evaluation criteria, client groups, and program alternatives considered in the analysis include those of prime importance;
6. have a work schedule prepared and periodically monitored; and
7. review results, and if findings seem valid, see that they are used.[1]

[1]Harry P. Hatry, Louis Blair, Donald Fisk, and Wayne Kimmel, *Program Analysis for State and Local Governments* (Washington, D.C.: Urban Institute, 1976), p. 11.

BUDGET EXAMINATION

An important activity in the budget process is budget examination, which uses other forms of analysis and specific analyses to review agency budget requests and make staff recommendations to legislative and executive political leaders. This section explains how budget analysts can perform sophisticated budget examination within the context of democratic government, complex technology, and current analytical techniques.

Information Sources

Reviewers are not limited to the agency budget submission in forming their analysis and conclusions. Information can be obtained from the budget submissions, hearings, reports which may be available, other information such as newspaper stories, and answers to specific questions prior to and after budget hearings. The most important information source is normally the agency budget request because it directly addresses the information needs of the budget reviewer. Hearings are also a valuable information source as they can be used to focus upon specific inquiries. Hearings permit direct oral interchange between the agency and the reviewers. Reviewers should also make use of any available reports, such as special analytical studies and program evaluation reports. This type of information often is not organized well for budget analysis purposes, but studies and reports do provide useful insight and suggest areas of fruitful inquiry. Other information sources, such as national media reports and books, can also be extremely helpful in framing inquiries.

Specific questions by reviewers and answers by agency officials are valuable to budget reviewers. These questions and answers can occur before and after hearings. They can be oral or written depending upon the reviewers' request. The major limiting factor is time. Rarely are questions asked prior to budget submissions because the submissions may contain the answers. If there is a short time interval between the submission and the hearing, then written questions and answers may be impossible—normally at least five working days are needed to develop answers, have them approved by top agency personnel, and have them typed and transmitted. If there is an equally short time interval between the hearing and the central budget office decision on the budget, then again written questions may not be possible. Time pressures dictate that the answers must not require new analysis but use existing information.

The key to an outstanding budget review is for the reviewer to gain the necessary program information and insight. No one source of information is adequate and many inquiries can be tailored for the situation. The advocate wishes to anticipate inquiries so that confidence in the agency budget personnel can be enhanced. Both the examiner and the analyst preparing the submission have in common a set of information. One wishes to know the information and the other should be ready to supply the information. What can a good budget examiner look for and what should a good agency budget analyst be able to provide?

Code of Ethics

Ethical considerations are significant and do tend to be overlooked until a crisis occurs. The code of ethics described here is part of the handbook for budget analysts in the state of Florida and its purpose is to guide the professional conduct of state budget analysts. The role of budget examiners and the proper carrying out of their responsibilities is critical to a successful budget process. Improper conduct can mean fraud, impotent and frustrated policy, inefficiency, counterproductive management practices, and an inability on the part of the examiners to develop and grow as professionals and as members of an organization.

The following code of ethics and its implications should guide professional conduct.

1. *No gifts or favors may be accepted by a budget analyst beyond minor social courtesies which have little or no significant value.* This first ethical principle is obviously intended to prevent corruption and improper influence on analysts by actors in the political process. It is critical (1) if objectivity, as well as the confidence of others in that objectivity, is to be maintained, and (2) if the policy issues are to be determined through the democratic process. As stated, it does not require the analyst's total separation from influencing factors, but such a separation is not inconsistent with this principle. Some budget offices do require total separation because of the importance of the analyst's being free from the possibility of any improper influence.

2. *The role of the analyst does not extend to independent action which establishes government policy.* Analysts are expected to gather information, analyze it, and recommend policy with appropriate supporting data and documentation. Their purpose is to raise the level of debate associated with policy-making, not to make policy. Budget analysts are staff functionaries whose job is to help the true policy makers—the elected officials and their appointees. They are called on to provide useful information to help the political decision makers arrive at more enlightened decisions. Often, examiners judge their success by how much they shaped policy rather than by their role in creating an environment in which more enlightened decisions are more likely to occur. As long as the budget analyst is part of a political system in which overriding policy is established by elected officials, the examiner should view his or her role as advisory. If the examiner's advice is not taken, no professional failure occurred unless his or her presentation of that information tended to inhibit enlightened decision-making.

3. *Examiners must maintain their objectivity, which includes presenting all aspects of issues fairly and excludes advocating an agency's position for any purpose other than to clarify the issues.* Being emotionally committed to the agencies under review is one of the hazards of budget examination. Analysts must avoid becoming staff advocates of agency requests; instead, they must remain detached so that they can critically examine budget requests. This presents a staffing dilemma for budget offices. On the one hand, examiners must be involved with a line agency long enough to know the complexities of that agency; on the other hand, examiners must not be coopted, which does tend to occur over time. There is no simple way to deal with this ethical principle, but it is important that the spirit of the principle be respected.

4. *Every attempt must be made to ensure that managerial decisions are made by the proper line officials.* Managers must make their own decisions, whereas analysts must be free to comment on those decisions and to facilitate a more thoughtful decision-making process.

5. *Analysts must avoid acting in an arrogant manner to anyone, including other government officials.* Analysts may have their own strong opinions, but these opinions must be kept under control. Sensitivity and respect for feelings must be shown to all individuals who are part of the budget process. Examiners are staff advisors and not managers of line government units. A professional problem stemming from the examiner's unique access to high officials and role as overseer of the budget process is a tendency to substitute his or her own decisions for those of the line manager. Sometimes the examiner will arrogantly demand information on some policy change from the line manager. Sometimes a line manager, as a ploy to escape responsibility, will ask the staff budget analyst to make managerial decisions (e.g., whether to buy or lease equipment). In either situation, the examiner must recall that his or her responsibility is primarily advisory and should maintain a cordial working relationship with the line manager.

6. *In framing recommendations and in dealing with the bureaucracy, the examiner must make every effort to foster and improve the quality of government management.* Recommendations and accompanying information should be sensitive not only to policy considerations but also to the managerial environment needed to accomplish that policy.

7. *The professional development and growth of the examiners is important.* Budget analysts must continually strive to understand the substantive policy and management issues associated with the units being examined. Analysts must also strive to improve their budget examination skills and knowledge so that better work can be performed. Improved government quality does not occur automatically and improvement usually comes only after a struggle. Given other policy and management concerns, budget analysts can easily overlook or fail to emphasize the improvement of government management as a continuing priority. Ironically, examiners are in a unique position to foster and encourage those improvements. For example, funds for professional development tend to be ignored rather than treated as one of the fringe benefits associated with employment for a progressive organization. The budget analysts should insure that such matters are not overlooked. Professional development also applies to the examiner. The tendency is to become involved in the daily tasks and neglect one's own professional development. Thus, this ethical principle calls upon analysts to recognize the importance of their own professional growth and to pursue it by means of formal education, training, and professional conferences.

Services Performed

Results of services performed are important. The budget examiner determines services or types of services which are anticipated from the planned budget. Historical information can be used to illustrate the type of service likely to be provided as well as to establish the reliability of the agency to perform as planned. The budget submission often indicates objectives and states likely products of the agency. The examiner looks beyond specific outputs and tries to ascertain the likely impacts on society and individuals directly and indirectly due to the program. Also, unanticipated good and bad effects are considered. It is helpful if the information is available in the budget request. If not, the information may be available in speeches or program evaluation reports.

The agency normally has an excellent explanation of its likely outputs. Any budget is a plan requiring forecasting so every budget must be tentative, since there is no guarantee the events will evolve as planned. This is accepted; if something else were said, the budget examiner would question the realism of the agency. The character of explanation of output and projected benefits depends upon whether the program is demand responsive or directed. Demand responsive programs react to individuals and groups which meet the agency's general criteria of need and seek assistance. In contrast, directed programs are established to fulfill a specific need and are managed directly by government. Demand responsive programs are grants-in-aid and direct benefit (e.g., food stamps) programs. In demand responsive programs, the government cannot control the rate or type of demand; thus it is conditioned by outside factors. In directed programs, the government has a high degree of control over exactly what it will do.

Budget examiners can probe direct programs for the management plan of the agency. The agency normally has a detailed plan of how it will use its resources to achieve specific outputs. It should have a definite fix on the likely benefits and spillover effects of the program. The examiner's role is first to make sure such a plan exists, and secondly to see that the plan has a reasonable chance of being successful. The plan and management should be flexible enough to meet likely contingencies.

Budget examiners handle demand responsive programs differently. Budget examiners probe these programs in terms of anticipated demands and likely outputs and benefits. Agency management should have excellent forecasts of likely demand. The agency should have prepared an analysis of various likely funding scenarios and estimated the likely outputs and benefits of each scenario. To the extent that the agency can control its ability to meet the program demand, the agency should be able to explain what it can do and the significance of its action in terms of the scenarios and resulting outputs and benefits. If the agency cannot provide these explanations, then the agency's ability to manage the requested funds properly can be strongly questioned.

If the budget examiner ever sees vagueness in the information provided, this can serve as a red flag to the examiner. Vague subjects can be carefully isolated because vagueness indicates possibly serious managerial problems. If agency management does not know how to deal with a situation or there is serious internal conflict, then agency budget officers must be vague about those situations in the budget request because the uncertainty cannot, by definition, be resolved. Good budget officers may be able to minimize the problem but they cannot hide the use of a vague answer.

Budget examiners can carefully probe the exact reason for the vagueness. The explanation may be merely a poor presentation rather than management difficulties. If the vagueness is isolated early enough, questions and hearings can be used to determine the exact nature of the problem. This probing requires skill; but unless the agency budget officer directly lies, the budget examiner can isolate the problem, given enough time. Even in the rare cases where the agency personnel lie, a skillful examiner can normally isolate the problem because logical consistency is difficult for liars to maintain.

Program Inputs and Outputs

The budget examiner should determine key input, process, and output measures. These concepts are explained in more depth in Chapter 5. Briefly, there are measures which tend to be more useful than other measures. These indicators show the resources going into the program, what activities are taking place, and the results attributable to the program. These measures are used for comparative and trend analytical purposes. By performing elementary analysis, the budget examiner can determine questionable program budget requests and poor management practices and can identify important changes in the program's environment which are not correctly reflected in the budget request.

Exhibit 6-2 is a checklist used by the city of Los Angeles to review performance reports. Notice how the budget examiner is sensitive to the interrelationship of input, process, and outputs. The examiner maintains a questioning, arm's length relationship with the agency.

The budget examiner can also check the accuracy of tables and data supplied by the agency. Exhaustive checks are not necessary, but any uncommon results, important statistics, and common places where errors occur can always be checked. Tables can be checked by observing if there is proper internal consistency among tables. Often totals of summary columns can be checked against other summary columns for internal consistency. Simple arithmetic errors do occur even in the most important budget requests. Commonly errors occur when incorrect pay rate scales are used or when personnel are placed into the wrong classification.

Budget examiners can carefully review the money requested and be sensitive to hidden revenue sources or "sleight-of-hand" tricks. This is a conventional spender's strategy and the diligent reviewer can determine when such strategy is being used. The examiner must be well versed in backdoor spending techniques and must know if any of them can be used by the agency. The examiner can profit from

---

EXHIBIT 6-2   Checklist for Review of Performance Reports

General

1. Check total gross man-hours for department with the combined total standard hours plus paid overtime hours as shown for each pay period on the IBM Personnel Audit Reports of the Controller (on file in Budget Administration Division).

Personnel

2. Have any new activities or sub-activities been added over those shown in original work program?
3. If so, how many positions are being used? Cost estimate?
4. Are any previous activities or sub-activities eliminated or curtailed?
5. If so, how many positions which were included in last year's work program have been eliminated? Cost estimate?

6. Net increase or decrease in cost as result of additions and deletions?
7. Are there any special projects on which work was performed on a one-time basis only?
8. If so, what sub-activities were affected and how many man-hours were devoted to such special projects?
9. How does the actual number of personnel utilized compare with the number of authorized positions?

Man-Hours

10. Where both net man-hours and gross man-hours are reported, what is the percentage of net total to gross total? Are there any sub-activities which have lower percentages than the overall average percentage? Which are they and how much variation from average is there? What are the causes? (Vacations, sick leave, other absences?)
11. How does actual work performed compare with the estimate for each sub-activity?
12. Has there been an increase or decrease in the number of personnel actually utilized over last month's figures?

Man-Hours Per Unit

13. How does the gross man-hours per unit for each sub-activity compare with last month's figures?
14. How does the net man-hours per unit for each sub-activity compare with last month's figures?
15. What is the reason for any increase or decrease?
16. In sub-activities where work performed and work unit are comparable, what is the variation between gross man-hours per unit for such sub-activities?
17. What is the variation between net man-hours per unit for such sub-activities?

Overall Appraisal

18. Based on the above analysis, could any employees have been transferred temporarily during slack periods?
19. If so, how many and in what classes of positions?
20. Based on the above analysis, were any additional employees required to handle peak loads?
21. If so, how many and in what classes of positions?
22. Were there any backlogs of work resulting from lack of sufficient personnel?
23. If so, how much?
24. What class of personnel and how many employees would be required to eliminate backlogs?
25. Are backlogs the result of seasonal variations? Of improper scheduling of vacations? Of greater than normal absences due to sickness? Of unfilled positions? If the latter, what is the recruitment situation?
26. At the end of each quarter, determine what percentage of last year's annual program has been completed for each sub-activity.
27. Will the remaining portion of the annual program be completed by the end of the current fiscal year if that rate of progress is maintained?
28. Will more or less personnel be required in each sub-activity to complete annual program?
29. If so, how many and in what classes of positions?

Source: Los Angeles, California, City Administrator's Office

the use of accounting reports. Use of fund transfer, lag time among administrative reservations, obligations, expenditures, and closing of accounts can be significant in determining hidden revenue. Other types of hidden revenue or improper expenditure estimates require considerable knowledge of the programs, but examiners can sometimes find such savings. For example, possibly the program can use existing government facilities rather than rent or lease new property. Another possibility is interagency or intergovernmental cooperative management agreements which allow savings as a result of economy of scale.

For the budget examiner, detailed tables from agencies isolate personnel by grade, type, unit, and status (permanent, temporary, part- or full-time). A critical resource is always personnel. Does the agency have too many or too few personnel for the assigned task? Maybe the agency has enough people, but they are of the wrong grade or type, or are poorly distributed among the units. Two common problems occur when an agency overexpands its highest ranks and fails to reallocate its personnel once a major task has been accomplished. Examiners cannot address such questions without detailed information on personnel. Another problem occurs when the personnel hired are not properly trained to do upgraded and more complex work requirements. Judgments in this area must be predicated on a knowledge of the personnel as well as of the new challenges facing the agency.

Budget examiners can often profit by comparing the agency's overhead and direct costs. A common mistake in bureaucracies is to allow overhead (i.e., those people and costs which serve to make the agency operate) to grow at the expense of direct costs (i.e., those people and costs which perform the activities directly associated with the agency's mission). Examples of overhead are personnel, legal, housekeeping, and budget activities. The proper size of overhead and even the definition of overhead are topics subject to debate. Ideally, overhead would be large enough to facilitate agency effectiveness and efficiency. In some situations, the overhead activities can grow to a point where agency effectiveness and efficiency are actually decreased. The budget examiner can examine the facts and determine if overhead is becoming excessive.

The data can be used to identify relationships between program demands and work load. For example, there tends to be a positive identifiable relationship between the population under the age of 25 in an area and the number of parole officers needed. If such relationships can be verified, then the examiner is in a much better position to judge the budget request.

Trends on program inputs and outputs are valuable information for the budget examiner. For example, if resources have been increasing and outputs decreasing, then serious questions must be raised concerning the efficiency and possibly even effectiveness of the program. What are the causes underlying trends and deviations from the apparent natural trend? Does there appear to be any positive or negative relationship between and among trends? For example, does salt tend to be more effective than sand in alleviating snow conditions? This information can lead to suggestions resulting in the use of cheaper substances while maintaining the same level of service to the public.

Comparative data on program inputs and outputs are also valuable information. What do comparable cities spend for the same type of services? What levels of output do they achieve? What explains the differences? Can those positive advantages be achieved in the budget examiner's city?

Emphasis and Change

Whether the budget request is presented in incremental or zero-base format, the budget examiner needs information on yearly budget emphases and changes in emphases from prior years. Decision makers wish to know how much stress is being placed on a given program relative to other program efforts. Balance is a political consideration, thus it is useful information for decision makers. They also wish to know if the agency is shifting its policy from previous years. This can best be determined by comparing the budget request with previous budget requests and actual obligation/expenditure patterns.

Budgets can be categorized into various logical subdivisions. A single categorization is probably inadequate for the variety of analytical needs of the budget examiner. One categorization should reflect the major agency tasks, projects, and continuing activities. Another categorization may be necessary to relate the inputs (e.g., dollars requested) to agency goals and intended benefits. However, often one categorization may be sufficient for both purposes if the agency is not handicapped by multiple inconsistent objectives. A categorization using line item information is normally not useful because various purposes can lie behind the use of the same items of expenditure.

Categorizations can provide comparative information over several fiscal years. Dollars requested and possible specific inputs and outputs can be presented in terms of the prior year, actual current year estimates, budget year estimates, and possibly budget year-plus-five estimates. Such a display of data permits comparative analyses by fiscal year. Thus program increases and decreases over time can be isolated.

Complex programs, involving contracts extending beyond the budget year, can be misleading in terms of increases and decreases. Obligations can be made for continuing, expanding, or starting programs. The decrease or increase in a given fiscal year only gives useful information on the rate of obligation, and says nothing about the use of the money. The categorization in such programs should indicate the changes in the funding level of programs divided into subcategories of continuing and expanded programs. Also any new programs can be identified as such. As noted in the previous chapter, the spender's strategy calls for the use of flexible definitions by the spender. The budget examiner can understand the nature of each program so that definitions and categorizations can be challenged.

The previous categorizations and related work are all designed to help the budget examiner identify emphases and shifts. What programs, projects, activities, or tasks are receiving greatest stress? This is judged in the context of the available resource, the maximum effort which could be given, and the relative emphases among the programs. Each is important in judging "emphasis." What programs, projects, activities, or tasks are receiving increased or decreased support? To answer that question fully, the budget examiner discovers whether changes are addressed to existing or new programs. Also, the examiner relates the change to program outputs, including anticipated benefits or harm to society and individuals. This analysis helps answer the followup question: Is the change worth it? Budget examiners seek *hard data* and get *written responses* to this type of inquiry in order to avoid later misunderstandings between the examiner and agency officials.

Program and financial plans (PFP) are required periodically (quarterly or semi-annually). They are summary tables of the budget, categorized by major programs and activities. In the federal government, the PFP includes both obligations and disbursements; but obligations are normally sufficient for state and local government purposes. The information covers the past year, current year, budget, and budget year plus five.

The PFP should be analyzed by the examiner for patterns reflecting policy and consistency with previously established management policy. The PFP should reflect any changes in policy and it is particularly useful prior to the budget call to forecast possible agency requests. Quick comparisons against past PFP's can be made to see if an evolution in policy is occurring. If changes are not occurring, the agency should be questioned, because agency policy is rarely constant and lack of change reflects a neglect to update the PFP. The PFP is an advance warning and the examiner can encourage the agency to use the PFP in that manner.

Responsiveness

A major concern of a budget analyst is to be sensitive to the concerns of elected political leaders and appointees and insure that existing programs are carrying out established policy. In gathering information and examining programs and their issues, budget analysts seek useful data which reflect upon the policy matters significant to the legislators. Budget examiners should identify all major policy concerns in their area which pertinent political officials would wish to understand in terms of their budget decisions. Examiners should try to identify desired new programs, changes in existing programs, and desired analyst follow-through on programs and projects considered legislatively important.

Even in unusual years when tax receipts are particularly high, few funds are available for all desired improvements in existing programs and for new programs. Resources for new and improved programs are normally small, but that does not mean that new programs should automatically be disregarded. Improved programs are prime candidates for funding if:

1. they result in unit cost savings in those programs where growth is inevitable (use unit cost analysis and marginal cost analysis);
2. the improved program can be an alternative to other current programs (use cost-effectiveness analysis);
3. the improvements can generate benefits in the area economy over the cost of program (use benefit-cost analysis); or
4. a case is made that intended political outcomes are significant in terms of the values of pertinent political officials.

New programs are prime candidates for funding if:

1.   they are mandated by current law to begin in the BY; or
2.   a cost-effective alternative exists to current programs (use cost-effectiveness analysis).

If the above conditions exist, the budget examiner should bring them to the attention of the political appointee when new or improved programs are being considered. An examination should identify the likely program outcomes, the groups positively and negatively affected, and the effect on those groups. This is particularly true of new or improved programs; political officials should be apprised of the implications of such programs so that they can take intelligent positions on them. In addition, examiners should be able to explain the theoretical linkages between direct budget amounts and government action, services and products produced, and program outcomes on society and individuals.

Analysts must be convinced such linkages exist and any doubts should be shared with pertinent political officials. The desired outputs should lead to the desired outcomes in the BY and specified years beyond the BY. Programs should be reviewed for timeliness, appropriateness, and necessity. The desired inputs and planned management activities should lead to the desired outputs in the BY and beyond. This requires the examiners to be sure each program is funded at least at the minimum level for viable operations. This is done by defining the minimum useful output level and by being sure the input level (e.g., salaries, expenses, and equipment) can produce that desired output level.

Examiners review current programs to determine outmoded, nonproductive, duplicative, overlapping, or very low priority programs or parts of programs. When this occurs, examiners should fully document and carefully justify recommendations because agency opposition is likely. If required, statutory, ordinance, or regulation revisions should also be recommended and all costs, including staff, should be deleted. Cost-effectiveness analysis might be especially useful here.

Effectiveness and Efficiency

A major concern of budget examination is program effectiveness and efficiency. The budget analyst's focus should be on the adequacy of the planned management processes to insure that the programs will be managed correctly. The examiner should be confident that intended outputs and outcomes will be achieved. The best evidence for this is the agency's established track record of achievement. Beyond that, the budget analyst should be confident that administrative or outside factors will not prevent the intended outputs and outcomes from occurring. Such confidence is normally acquired by site inspections and inquiries to agency officials to see if they have properly anticipated the likely administrative and outside factors which could interfere. Examiners should review programs for documented workload change. Was there unavoidable growth in workload which cannot be absorbed? Conversely, workload decreases should be noted. In both situations, adjustments in staffing, expenditures, and other resources should be considered. Unit cost and marginal cost analyses might be particularly useful. Input to output ratios (productivity measures) are very useful and can be of interest to political officials. Marginal analysis is particularly helpful in determining the optimal input level for the most effective program operation.

Normally, maximum use should be made of nongeneral revenue sources rather than the general fund. Examiners should examine user fees, grants, trust funds, and internal service funds to be sure that they cover the maximum amount of expenses permitted in order to take pressure off the general fund. Unit cost analysis is useful in determining proper user fee charges. At the state and local levels, analysts should seek full justification from former or reduced federally funded programs.

A common failure of government agencies is not to aggressively recruit and develop employees, especially professional employees. Specific sums of money should be earmarked for professional development, including education, training, and professional conferences. Care should be taken to document carefully how the professional development improves employees. Politically inappropriate travel must be carefully avoided.

Interagency staff harmony and inter- and intra-agency cooperation can achieve efficiencies. Examiners should determine if agencies' support processes (e.g., budget, personnel, general services) work in harmony and provide consistent management direction and control. This can be done by site visit or by questioning agency personnel.

In this day of rapidly advancing technology, analysts should be sure that each agency is taking advantage of modern technology to improve the quality of government services and achieve greater efficiencies. Examiners should determine if capital purchase or leasing can be used to improve program output and efficiency.

Forecasting

Budgeting is always future-oriented and predicting the future is important in terms of both revenues and expenditures (see chapter 5). Normally, a government has many revenue sources, of which the largest are usually forecasted by a central authority such as the chief state economist or county budget office. The smaller revenue sources tend to concern specific departments and are forecasted by them. Analysts should verify department forecast accuracy by comparing past forecasts and actual money received. In addition, the examiner should verify agency expenditure forecasts by checking past year accounting reports, developing comparative cost data, and checking to avoid improper inventory buildup. For demand responsive programs, analysts should normally use marginal utility analysis; but for one-time projects, analysts should review cost estimates, especially in relationship to construction time assumptions. Careful examination of Program Evaluation and Review Technique (PERT) time and PERT cost can be particularly useful in determining the reasonableness of the expenditure forecast. Care should be taken to review prior year nonrecurring expenditure summaries in order to ensure that CY projects and programs do not improperly extend into the BY. Care should also be taken to identify actual and potential nonplanned cost escalations.

An interesting approach to government forecasting is called "consensus forecasting" by the state of Florida. The legislature's Division of Economic and Demographic Research prepares revenue forecasts, recommends formula budgeting, and prepares expenditure forecast models for approximately 25 percent of the state's programs. In doing this, the unit uses a remarkably large database, extensive computer capability, and complex economic models. Economic data are acquired from major national economic forecasting organizations and are added to the unique data collected from state sources. In addition, data are gathered on state education, criminal justice, and social services. All these combine into a Florida database and are used with an econometric model containing 123 simultaneous equations. The result is a Florida economic forecast which is critical in developing forecasts for state revenue, education expenditures, criminal justice expenditures, and social service expenditures. The data are also used to develop education, criminal justice, and social service formula budgets.

Whenever possible, analysts should seek comparative program data. Often, other public or private agencies are doing something similar to the agency being examined. By contrasting input, process, output, and outcome data, the analyst is in a much better position to judge forecasting accuracy. If another agency in a comparable government is doing the same thing for less money, that fact is helpful.

A common mistake made by examiners is not to demand and receive an accurate analysis of future year operating expenditure implications of large capital and nonrecurring cost projects. Building a new facility is one consideration, but maintaining it properly is yet another matter. Budget examiners should seek such analyses, and fiscal implications should be carefully explained to the political decision makers.

Politically Sensitive Subjects

Both political and professional officials discover that there are sensitive management practices in which error can lead to serious political or managerial consequences. Examiners should identify those areas, check on the frequency of errors in those areas, and be sure that existing control procedures are adequate. Budget analysts should identify any occurrences of politically or managerially embarrassing or illegal actions, especially in such sensitive areas as travel (with special stress on out-of-state travel), energy use, authorized positions, capital outlays, consulting, and mainframe computers. An analysis of such matters should isolate inadequate control procedures and determine if existing or planned control procedures create a counterproductive management hardship on line officials.

Two expense items normally should be zero based and fully documented. Temporary employment and consulting are not meant to be a regular personnel expense, but that can occur. Careful attention should be paid to ensure that this line-item category is not being abused. Data processing is not only an expensive line-item category, but one which should be watched carefully. Early decisions tend to commit management to certain future computer hardware and software decisions. However, given the extreme rate of technological advancement, care must be taken to ensure that proper decisions are being made and reviewed each year.

Detailed Budget Examination

Detailed budget examination involves looking carefully at (1) salaries, benefits, and temporary employee expenses, (2) price level increases for expenditures, and (3) operating capital outlays and trust fund schedules. Normally, across-the-board cost-of-living expenses are calculated separately by the central budget office. Agencies are commonly asked to continue CY annual rates for authorized positions, modified for any appropriate productivity improvements. Budget analysts normally use agency information to calculate lapsed salaries rather than use an overall lapse factor. Care should be taken to examine vacancy rates as well as salary funds that have been transferred or have reverted to other line categories. Commonly, new positions are assumed to be at minimum current pay rates, with all necessary benefits included; benefits are calculated as percentages of the salary base. Examiners should confirm the rates and calculations. Budget analysts may find matrix algebra to be extremely useful in making these adjustments.

In calculating current program expenses, examiners normally start with CY levels and adjust them for program reductions and modifications. Care should be taken not to drop the input to levels below which desired output becomes impossible. Deductions from current estimated expenditures should include nonrecurring and nonessential items, nonessential inventory buildups, and expenses for deleted or lapsed current positions. In normal years, inflation increases are allowed at the wholesale price index level, but these may not be at a flat percentage. If one or more categories dominate the expenses, price increases for those categories should be treated separately. If unusual price changes occur in significant items (e.g., insurance, telephone, travel), they should be calculated separately. Data processing expenses also must be carefully reviewed. Budget analysts should balance user unit costs against the data center's information. Examiners should use a general services schedule for rental space and the current market rate for private space. Rates can be unnecessarily high due to choice location or unnecessary co-location requests.

Budget analysts should be sure that each equipment item is justified. State or local contract prices should be used and additional equipment requests should be fully documented and verified. Equipment replacement should be done by means of standard rules unless specifically requested with full documentation. Examiners should be sure that inventory levels and practices are justified. Often governments use general and specific guidelines for commonly purchased items. These guidelines should be used in judging equipment requests.

Special attention should be given to grant and trust programs. Normally, policy makers prefer not to replace federal cuts with general revenue funds unless the basic intent of a necessary program is seriously jeopardized. State and local governments prefer funding "in kind" rather than "cash matching." Budget analysts should ensure that jointly funded programs maximize federal and trust (e.g., user fee) receipts as well as leave justifiable ending balances. All calculations which produce beginning and ending balances, including trust fund investments, should be carefully examined. Normally, small working capital amounts are allowed to cover cash flow requirements.

Automation

The budget preparation process can be automated, and various activities in that process are commonly automated. For example, revenue forecasting and preparation of budget allocation formulas are often automated. The former activity often involves a great deal of data, and the latter involves not only large data sets, but also "what if" types of analysis using those data sets. Some jurisdictions use computers to "roll up" the data from the lowest units to higher levels of aggregation. A few jurisdictions have a comprehensive automated budget preparation process. Normally, the weakest aspect of the system relates, not to computers, but to failure to acquire good performance (output or outcome) measures.

Regardless of the scope of automation, the keys to understanding automation are to use systems theory and to think backwards from the products of the automated system. A simple input-process-output system model is central to automation. One defines the products and then designs the process and inputs to get the desired outputs (products). In budget preparation, the most important output can be the appropriation act. However, it can be the revenue estimate report. Hardware (i.e., the computer and related equipment) and software (i.e., the instructions to the computer on how to manipulate the data) should be defined in relationship to the desired output reports. The input reports are the means to get the necessary data into the computer.

Automation can mean that "data crunching," consideration of "what if" possibilities, preparation of complex multiple consistent crosswalks, and even performance of various types of analysis can be done more accurately and faster with a computer. It permits much more sophisticated analysis and higher-quality budgeting. Automation also means a new set of complexities, including frustration when massive data sets are "lost" and computer breakdowns occur. Increasingly, automation will be more common as hardware becomes less expensive and more useful software is developed.

The microcomputer has particular relevance to the budget process and the electronic spreadsheet is especially significant software. Given the many tables employed in budgeting, commonly used tools are the multiple-column and row light-green paper, plus the calculator. The electronic spreadsheet is the modern replacement for those tools. The grandfather of the electronic spreadsheet is the VisiCalc® program which was conceived in 1978 by Daniel Bricklin and Robert Frankston. The VisiCalc program produces spreadsheets of 63 columns or more by 254 rows. However, the advantages go much beyond a very big sheet of data. The sheet is organized with A, B, C labels for columns and numbers for rows. Thus, one can

VisiCalc is a registered trademark of VisiCorp.

identify each cell of this very large matrix (e.g., A24, G2, M150, AA50). One of the strengths of the electronic version is that the user can use a formula to derive the answer for each cell and the formula can be stated with other cells as variables in the formula. Thus, a cell's value can be calculated by entering 7 + 13 or entering "add cell B24 (with a value of 7) to cell G177 (with a 13 value in it)." This permits use of complex interrelations of data which we commonly need for analysis and accounting. Analytical problems, such as purchasing decisions, often use sets of data arrayed by columns and rows. Thus, they are well suited for the electronic spreadsheet. Some analytical tools, such as the crosswalk, are ideally suited.

The major frustration with light-green ledger paper is the reality that mistakes are made, new ideas require major changes, and "what-if" analyses are often needed. The results are many erasures and versions of the first spreadsheet. The power of the electronic spreadsheet is the ease of making modifications. Rows and columns can be added even in the middle of the spreadsheet. Any data changes are automatically recalculated, saving time and eliminating mistakes. Thus, errors can be changed quickly and new ideas can be added easily. The most dramatic strength is that "what-if" analysis becomes dramatically easier. Instead of preparing new sheets and running the calculator on all the new numbers, the user merely finds the cells that contain the key variables, and makes the changes. Automatically and within seconds, all the numbers are recalculated. Some electronic spreadsheets, such as Lotus 1-2-3, can even take a set of cells and convert them into graph, pie, and bar charts.

PROCESS ANALYSIS

Focus

The purpose of **process analysis,** in the context of public budgeting, is to help the line managers and the budget analyst understand the existing bureaucratic process between organization input and output. It is not an attempt to define the optimal process which will most effectively use available resources, although a by-product might be that determination. It does seek to determine if the existing process is an effective use of resources and to identify idle or poorly used resources.

This subtle stress in process analysis for public budgeting can be overlooked. When examining a budget, the analyst is seeking insight that will help higher-level decision makers and foster improved management within the organization. The budget analyst must always appreciate that a staff function is being performed and that the line-unit supervisor is responsible for managing his or her unit. The analyst is only an aid to the manager *and* other higher level managers and policy makers in the government. Thus, process analysis in the context of budget examination is not striving to necessarily find the optimal process as that task is really the responsibility of the line manager. Instead, process analysis here is used only to help others make reasonable judgments on the effectiveness of the existing process and the quality of management in that unit.

Steps

The steps in process analysis are as follows:

1. define programs within the organizational divisions of the government;
2. define the minimum level of service for each program; and
3. develop a flow chart for the process of each program.

Defining programs and minimum levels of service are difficult professional challenges. In order to foster greater managerial accountability, programs normally should be defined within specific lowest-level organizational units in a government. The defined programs should be the major sets of activities in an organizational unit which produces specific projects and services. If programs cut across organizational units, then both managerial and fiscal accountability are much more difficult to establish and maintain. A major problem in defining sets that are identified as programs and sometimes forcing such "fits" is that it may discourage needed managerial cooperation. Nevertheless, defining programs is very useful and managerially helpful for most administrative situations.

The problem of defining a program's "minimum level of service" is often a difficult challenge. "Minimum level of service," as notably used in ZBB, is the lowest amount of resources needed to conduct the program as a viable administrative undertaking. The professional challenge for the budget analyst is that line managers nearly always consider their present level minimum and they tend to refuse to consider the possibility of lesser amounts than what they are currently using. The best approach to take is to define with the manager the existing inputs and outputs. Then, the analyst starts posing "what if five percent less, 10 percent, and so on" situations to seek clarification of what would happen to the outputs. Next, the analyst should attempt to determine the impact of those smaller outputs upon the program outcomes. This may become a problem because some managers have difficulty conceptualizing their program and program outcomes. Normally, some reasonable minimum level of service becomes apparent after some discussions.

Flow charting the process of each program involves identifying, first, what activities take place in the unit, and secondly, who does what aspect of each activity. The latter should include an estimate of the percentage of time in a work week devoted to each activity by each person or class of employees in the unit. Flow charting gets the line manager away from broad superlatives about the virtues of programs and focuses on exactly what the unit does. The first document presents the unit's activities; normally, this is best defined by stating the trigger actions within the unit (e.g., a phone call from a client) and charting what follows until the unit produces a specific service or product. The chart, which can be done in several ways, should show the relationship of the steps to each other. The chart shows the activities done on a day-in and day-out basis. (See Exhibits 6-3 and 6-4.) The second document identifies who does what activity, the payload and position descrip-

EXHIBIT 6-3   Daily Activities

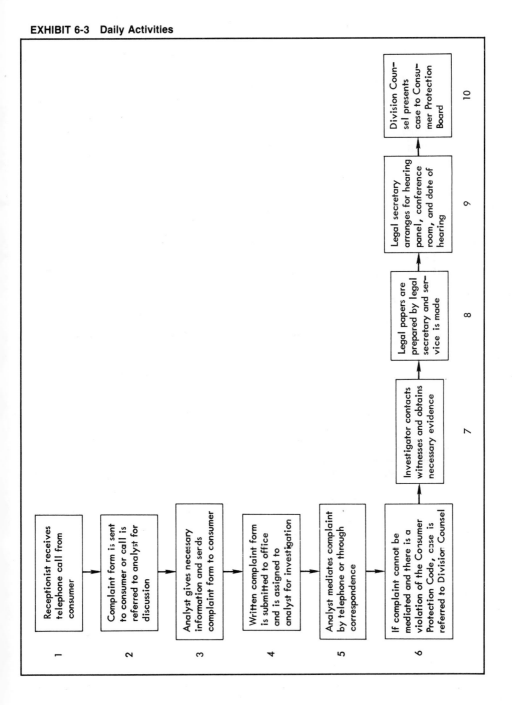

1. Receptionist receives telephone call from consumer

2. Complaint form is sent to consumer or call is referred to analyst for discussion

3. Analyst gives necessary information and sends complaint form to consumer

4. Written complaint form is submitted to office and is assigned to analyst for investigation

5. Analyst mediates complaint by telephone or through correspondence

6. If complaint cannot be mediated and there is a violation of the Consumer Protection Code, case is referred to Division Counsel

7. Investigator contacts witnesses and obtains necessary evidence

8. Legal papers are prepared by legal secretary and service is made

9. Legal secretary arranges for hearing panel, conference room, and date of hearing

10. Division Counsel presents case to Consumer Protection Board

tion of each person, and the percent of time on each activity (see Exhibits 6-5 and 6-6.)

The limitations of process analysis for the budget analyst are primarily those of time and organization size. The budget calendar forces the budget analyst to work within a finite time frame. Thus, normally the necessary time is not available to do this time-consuming analysis. Priority of the analyst's time is decided by the current politically hot or managerially sensitive units. Depending on the nature of the political or managerial concerns and the budget offices' appropriate role, those factors will determine which programs should or should not be analyzed by the budget analyst.

Organizational size is a limitation because the technique is most effective with small units (less than 20 persons). For larger organizations, techniques such as regression analysis of specific inputs and outputs are effective. For example, in a large decentralized urban library system, a regression analysis (see page 153-154) was used which related input (i.e., full-time positions used in circulation) to output (i.e., books circulated by specific branch libraries). A scatter diagram was used and a linear regression line was drawn. The line represented the system's productivity

EXHIBIT 6-4   Daily Veteran's Office Activities

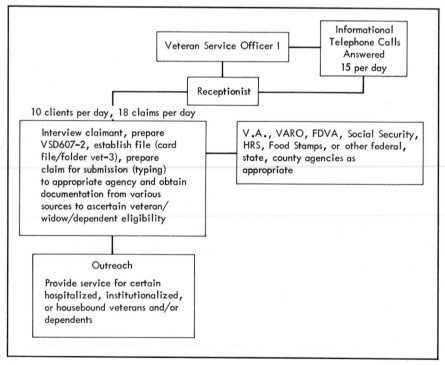

EXHIBIT 6-5   Staff Analysis

Section			
Supervision		1	Assistant Director
		1	Secretary 1
	Total	2	
North Network:		4	Family Counselor I
		2	Family Counselor II
		1	Family Counselor III
		1	Network Supervisor
		1	Secretary - I
Central Network		3	Family Counselor I
		2	Family Counselor II
		1	Family Counselor III
		1	Network Supervisor
		1	Secretary - I
South Network		3	Family Counselor I
		1	Family Counselor II
		1	Family Counselor III
		1	Network Supervisor
		1	Secretary - I
	Total	24	+ 1 psychologist = 25 employees
Child Care Program:		1	Child Development Specialist I
		4	Child Development Specialist II
		1	Program Supervisor (C.D.S. III)
		1	Secretary - I
	Total	7	
Directed Job Search:		1	Special Projects Coordinator
		1	Secretary - I
	Total	2	SECTION TOTAL: 36

Average client service per direct-service employee = 643 clients which provides only 2.7 hours per client per employee, based on a (1) one-time service frequency. Average client is seen eight (8) sessions (8 hours of direct services, plus required indirect services).

Source: Broward County, Florida, 1983.

for the book circulation program. Deviations identified successful and unsuccessful ''program management'' and permitted longitudinal and comparative data analyses. The process-analysis tool should be used, in connection with the regression analysis, to determine the most and least successful units.

EXHIBIT 6-6 Performance Time Analysis

This analysis reflects performance on a monthly basis. The "available" hours are calculated by multiplying 37.5 × 4 which equals 150 available working hours.

STAFF: Family Counselor II - 5 employees.

Screening:	Attendance is required because of therapeutic knowl-edge	
	Average screening time is 2 hours per week	
	Average time per month:	8 hours
Counseling Services:	Individual and family counseling with a caseload of 38 cases	
	Average time required per session:	1 hour
	Average time estimated per month	80 hours
	(some clients require additional time if family is in critical state or has several members)	
	Average time estimated per month in recording/case documentation (3 hours per week): (entry in case file per session is required	12
Group Counseling:	These are not youth groups as facilitated by Family Counselor I; these groups are multi-problem family groups whose children are acting out with evidenced delinquency.	
	Average number of groups per quarter is 4	
	Average number of hours estimated per month:	32 hours
	Average recording time per month:	1 hour
Special Community Assignments:	Respond to communities who need assistance in developing youth programs and preventing local juvenile crime. Communities request speakers and parent/community groups request a one-time parenting skills or problem solving workshop.	
	Average number of engagements, workshops, meetings attended per month is at 3 hours per session.	2
	Average number of hours per month	6 hours
Support Services:	Attend case staffings at school, attend-in house staffings (attendance required).	
	Participate in case consultations with psychologist. (Average staffing attended = 4 per month; average length of staffing is 2 hours)	12 hours

Crisis Counseling:	Provide immediate intervention to walk-in clients.	
	Average walk-ins for crisis counseling is 15 clients per month.	
	Average counseling session in crisis counseling is 2 hours	30 hours
	Total # of workload hours required vs.	181 hours
	Total # of work hours available	150 hours

This difference in hours required and hours available has made it necessary for us to minimize assistance to community groups. It has further reduced the quality in case documentation and has required some clients to be placed on every-other-week and sometimes monthly service cycle. Our involvement in multi-problem family groups has already been reduced. This continued cutback will result in less effective results of diverting youth from the juvenile justice system.

Source: Broward County, Florida, 1983

The limitations of time and organization size are largely mitigated by a patient budget office. The constraint of a fiscal budget year is limiting for that period, but over time, the entire government can be carefully examined using process analysis. Any information acquired but not used in one set of budget decisions can be used in subsequent budget decisions. Even the limitation of organizational size can be overcome. A regression analysis can be used to isolate the best and the worst. With that insight, process analysis can be targeted and, thus, used more effectively. If in a large organization, the necessary data is not available to do the desired regression analysis, a patient budget office will seek to develop the necessary data and then to use it.

Advantages

The advantages of process analysis are that it provides a useful snapshot in time which (1) helps us to understand the inner workings of an organization, (2) identifies ineffective use of resources, and (3) leads to management inprovements. The snapshot in time is analytically important because it permits both longitudinal and comparative analyses. Line managers are often not trained in public administration. Thus, process analysis provides them and the budget analyst with a significantly heightened awareness of the activities that take place in a program and the role of each employee in those activities. Often, prior to that analysis, the line manager was not even aware of those facts and their implications on his or her role as a manager. Managers are often surprised by what they find. This analysis particularly and immediately identifies weak and strong programs. Weak managers cannot provide necessary information; whereas strong managers normally overwhelm the analyst with relevant information. Process analysis also helps mediocre programs as it permits their managers to understand the internal processes more logically.

Process analysis helps identify ineffective use of resources (inputs). For example, a government's youth services activity in a large urban county had been trimmed back over the years, and its administrative management section with higher priced positions was quite large. A process analysis showed that the organization was top heavy with too many leaders and not enough workers. In another program in that same county a process analysis identified activities that were being done by regular personnel but which could be done just as effectively by unpaid volunteers.

Process analysis significantly contributes to management improvement because it:

1. helps line managers understand management and the need to justify their resource requests;
2. fosters a sensitivity to the importance of and the meaning of productivity;
3. helps identify weak management;
4. helps identify managers who need management training;
5. identifies managers who have taken their organization away from policy determined objectives; and
6. trains managers in techniques which can help them manage their own programs.

Line managers, are not normally educated in public administration, and have no exposure to public management except for what they experience or deduce from their own values and attitudes. Budgets and the need to justify them are a new side of life as are other day-to-day management activities. In smaller governments, central budget offices may have prepared budgets for unit managers without their involvement. Process analysis treats unit managers, not as children on an allowance, but rather, as adults who must justify their resource requests and manage those resources correctly once they are received.

Process analysis coupled with budget examination fosters a unit management sensitivity for the meaning and importance of productivity. Managers are asked to think in terms of input and output relationships. That type of thinking may not be present in a line manager, but is required by process analysis. It must be learned by the managers, or process analysis cannot be done intelligently.

Weak managers are frustrated by process analysis because they cannot justify or even explain what they do with their resources. Budget analysts must normally spend a great deal more time working with weak managers. In one situation in a local government, a unit withdrew its $1.5 million request for added resources when upper levels of management in the division realized that the program manager could not explain how the additional monies would improve the program. A useful by-product is that specific and general managerial training needs become more apparent with process analysis. If a manager has difficulty understanding "input," "output," and how to flow chart activities, then specific education or training should be provided for that person. If managers cannot understand the essential concepts, then wherever possible they should be counselled in their career development and encouraged to move into areas more suited for their talents.

Another management plus of process analysis coupled with budget examination is the identification of organizational units that have deviated from their intended function. For example, a local government provided a mobile social service van on location in poor neighborhoods. On examination of the unit's process, the real services provided by two professional social workers were voter registration and a check of pulse rates. Obviously, the unit had abandoned its stated purpose, and professional social workers were being misused. Providing voter registration service is not inappropriate, but costs for such services should be correctly reflected in the voter registration section of the budget or policy makers are being misled.

The final above cited management improvement is training line managers on useful managerial and analytical techniques. Line managers are exposed to and learn to appreciate the techniques. For example, the urban library's management was impressed with the earlier cited use of regression analysis in the library circulation activity. They are now using the technique in other library programs.

Context Is Important

The previous discussion may leave the false impression that successful process analysis application is merely a central budget office decision. Top-level management should strongly support the whole concept and demand line management cooperation. Organizational resistance is difficult to overcome without that type of support. In a period of tight or declining budgets, one can often find more serious and useful cooperation and desire, especially from higher-level officials.

Another possible misunderstanding is that there is some cookbook set of approaches which can be applied uniformly from jurisdiction to jurisdiction. Although this chapter suggests what can be done, the actual doing must be tailored to the unique situation of each jurisdiction. A creative approach to professionalism is needed to adapt the concepts and techniques to new situations. Normally, the biggest practical problem inhibiting process analysis is a lack of adequate data. A proactive solution for a central budget office is to support budget requests for data collection as long as the data collected can also be useful for budget purposes.

Needed Interpersonnel Skills

A working assumption of a budget analyst should be that the analyst is part of a team attempting to provide the desired levels of service at the lowest cost. To the extent possible, the analyst strives to have the line managers use the same assumption. For this mind setting process to be most effective, top level officials must articulate this perspective and promote that attitude with their policies, decisions, and actions. The analyst should extend the mind set so that line managers become a part of the "we" and "team."

To properly work as a "team player," the analyst should strive to appreciate and understand the manager's perspective. The difficult character of the job and the commitment to public service must be emotionally as well as intellectually understood. Analysts should strive to appreciate how the manager feels when employees must be cut and to understand the difficult challenge of supervising employees who continue to work for long periods after they have received termination notices. Budget analysts must attempt to make the line manager's tasks easier whenever possible.

A pro-active posture is best. The analyst and line manager should recognize that they can positively contribute to better policy-making and better management of the organization. They should not be merely passive or reactive. In fact, one of the distinctive characteristics of most successful top level line managers is being pro-active especially in the budget process. Reactive managers tend to be the weak managers.

Another useful working assumption is that every organization, regardless of size, can have its funds cut to some extent without loss of service. The challenge for the budget analyst is to discover "how": The challenge for the line manager is to take the existing resources and maximize output levels. Thus, tension can and does exist between the two organizational actors, but it can be constructive. The analyst should carefully decide how to approach dealing with specific line managers in order to create the necessary mind set and get the needed information. The line manager should decide how to respond to those data requests so that effective program management can be achieved at minimum overall commitments of the line personnel.

Honesty

Budget analysts must earn their reputation for being honest and cooperative with line managers. Being doctrinaire and having a know-it-all personality can poison a useful professional relationship. Constructive cooperation is essential. Analysts must appreciate that the line manager's budget is much like their own paycheck. Managers are sensitive to any changes affecting their unit's budget. Analysts must strive to achieve a trust relationship in which both parties appreciate the other's perspective. Such relationships take time to develop, thus a wise office policy is to have budget analysts assigned to the same units for at least two years.

The following simple practices can be very useful in establishing professional line manager/analyst relationships:

1. Phone calls and other messages should be returned promptly.
2. When possible, the analyst should strive to attend line manager's internal group meetings as well as to read their reports and studies.
3. Normally, an analyst knows more about top-level developments than does the line manager. A simple sharing of information can thus be quite useful to the manager and help in establishing the desired rapport.
4. An analyst should often go the extra step of initiating the news-sharing rather than waiting for specific inquiries.
5. Nothing should be printed in the budget document without the line manager's knowledge. Agreement isn't always possible, but the manager should not feel that the analyst is acting unilaterally.
6. If there are any dollar or word changes, the line manager should be notified. Again, surprises should be avoided.
7. If the budget analyst does make a mistake, such mistakes should be freely, quickly, and openly acknowledged. To do otherwise, can deepen any feelings of distrust and unfortunately contribute to a conspiracy explanation of events.

Obviously, there can and should be exceptions to these "proverbs." How-ever, if the spirit of them is followed the working relationship between the analyst and the line manager should be good.

Cooptation

One concern in budget offices is that the relationship can become so strong between the analyst and the line manager that cooptation takes place. Analysts must be able to scrutinize but not be overly tolerant of managerial mistakes. Cooptation problems can be avoided if analysts are given new division assignments every two to three years. In fact, in order to avoid boredom better analysts will seek rotations. One interesting phenomenon is the subtle and sometimes not-so-subtle different ways that line managers treat their ex-budget analysts once the relationship has changed.

PROGRAM EVALUATION

Program evaluation focuses upon program outcomes (the impacts of government programs on individuals and society) and essentially deals with the question of pro-gram effectiveness. As a way to conduct inquiries, it is very much influenced by logical positivism or what is commonly called the scientific method. Most evaluators believe that evaluation is first and foremost an application of rigorous scientific procedure to reach reliable and valid conclusions on the impact of pro-grams. Program outputs are considered independent variables, and program out-comes are considered dependent variables. For example, to evaluate a new vaccine, one could use an experimental design which calls for measurements to be taken be-fore and after the vaccine is used. Two groups would be part of the experimental design, but only one would get the vaccine. The research design is graphically ex-plained as follows:

experimental group $\qquad$ $0_1 \times 0_2$
control group $\qquad$ $0_1 \quad 0_2$

Conclusions on the causal effectiveness of the vaccine would be made by comparing first the "before" and "after" observations and then the difference be-tween the observations of the experimental and control groups. There should be sig-nificantly less disease in the vaccine group. One of the problems with such a re-search design is that withholding treatment from the control group is ethically wrong since the patients in the control group are not informed that they have re-ceived a placebo rather than the vaccine; but without a control group the evaluators cannot be certain of their conclusion. The "solution" to evaluative problems when better research designs cannot be used is to apply quasi-experimental designs. They do not allow one to reach definitive conclusions on program effectiveness, but they are better than no design at all.

The typical evaluation question is: "To what extent is the program succeeding in reaching its goals?" The steps in evaluation consist of the following:

1. find out the program's goals;
2. translate the goals into measurable indicators of goal achievement (desired outcomes);
3. collect the data on the indicators for those who participate in the program and control group; and
4. compare the data on the experimental and control groups with the desired program outcomes.

Commonly, identifying "measurable indicators of goal achievement" is very difficult and such efforts result in anything but the desired characteristics of clarity, specificity, measurability, and behaviorally oriented data, leaving the evaluator in no position to determine if the desired program outcomes were accomplished. The challenge for evaluators is to counter that natural tendency. They can do that by investigating the program, specifying reasonable goals, and seeking confirmation. Sometimes, they use elaborate, consensus-building exercises. Despite the difficulty, most approaches to program evaluation require the evaluator to develop some definition of program goals.

The next step is developing the measures, a process which is sometimes called instrumentation. The process is "modeled" by identifying attributes and describing the program outputs and outcomes as well as interim steps between them. The Urban Institute publication *How Effective Are Your Community Services* provides a detailed list of useful attributes and measures of government services. Measures selected can deal with attitudes, work behavior, services, turnover, budgets, changes in the environment, and so on. Measures can focus on people and deal with values, attitudes, knowledge, and skills. They can focus on institutions and deal with responsiveness. Normally, evaluators attempt to conceptualize the entire chain of cause and effect from acquisition of dollars to fund the program to ultimate program outcomes. In addition, possible intervening variables are isolated. The ultimate purpose is to be able to assert as definitive a conclusion as possible about the program's effectiveness.

AUDITING

Purpose of Auditing

Auditing is a vital activity. Its most important function is to validate the correct operation of the accounting system. This includes verifying the accuracy of inventories and existing equipment; determining that proper legal authority exists to perform current government activities; checking the adequacy of internal control practices and procedures; uncovering fraud; and isolating waste and mismanagement. Political accountability and democracy become largely meaningless unless the general public and the political leadership have a reasonably effective means to validate the correct operation of the accounting system and to establish that democratically established policy is being followed. A 1983 news story about a rash of mysterious fires in Nigeria illustrates the central importance of auditing. The fires not only destroyed several buildings, including a 37-story building as distinctive to the Logos skyline as the twin World Trade Center skyscrapers are to New York's, but also derailed an investigation into government corruption. They occurred in buildings housing departmental accounting records, and they seem to have been set to cover up embezzlement, provoking violent antigovernment protests by university students.[2] Such acts of arson are not limited to places outside the United States.

Beyond being an essential safeguard of government accountability, auditing is also important in establishing credibility and in improving government management. It provides independent judgments of the manner in which public officials carry out their responsibilities as well as of the credibility and lawfulness of their financial statements. This is particularly important to investors when they are deciding to buy a government's notes and bonds. Auditing improves efficiency and economy by examining and reporting on government procedures, operations, and management policies. Auditing helps decision makers improve effectiveness by evaluating whether a program was carried forward as planned, met its program objectives, and produced desirable changes.

Two common varieties of audit are the pre- and post-audits. Pre-audits are done before obligations are made. In many states, the elected auditor performs essentially pre-audit functions. Pre-audits focus upon determining legality and examining vouchers. The depth and detail of a pre-audit vary, but the importance of independence is always present. The disadvantages associated with pre-audits are that they:

1. reduce the level of responsibility;
2. lead to red tape;
3. foster interagency friction; and
4. are costly.

The post-audit is the more common form of auditing. It also should be done by an independent group. It can focus upon verifying documents, checking transactions and procedures, or examining administrative effectiveness and efficiency. Post-auditing is not a closing of accounts. However, sometimes accounts cannot be closed without an audit.

Audits can be conducted within an agency. If that is done, the audit should be independent and focus upon evaluating legality of actions and effectiveness of administrative controls. Such audits commonly:

1. review compliance with and appraise performance under policies, plans, and procedures established by management for carrying out its responsibilities;
2. examine financial transactions;
3. test the reliability and usefulness of accounting and other financial and program data produced in the agency;

4. review the effectiveness with which the agency's resources are utilized; and
5. examine the effectiveness of safeguards provided to prevent or minimize waste or loss of agency assets.

Internal versus External Audits

Internal audits can be distinguished from internal inspections. The latter are designed to confirm that policy, procedures, and reporting are being carried out correctly. They are addressed to employees who are responsible for carrying out particular operations such as meat inspection, food stamp applicant screening, and unemployment insurance interviews. Internal auditing addresses broader concerns of legality, effectiveness, and efficiency.

External audits are similar to internal audits, but they are done by independent agencies. A typical external audit examines accounts, checks on the accuracy of recorded transactions and inventories, does on-site review of stocks, verifies physical existence of equipment, and reviews operating procedures and regulations. The Congressional audit agency for the U.S. federal government is the General Accounting Office (GAO). This agency reports directly and is responsible to the Congress. By law, an agency must respond to GAO reports, forcing it to comment on the problems raised by GAO and encouraging a statement of how the agency will resolve the problems. GAO investigates fraud, waste, and mismanagement. Its audits often focus upon delegation of responsiblity, policy direction (including program evaluation), budget and accounting practices, and the adequacy of internal controls, including internal auditing. Legislative audits are commonly post-audits; thus the group appropriating the money often makes the final check on its expenditures.

Auditing Principles

Governmental auditing principles have been established by the American Institute of Certified Public Accountants (AICPA), a nonprofit professional association, and the U.S. General Accounting Office (GAO). In addition, the National Council of Governmental Accounting (NCGA) has issued standards drawn from the AICPA auditing standards. The publications *Audits of State and Local Governmental Units* by AICPA and *Standards for Audit of Governmental Organizations, Programs, Activites and Functions* contain the accepted auditing standards. Exhibit 6-7 gives the GAO audit standards which serve to guide both accountants and auditors. Stress is placed on assuring legal compliance and complete disclosure of government financial position and operations. Legal provisions take priority over accounting principles, and accounting systems are to provide budgetary operational control. The auditing standards adopt the fund accounting concepts; value fixed assets at their original cost; do not use depreciation in fund accounts; adopt the modified accrual method for the major funds and for other funds such as enterprise and trust; call for revenues to be classified by fund and source and expenditures to be classified by fund, function, organizational unit, character, and object class; assert that common terminology and classifications should be used; and specify that periodic and annual comprehensive financial reports be prepared, with the latter showing all government funds and financial operations.

Auditing procedures are spelled out in the AICPA and GAO publications so that specific questions are uniformly asked and the role of the auditor is clearly defined. The two keys to understanding auditing are professionalism and documentation. The guide stresses the importance of an independent, highly educated audit staff which systematically and carefully reviews the financial and related managerial facts in the audited unit. Audit workpapers are critical. For example, they must show the following:

1. that the audit staff obtained an understanding of the audited entity before determining specific audit tests and procedures;
2. that the audit staff followed up on findings;
3. that the following were considered:
   a. internal control evaluation results,
   b. completion and accomplishment of audit objectives,
   c. consideration of matters related to audit objectives,
   d. conformance with standards;
4. that the audit program was followed;
5. that the workpapers show sufficient data and support findings and conclusions; and
6. that the auditor's time was budgeted and recorded.

EXHIBIT 6-7   GAO Audit Guide Outline

Questions on the General Standards

I. Audit Scope
   A. Statutory Provisions
   B. Fulfillment of Responsibilities
   C. Audit Planning
II. Staff Qualifications
   A. Education
   B. Professional Achievements
   C. Training Program
   D. Staff Appraisal System
   E. Use of Consultants
III. Independence
   A. Head of Audit Organization
   B. Organizational Independence
   C. Audit Freedom
   D. Availability of Audit Reports
   E. Conflicts of Interest
   F. Selection of External Auditors

IV. Due Professional Care
    A. Organization and Responsibility
    B. Policies
    C. Planning System
    D. Quality Control System

Questions on the Examination and Evaluation Standards

  I. Audit Planning
    A. Preliminary Planning
    B. Audit Program
  II. Staff Supervision
    A. Clearly Defined Responsibilities
    B. Audit Program
  III. Compliance with Statutory and Regulatory Requirements
  IV. Evidence and Auditing Procedures
  V. Evaluation of Internal Control
  VI. Financial and Compliance Audits—General
  VII. Audits of Economy and Efficiency Matters
VIII. Audits of Program Results
  IX. Work Papers
  X. Exit Conference

Questions on the Reporting Standards

  I. Form and Distribution
    A. Form
    B. Distribution
  II. Timelines
  III. Content
    A. Clarity and Conciseness
    B. Objectivity and Constructive Tone
    C. Scope
    D. Adequacy of Support and Persuasiveness
    E. Recommendations
  IV. Financial Reports

The workpapers serve as the basis for the audit findings and recommendations. In well-prepared workpapers the above and other considerations are reflected so that any problems are completely documented. Focus is placed upon determining the adequacy of internal control, compliance with statutory and regulatory requirements, adequacy of accounting system, existence of economy and efficient conduct, and program effectiveness. An audit includes not only a report of findings and recommendations but also an exit conference in which auditors explain their conclusions.

REVIEW QUESTIONS

1. Explain how one goes about developing a useful list of major program issues and then selects from that list. Explain the usefulness of an issue assessment and what should be considered in such an assessment.
2. What factors influence an analysis? Why is the chief executive particularly significant? What type of chief executive support is important?
3. Explain some of the common mistakes made in the analysis and presentation of analytical results.
4. What is the rationale behind ethical codes in general and the one described in this chapter in particular?
5. How does a budget examiner isolate services performed? Why is this important? What key program input, process, and outputs should be especially examined? How does a budget examiner identify program emphasis and change?
6. From a budget examiner's perspective, how does one attempt to achieve responsiveness to duly elected political leaders? What concerns are commonly significant?
7. What does one examine in order to help establish economy and efficiency in government?
8. Explain how a budget analyst should use forecasts in his or her budget examination.
9. What types of queries are common in a detailed budget examination?
10. How does one go about automating a budget examination process?
11. Explain how to do process analysis. Why are context, interpersonnel skills, and honesty important in process analysis?
12. What is the focus of program evaluation and how does research design relate to that concern? What challenges do program evaluators face?
13. What is accomplished in auditing? What are the types of audits?
14. Explain the relationship between accounting and auditing. Explain auditing procedures, especially their purpose.

REFERENCES

FOSS, THOMAS C. and THOMAS D. SUTTBERRY (eds.). *State Budgeting in Florida: A Handbook for Budget Analysts*. Florida State University, Public Managers Training and Advisory Service, 1983.

GOODNOW, FRANK J. "The Limits of Budgetary Control," in *Proceedings of the American Political Science Association*. Baltimore, 1983.

LINDBLOM, CHARLES E. *The Policy Making Process,* 2nd ed. Englewood Cliffs, N.J.: Prentice Hall, 1980.

LYNCH, THOMAS D. AND SHERRY A. "Practical Tools For Budget Examination." Paper for Southeastern Regional Conference of the American Society for Public Administration. Tallahassee, Florida. October, 1983.

McCAFFERY, JERRY. "MBO and the Federal Budgetary Process," *Public Administration Review,* 36, 1 (January/February 1976), 33–39.

MILLER, ERNEST G. "Implementing PPBS: Problems and Prospects," *Public Administration Review,* 23, 5 (September/October 1969).

MOAK, LENNOX L. and KATHRYN W. KILLIAN. *Operating Budget Manual.* Chicago: Municipal Finance Officers Association, 1963.

ROUSMANIERE, PETER F. (ed.). *Local Government Auditing.* New York: Council on Municipal Performance, 1979.

SCHWARTZ, ELI. "The Cost of Capital and Investment Criteria in the Public Sector," *Journal of Finance,* 25 (March 1970), 135–42.

SCOTT, CLAUDIA DEVITA. *Forecasting Local Government Spending.* Washington, D.C.: Urban Institute, 1972.

SPENCER, BRUCE P. "Technical Issues in Allocation Formula Design," *Public Administration Review,* 42, 6 (November/December 1982), 524–529.

THAI, KHI V. "Government Financial Reporting and Auditing," in Jack Rabin and Thomas D. Lynch (eds.), *Handbook on Public Budgeting and Financial Management.* New York: Marcel Dekker, 1983.

WACHS, MARTIN. "Ethical Dilemmas in Forecasting for Public Policy," *Public Administration Review,* 42, 6 (November/December 1982), 562–567.

WEISS, CAROL H. *Evaluation Research.* New York: Prentice-Hall, 1972.

WILDAVSKY, AARON. *The Politics of the Budgetary Process.* Boston: Little, Brown, 1964, 1984.

SEVEN
OPERATING BUDGETS
AND ACCOUNTING

The actual execution of the budget and fund management are not as politically and behaviorally oriented as the budget formulation phase, but they are complex and important. Control is the most significant emphasis in budget execution because both the executive and legislative officials demand that the agency follow the established policy set down in the budget. A significant concern is the correct use of idle cash due to the lag between collecting taxes and spending money. Idle cash can be invested, thus earning extra revenue for the government.

This chapter also discusses the fundamentals of government accounting. Stress is placed on explaining those accounting and auditing concepts which are particularly useful to public budgeting. A large section of the chapter is devoted to describing an elementary set of accounting reports which greatly aid the public budget process. Topics covered in this chapter include:

1. how responsibilities can be fixed on key officials and why that designation is helpful in ensuring proper control;
2. budget execution suggestions which reflect an appreciation of common management problems;
3. factors and pitfalls which should be weighed in developing the operating budget;
4. current year adjustment and policy reinterpretations;
5. administrative reservations, allotments, and other budget concepts;
6. expenditure controls;

7. cash internal control;
8. management information systems;
9. significance and procedures for cash management;
10. techniques used to determine proper cash and security positions;
11. basics of investment in marketable securities;
12. the fundamental definitions, beliefs, and norms of government accounting;
13. the fundamental concepts upon which government accounting is developed, including fund accounting, accounting systems design, and internal control systems;
14. financial reports which are particularly useful for public budgeting;
15. computerization of accounting systems;
16. the various types of auditing.

DESIGNING CONTROL

Fixing Responsibility

If control is to be established, careful consideration must go into designing procedures and fixing responsibility. One of the most effective ways to achieve control is to associate a specific program or programs with an office. Only the person holding that office has the power to obligate or control expenditures. Care is taken to avoid having more than one person authorizing obligations for the program; thus errors or fraud can be traced to the responsible person. If responsibility is split, then mistakes are more difficult to correct and legal actions are more difficult to pursue.

The Federal Anti-deficiency Act is designed to focus responsibility. The director of the Office of Management and Budget must apportion appropriated money and other funds into specific amounts available for portions of the fiscal year for particular legally sanctioned projects or activities. The appropriation and funds are apportioned to the agencies. Two officers are given special responsibilities. The agency head is responsible for obligations and the integrity of the budget control system. The agency budget officer is responsible for ensuring the money is not over obligated. The Anti-deficiency Act states that a person knowingly and willfully violating the apportionments can be fined and imprisoned. If the person violates the apportionments without knowledge, then that mistake subjects the person to administrative discipline such as a reprimand, suspension from duty without pay, or removal from office. This Act fixes responsibility quite clearly and it has been an effective device.

Budget Execution

Budget execution depends on top level support. Top management must recognize the importance of proper budget execution and support the budget office. No procedures can work unless top management uses them. If the agency head is willing to overspend the budget or refuses to insist that useful budget forms be followed, then budget execution will be chaotic and lack control. The agency head need not develop the procedures or take an active role, but that agency head must support the budget officer who does develop the procedures. Ideally, the agency head would understand public budgeting sufficiently to demand proper budget execution, but that is not essential to the budget officer who is highly competent. If the agency head supports the budget officer, then budget execution can work effectively. The operating managers in the organization must also support the budget system. They must understand the system in terms of how it affects them and what they must do in support of the system. Ideally, they should understand the larger context of the system and public budgeting in general so that problems and requests can be anticipated. If operating managers do not support the system, then reports and other needs are not timely or are incorrect, thus causing embarrassment and possibly even causing administrative hardships.

Budget execution also depends on a qualified budget staff and a positive attitude toward the concept of public trust. If the budget staff is unaware of the needs of budget execution, then serious management problems are likely to occur. If there are insufficient people on the staff, then they will be overwhelmed, thus forcing them to concentrate on major problems and allowing some routine matters to become major problems. Many employees, especially top management and budget office employees, have a sense of public trust. If they view their job as a means to further private interests, then the possibility of corruption is increased. In addition, employees should be concerned with economy and efficiency. The first concern should be program effectiveness, but economy and efficiency are important if the government is to get maximum use for its tax dollar. Also budget behavior tends to foster a maximum spending approach, and an economy-efficiency ethic is necessary to overcome this natural tendency in budgeting.

A budget execution system should be established which gives direction to agency activities and permits continuous and current reviews to determine if planned objectives are being met. One approach is to link an operating budget with management-by-objectives (MBO). If this is done, each agency unit is asked to develop objectives and progress reports. A crosswalk (explained in chapter 7) is used to link MBO and the operating budget. The operating budget should be keyed to the major line units in the organization so that programs, objectives, and dollar amounts are related to line organizational units.

In order to work smoothly as an organization and to avoid intercommunication difficulties, established procedures are needed to change work plans, schedules, and use of funds. Those procedures should be designed to ensure all factors are considered and all key people in and outside the organization are notified of the decision in a timely manner. Circumstances do arise where procedures must be short-circuited; but if the procedures are designed properly, short-circuiting of procedures will be infrequent. The design of procedures is always a difficult task and care must be taken to make them as simple and effective as possible.

To fix responsibility, formal authorization is given each official who will order the spending of money. The authorization is reviewed to be sure such delegations of authority are permissible under law. The authorization is written carefully so that any later confusion and misunderstandings about the authorization are eliminated. Allotments and operating budgets can be coordinated with the formal authorizations so that officials know how much money they must deal with as well as any other guidance necessarily associated with the dollar amounts.

The accounting and related record systems can be designed to serve prescribed budgetary needs. Accounting is described in more depth in an earlier chapter. Briefly, the budget execution activity is carried out in a larger context than accounting, but the actual recording of transactions should be done so that analysis can compare actual practice with planned practice as defined in the budget. This comparison is essential if the analyst is to know if the policy was carried out.

Another concern in budget execution is to develop a system which monitors considerations such as legality, propriety, and economy. In some governments, the legality and economy issues are monitored by means of pre-audits. The advantages of catching these errors must be considered against the complex, expensive procedures added to government operation. In many grant-in-aid programs, an elaborate procedure to check legality, propriety, economy, equal opportunity, and environmental quality is probably justifiable. If the program is a routine daily operation such as street maintenance, then an elaborate clearance procedure would be foolish. In those circumstances, management judgment would be needed to seek special advice on matters like environmental issues when unusual conditions warrant such advice. The use of special clearance procedures can be institutionalized if the issue becomes common; thus overall time and effort can be saved by checking the matter before obligations are made.

Once the budget execution system has been designed, there are three helpful operational considerations. First, if possible, performance standards—maybe in connection with management-by-objectives—can be established in connection with the operating budget. This would greatly aid in productivity studies and performance budgeting. Second, the nature of the unit's activity often does not lend itself to performance standards; but if it does, advanced planning linking performance estimates with available funding levels is also a useful management method. Third, regardless of the type of government activity, financial obligations can be scheduled in advance to achieve a desired rate of expenditure and avoid a final month deficit.

In developing and using a budget execution system, several factors are weighed carefully. Must the operating budget be prepared under unusual legislative appropriation conditions, or is a revision (e.g., supplemental appropriation) likely? Is a continuing resolution in effect? What size and structure is the organization (e.g., field, regions, area offices)? What type of financial concepts (these are explored later in this chapter) are appropriate to use in the context of the organization? What are the sources of funds and how is that important to the budget execution system? What financial, quantified work unit data, personnel, and manpower measures should be collected, and how? How should personnel ceilings and personnel restrictions be enforced or reflected in the budget execution system? What should be the frequency, level, and coordination means for budget execution reporting? Each of these questions must be considered and answered in the context of the work environment. Each answer can help budget officials better design and operate the budget execution system. Follow-up is essential. Frequent and regular reports are needed to check on work progress, objectives yet unaccomplished, and the status of the various funds (funds are explained in the chapter on accounting). If a problem or question arises from the reports, then prompt, regular, and careful follow-up is needed or the problems and questions tend to be forgotten until they become major problems. An organized system of audits and inspections must be established to verify and supplement the reporting system. If audits and inspections do not exist then fraud, cheating, or merely poor operational practices are more difficult to isolate before they become a widespread problem.

Pitfalls to Avoid

An operating budget can:

1. become unmanageable to top, middle, and first line managers if it is not carefully designed for each level of management;
2. be too complex and detailed for management and thus become cumbersome or useless;
3. be too late or too inaccurate for decision-making purposes;
4. be out of synchronization with the accounting system;
5. be out of touch with the rest of the budget process; and
6. be ignored by top management, thus guaranteeing its ultimate failure.

Some of these major pitfalls were discussed in the previous section, but they should be stressed again. Designing an operating budget requires careful attention. For example, the budget and accounting offices involve various people who are trained differently. Each group views its needs separately and often the operating budget system is developed or becomes nonsynchronized with the accounting system. Care must be taken to avoid this natural tendency.

An operating budget must serve all levels of budgeting. The tendency is to be too demanding of the first line managers and thus make their tasks even more complex. Care can be taken to understand the needs and burdens placed on each level of management. However, the operating budget must provide information in a timely manner, especially to top management, and it should provide essential information for other phases in the budget cycle.

If the operating budget is ignored by top management, then the whole process is likely to be a failure. The key person in the agency is the head, and that person has the power to make exceptions to the operating budget. This power is essential in order to provide managerial flexibility to adapt to unusual circumstances which can and do arise. If that power is abused by frequent needless exceptions, then the discipline of the operating budget breaks down and advantages of the procedures are lost. An equally serious matter is when the agency head does not even create a budget execution system or does not update the system. The agency cannot be protected from bad management when it occurs at the highest levels.

Current Year Adjustments

Regardless of how well a budget is planned, adjustments are made in the current year. Sometimes the adjustments involve transferring funds from one fund or appropriation to another. Sometimes the adjustment involves new appropriations and the legislature must pass supplemental appropriations. The reasons for changes vary from poor management to unanticipated events (e.g., heavy snowfalls) to political strategies (e.g., legislative approval is more likely in a supplemental request). In many state and local governments, the law requires almost all changes to be approved by the legislature. In some local governments, the executive has greater latitude and does make changes unilaterally to such an extent that the changed operating budget is significantly different from the legislatively approved budget.

Normally, changes are small and appropriations are written broadly enough so that legislative approval is not needed. If significant changes do occur and new legislation is not needed, the agency is still wise to inform the legislature of the change. Otherwise, a poor relationship can develop between the agency and its appropriation committees.

Often transfer of appropriations occurs when functions are transferred to other agencies. The sums do not change, but a different person is given control of the funds. This often occurs in government reorganizations.

Requests for budget adjustments are rigorously reviewed, except when functions are transferred. Budget adjustments should be rare or both the executive and the legislature will spend most of their time reconsidering most of their decisions. Such requests should involve an emergency. Also, supplementals are not consistent with uniform budget considerations which weigh all budget demands at the same time. Exhibit 7-1 illustrates a request form for budget adjustments (see page 210-11). Answers are needed to the following questions:

1. Was the item in the original budget request?
2. Is the money for a recurring or nonrecurring expenditure?
3. What type of adjustment is requested?
4. What is the account number, title, and amount of adjustment?
5. Has a certificate of unencumbered balance (explained in the next chapter) been secured?
6. What is the reason for the request?

BUDGET CONCEPTS AND REPORTS

Allotments and Budget Concepts

After the money has been appropriated by the legislature and apportioned by the central budget office to the agency, then the agency has control over the funds and agency budget controls are used. The primary control is the allotment. It provides authority from the agency head to the operating officials to incur obligations within prescribed amounts for a specific period of time. The allotments must be consistent with appropriations and apportionments. Allotments and operating budgets can be melded because the operating budget fulfills the function of an allotment and more. Allotments can be made using organizational units, activities, geography, or object classification as the categories, depending upon management needs. Allotments are normally made at the highest practical operating level in order to focus managerial responsibility. The level depends on the amount of authority delegated in the particular organization.

Allotments can be designed to complement the management structure of the agency and the problems faced by the agency. Normally, allotments are quite specific on highly sensitive controllable object classifications such as travel. Often the agency must cut current year funds severely and the controllable items receive the burden of such decisions. Thus the controllable items must be "controlled" through the use of specific allotments. Also allotments often are subdivided in terms of "targets," "allowances," "work plans," "financial plans," or other categories, depending upon the management devices used by the agency. The categories and names of categories are not significant as long as management control and delegation of responsibility are facilitated. Exhibit 7-2 is an example of an initial allocation and allotment schedule used in a city government (see page 212-13).

The use of budget terminology is not uniform; but regardless of the terms used, the concepts are important to understand. Thus far, authorization, appropriation, apportionment, and allotment have been explained. These terms are used uniformly. Each represents a different hurdle which must be passed before money is actually spent. Other useful concepts (labels based on common usage) along the way to spending the funds are administrative reservations, obligations, accrued expendutire, and outlay or disbursement. To this list should be added inventory and cost even though they occur after money has been spent.

Administrative reservation means setting aside some funds for a specific purpose. This technique is commonly used by agencies which grant money, but it can be used by other groups which have a lag between deciding who should receive the money and drafting the legal obligating documents. Some certitude is needed as to the availability of funds and the administrative reservation provides that assurance. In a few instances, the legal obligating documents cannot be written. Thus, the possibility exists that funds will not be forthcoming in spite of the administrative reservation. The lag between reservation and obligation can be only a matter of minutes or it can be several weeks, depending on administrative circumstances and requirements.

Expenditure Controls

Expenditure controls are techniques which help to ensure that expenditures are made only in the amounts and for the purposes specified in the appropriation act. There are two types of expenditure controls: budget and administrative. Budget controls are geared to the appropriations and apportionments. Administrative controls

EXHIBIT 7-1 Request Form for Budget Adjustments

DEPARTMENT: CODE #: _____   NAME: _____
SUB-ORGANIZATION UNIT: CODE #: _____   NAME: _____
ACTIVITY: CODE #: _____   NAME: _____

1. Item was ___ was not ___
   included in the department's
   original budget request

2. Type of Expenditure
   Recurring _____
   Non-recurring _____

3. Type of Adjustment
   ___ Inter-Classif. Transfer
   ___ Inter-Divisional Transfer
   ___ An Allocated Reserve Transfer
   ___ Supplemental Appropriation

The Budget Adjustment Requested will Require the Following Revisions:

4. From: 5. For Accounting Dept. Use Only

Account No.	Account Title	Amount	Unencumbered Bal. Before Adjustment	Unencumbered Bal. After Adjustment
	CROSS TOTALS			

6. To:

TOTAL TO BE ADJUSTED TO ABOVE

7. Reasons for Adjustment Request: (Set forth reasons the adjustment is required, the factors involved in arriving at costs, and the status of the account from which transfer is made.)

Approval Requested by: _____ Date: _____

Approved as to Availability of Funds by the Central Accounting Office:

Approved by Budget Officer: _____ Date: _____
Approved by Chief Executive: _____ Date: _____
Approved by President of Council: _____ Date: _____
                                                  Date: _____

Source: Lennox L. Moak and Kathryn W. Killian, *Operating Budget Manual* (Chicago: Municipal Finance Officers Association, 1963), p. 311.

EXHIBIT 7-2 Schedule of Initial Allocations, 1963 General Fund Appropriations (000 Omitted)

Appropriation Title Account Code	Personal Services 100 Class		Purchase of Services 200 Class		Materials and Supplies 300 Class		Equipment 400 Class		Other Classes		Total Allocation
	Allocation	Allotment Reserve	Class	Amount	Class	Amount	Class	Amount	Class	Amount	
Streets											
Administration	$ 394	$ 313	200	$ 7	300	$ 6	400	$ 2			$ 409
Highways	2,265	1,932	200	28	300	55	400	9	500	$ 6	2,872
			261.61	46	305.05	69	405.05	24			
					307.07	74	411.11	31			
					314.14	36	428.28	100			
					315.15	96					
					328.28	33					
Sanitation	12,462	9,877	200	1,000	300	59	400	39			15,807
			205.05	31	305.05	82	428.28	1,080			
			211.11	111	310.10	29					
			260.60		311.11	66					
					314.14	33					
					315.15	519					
					316.16	41					
					318.18	43					
					323.23	38					
					328.28	168					
Survey and Design	1,308	1,043	200	13	300	28	400	20			1,429
			250.50	60							
Traffic Engineering	984	770	200	8	300	37	400	8			1,549
					305.05	189	410.10	108			
					310.10	139	428.28	46			
					316.16	30					

Appropriation Title Account Code	Personal Services 100 Class		Purchase of Services 200 Class		Materials and Supplies 300 Class		Equipment 400 Class		Other Classes		Total Allocation
	Allocation	Allotment Reserve	Class	Amount	Class	Amount	Class	Amount	Class	Amount	
Streets (continued) Street Lighting	$ 349	$ 277	200 220.20 260.60	$ 1 2,653 688	300 305.05 310.10	$ 12 26 97	400 428.28	$ 13 21			$ 3,859
TOTAL	$17,762	$14,232		$4,652		$2,005		$1,501		$ 6	$25,926
Public Welfare Administration & Social Services	$ 690	$ 534	200 290.90	$ 13 8,194	300	$ 8	400	$ 2	505.05	$ 495	$ 9,402
Surplus Foods Distribution Program	171	132	200 210.10 285.85	11 38 310	300	10					540
Children's Reception Center	131	101	200	1	300	23	400	1			155
Child Welfare Center	413	320	200	13	300 313.13	32 36	400	3			498
Youth Conservation Services	421	329	200 250.50	26 143	300 313.13 1	10 12	400	3	505.05	120	734
Total	$ 1,826	$ 1,416		$ 8,748		$ 131		$ 9		$ 615	$11,329

Source: Philadelphia, Pennsylvania, Budget Bureau.

are applied generically to specific operations of the agency, to ensure funds are spent correctly. Administrative controls are intended to prevent the waste or misuse of public funds at the operating level.

There are two types of budget controls: allotments and reports. Allotments were explained earlier in this chapter. They are a device to regulate the timing of obligations and expenditures during the year. Reports are used to show what expenditures have been made and how this compares with what should have been made. A set of reports which could be used in many different governments is published by the Government Finance Officers Association.

There are a variety of reports commonly used: daily financial reports, monthly financial reports, quarterly financial reports, monthly performance reports, revenue reports, and annual reports. Daily financial reports are listings showing all transactions by department account. Monthly financial reports are cumulative daily reports which summarize (1) personnel costs by full-time, part-time, temporary, overtime, and other, and (2) costs by major object of expenditure. Quarterly financial reports point out variances between the current and prior year's expenditures. The monthly performance reports contain code numbers, descriptions, selected key work units, number of persons engaged in producing units, and explanations of significant variances. Common data elements include budgeted work units for the year, units programmed for the current month, amount during the first prior year and current year, percent already completed, and percent of variance from that programmed to date.

There are two common types of administrative controls: encumbrances and competitive bids. An encumbrance is a claim on money; thus encumbered money is not available for new commitments. The administrative reservation defined earlier is an encumbrance. The advantages of encumbrances are (1) they keep officials in government from overspending, and (2) the use of the concept enables officials to be certain of how much money is available for new commitments. Competitive bidding requires that the government solicit price quotations for goods or services from potential vendors or contractors. The normal advantages of competitive bidding are (1) the procedure tends to avoid careless and possibly costly awarding of contracts, and (2) the procedure reduces the danger that contracts will be awarded in return for kickbacks or political favors.

Expenditure controls and other administrative practices such as pre-audits should be carefully considered. The common reasons for detailed expenditure controls are to minimize fraud and insure that higher level policy is carried out. Detailed expenditure controls can also be called "red tape." The use of these controls means time and money must be used to write and review the reports. Also the controls tend to inhibit operating departments and their officials from taking initiatives and being creative because so much paper work must be done.

A fraud/red tape dilemma exists. Does the government wish to risk fraud (or cries of nonresponsiveness to politial leaders) or add more red tape? Neither is pleasant, but the lesser evil is red tape. In the case of fraud, analysis can be used to determine the optimal point of costly control. Expensive administrative controls should be added up to the point that the cost of fraud is equal to the cost of the controls. Such an analysis would be difficult to accomplish given the uncertainties; but even if it were possible, the political wisdom of minimizing would tend to force administrators to opt for more controls—red tape. Politically, no politician wishes to be placed in the situation where any fraud was said to be condoned.

Cash Internal Control

The budget officer must be sure that proper cash internal control exists. Fraud and misuse of funds cannot be prevented completely, but they can be discouraged to the point where only rare cases occur. Twelve simple practices can make a significant difference.

1. All disbursements, except for petty cash, should be made by check. Cash invites theft and fraud because it is much more difficult to trace and associate with specific persons. Also cancelled checks provide a receipt. Petty cash is an exception in that detailed controls for small items can cost more than the items.

2. The signing of checks in advance should be prohibited. Signed checks are similar to cash. Delaying the signing of checks shortens the time they are negotiable and makes it easy to ensure that the checks do correspond to the purchase.

3. Checks should not be drawn to "cash." The checks should be used to create a trail so that if there is a fraud, investigators can isolate the illegal transaction. Also, a check made out to "cash" is more difficult to associate with a specific voucher and invoice; thus confusion is not lessened but compounded.

4. Bank accounts should be reconciled independently. If that is done, errors can be detected more easily because a second independent person is not likely to make the error in the same manner. More important, the likelihood of fraud is lessened because two people instead of one would have to be involved in the crime.

5. Checks should be reconciled with the statement using sequenced (numbered) checks. This permits tighter control of the checks and uncovers omissions much more easily. Also, if the checks are not numbered, theft of checks is much more difficult to detect.

6. Checks should be issued only on written authority. Checks should be traceable to invoices, purchase orders, and encumbrances. This is best done with a written record. More significantly, confusion about issuing of money should be minimized and written authority is the best way to avoid misunderstandings. The protection of the disbursing agent is enhanced if the agent *can prove* all disbursements were proper, and that can best be done with a written record.

7. An inventory control should exist over blank and voided checks. Without such control, fraud and theft is made easier and a good criminal investigator would question the person who did not maintain such control for possible criminal involvement.

8. Separate bank accounts should be maintained for every fund. As explained in the chapter on accounting, each fund must be maintained separately, and this is done through separate bank accounts. This prevents a mingling of money and facilitates separate accounting and auditing.

9. Surprise counts should be made of the petty cash. Elaborate controls are by definition not desirable, but some means is necessary to encourage honesty on the part of those responsible for the fund. No one should be placed above or beyond suspicion. Surprise counting of petty cash is a sufficient and inexpensive control. Care should be taken to stress that the surprise count is a standard operating procedure which should not be taken as a personal questioning of honesty.

10. Checks should be matched with vouchers. If one cannot trace a check to an invoice to a purchase order, then confusion exists which can lead to paying bills twice, not paying some bills, and other problems.

11. Vouchers and supporting documents should be marked once a check has been issued. This prevents mistaken or fraudulent multiple use of the same justifying documents.

12. Cash receipts and deposits should be recorded daily. The logging of cash receipts provides an essential proof that money has been received and a record of when it was received. Depositing the receipts in the bank discourages large losses through theft. Also, once in the bank, the idle cash can be invested, thus earning extra revenue for the government. Even a day's interest on large sums is an extremely significant revenue source for a government.

Management Information Systems

Budget information can be part of a management information system (MIS) or it can be a separate system. An MIS uses sophisticated computerized procedures and routines. The advantage of a computerized system is that it offers speed and reliability in dealing with massive volumes of information. However, an MIS is only a tool which must be programmed correctly and given valid information. Ideally, a budget information system fosters the following:

1. *Control:* ensuring that operations take place in conformance with the budget and that frauds are not expended in excess of available revenues.

2. *Planning and analysis:* evaluating with accurate, reliable, relevant information alternative allocations of resources and the efficiency of government operations.

3. *Accountability:* ensuring public monies are collected and disbursed properly and that an auditable record is kept of all transactions.

The parts of a budget information system depend on the complexity of the government. A few possible subsystems are budget preparation, budget status, legislative tracking, and treasury. A budget preparation subsystem would permit quick access to critical data. A budget status subsystem would provide current data on appropriations, administrative reservations, outlays, and so on. A legislative tracking subsystem would permit a quick comprehensive monitoring of legislative actions. A treasury subsystem would prepare the data and reports required on disbursements and outlays. If the data involved are not overwhelming, the agency or government may be wise to process such information manually. If speed or processing of large amounts of information is needed, then a computerized system should be implemented.

Pitfalls do exist. A good budget information system is complex and quite difficult to design as every detail must be decided in order to program the computer properly. The budget process demands timely information, so system failures and breakdowns cannot be tolerated. Also computer errors can often be most embarrassing as they tend to affect groups (for example, giving each member of a group too much money because a decimal place is misprogrammed). Computerized information systems can provide greater productivity to routine operations, but they require valid information and programmers who understand the complexities of budgeting.

In a few governments, integrated financial management systems (IFMS) are being used. The exact design varies, but Exhibit 7–3 is a good illustration of an IFMS. It was designed for New York City partly in reaction to that government's mid-1970 fiscal problems. Like other information systems, it accumulates, organizes, stores, and makes information available when needed. It contains a number of subsystems which are linked in the sense that information is shared among the subsystems.

The structure of the New York City IFMS is based upon integrating elements and a group of subsystems. The integrating elements are a chart of accounts, standardized formats for transactions, and master tables. The chart of accounts is the basic dictionary for characterizing transactions throughout the system. The standardized formats for transactions permit the system to track and monitor its own

EXHIBIT 7–3   IFMS Integrated Data Base

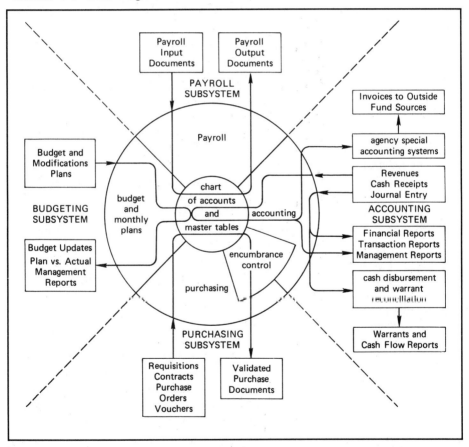

(Urban Academy, *An Introduction to IFMS.* New York: New York City Urban Academy, December 1976, p. 39.)

activities. The master tables permit the cross-referencing of data. The group of subsystems is composed of budget and monthly plans, accounting, payroll, and purchasing. The first two subsystems are most important as they provide guidance to the other systems. The make-up of the subsystem is suggested in Exhibit 7–3.

CASH MANAGEMENT AND INVESTMENTS

Cash Management

The government does not collect and disburse money at the same time. There is a time lag and it is sometimes referred to as *cash flow*. A *cash flow problem* is when the amount which should be paid exceeds available cash even though there are enough government assets. Normally, those assets are in the form of obligations or taxes owed to the government which have not yet been paid or collected. The opposite of a cash flow problem is idle cash. Governments usually do not have cash flow problems unless they are highly dependent upon transfer payments (e.g., grants from other governments).

The more common situation involves determining the best cash position so money is available for payrolls as well as for payment of debts and "extra" cash is invested until it is needed in the current year. For this to occur, forecasts must be made of the monthly cash balance needed to meet obligations. Government revenue does not come in evenly and is collected from several sources. For example, at the federal level, 25 percent of the revenue is not collected by the treasury. When and how much money is collected must both be forecasted as well as the expenditure rate by month for the government.

The cash position is determined by either of two factors. One is the minimum compensating balance requirement imposed by the commercial bank used by the government. The other is the self-imposed transaction balance developed considering risks and current interest rates on that idle cash. The desirable cash position is the larger amount determined by those two factors.

There are several approaches for determining the best balance. The most common practice is to hold a certain number of days' expenditure as a cash balance. The exact number of days will depend upon the judgment of the budget officer or treasurer. This practice is useful for most small governments. A second approach is called Economic Ordering Quality (EOQ). In this mathematical model (see Exhibits 7–4 and 7–5), carrying costs represented by the forgone earned interest are weighed against the total cost of the transactions. The government incurs an opportunity cost for holding rather than investing the cash. Also each bank transaction (e.g., transferring from securities to cash) involves an administrative cost to the government. If the number of transactions drives up the cost, then more money can be saved by having a higher cash amount available. A formula helps determine the optimum size cash balance.

A third approach is called the Miller-Orr Model. The same basic concepts are involved except the focus is placed upon the upper dollar limit needed for cash pur-

EXHIBIT 7–4   Economic Ordering Quality Formula

$$P = b\left(\frac{T}{c}\right) + vT + i\left(\frac{c}{2}\right)$$
where

P = total cost of cash management

b = fixed cost per transaction of transferring funds from marketable securities to cash or vice versa

T = total amount of cash payments or expenditures over the period involved

c = size of transfer, which is the maximum amount of cash

v = variable cost per dollar of funds transferred

i = interest rate on marketable securities

The formula used to solve for the optimal transfer size and initial cash balance is

$$C = \sqrt{\frac{2bT}{i}}$$

The average cash balance is computed by dividing C by 2.

poses. When the cash balance touches the upper boundary then a predetermined amount of securities is automatically purchased. When the cash balance touches zero or an amount slightly above zero, then a predetermined amount of securities is sold, thus increasing the cash balance. The upper and lower boundaries are determined with transaction cost and lost earned interest in mind. The greater the likely

EXHIBIT 7-5   Illustration of the EOQ formula used by J. Richard Aronson and Eli Schwartz in *Management Policies in Local Government Finance.*

A city has total cash payments of $6 million for a six-month period. During this period, the payment (T) will be made at a steady rate, the cost per transaction (b) is $50, the interest rate (i) is 3 percent, and the cost per dollar of funds transferred (v) is 0.05 percent. Therefore:

$$c = \sqrt{\frac{2bT}{i}} = \sqrt{\frac{2(50)\,(6,000,000)}{.03}} = \$141,421$$

The optimal initial cash balance and transfer size is $141,421 and the average cash balance is $141,421 divided by 2 or $70,710. By dividing 6,000,000 by 141,421, the number of transfers (42) can be calculated. The total cost of cash management for the six month period is:

$$P = \$50\frac{(\$6,000,000)}{\$141,421} + \frac{.0005\,(\$6,000,000)}{} + \frac{.03\,(\$141,421)}{2} = \$7,242$$

cash fluctuations, the greater the control limits. The Miller-Orr Model is best applied when cash balances fluctuate randomly.

Commercial Bank Services

Which bank should a government use? There is a difference in earned interest and extra bank services which can lower government administrative cost. Also, there is the fact that local banks are likely investors in local or state government securities. Political factors must be weighed. Local banks do provide local jobs. Also bank officials are often heavy political contributors. Often all those factors are weighed when decisions are made on which bank a local government should use. Because a government uses many accounts, one possibility is to spread the business among all the local banks.

An unusual service provided government is the warrant. It is mentioned in Exhibit 8–3. A warrant is a draft payable through a bank and it is used to slow disbursements. When a warrant is presented for payment, the bank will not pay until the warrant is accepted by the government. This device can be used in cash management to help regulate the amount of cash available. The disadvantage is the higher bank service charge and government cost to manage the use of warrants.

A practice which is becoming obsolete is "playing the float." A float is the difference between the total amount of checks drawn on a bank account and the amount shown on the bank's books. If the size of the float can be determined accurately, then the bank balance can be lower and the idle cash can be invested. For small governments this is not significant, but for large governments the amount of money can be large and the earned interest on only a few days' investment is significant and worth the effort.

The practice of playing the float is becoming obsolete with the greater use of electronic fund transfer systems which tend to eliminate the float. The Federal Electronic Funds Transfer System illustrates the new practice. It was implemented by the Treasury Department and Federal Reserve System in 1976. A computer link is established between the Treasury Department and the New York Federal Reserve Bank. The system provides the capability for automatic receipt of fund transfers as well as computer assisted generation of fund transfers amoung Treasury, Federal Reserve Banks, member banks, and others using the Federal Reserve Communication Systems. Thus processing of checks can be done instantly instead of taking several days.

Controlling Payables

Paying bills can mean saving money. Given the fact that idle cash is earning interest, bills should not be paid until they are due unless the discount for early payment is higher than the earned interest. In order to maximize earned interest, governments often make grants using a letter of credit. This enables the government to draw interest instead of the grantee.

Care should be taken to ensure knowledgeable people are paying the bills. Normally, the management and control of payables is centralized to provide that expertise. In larger governments, another method used is to use field units, with headquarters establishing spending and disbursement levels. The following general guidelines[1] are useful in tailoring agency or government disbursement and collectibles policies and procedures:

1. Each agency should have a carefully developed disbursement plan as a part of its forecast of outlays. The plan should be consistent with the agency's objectives, strategies, program plans, and budget.

2. A payment schedule and control system should be established.

3. Procedures should be established for evaluating economic factors, including the time value of money, in establishing payment schedules. Unless there are significant programmatic or policy factors, payments should generally be made at the time they are due.

4. Except for very large purchases where special analyses might be warranted, cash discounts are usually desirable.

5. Procedures should be reviewed to assure that payments to small vendors and for occasional purchases are not delayed beyond the due dates.

6. Fuller use should be made of letters of credit and other established procedures for managing the timing of payments for government programs.

7. Procedures should be established for regular comparison of actual and planned disbursements.

8. The causes and impact of significant variances from disbursement plans should be evaluated and plans adjusted when necessary.

9. Agencies with significant amounts of receipts should have a collections plan which is a part of the overall forecasts and consistent with the agency's objectives, strategies, program plans, and budget.

10. Collection schedules and control systems for billing and cash processing should be established.

11. Economic factors, including the time value of money, should be considered in development of billing cycles and collection procedures. The importance of prompt collection and deposit of cash should be recognized.

12. Procedures should be established for regular comparison of actual with planned collections.

13. The causes and impact of significant variances from planned collections should be evaluated and plans adjusted when necessary.

Investment in Marketable Securities

Once the cash and security position has been determined, then the government is ready to invest the money for the desired short period of time. Often as much as 70 percent of the total liquid assets can be invested in securities. State law often limits the choice of securities to "safe" investments such as U.S. Treasury securities, U.S. agency securities, obligations of other municipalities within a state, and bank certificates of deposit. Permissible investments do not include common stock.

[1]The guidelines were prepared by the U.S. Joint Financial Improvement Committee.

The safeness of some government securities (e.g., New York City bonds in 1975) is more questionable today. Investing in such securities may be permitted under law, but such investments are unlikely until the risk of default on the securities is nearly eliminated.

Not all securities will earn the investor the same return on investment. That return is called "market yield" and it is determined by a combination of:

1.   length of maturity;
2.   default risk;
3.   marketability;
4.   call provision; and
5.   tax status.

If a government is to invest, then the security market must be watched to determine what is a reasonable market yield and that yield should be sought. Long-term securities tend to receive higher yields, but yields of 15 to 30 years are not significantly higher. The key influence is the expectation of what will happen to the interest rate. Generally, when interest rates are expected to rise, the yield also rises. In poor market conditions, investors may be offered a risk premium to induce them to invest in long-term securities. Only when interest rates are expected to fall significantly in the future do long-term securities—currently yielding less than short-term securities—become attractive.

Default risk is the possibility that the borrower will fail to pay the principal or interest. All other factors constant, the greater the possibility the borrower will fail to meet the obligation, the greater the premium or market yield on the security. U.S. Treasury and U.S. government agency issues are considered default free so they establish the lower limit for securities. The credit-worthiness of other issues is judged by the major security rating firms such as Moody's Investor's Service and Standard and Poor's. Sometimes investors demand a risk premium before investing in issues other than default-free securities.

Marketability involves the ability of the security owners to convert the security to cash. This is particularly important when idle cash is used to purchase the security, because the government may wish to convert the security quickly back into cash. Marketability concerns both the price realized and the amount of time required to sell the asset. The more marketable a security, the greater will be the ability of its owner to execute a large security transaction. Less marketable securities require higher yields.

A call provision on a security allows the issuer to buy the security back at a stated price before maturity. The call provision is to the borrower's benefit because the borrower can refund the issue if interest rates move significantly lower. The investor is disadvantaged because the security is called in a period of low interest rates and the investor's funds must then be placed in securities returning a lower yield. Not surprisingly, investors demand a yield inducement and maybe a premium as well to invest in callable securities. Callable government securities are becoming more popular but are unusual in federal government securities.

Tax status has two effects on market yields. In the first place, governments do not have to pay taxes on investment income, thus this is not an expense to them. Secondly, state and local government securities are tax havens for many private investors; this affects the government security market by driving the yield down. Generally speaking, the fact that local governments do not pay federal income tax means that they should invest in higher yield federal securities rather than state and local government securities. Another difference in investment strategy involves deep discount bonds and the tax rates on ordinary and capital gains. This distinction is significant to the individual who is a taxpayer but is not significant to the investing government. Thus a government should not take advantage of the "bargain" yields on coupon bonds selling at par or above. In general, governments should simply invest in securities showing the highest pretax return.

Types of Marketable Securities

There are four types of securities commonly used by state and local governments. They are U.S. Treasury obligations, federal agency securities, repurchase agreements (REPO), and negotiable certificates of deposit. Each has its special advantages.

There are two major types of U.S. Treasury obligations: treasury notes and treasury bills. Treasury bills pay about 6 percent interest and are auctioned weekly for 91- to 182-day maturities. One-year bills are sold separately. Treasury bills carry no coupon but are sold at discount. These securities are extremely popular as short-term investments. The secondary market is excellent and transaction costs are low. Treasury notes hold one- to seven-year maturities but they are used in the secondary market for short-term investments. In general these two types of securities are the safest and most marketable, and yield the lowest return on investment.

There are other types of securities issued by the federal government carrying the same assurances as U.S. Treasury obligations but having slightly better yields. Principal agencies issuing securities are the federal land banks, federal home loan banks, federal intermediate credit banks, the Federal National Mortgage Association (called "Fannie Mae"), the Government National Mortgage Association ("Ginnie Mae"), and the banks for cooperatives. Maturities range from a month to 15 years, but about two-thirds of the issues are for less than a year

The repurchase agreement (REPO) is an innovation of government security dealers who recognize the selling potential of securities tailored to specific short time periods. With REPOs, dealers agree to repurchase the security at a specific future date, thus increasing the number of transactions and the resulting total fees from those transactions. Government investors benefit because they can get securities for the specific time periods they need, thus gaining the desired earned interest. There is little marketability but that is unimportant because REPOs are normally only for a few days. There is no default risk because the securities are almost always U.S. Treasury securities.

Another commonly used short-term investment is the negotiable certificates of deposit (CD). A CD is the deposit of funds at a commercial bank for a specified period of time at a specified rate of interest. This investment device was originated in 1961 and it normally provides a yield better than treasury bills, with maturity in 30 to 360 days. A sizable secondary market exists but marketability is usually non-existent for small bank CDs. The default risk is related to the possibility of bank failure, which is normally a low risk for most banks. Commonly local governments use CDs from local banks to support the region economically.

Portfolio

A portfolio is merely the collection of securities one holds. Government investors, as noted before, are limited to the legally sanctioned list of securities. The key consideration for a government's portfolio is to have the cash available when needed for the operations of the state, city, county, and so on. Default risk is minimum and a call risk is unusual. Taxability is not a direct factor; therefore, computations are simplified to the return on investment. Government investors should concentrate on maturity and marketability.

For the short term, needs are best satisfied by treasury bills, REPOs, and CDs. A significant portion of the emergency liquidity needs should be met with treasury bills and REPOs.

Intermediate and long-term needs are handled differently. Treasury notes and bonds as well as U.S. securities are used for intermediate purposes. Again, the key is to ensure cash is available when needed, so maturities must be timed correctly or marketability must be excellent if the timing is not correct. U.S. agency securities provide better yields but this advantage must be weighed against their marketability. In some cases, long-term investments are used, especially for larger potential emergencies or when funds are accumulated over years for a given purpose. In such cases, long-term treasury and agency securities are normally used. The most important consideration for long-term investments must be the future course of interest rates. The highest yield is not as important as the date of maturity or possible marketability. Often governments take the more conservative approach of confining their investments to short-term securities.

In summary, investments of idle cash should be made, but expertise is needed to do it correctly. This section gives the reader some of the basics, but much more knowledge and experience are needed to deal properly in government securities. A better knowledge of both chapters will be obtained by reflection on the complementary character of the two.

ACCOUNTING FUNDAMENTALS

Accounting consists of *recording transactions* of an agency in financial terms, including classifying, summarizing, reporting, interpreting, and analyzing those transactions for the user of the data. The key words are "recording transactions." Transactions are financial decisions, such as obligating money, deciding to disburse, and setting aside funds for a purpose. Accounting is merely keeping track of and analyzing those transactions by using summaries and classifications. Accounting provides management with a means to evaluate management performance, to plan for future operations, and, lastly, to achieve financial control.

Principles of Governmental Accounting and Reporting principles are deceptively simple. They stress that accounting should complement legal requirements and budgets. Fund accounting is used. Under the principles, government assets are not to be depreciated as in private sector accounting and a modified accrual method of accounting is recommended. Standard classification, terminology, and reports are suggested. Financial reports are to show current conditions and yearly reports should be prepared and published.

Government accounting is predicated upon disclosure and integration with other management activities. Full disclosure of the financial results of government is essential or abuse can go undetected. Accounting produces financial information for management purposes which permits effective control over and ensures the accountability of all funds, property, and other assets. Reliable accounting serves as the basis for preparing and supporting budget requests, for controlling the execution of the budgets, and for providing needed financial information for reviewing groups. Government accounting, which is integrated and consistent with all accounting operations throughout the government, permits comparative analyses, thus strengthening the analytical ability of management.

Accounting Norms and Budgeting

Certain norms are accepted in government accounting. The control accounts or fiscal accounts—which record receipts, obligations, and disbursements—must embrace the detail that supports the budget. If that is not the case, then the budget and accounting information cannot be related. Decisions on the forms of accounting records should be centralized, but the routine decentralized. Standard definitions and classification cannot be achieved without centrally controlled decisions on such matters, but the actual routine of accounting should be handled in the field where the action is taking place. Accounting must accompany a pattern of internal audit and control. Unless some inspections occur which verify that the required accounting practices are being used, the organization will not take the requirements seriously. Actual costs and measures should reflect management success and failure. Accounting is merely a reflection of performance and the reflection must show the good and bad news in order to help managers understand their true situation. Flexibility in accounting is desirable, but only in the context of overall uniformity. If useful summary information is to be compiled, then accounting uniformity is essential. On the other hand, accounting requirements can inhibit the organization from responding to its environment. This dilemma is always the challenge of top government accountants who must design the accounting systems.

A key step in accounting is obligation. If an item is being bought, then the agency normally issues a purchase order or a more formal contract. The purchase order is a valid offer. The vendor will send the goods requested and the bill to the agency based upon a valid purchase order or contract. In the case of personnel, a contract or a mere agreement to work for certain remunerations constitutes the obligation. The agency must pay for services rendered and tenure protections commonly exist for government employees. Once an order is placed and has been accepted by the vendor, then the government is obligated to pay—given that the contract is fulfilled by the vendor. At this stage, the agency records the order as an *accounts payable* item when the purchase order is sent. Normally, not all the money obligated must be paid because some orders are deficient in some manner and the government is not obligated to pay in such circumstances.

Once the goods have been received and placed in inventory, then an accrued expenditure exists until such time as the check is issued. This concept is useful if there is a large purchasing function because the demand on cash and government liability would be monitored more closely. In many other types of government functions, this concept is not needed. In this chapter the reports cited do not use "accrued expenditure" because the concept normally is not needed.

Expenditures is another step. This is when the invoice has been received from the vendor, and money—in the form of a check—is actually issued by the government. Today, expenditures are controlled closely. In the federal government, the rate of disbursement, especially on grants, is monitored and controlled for fiscal policy reasons. In all levels of government, but to a lesser extent in the federal government, the rate of disbursement is monitored and controlled in order to avoid shortages of cash and to take advantage of short-term idle cash investments.

Two additional budget and accounting concepts can also be applied. Once the goods are in hand but not being used, they are considered *inventory*. This concept is useful because inventory can be converted to cash if necessary; thus separate treatment helps the decision maker have a better understanding of agency convertible assets. Another concept is *cost*. Once the goods are taken from inventory, they are considered used and are a cost. At this point, the item is no longer an asset.

Government accounting is keyed to the operating budget. Accounting is especially useful in tracking the obligations and expenditures against the budget. In government accounting, the term *encumbrance* is used. It is a claim on money. As soon as an obligation is made, the money needed to pay the obligation is set aside and no longer included in the balance of money available for new commitments. In budgeting for personnel costs, encumbrances are sometimes not essential because the cost is highly routine and regular in its flow. However, in budgeting for purchases of equipment, materials, supplies, other contracts, and grants, encumbrances are quite important and the accounting system should provide data on those encumbrances as well as later related expenditures. This point shall be made again in the discussion concerning Exhibits 7-7 and 7-8.

In state and local government, a large share of the funds used comes from grants from the federal government. Federal requirements normally stipulate that each grant should be treated as a fund, with separate records maintained on all receipts and expenditures. The permitted cost and required supporting documents are spelled out in federal guidelines. Generally, the requirements are similar to those for normal government accounts. The appropriate local share of the grant is a unique feature of the federal guidelines. Normally, the local government can use cash gifts as well as value of goods and services for the local share. Also federal regulations include provisions for auditing of financial records plus acceptable internal control procedures such as those discussed later in this chapter.

FINANCIAL ADMINISTRATION

The key to good financial administration is good account records. All financial transactions must be recorded. They must then be summarized and classified. Also all such transactions must be related to the appropriate fiscal year.

Government accounting uses the accrual rather than the cash method of accounting. In the cash method, income is recorded when it is received and expenditures are recorded when they are paid. In other words, transactions are recorded as of the date the cash changes hands. The advantages of the cash method are that it is easy to administer and the cash balance is easily determined. The critical disadvantage is that expenses and revenues cannot be related to the budget and its fiscal year. Thus accountability is impossible.

In the accrual method of accounting, revenues are recorded when they are earned or billed and expenditures are recorded when they are obligated. The accrual method does permit accountability but it also distorts the revenue and cash position of the government. The cash position must be calculated separately, as described earlier. Governments use a modified accrual method primarily because there are fundamental differences between a private enterprise operation and a government undertaking. This difference will become apparent when the various financial reports are discussed.

Accounting is built upon three operational tools: vouchers, journals, and ledgers. A *voucher* is a document which confirms the fact that a financial transaction has taken place. For example, payroll checks, purchase orders, receipts for rent payment, and even appropriation laws are vouchers. The *journal* is the first record book (now sometimes a computer printout) of the transactions. It is a chronological listing of the transactions and shows the date of the transaction's occurrence, the dollars, and a brief explanation of the transaction. A *ledger* is a group of accounts which pertain to the same subject, that is, a subject matter listing of information. These tools are important because together they provide the means to record usefully, summarize, and classify the transactions.

Government accounting uses the fund concept. A fund is a sum of money set aside for a particular purpose and accounted for separately from the other monies of the government. The purpose behind fund accounting is to control the handling of money to ensure that it will be spent only for the purposes intended, such as highway construction. The concept is extensively used but it does reduce management flexibility, thus making public management more difficult.

There are three fund classifications and two sets of fund types. The three-way classification of funds is governmental, proprietary, and fiduciary. The federal government uses a different set of funds than do state and local governments in America. The two federal government funds are general and special. For state and local government, there are six governmental funds: general funds, special revenue funds, debt service funds, capital project funds, special assessment funds, and some types of trust funds. The only type of proprietary federal government fund is a revolving fund. The state and local level proprietary funds are enterprise funds, internal service funds, and some trust funds. There are three federal government fiduciary funds: trust funds, deposit funds, and management funds. The state and local level fiduciary funds are called trust funds and agency funds.

Basic Governmental Accounting

An important accounting convention is to use a double-entry system, with documents as the basic record. Original entries of transactions are recorded in journals and posted to general and subsidiary ledgers. Recording and posting are done with the objective of keeping both sides of the accounting equation always balanced. The fundamental accounting equation starts with assets equaling equities. Assets are owned items, such as cash, tax receivables, equipment, and buildings. Equities are claims against those assets; they include liabilities (e.g., claims of creditors for goods and services purchased, amounts due to employees for unpaid wages, amounts due on loans) and residual equity (in the public sector, the latter is called fund balance). Some forms of equity are not available for potential obligation and they are separated from fund balance and called reserves. The revised account equation, which can be seen in Exhibit 7-6, is as follows:

EXHIBIT 7-6

$$A = L + R + FB$$

where

A = assets
L = liabilities
R = reserves
FB = fund balance

The double-entry system is designed to isolate entry and arithmetic errors. In posting entries, each transaction must be both a debit and a credit. A debit of one account must be accompanied by a credit in the same amount on another account so that the accounting equation always remains balanced. As a rule, any increase in an account on the left side of the accounting equation must be debited, whereas an increase in the same amount on the right side is credited. For example, debts are increases in assets and decreases in liability accounts. Credits are decreases in assets and increases in liability. To check for errors, trial balances of the equation are used, but finding simple entry and arithmetic errors can be time-consuming. Fortunately, the use of the computer permits greater speed in calculation and reduces the likelihood of arithmetical error. Thus, the computer has become an essential tool for large accounting systems.

Accounting System Design

There are several factors to consider when designing an accounting system. Information should be timely, accurate, and objective. Obviously, this is an ideal and trade-offs must be made, especially between timeliness and accuracy. The system should be consistent with all legally established minimum requirements. Particular attention should be given to the collection and recording of information because this is the place where most errors occur. Care must be taken to design cross- and double-checks to isolate and correct such errors. Another concern is classification, summarization, and storage. Proper design here rests upon an excellent grasp of how the information can best be used. Thought also goes into evaluating the use of electronic data processing. The advantage is speed and enhanced analytical capability. The risks to consider are computer assisted fraud and the possibility of massive, extremely embarrassing mistakes.

The final factor to weigh in designing an accounting system is internal control. The system should fix responsibility on specific individuals. Policies and procedures should be written to avoid misunderstandings. Only designated personnel should be authorized to perform certain key functions such as disbursement. Forms should be carefully considered so that they reduce the likelihood of error and fraud. All reporting should be regularly and carefully analyzed or else the reports should be eliminated. Care must be taken to establish built-in cross- and double-checks of forms, people, and units in order to isolate errors and prevent fraud. For example, independent record keepers can be used to act as cross checks on each other. A further safeguard is to use independent auditors. One final but key point to internal control is to get, train, and keep good people in the accounting unit.

REPORTS AND ANALYSES

Accounting is one of those subjects that can best be understood by example. The previous portions of this chapter explain accounting and financial administration fundamentals. This portion explains specific reports which illustrate some of the fundamentals and demonstrate the usefulness of accounting. The reports and analyses are drawn from chapter 15 of Aronson and Schwartz, *Management Policies in Local Government Finance*. The following five financial reports are discussed:

1. statement of revenue: estimated and actual;
2. appropriation and expenditure ledger account;
3. statement of encumbrances and authorization;
4. fund balance change; and
5. balance sheet.

Statement of Revenue

Exhibit 7-7 compares estimated with actual government revenue. This accounting report provides highly useful information to help analysts judge the accuracy of forecasting techniques. This report should be keyed to funds, tax source, and fiscal year. As the reader may recall, separate estimates must be made for each tax source and separate accounting forces us to examine the estimates by funds and fiscal year. The recorded estimate should be the official one used by the government in computing its budget. Again, the reader may recall, the government should pass a resolution indicating the assumed (projected) revenue. The actual revenue should be that amount actually collected.

In examining Exhibit 7-7, the reader will notice where estimation errors were made. The important errors are those which result in significantly less revenue for the government. These errors are particularly harmful and result in using tax anticipation notes. If the revenue source is small, then large errors can be tolerated. If the revenue source is large, then even small optimistic errors cannot be tolerated. In Exhibit 7-7, the intergovernmental revenue (e.g., state payment, revenue sharing, or grant-in-aid) was significantly in error. Fortunately, the conservative estimates on the other revenue sources more than offset the mistake so that the entire estimate was off about 9 percent. Exhibit 7-7 tells the analyst that more effort must go into correctly forecasting revenue.

The subsequent exhibits (7-8, 7-9, 7-10, 7-11) are complementary. Each tells the analyst a part of a story, but together they tell a reasonably comprehensive story about the whole government. For example, each is concerned with encumbrances and expenditures. If a question is raised on encumbrances in the balance sheet (Exhibit 7-11), the ultimate answer may be found in the appropriation and expenditure ledger account (Exhibit 7-8) or the statement of expenditures and encumbrances (Exhibit 7-9). The analyst must be able to read all the financial reports and understand their interrelationship.

EXHIBIT 7-7   Milesville General Fund Statement of Revenue—Estimated and Actual Fiscal Year Ended June 30, 1977

Revenue Source	Estimated Revenue	Actual Revenue	Actual over- or (under) estimated
Taxes	$240,000	$290,000	$50,000
Licenses and permits	30,000	36,000	6,000
Intergovernmental revenue	120,000	90,000	30,000
Charges for services	40,000	45,000	5,000
Fines and forfeitures	6,000	9,000	3,000
Miscellaneous	4,000	10,000	6,000
Total	$440,000	$480,000	$40,000

Appropriation and Expense Ledger

Exhibit 7-8 is a subsidiary or partial appropriation and expenditure ledger account. As defined earlier, a ledger concerns a subject and in this case the subject is a specific account (or fund), including information on encumbrances, expenditures, and essential voucher information. This report uses regularly and routinely collected voucher information.

Exhibit 7–8 tells us a story. On July 1, 1986, the fiscal year began, with $125,000 being appropriated to the supplies account of the general fund. This meant that $125,000 was available to be obligated and spent. On July 10, 1986, some laboratory equipment was ordered which cost $25,000, thus reducing the amount to be obligated to a total of $100,000. Details of the order can be found on purchase order number 104 and this order constitutes a voucher. On October 15, 1986, an automobile or parts for automobiles were ordered costing $10,000. This increased the encumbered balance to $35,000 and reduced the unencumbered balance to $90,000. On November 3, 1986, the ordered laboratory equipment finally arrived and was paid for. However, either some of the merchandise was damaged or a discount was given because the actual expenditure was $24,500. This meant that the total encumbrance was reduced by $25,000 to $10,000. The difference of $500 between the encumbrance and expenditure required a $500 upward adjustment in the unencumbered balance because that money was again available for obligation.

This type of financial report is quite useful. The analyst always knows how much money is available in each account for obligation, how much has already been spent, and how much is obligated but not yet actually spent. At any time in the current year, the operating budget may have to be revised. A summary appropriation and expenditure ledger account is essential for an intelligently done revision. Also the account tells managers how much they can plan on using and how much can be (or should be) spent before the end of the year.

Exhibit 7–9 is an elaborate summary statement of appropriations and expenditures. It is done for each separate fund, and compares appropriations with expenditures and encumbrances involving a two-year period. This statement assumes that the fund balance is closed at the end of two years, thus providing sufficient time to pay obligations from the previous year. A two-year period is a reasonable time, but a shorter or longer time period can be selected. The reader may notice that the $800 "close to fund balance" and other information appear in Exhibit 7–10. The reader may also note that the information can be further subdivided into activities and objects.

Exhibit 7–9 helps identify expenditure forecasting errors, but a serious problem is not apparent in the example cited. Out of $425 appropriated, there was left unobligated only $11,200, or about 2 percent of the total. However, most of the money was in the welfare category and the expenditure forecast error in that category was 16 percent. This error, coupled with a zero encumbrance, would raise a question for a budget analyst. The low 1987 encumbrances total is a pleasing sign that last of the year spending was low and proper pacing of obligation probably took

EXHIBIT 7-8 Milesville General Fund—Supplies Account Appropriation and Expenditure Ledger Account Starting July 1, 1986

Date	Explanation	Encumbrances			Expenditures		Appropriations	
		Increase	Decrease	Balance	Amount	Total	Amount	Unencumbered Balance
Jul. 1	Budget						$125,000	$125,000
Jul. 10	Lab. equip.—P.O. #104	$25,000		$25,000				100,000
Oct. 15	Autos—P.O. #410	10,000		35,000				90,000
Nov. 3	Lab. equip.—P.O. #104		$25,000	10,000	$24,500	$24,500		90,500

EXHIBIT 7–9 Milesville General Fund Statement of Expenditures and Encumbrances Compared with Authorizations, Fiscal Year Ended June 30, 1987

	Prior year reserve for encumbrances	Expenditures chargeable to prior year reserve for encumbrances	Close to fund balance	1977 Appropriations	1977 Expenditures	1977 Encumbrances	1977 Unencumbered balance
General government	$1,500	$1,500		$ 45,000	$ 41,000	$2,000	$ 2,000
Public safety	750	750		100,000	98,000	500	1,500
Highways and streets	450	400	$ 50	60,000	60,000		
Sanitation	250	275	(25)	40,000	39,000		1,000
Health	150	140	10	20,000	18,000	1,300	700
Welfare	1,000	800	200	30,000	25,000		5,000
Culture-recreation	400	100	300	16,000	13,200	2,000	800
Education	500	235	265	14,000	12,600	1,200	200
Transfer of funds				100,000	100,000		
Service fund	$5,000	$4,200	$800	$425,000	$406,800	$7,000	$11,200

*The NCGA would prefer breaking down expenditures by activity and object as well. This has been omitted for the sake of brevity.

†If there has been material revision of appropriations since the adoption of the original budget, this should be indicated here, with columns showing the original budget and revisions.

place. The prior year was even lower so the manager might watch for a possible laxness developing in this area, but there certainly is no cause for alarm.

An analysis of the closing entries is particularly interesting. The sanitation function had a negative closing entries so that more money was spent than encumbered. This is a matter of note. Other interesting occurrences were the large $300 and $265 amounts in two categories. They represent 75 percent of one category and 48 percent of the other. Both percentages are high but the amounts are low. Possibly further investigation is warranted, but such an investigation is not strongly recommended. The total percentage of encumbrances to the closing entries is high at 16 percent but the amount is low so nothing extremely serious appears to be wrong beyond the antideficiency error.

Exhibit 7–9 also helps identify managers who may be obligating end of the year funds in an attempt to argue that they needed all their requested appropriations. If the encumbered balances are large, this implies large last of the year obligations which have not been paid yet. Also, large close to fund balances indicate sloppy purchasing practices which may be due to hasty obligations in the previous year. Analysts should check the ledger accounts to see when obligations were made, and then confirm if they were necessary. An examination of increases in inventory would also be wise.

Fund Balance Change

Exhibit 7–10 focuses attention on available assets and the fundamental changes which occurred during a fiscal year. It is done for each separate fund and highlights the key additions and subtractions associated with the fund change during

EXHIBIT 7-10   Milesville General Fund Analysis of Changes in Fund Balance, Fiscal Year Ended June 30, 1987

Fund balance, July 1, 1986		$ 84,500
Add:		
Excess of revenues over expenditures, 1987		
Revenues	$480,000	
Expenditures	406,800	
		73,200
Reserve for encumbrances, June 30, 1986	$ 5,000	
Less: Expenditures charged to prior year reserve for encumbrances	4,200	
		800
		$158,500
Deduct:		
Reserve for encumbrances, June 30, 1987	7,000	
Increase in reserve inventory and supplies	2,000	
		9,000
FUND BALANCE, JUNE 30, 1987		$149,500

the year. The excess of revenue over expenditure is added after it is adjusted upward for the prior year reserve for encumbrances. Deductions are made from the reserve for encumbrances and additions are made for increases in reserve inventory and supplies. The revenue in the computation is cited in Exhibit 7–7 and the expenditure cited in Exhibit 7–9. Also the reserve for encumbrances can be found in Exhibit 7–9. The increase in reserve inventory and supplies is reflected in Exhibit 7–11, and will be discussed more later.

The fund balance tells us how much money can be spent without fear of overspending. It also explains the component parts of that figure. The revenue less expenditure tells us there is a 15 percent surplus, which is certainly unusual in most governments. The fund increases by $65,000, which constitutes a 177 percent yearly increase. Some questions about this increase should be raised by a budget examiner as either taxes can be cut or expenditures can be increased. Certainly, the fund is in a healthy position in which to be starting the next year, unless some unusual expenditure increase is forecasted.

Balance Sheet

The balance sheet is illustrated in Exhibit 7–11. The government balance sheet is similar to a private business balance sheet, and is based on the simple formula: total assets equal total liabilities, reserves, and the fund balance. Assets include cash, short-term investments, property tax receivables, amounts due from other funds, and inventory. Liabilities include accounts payable and payroll taxes payable. Reserves include reserve for encumbrances and inventory of supplies. The balance sheet is designed to emphasize available assets, especially quickly available assets. A balance sheet must be prepared for each fund and each fiscal year.

The interesting feature of the government balance sheet is the items not found in it. The balance sheet does not include depreciation, profit, or stocks. Government accounting normally does not include depreciation. Capital items are reflected in the capital budget and debt administration. Government can have a surplus but not a profit. If money is returned to the taxpayer, it is called a rebate, but that is unusual. Government programs provide a service and normally are not also designed to make a profit. The initial capital or designated paper representing ownership in a private business is called stock. By definition, a government is owned and controlled by the people through the political process; therefore the notion of private ownership is logically impossible. Instead, the fund balance is used to indicate available resources in the fund.

The balance sheet is informative, especially if it is presented in a comparative format. In Exhibit 7–11, the fund has grown significantly with little growth in total liabilities. Not a great deal of money is held in cash and idle cash is invested in short-term investment. The reader will note that the investment is cited at cost rather than at the higher market value. This is to provide the safest conservative estimate, but both cost and market value should always be shown. This information shows the loss of profit anticipated from the investment. The amount of property tax receivables and allowances for uncollectible taxes has declined. This is a good sign because it indicates a sound tax base and good collection practices. The inventory of sup-

EXHIBIT 7-11 Milesville General Fund, Balance Sheet, June 30, 1986 and 1987

ASSETS	1987		1986	
Cash		$ 15,000		$ 8,000
Short-term investment— at cost (market value $123,000)		120,000		50,000
Property taxes receivable	$35,000		$45,000	
Less Allowance for uncollectable taxes	3,000	32,000	4,000	41,000
Due from other funds		1,500		2,200
Inventory of supplies		10,000		8,000
Total Assets		$178,500		$109,200

LIABILITIES, RESERVES, AND FUND BALANCE	1987	1986
Accounts payable	$ 10,000	$ 9,200
Payroll taxes payable	2,000	2,500
Total Liabilities	12,000	11,700
Reserve for encumbrances	7,000	5,000
Reserve for inventory of supplies	10,000	8,000
Total Reserves	17,000	13,000
Fund balance	149,500	84,500
Total Liabilities Reserve and Fund Balance	$178,500	$109,200

plies and its mirror reserve have not grown radically, so unnecessary purchases probably did not take place. The significant increase was in the fund balance. An analyst would question this increase and wish to examine the fund balance in more detail.

In a balance sheet, the "due from other funds" amount is a significant item. In this particular balance sheet (Exhibit 7–11) there is no apparent problem, but problems can exist. The use of many funds means that some interfund transfers are necessary. It is possible to abuse these transfers for the purpose of confusing or hiding the real condition of the various funds. Fraud, poor management, or deliberate attempts to present a better picture of financial conditions are some of the reasons for an abuse of transfer. An analyst can be aware of this potential and can make an inquiry if the "due from other funds" amount distorts the total assets in the balance sheet. The inquiry would involve the legality and motivation behind any unusually high assets acquired as a result of the transfer.

The financial reports are an important use of the accounting system. They provide information useful in budget preparation, operating budgets, and auditing. Knowledge of the complexities of public budgeting and government are essential if the financial reports are to be interpreted correctly. Each financial report is read in the context of the other reports and knowledge of the budget process.

This section of the chapter explains the fundamental decisions to be made in computerizing an accounting system. Many small governments can save a significant amount of operating expenses and greatly improve their management capabilities by shifting from a hand-posted accounting system to computerized operation. Often, small governments may have only bank statements or small bookkeeping activities which are difficult to maintain owing to high personnel turnover. A standard computer software package can be designed for small government in each state. Such a system could be used by most cities in a state, require a minimum amount of effort to operate, and provide adequate financial data to local public managers. Such a system was developed in Tennessee. Their computerized "General Ledger and Budgeting Accounting Program" costs $600 to $2500 to operate, depending on the number of transactions. It serves as an example of what can be done.

A fundamental ingredient of the Tennessee system is a codification of the accounting fields based on the state uniform standardized chart of accounts. The use of the code does assume correct coding of the transactions. A qualified person is needed to analyze the reports, correct coding mistakes, and isolate problems in coding. The codification in Tennessee was as follows:

XX—XXX—XXXXX—XXX—XXX—XX

City code: to identify the city on the computer file;
Fund code: to identify groups and specific funds;
Basic account or purpose account: to identify accounts such as assets, liabilities, revenues, expenditures, reserves, etc.;
Object account: to identify primary and secondary objects of expenditures;
Optional code: for project cost accounting;
Second optional code: to identify responsibility centers.

Input and Output

The input for the Tennessee system is in the form of vouchers. A copy of the checks plus entry information (e.g., fund, function, object, debit, credit, description) go to the computer center. Cash reports on deposits, budget, and a general journal form (for corrections, adjustments, recordings of accounts payable, and encumbrances) are also sent to the computer center with the appropriate entry information. Data are batch processed and the sending unit is responsible for the accuracy of the input. The computer center does run an input edit on the cards to ensure that (1) each transaction is entered dually according to accounting practice, (2) each expenditure and encumbrance has an object code, and (3) no code number has been used that is not in the chart of accounts. The edit is only for easily caught errors. More significant errors must be caught with an inspection procedure and an examination of the reports produced with this data.

The computer can generate an amazing number of useful reports based on the previously described input. These include:

1. the balance sheet;
2. trial balance;
3. general journal entry register;
4. budget entry register;
5. cash receipts journal;
6. cash disbursement journal;
7. deposit register;
8. analysis of change in cash on hand;
9. statement of estimated, realized, and unrealized revenue by specific source;
10. statement of expenditures compared by appropriation (function and object);
11. statement of object expenditures by account number; and
12. detailed general ledger analysis (helps trace transactions for each account).

Much more complex computerized accounting systems than the Tennessee example exist. By examining a simple system, however, the relationship of the computer to fundamental accounting concepts and financial reports can be understood more easily. Also the usefulness of computers becomes more apparent. The task of preparing reports on each fund is time-consuming. A computer can take much of the dull routine out of accounting work and do it much more accurately.

REVIEW QUESTIONS

1. Compare and contrast apportionment, allotment, and administrative reservations.
2. What are the common pitfalls one can anticipate in budget execution, and how can budget execution system design assist in minimizing these pitfalls? Compare and contrast budget and administrative controls.

3. Explain the fraud/red tape dilemma. Explain the importance of and how to achieve cash internal control.
4. Explain cash management and its importance. Why are guidelines for disbursement and collection significant, and what are their implications? What knowledge is particularly useful in investing idle cash?
5. Explain the fundamentals of accounting. How does accounting support budgeting?
6. Explain how one can go about making an analysis of a city's financial situation using each of the key financial reports discussed in this chapter.

REFERENCES

American Accounting Association. "Report of the Committee on Accounting for Not-For-Profit Organization," *Accounting Review*, Supplement to vol. 46 (1971), pp. 81–163.

APPLEBY, PAUL. "The Role of the Budget Division," *Public Administration Review*, 18,3 (Summer 1957), 156–59.

ARONSON, J. RICHARD and ELI SCHWARTZ (eds.). *Management Policies in Local Government Finance*. Washington, D.C.: International City Management Association, 1975.

BARTIZAL, JOHN R. *Budget Principle and Procedure.*. Englewood Cliffs, N.J.: Prentice-Hall, 1942.

BATER, FRANCIS M. *The Question of Government Spending*. New York: Harper & Row, Pub., 1960.

BIERMAN, HAROLD, JR. and SEYMOUR SMIDT. *The Capital Budgeting Decision*. New York: Macmillan, 1966.

BLOCKER, JOHN GARY. *Budgeting in Relation to Distribution Cost Accounting*. Lawrence, Kansas: School of Business, 1937.

BUCK, ARTHUR EUGENE. *The Budget in Government of Today* New York: Macmillan, 1934.

BURKHEAD, JESSE. *Government Budgeting*. New York: John Wiley, 1956.

CRECINE, JOHN P. *Governmental Problem Solving: A Computer Simulation of Municipal Budgeting*. Chicago: Rand McNally, 1969.

ERNEST, E. "The Accounting Preconditions of PPB(S)," *Management Account*, 53 (January 1972), 33–37.

FISHER, G. W. *Financing Local Improvement by Special Assessment*. Chicago: Municipal Finance Officers Association, 1974.

FREEMAN, ROBERT J. and EDWARD S. LYNN. *Fund Accounting*, 2nd ed. Englewood Cliffs, N.J.: Prentice-Hall, 1983.

HENRY, M. L. et al. "New York State's Performance Budget Experiment," *Public Administration Review* (July/August 1970).

JOINES, W. W. "Computerized General Ledger and Budgeting Accounting Systems," *Government Finance*, 5, 2 (May 1976), 27–32.

MOAK, LENNOX L. and KATHRYN W. KILLIAN. *Operating Budget Manual*. Chicago: Municipal Finance Officers Association, 1963.

National Committee on Government Accounting. *Governmental Accounting, Auditing, and Financial Reporting*. Chicago: Municipal Finance Officers Association, 1968.

RONDINELLI, DENNIS A. "Revenue Sharing and American Cities: Analysis of the Federal Experiment in Local Assistance," *Journal of the American Institute of Planners*, 41, 5 (September 1975), 319–33.

STOIN, A. W. *Local Government Finance*. Lexington, Mass.: Lexington Books, 1975.

———. "Symposium: Performance Budgeting: Has the Theory Worked?" *Public Administration Review* (Spring 1960).

THAI, KHI V. "Governmental Accounting," in Jack Rabin and Thomas D. Lynch (eds.), *Handbook on Public Budgeting and Financial Management*. New York: Marcel Dekker, 1983.

———. "Government Financial Reporting and Auditing," in Jack Rabin and Thomas D. Lynch (eds.), *Handbook on Public Budgeting and Financial Management*. New York: Marcel Dekker, 1983.

THIERANF, R. J. and RICHARD A. GROSSE. *Decision-Making Through Operations Research*. New York: John Wiley, 1970.

TURNBULL, AUGUSTUS. *Governmental Budgeting and PPBS: A Programmed Introduction*. Reading, Mass.: Addison-Wesley, 1970.

U.S. Civil Service Commission, Bureau of Training, The Management Science Training Center, *Budget Formulation*, Washington, D.C.: 1976.

U.S. Joint Financial Management Improvement Program. *Money Management*. Washington, D.C.: U.S. Joint Financial Management Improvement Program, 1976.

U.S. Joint Financial Management Improvement Program. *Operating Budgets*. Washington, D.C.: U. S. Joint Financial Management Improvement Program, November 1975.

Urban Academy, *An Introduction to IFMS*. New York: New York City Urban Academy, December 1976.

EIGHT
CAPITAL BUDGETING
AND
DEBT ADMINISTRATION

This chapter discusses state and local debt, capital budgeting, and issuances. The concept of debt is defined and classifications commonly used are explained. Capital budgeting is contrasted to operating budgeting, with emphasis placed on capital facility planning and the capital budget cycle. The practical aspects of state and local bonding are explained, including designing an issue, the prospectus, notice of sale, debt records, reporting, and bond ratings. Capital budgeting and debt administration are introduced, with emphasis placed on the specific knowledge particularly useful to a person dealing with these challenging subjects. At the completion of this chapter, the reader should understand:

1. the commonly used definition of debt;
2. why debts are incurred;
3. alternatives to debt;
4. types and forms of debt;
5. revenue bonds;
6. creative capital financing and its origin;
7. nontraditional capital financing;
8. commonly used tests and limits on debt;
9. early warning guidelines for municipal financial operations;
10. significance of the New York City financial crisis on debt administration;

11. municipal bankruptcy, financial problems, and remedies;
12. the difference between capital and operating budgets;
13. capital facility planning and its significiance;
14. the essential decisions and expertise critical in designing a municipal bond issue;
15. what is and should be in a bond prospectus and notice of sale;
16. investment syndicates and their significance;
17. the importance of good bond administration and data associated with debt reporting; and
18. bond ratings, what influences them, and why they are significant.

STATE AND LOCAL DEBT

Definitions

When persons charge items on Master Card or Visa, they are incurring a debt. They normally receive the items and pledge that they will pay for these items within a certain time period. When they get a bank loan for a car, they have incurred a debt. They have agreed to pay back the loan amount (called principal) plus an extra amount (called interest) for the privilege of borrowing the money over an extended period of time.

Governments also borrow money; thus they incur short- and sometimes long-term obligations to pay back the principal and interest. However, some types of debt (e.g., trade accounts payable and conditional repayment loans) sometimes do not involve interest payments. Debt constitutes an obligation which must be paid under the established legal conditions. The Bureau of Census uses the following definition, which stresses interest bearing obligation:

> All long-term credit obligations of the government and its agencies, and all interest bearing short-term (i.e., repayable within one year credit obligations. Includes judgments, mortgages, and "revenue" bonds, as well as general obligation bonds, notes, and interest bearing warrants. Excludes noninterest bearing obligations, amounts owed in a trust or agency capacity, advances and contingent loans from other governments, and rights of individuals to benefit from employee-retirement funds.

Governments incur debt for several reasons. In some cases, cash is needed before the actual revenue is collected. Debt is used to harmonize those divergent patterns of current expenditures and revenues. Often, the government wishes to finance a significant capital construction project or even large equipment purchases. Current revenues cannot pay for such large purchases so a loan is negotiated. Sometimes a debt is incurred in order to refinance an existing—e.g., short-term—debt. On occasion, debt is incurred to finance operating deficits. A form of debt which is not often recognized as such is a government's pension benefit obligation. Bonds are not normally sold for this purpose but pensions are an increasingly significant government obligation which places severe financial pressure on governments.

Governments do not have to incur debts but the alternatives to debt are difficult to use effectively. One alternative is to accumulate funds over time, much like an individual's Christmas savings plan; this is called a sinking fund. The funds are invested until such time as the money is needed. Another alternative is to pay as-you-go—to pay for the equipment or building costs out of operating expenses. The difficulty with both alternatives is that capital facility needs of governments often do not fit the pace of financing of the funding techniques. A city which needs to build a water purification plant sometimes cannot wait the 10 or 20 years required for a sinking fund or pay-as-you-go financing approach. Emergencies and irregular expenditure demands do occur and debt is sometimes the only practical alternative under the circumstances.

Classifications of Debt

Most of the liability items in the state and local government balance sheet are debts of the government. They include bonds, certificates of indebtedness, mortgages, notes, accounts payable, warrants payable, liens, judgments, unfunded pension obligations, and selected contingent liabilities. Excluded are contingent items and reserves for encumbrances.

The largest amount of debt is in the form of bonds. They are a written promise to pay a specified sum of money (called the face value or principal amount) at a specified date or dates (called the maturity dates) together with periodic interest at a specific rate. Serial bonds, which are the most common type of bond, are designed so that a specific number of bonds are retired each year. In contrast, term bonds, which are infrequently used, are normally designed to pay the interest over time but pay the principal when the loan period has applied. Sinking funds are normally used by the borrower to collect the necessary large principal payment at the end of the loan period. Before 1983, most bonds were payable to the bearer and they had detachable coupons representing the interest payments. Upon presentation of the matured coupon to the bond maker's paying agent, the proper interest represented on the coupon was paid. All bonds must now be registered on the books of the issuing government or paying agent to provide protection to the bond holder.

The other forms of debt are normally not as significant unless they happen to involve large obligations. Certificates of indebtedness vary from state to state, but they are frequently used in connection with agency resources or assets. Mortgage bonds use property to secure the obligation without transferring title, but most of them still do not give the government's creditor the right to foreclose. Notes are widely used to represent evidence of financial obligation, normally of a short-term nature. Accounts payable include government firm liabilities such as wages earned but not yet paid as well as the common unpaid bills. The now uncommon warrant is a government-issued document to the bank upon which payment is made with the approval of the government. A lien is a claim upon property arising from failure of the owner to make timely payment of a claim. A judgment is a court decision that the government has a liability or debt to a person who has sought redress through the courts. An unfunded pension liability is incurred when a government does not place sufficient funds in an appropriate pension fund but is still liable for those pensions. A contingent liability is incurred when an agreement stipulates that a liability will occur if a certain condition is met. For example, a city agrees with the area-wide transit board to help finance a transit system once the population density and traffic congestion reach a given level. Controversies often arise over the condition and the fulfillment of the agreement.

Debts can be classified by pledge of security. One type is the "full-faith-and-credit" debt in which a government's credit, including the implied power of taxation, is unconditionally pledged. For example, a city states it will pledge itself unconditionally to pay a bond obligation. Another type is a moral debt in which the issuer or a guaranteeing government has a moral but not a legal obligation to pay. The financial community would rarely be interested in a moral debt unless a government was responsible for that debt. What commonly occurs is some government body (e.g., a housing authority) pledges its user charges or some other revenue source to pay the debt and another unit of government (e.g., the state) gives its moral backing to the debt. The financial community normally requires a default remedy to be spelled out by the government. The best pledge from the investor's point of view is a full-faith-and-credit obligation plus a specific user charge to pay the indebtedness.

Short-Term Debt

Short-term borrowing is normally done for the following reasons:

1. The community is short of the necessary revenue to pay for services. For example, the city forecasted the revenue incorrectly and there is not enough money to pay for planned expenditures.

2. A brief loan is needed and will be paid back as soon as taxes are collected. The money owed to the city may have been collected, but obligations must be paid. A brief loan is needed to bridge this cash flow problem until the debts owed the city are paid.

3. The community has an emergency and necessary funds are not available.

4. The funds are needed to start a capital improvement project, but a long-term bond issue has not yet been approved.

At one time, short-term debt vocabulary included only tax anticipation notes (TANs), revenue anticipation notes (RANs), and bond anticipation notes (BANs). Under Internal Revenue Service arbitrage regulations and under specific circumstances proceeds from government short-term securities can now be invested, yielding significant revenue. Thus there is a fifth reason for short-term borrowing: to raise revenue, as the government can borrow at a lower rate than it can earn in the security market. In addition, there are new forms of short-term borrowing, including tax and revenue anticipation notes (TRANs), grant anticipation notes (GANs), and tax-exempt commercial paper (TECP), which will be explained later.

Given that they have very tight budgets and that they collect revenue primarily in the third and fourth months of a fiscal year, most large and many medium-size governments have discovered that short-term borrowing is essential. Because instruments such as TANs can actually be a money source—an added bonus—previous approaches by finance officers to short-term borrowing have been turned upside down. Certainly BANs have become more popular, given their money-making potential plus their remarkably high long-term interest rates. Regardless of the motivation for short-term borrowing, a formal payment calendar should be established so that the debt can be properly managed to maximize the benefits to the local government.

Early Developments in the Debt Concept

Innovation can clearly be seen in the use of debt in the past 30 years. The most well-known innovative debt concept is the revenue bond. It was first used in 1897 to support the construction of the Spokane, Washington, Water Works. This debt mechanism, coupled with a means to raise revenue, was not popular until after World War II. Then court decisions held that authorities (e.g., Port of New York and New Jersey and Triborough Bridge Authority) had separate legal status. People in government were seeking new ways to finance public facilities without increasing taxes, and revenue bonds provided an answer. Briefly, the reasons for increased use of revenue bonds are as follows:

1. Although revenue bonds had a higher interest cost than general obligations bonds, that cost decreased significantly.
2. There was more use of public authorities and an expansion of types of authorities (e.g., airports, public parks, recreation areas and facilities, stadia and public sport facilities, power projects, housing, public markets, college dormitories, port facilities, etc.).
3. Restrictions on general obligations closed this mechanism, forcing the use of revenue bonds.
4. It was relatively easy to obtain revenue bond approval, especially because of the non-referendum requirement.
5. The ability to apply user charges to pay for debt services was appealing.

A lesser used version of the revenue bond is the lease rental bond. Let us say a school district cannot get voter approval for a bond issue. One ploy used is to create a nonprofit authority to build and then lease the new school to the school district. A long-term school board lease with the authority provides the necessary security so that revenue bondholders know that debt services will be paid. Thus the school is built and financed by a revenue bond. Because the authority is merely a financing mechanism, some financial groups treat these governments as general obligation bonds. The same type of authority is sometimes created to help industry in plant and equipment acquisition. These industrial aid revenue bonds are paid off through a lease which exists between authority and industry. Industrial aid bonds were started in Mississippi to encourage industrial growth in the state. Most states use such revenue bonds, but Mississippi and a few other states are unusual in that even general obligation borrowing authority can be used to assist industry. The bonds are retired through revenue generated from leases between the government and industry.

An interesting cousin of the revenue bond is the special obligation bond. A revenue bond is tied to the revenue-generating capacity of a government's ability to produce a service, as well as to the demand for that service. A special obligation bond is tied to the revenue-generating capacity of a government revenue source, which can be entirely outside the control of the local government and may have no logical relationship to the reason for the bond. For example, general revenue-sharing receipts from the federal government can be the pledged revenue source for a special obligation bond which can be used to build libraries, schools, roads, or piers.

Capital Financing in the 1980s

The early 1980s saw a remarkable change in the tax-exempt securities market. On the one hand, the need for state and local spending on public facilities became very significant (i.e., $3 trillion). On the other hand, the supply of long-term investment capital decreased. No reasonably accurate estimates can be made of public facilities' needs, but Pat Choate, a senior economic policy analyst for TRTW, Inc., estimated in *America in Ruins: Beyond the Public Works Pork Barrel* (Washington, Council of the State Planning Agencies, 1981) that $3 trillion was needed for repair, replacement, and construction of new public facilities. This was in a period in which Reagan's Republican administration was successfully reducing federal domestic programs, many state and local areas were experiencing tax revolts which were limiting government revenue, and the economy was going through the worst recession since the Great Depression. This left state and local governments with debt as the only alternative in a very unstable credit market in which traditional debt instruments were inadequate.

The municipal bond market was affected both by the recession and by legal changes instituted by the Reagan administration. As a counter to high inflation rates prior to the recession, the Federal Reserve System had imposed extremely restrictive monetary policies. That, combined with the Reagan administration's massive yearly deficits, produced record high interest rates which came down slowly as economic recovery started to take place. Changes enacted in the Economic Recovery Tax Act of 1981 (ERTA) contributed to the higher interest rates by reducing the incentive for persons in higher tax brackets to use the municipal bond tax shelter and by expanding other income-sheltering opportunities (e.g., Individual Retirement Accounts and All Savers Certificates). In addition, ERTA permitted firms to sell tax benefits to the highest bidders, which created billions of dollars of alternative tax shelter investment opportunities. Further, the Investment Tax Credit (ITC) and Accelerated Cost Recovery Schedules (ACRS) enhanced the after-tax rate of return on private investment, thus lessening the need for tax shelters because less income was taxable. The 1982 Federal Tax Act (TEFRA) further changed the municipal security market by the partial removal of the deductibility of bank interest costs used to finance tax-exempt securities and the requirement that all new municipal bonds must be registered. The latter change was extremely significant, as coupon bonds were very popular among investors.

The biggest influence on the market, however, was the poor economy, which resulted in fewer business and individual profits that normally would have been attracted into the municipal bond market in tax shelters.

Given those environmental factors, the character of the municipal bond market changed radically. Demand for tax-exempt bonds by the two major institutional investors, namely commercial banks and property and casualty insurance companies, practically evaporated after 1979. The tax-exempt market reacted by stressing and more aggressively marketing to individual investors. The percentage of bonds held by individual and mutual funds in the tax-exempt market shot up in 1981 and 1982. This was particularly true for short-term tax-exempt paper, which appealed to the money market mutual funds. During 1981, tax-exempt money market holdings grew by $3 billion, which represented an increase of approximately three-fourths. By the end of 1982, there were $13.2 billion in aggregate holdings.

The factors cited above, plus the extensive use of private-purpose tax-exempt borrowing, has narrowed the gap between the tax-exempt and taxable market, with the notable exception of the short-term market. Historically, tax-exempt interest rates run from 65 to 70 percent less than comparable taxable bond yields. In 1981 and 1982, the spread shifted to 80 to 85 percent. This means that the arbitrage advantage does not result automatically in lower bond interest charges for local and state governments. The cost of borrowing for long-term issues is about the same for government as for the private sector. This radical change was partially the result of industrial revenue bonds, which enables local government to attract industry through its lower interest cost advantage. The extensive use of that technique, plus scattered defaults (e.g., Washington Public Power Supply System), have shaken confidence in user revenue. The result is higher tax-exempt borrowing rates.

CREATIVE CAPITAL FINANCING

For the finance officer, there is a new world. Since the beginning of the century, the municipal bond market was staid, straightforward, and conservative. Most financing was general obligation (GO) debt, with a gradually increasing use of revenue issues backed by either a user fee or a dedicated tax source. In 1960, total long-term financing was approximately $7.5 billion, of which 70 percent was general obligation. By 1975, non-GO debt accounted for 50 percent of the total new issues; and by 1981, it accounted for 70 percent, a complete reversal of the 1960 situation. Exhibit 8–1 illustrates the rate at which revenue bonding replaced tax-supported debt. Only the most popular subjects (e.g., building of police stations and jails) tend to be financed by GO debt because they alone get voter referendum approval. As Exhibit 8–2 shows, 29 percent of the issues submitted to the electorate received voter approval in 1975, and only 15–18 percent of the total debt actually issued was approved in 1976–1978.

Historically, municipalities have not been active in the short-term market, but disclosure requirements and economic pressures channeled them in the 1980s into the public market. Lower cash reserves have forced municipalities in record num-

EXHIBIT 8-1 Recent Trends in Revenue Bond Financing

| | | PERCENTAGE OF VOLUME SOLD AS: | |
YEAR	TOTAL VOLUME (MILLIONS OF DOLLARS)	REVENUE	GENERAL OBLIGATION
1969	$11,702.0	30.53%	69.47%
1970	18,082.5	33.74	66.26
1971	24,929.1	34.94	65.06
1972	23,692.4	39.69	60.31
1973	23,821.5	44.62	55.38
1974	23,560.4	42.44	57.56
1975	30,699.4	48.00	52.00
1976	35,415.7	48.77	51.23
1977	46,705.9	61.33	38.67
1978	48,352.0	63.37	36.63
1979	43,365.4	72.07	27.93

Source: Philip J. Fischer, Ronald W. Forbes, and John E. Peterson, "Risk and Return in the Choice of Revenue Bond Financing," in *Creative Capital Financing.* Edited by John E. Peterson and Wesley C. Hough. Chicago: Municipal Finance Officers Association, 1983, p. 140.

EXHIBIT 8-2 Trends in Bond Election Results

YEAR	PERCENTAGE APPROVED OF VOLUME SUBMITTED TO ELECTORATE	PERCENTAGE APPROVED OF TOTAL VOLUME OF DEBT SOLD
1968	54%	53%
1969	40	37
1970	63	30
1971	35	13
1972	64	34
1973	52	28
1974	62	35
1975	29	12
1976	59	15
1977	61	12
1978	63	18

Source: The Daily Bond Buyer

bers to seek short-term financing in order to reduce interest cost on capital projects, to meet short-term cash flow deficits, and to generate new revenues through wise cash management. Even with arbitrage regulations, municipalities are discovering remarkable cash management advantages in short-term borrowing within the existing market. For example, if a $5 million tax and revenue anticipation issue is sold in July (the first month of the fiscal year) and matures the following June (the last month of the fiscal year), the city receives the financial benefit of additional revenue while it covers its cash flow deficits. The following explains how this is possible:

Proceeds in July: $5 million
Less insurance cost: ($30,000)
New proceeds: $4.97 million
Interest expense (11 months at 9 percent): $412,500
Interest earnings (10 months at 13 percent): $538,417
Net New Revenue: $125,917

The key for the finance officer seeking the lowest finance charges is to tailor the municipality's issue to attract a significant portion of the municipal bond market. The reality is that GO debt is not as viable a means to finance huge capital needs in periods of economic hardship. This leaves the finance officer with the challenge of making the debt issue as attractive as possible to potential investors at a time when a radical shift to the individual investor is taking place. One type of creative capital financing—zero coupon bonds (ZCBs)—illustrates the more individually tailored market orientation useful to a finance officer. ZCBs are bonds without current interest coupons which are at substantial discount from par and provide return to investors through accretion in value at maturity. Thus, they can be sold for $602 when issued and can be redeemed in five years for $1,000. The heads of the approximately 2.5 million households in 1982 with incomes between $50,000 and $100,000 should be interested in smaller original tax-exempt investments. They are looking forward to retirement or to financing college educations. A package of ZCBs could provide these investors with the equivalent of a tax-free annuity stream that would be attractive compared with taxable alternatives. Exhibit 8-3 provides an example.

NONTRADITIONAL

The nontraditional ways to package bond issues more attractively include external credit supports, tax-exempt commercial paper, put option securities, original issue discount bonds including ZCBs, variable rate securities, and leasing. These are means to attract new or retain old investors in the tax-exempt market. With these instruments, a negotiated sale may become superior to a competitive sale owing to the complexity of this type of sale. Regardless, technical advice is important to obtain in meeting the following goals:

1. targeting the investment vehicle toward a specific group of investors (those who have money and have a preference which can be satisfied);
2. designing the instrument features, such as where to place the put option, what index to employ in a variable rate, and how to construct a lease-purchase agreement (these will be explained later);
3. timing the transaction; and
4. considering objectively the alternative approaches.

EXHIBIT 8-3 Tax-Exempt ZC "Annuity" Bonds

MATURITY (IN YEARS)	AMOUNT AT MATURITY	PRICE TODAY FOR ANNUITY PAYMENT	EFFECTIVE YIELD
1	$ 1,000	$ 915.73	9.00%
2	1,000	830.58	9.50
3	1,000	746.22	10.00
4	1,000	671.70	10.20
5	1,000	602.34	10.40
6	1,000	538.10	10.60
7	1,000	478.89	10.80
8	1,000	424.58	11.00
9	1,000	375.02	11.20
10	1,000	329.99	11.40
11	1,000	289.28	11.60
12	1,000	252.64	11.80
13	1,000	219.81	12.00
14	1,000	189.28	12.25
15	1,000	164.54	12.40
16	1,000	143.71	12.50
17	1,000	125.28	12.60
18	1,000	109.01	12.70
19	1,000	95.52	12.75
20	1,000	83.62	12.80
	$20,000	$7,585.84	11.76%

Equivalent Taxable Returns:

50% Tax Rate	$40,000	$7,585.84	26.11%
30% Tax Rate	28,710	7,585.84	18.16%

Source: Ronald Forbes and Edward Renshaw, "Tax-Exempt Zero Coupon Bonds," in *Creative Capital Financing.* Edited by John E. Peterson and Wesley P. Hough. Chicago: Municipal Finance Officers Association, 1982, pp. 153.

The forms of external credit support include a bank line of credit, a letter of credit, municipal bond insurance, state credit assistance, and federal guarantees. A line of credit is a contingent loan arrangement with a bank in which the bank agrees to lend funds required by the government for a fixed time period. The similar letter of credit (LOC) is an unconditional pledge of the bank's credit to make principal and interest payments of specific amount and term on an issuer's debt. Both provide a guarantee that future liquidity needs will be met. Normally, they are used for smaller amounts than are found in bond insurance, and the size and type of issue are generally unrestricted; banks usually charge an annual fee for the LOC plus normal interest charges on the principal. In contrast, the bond insurance premium is a one-time, up-front fee. The LOC and letter of credit can lower interest cost because the credit-worthiness of the bank is substituted. Also, it may be necessary to use the LOC in connection with other creative capital financing devices (e.g., put options). A major private insurance group such as the Municipal Bond Insurance Association (MBIA) or the American Municipal Bond Assurance Corporation (AMBAC) can also as-

EXHIBIT 8-4 Selected Features: Private Municipal Bond Guarantees

| | Features Which Issues Must Possess to be Eligible for Guarantee | | | |
PROGRAM	TYPE OF ISSUE*	SIZE OF ISSUE (IN MILLIONS)	QUALITY LIMITATIONS	COST OF GUARANTEE (PD. AT TIME OF ISSUE)
AMBAC	G.O.'s & Rev. Bds. of existing facilities	$0.6–$22.0 (tot. prin. & int.)	S&P BBB or better	½%–1½% of original principal *and* interest
Indemnity Corp.	G.O.'s & Rev.'s	$0.6–$18.0 (tot. prin. & int.)	none	½%–3½% of original principal *and* interest
MBIA	G.O.'s & Utility Rev. Bds.	$0.6–$20.0 (prin. only)	Generally, S&P BBB or better	1%–2% of original principal only

*With the exception of Indemnity Corp., all guarantees are for *new* bond issues. (Indemnity Corp. will also guarantee portfolios of outstanding bonds.)

Source: Michael O. Joehnk and David S. Kidwell. "Determining the Advantages and Disadvantages of Private Municipal Bond Guarantees," in *Creative Capital Financing.* Ed. by John E. Petersen and Wesley C. Hough. Chicago: Municipal Finance Officers Association, 1983, p. 214.

sume the default risk of a government for a specific fee. Exhibit 8-4 presents selected features of the three private bond guarantee programs available to state and local governments.

The result of purchasing insurance should be a lower interest rate than could be obtained without insurance. That benefit, using a present value method, must exceed the premium cost. Normally, the insurance premium accounts for 20 to 30 basis points (100 basis points equals 1 percent interest). Cost saving can be as high as 40 to 95 basis points on new bond issues. States can provide municipal credit assistance by guaranteeing local debt issues, much as a private insurance company would do; by acting as a financial intermediary via a state municipal bond bank; and finally by providing grants to subsidize local debt service requirements. Each activity can lower subjurisdiction interest and possibly administrative costs. The last external source of support is the federal government, which has provided guarantees in the areas of housing and urban renewal.

An interesting creative finance development is "loan-to-lender" financing, which marries federally insured certificates of deposit to tax-exempt industrial revenue bonds. An industrial tax exempt revenue bond is issued, with the proceeds deposited in exchange for federally insured certificates of deposit with triple-A credit ratings. Those proceeds which result from negotiation at the same rate and term as the industrial bonds are used, by contractual obligation, to make mortgage loans to third party developers to finance publicly desired projects (e.g., low income housing). These increasingly popular instruments carry remarkably low interest rates (e.g., 10.5 percent for a 10-year term with a 30-year amortization schedule).

Tax-exempt commercial paper (TECP) can be used for purposes similar to those of TANs and BANs, but the paper must be supported by a bank line of credit which enhances cash liquidity. This new security has recently increased in popularity, especially because the interest earned is exempt from federal taxes. The variety of maturities available and the ready liquidity make TECP an especially convenient instrument for those wishing to tailor maturities to future needs. There is a drawback: TECP has higher start-up and operating costs than traditional short-term instruments have (e.g., TANs and BANs). Thus, a government should have at least $25 million of short-term borrowing a year to justify the TECP costs. If the government has large short-term borrowing needs, TECP normally costs less than traditional short-term instruments. However, TECP must be retired when funds become available and this may eliminate important reinvestment earning opportunities. The latter can be an important source of local revenue.

A put, or tender, option in the issue offering can attract long-term investors as well as take advantage of lower short-term interest rates. The tender option permits the investors to convert the investment to a shorter maturity, much as the call provision permits the government to do the same. The put option places liquidity demands on the issuer; hence a letter of credit is needed. The so-called "window put," or European option, can be exercised once during a certain period. In contrast, the "anniversary put," or American option, allows the investor to put their bonds back to the issuer periodically, generally on a given date once every year. Other things being equal, investors should value a 25-year bond with a five-year window put option higher than they would a traditional 25-year bond. The former represents a very strong protection against rising rates and falling bond prices. In high interest periods, it saves the issuer at least 275 basis points. Beside external liquidity support, the put option requires a remarketing agreement with a bank or underwriter by which the option is exercised.

An original issue discount bond (OID) is a long-term bond offered at a discount of the stated par value. The return occurs through gradual accretion to the bond's maturity when par is met. This is in contrast to traditional bonds, with which investors pay the par value to the municipality and receive back the principal plus the stated interest by the time of maturity. The IRS treats the difference between the par value and the purchase price as tax-exempt income. The "ultimate" original discount bond is the ZCB explained earlier. Another type of bond is the compound interest bond (also called the municipal multiplier and capital appreciation bond), which is initially sold at its par value. At maturity, investors receive payment of principal invested plus the amount of earned interest that has been accumulated over the life of the bond at a semi-annually compounded rate.

Variable rate securities attract investors who believe that market rates will continue to rise and wish to maintain their investment capital value. This is accomplished by offering securities which have floating rates; the yield is tied by a formula to some other market factor, such as the prevailing interest rate on treasury notes. An added plus is the inclusion of a put option to increase liquidity as a trade-off for lower interest charges. The key to this type of issue is the choice of indexes by which the floating rates are determined and the frequency with which the rate is readjusted.

A nondebt instrument which can accomplish the same purpose as a debt is the lease. The category includes the operating lease, the sale-leaseback, the safe-harbor lease, and the leverage lease. In the past, a lease was merely an agreement between a government unit and a private owner for the use of property or services over a period of time in exchange for rent or a fee. With creative capital financing, there are much more complex agreements which take advantage of recently enacted federal tax incentives for private investment in capital goods. In a true or operating lease, a government unit acquires the use of an asset, with a private investor having title, a 20 percent equity investment (under IRS rules), and the use of a tax-exempt debt (e.g., an industrial bond) to cover the other 80 percent. Often the government purchases the asset at fair market value when the lease expires. The result of this complex arrangement is that the private person is able to "share" the accelerated depreciation and investment tax credit advantages at a lower lease rate and an agreed-upon fair market value selling price.

A sale-leaseback involves the sale of government property to private investors, who receive tax advantages from the purchase while leasing back the asset to the government for its use. The value of the tax benefits can be shared, with the "sale" proceeds used to renovate the asset. In a safe-harbor lease, made possible by ERTA, the government sells property (e.g., mass transit vehicles) in a traditional sale-leaseback, with the advantage that the tax write-offs can be sold to and used by profit-making companies to reduce their taxes. At the end of the lease, the asset may be repurchased for a nominal amount. In a leverage lease, a third party finances a large purchase. The lessor uses borrowed capital to purchase the asset leased to the local government. The lender is repaid with a tax-exempt interest and a security interest in the property. Exhibits 8-5 and 8-6 present the investor's and the government's respective advantages from a possible sale-leaseback situation using the new present value concept.

Two more ideas associated with creative capital financing—warrants and small denomination bonds—may also be useful in designing issues. "Warrants" have acquired an additional meaning with the use of that term by the Municipal Assistance Corporation's February 1981 issue for the City of New York. Warrants are special certificates attached to bonds that permit investors to purchase future bonds at the same price and interest as the original issue. This is normally referred to as an "option to buy." Such certificates are treated as bearer-redeemable securities that may be detached from the original bonds and sold separately. Edward Anthony Lehan champions mini-municipal bonds, which are sold in $100, $500, and $1000 par amounts rather than in the traditional $5000 par amount. He points out that they have been successful when tried and that they give the added advantage of permitting local citizens to invest directly in their community more easily. The mini-bonds, in some instances, were modeled on U.S. savings bonds and were essentially mini-ZCBs.

Tests and Limits

At the local and state levels, questions are raised when an increase in the local or state public debt is contemplated. Some argue that no debt is best. Others say that if the services can be greatly increased by substituting capital for current expenditures such as labor costs, then such investments are wise. Others argue that capital

EXHIBIT 8-5 Sale-Leaseback from the Investor's Perspective

TOTAL PRICE TO INVESTORS: $5,000,000
SOURCES OF FUNDS: $3,850,000 Industrial Revenue Bond
$1,150,000 Investor Equity

	YEAR 1	YEAR 2	YEARS 3–14	YEAR 15	TOTAL (000'S)	NET PRESENT VALUE @ 15% (000'S)
(A) Operating Expenses						
Rental Income	$ 585,000	$585,000	$7,020,000	$ 585,000	$8,775	$3,421
Sale Price at End of Lease	—	—	—	1,150,000	1,150	141
Administrative Expense	5,000	5,000	60,000	5,000	75	29
Debt Service on IDB	565,273	565,273	6,783,276	565,273	8,479	3,307
Income before Taxes	14,727	14,727	176,724	1,164,727	1,371	226
(B) Tax Advantages						
Tax Liability or Savings at 50%						
Bracket**	77,667	71,470	−11,535	−493,051*	−355	148
Investment Tax Credit	950,000	—	—	—	950	826
Total Return on Investment after Taxes (Income before taxes plus tax advantages)	$1,042,394	$ 86,197	$ 165,189	$ 671,676	$1,965	$1,200

*includes capital gains tax
**tax on income after deductions for straight-line depreciation, administrative expenses, and interest paid on IRB

Source: Creative Capital Financing, p. 89.

254

EXHIBIT 8-6   Sale Leaseback from the Government Unit's Perspective

	ANNUAL	15-YEAR TOTAL	PRESENT VALUE @ 15%
Cost of Sale-Leaseback Financing Alternative:			
(1) Lease Payments (net of ground lease)	$585,000	$8,775,000	$4,449,556
(2) Earnings from Escrow Account ($1 million invested at 11%)	110,000	1,650,000	836,669
(3) Repurchase of Building at End of Lease ($1.15 million less $1 million in escrow account)		150,000	35,909
(4) Net Cost of Sale-Leaseback	$475,000	$7,275,000	$3,648,796
Cost of General Obligation Bond Financing Alternative:			
(5) Debt Service if $4 Million, 15-Year Bonds at 10% Were Issued	$525,895	$7,888,425	$3,999,999
Savings from Sale-Leaseback:			
(GO debt service less total cost of sale-leaseback)	$ 50,895	$ 613,425	$351,203

Source: Creative Capital Financing, p. 90.

expenditures benefit tomorrow's taxpayers and paying a debt appropriately shifts the cost of the project to them. Others use a more pragmatic test: If the government (1) can service the debt (i.e., meet the payments as well as meet other normal expenses of government) and (2) can refinance its debt through the market, then the debt is acceptable.[1] Servicing a debt can be a tremendous burden on a community. A commonly used danger sign is when the debt service approaches 20 to 25 percent of the total budget. In some communities this limit is exceeded, but nationally the aggregate debt figures for state and local governments are less than 10 percent of the total budgets.

Exhibit 8-7 shows the federal, state, and local debt as a percentage of general revenue. In the aggregate, state and local debt is not a significant proportion of general revenue. In contrast, the percentage of federal debt has grown steadily since 1969 and it is approaching the undesirable 20 to 25 percent level.

Governments which have the most difficulty in financing their activities are usually those experiencing weak economic growth. If an area is growing, then there is demand for borrowing, but there is an improving tax base with which to pay that debt. If the tax base is shrinking but the cost of government is increasing, then the government is more likely to be classified as weak and not able to attract investors when refinancing is sought.

[1]Some argue that even this test is not appropriate given the changing municipal market demands and conditions. There is no uniform acceptance of any single simple test.

**EXHIBIT 8-7 Federal, State and Local Debt,
Selected Years 1954–1981**

AMOUNT (IN BILLIONS)			
FISCAL YEAR	GROSS FEDERAL DEBT	TOTAL STATE DEBT	TOTAL LOCAL DEBT
1954	$ 270.8	$ 9.6	$ 29.3
1959	284.7	16.9	47.2
1964	316.8	25.0	67.2
1969	367.1*	39.6	94.0
1974	486.2**	65.3	141.3
1979	833.8	111.7	192.4
1980	914.3	122.0	213.6
1981	1,003.9	134.8	229.0

*During 1969, three government-sponsored enterprises became completely privately owned and their debt was removed from the totals for the federal government. At the dates of their conversion, gross federal debt was reduced by $10.7 billion.
**A 1973 procedural change in the recording of trust fund holdings of treasury debt at the end of each month increased gross federal debt by about $4.5 billion.

Sources: ACIR staff compilations and computations based upon U.S. Bureau of the Census, Governmental Finances In (Year) (State and local debt figures: Tables 19 in 1980–81 edition).

An associated problem is refinancing the short-term debt, which must be either retired or refinanced each year. This places pressure from the market on weaker governments when refinancing needs are high and investor confidence is low. Weaker governments find themselves unable to pay off the short-term debts, so default becomes a very real possibility in spite of the fact that normally they can meet the interest payments.

Investors' views are significant. They wish to buy safe bonds or notes which will earn them some money. There are no ideal indicators; however, investors do use the following indicators in making decisions:

1. Does the ratio of debt to full value exceed 10 percent?
2. What is the ratio of debt to market value of the real property? How does that compare with other governments?
3. What is the debt per capita? How does this compare with other governments?
4. What is the ratio of debt to personal income (per capita income)?
5. What is the ratio of debt service to total budget?

Standard and Poor's (a major bond firm) has developed a series of early warning guidelines which municipalities would be wise to consider carefully in monitoring their own financial operations. They are:

1. current year operating deficit;
2. two consecutive years of operating fund deficit;
3. current year operating deficit that is larger than the previous year's deficit;

4.   a general fund deficit in the current position on the current year balance sheet;
5.   a current general fund deficit (two or more years in the last five);
6.   short-term debt (other than BAN) greater than 5 percent of main operating fund revenues outstanding at the end of the fiscal year;
7.   a two-year trend of increasing short-term debt outstanding at fiscal year end;
8.   short-term interest and current year debt service greater than 20 percent of total revenues;
9.   property taxes greater than 90 percent of the tax limit;
10.   net debt outstanding greater than 90 percent of the tax limit;
11.   total property tax collections less than 92 percent of total levy;
12.   a trend of increasing tax collections during two consecutive years in a three-year trend;
13.   declining market valuations during two consecutive years in a three-year trend;
14.   overall net debt ratio 20 percent higher than previous year; and
15.   overall net debt ratio 50 percent higher than four years ago.

State constitutions and laws do establish artificial limits. They vary greatly from state to state as well as by type of local government. Normally, they express the limit as a percent of the property tax base. Often state laws add provisions so that jurisdictions which tax the same citizens have lower limits. This avoids greater taxpayer liabilities for citizens from two or more overlapping jurisdictions. Also state laws sometimes establish artificial limits based on the tax imposed for servicing the debt. Another common state limitation is the procedural requirement calling for a referendum on long-term indebtedness bond issues.

Revenue bonds are treated by investors much like corporation bonds. State law often does not prescribe limits and the limits are established by the market. Investors examine forecasts of income to ensure debt services will be met and their investments will be safe.

New York City Financial Crisis

In April 1975, New York City hovered on the brink of default on its obligations. With help from New York State, the federal government, and others, default was averted, but two significant consequences have emerged:

1   interest rates are higher for state and local government since the crisis;
2.   more elaborate financial disclosures are now required.

The effects of the New York crisis were felt throughout the nation and North Carolina is one example. In *Southern City*, Kenneth Murray reported in January 1976 that:

A recent study by the Municipal Finance Officer's Association (MFOA) shows that the New York City financial crisis has already cost local governments in North Carolina $424,000 in first-year added interest costs on bonded indebtedness and $5.1 million total in interest over the life of municipal bonds issued in 1975.[2]

[2]Kenneth Murray, "New York Crisis—Its Effect on North Carolina," *Southern City* (Raleigh, N.C.: North Carolina League of Municipalities, January 1976), p. 6.

In the pre-crisis era, state and local governments were able to sell their bonds without revealing much about their financial situation. Since the crisis, investors are demanding greater disclosure of facts about the community and bonds.

Government Financial Emergencies

There are rather clear warning signs for a municipality which is in financial trouble:

1. an operating fund revenue/expenditure imbalance in which current expenditures significantly exceed current revenues in one fiscal period (a well-managed government, under some conditions such as an excessively large fund balance, could properly have this type of imbalance);
2. a consistent pattern of current expenditures exceeding current revenues by small amounts for several years;
3. an excess of current operating liabilities over current assets (a fund deficit);
4. short-term operating loans outstanding at the conclusion of a fiscal year, the borrowing of cash from restricted funds, or an increase in unpaid bills in lieu of short-term operating loans;
5. a high and rising rate of property tax delinquency;
6. a sudden substantial decrease in assessed values for unexpected reasons;
7. an unfunded or underfunded pension liability, unless done over a long period of time such as 40 years; and
8. poor budgeting, accounting, and reporting.

Once there is recognition of the financial problems, financial management improvements can be considered. The most common remedy is to eliminate the imbalance between revenues and expenditures. Often, an appropriate remedy is to develop safeguards against misuse of short-term operating funds. The remedy could be to fund the retirement system adequately. Commonly, improvements must be made in municipal accounting and reporting systems.

If self-remedies are ineffective, then more significant steps can be taken. Some states have administrative bodies created to assist troubled local governments. If that is inadequate, the courts can demand that consultants such as Morgan Guarantee Trust be hired and, if necessary, can arrange for direct agreements with creditors. This is usually adequate for temporary or technical financial emergencies. If the problem continues, states sometimes have the power to force special remedies on a local government. Agreements usually undergo state review, approval, and supervision. The federal role is to provide a means to devise financial adjustments which a majority of the creditors approve.

Under chapter 9 of the federal bankruptcy law, a plan of composition or financial adjustments is developed. First, a voluntary petition for bankruptcy is filed by the eligible local government unit. A plan of composition must be filed with the petition. The plan must be accepted by those holding 51 percent of the securities affected by the plan. Upon filing, an order is entered by the judges either approving or dismissing the plan. If approved, the resources of the debtor come within the jurisdiction of the court and a time and place is fixed for a hearing. Notice is given to the creditors, answers can be filed, and the hearing is held. After the hearing, the court may confirm a plan of composition that has been accepted by the creditors involved in two-thirds of the aggregate amount. The court may but seldom does continue jurisdiction after the confirmation of the plan.

CAPITAL BUDGETING

Operating versus Capital Budgeting

Most local governments have two types of budgets: operating and capital. The operating budget deals with everyday types of activities. The capital budget deals with large expenditures for capital items. They differ in the nature of items purchased, methods of financing, and even the accompanying decision-making process. In most instances, operating expenses are depleted in a single year. Normally, capital items have long-range returns and useful life spans, are relatively expensive, and have physical presences, such as a building, road, water supply system, or sewage system.

The most significant difference is the method of financing. Capital budget items are often financed through borrowing, but they can also be funded by saving over a period of years for the capital item or by using grants, special assessment, and the general revenue fund. Because government debts are involved, state laws, not surprisingly, do establish debt limits (normally associated with the assessed value of property). Also states often require equalization rates to ensure consistent treatment throughout each state. The debt limits vary from state to state and there are exceptions to the limit and application of equalization rates.

Some local governments shift as many expenses as possible from operating to capital budgets. For example, in both West Point, Mississippi, and New York City, band uniforms have been called capital budget items by public officials. This tendency can lead to corruption of the concept of a capital item to such an extent that the government has two operating budgets, with one financed through borrowing. That situation in turn leads to overuse of bonding, greater government resources used for debt retirement, and proportionately less money used to meet operating budget demands. Eventually the debt can become large enough that payments cannot be met and the community must face the possibility of municipal bankruptcy. Traditionally, debt is used to finance items with a life expectancy that lasts as long as the debt payments. The effect of this practice is to limit the overuse of debt financing and to make the debt more politically defensible as the future taxpayers are able to identify how they benefited from the decision to finance the item by borrowing money.

In capital budgeting, planning and careful, deliberate action are essential. Planning is needed to integrate the capital items with the remainder of the physical structure in the community. Capital improvement plans are essential to coordinate the work by time, funding possibilities, and physical plans. If building is involved, then the process of executing decisions involves study of the possibilities, site selection and acquisition, and planning and design as well as construction financing. Delays translate to higher construction costs owing to inflation, especially rising labor costs; thus, delays are to be avoided. Also, the increased operating and maintenance expense incurred on account of the new facility is an important factor which can be considered in the planning phase. Communities have built facilities they cannot afford to operate or maintain (e.g., stadiums).

Capital Facilities Planning

Decisions to add a public facility or make extensive repairs can be made on the basis of understanding the needs of the community and the resources available. The best approach to identifying the resources is to inventory the existing public facilities. The next step is to catalog the proposed public facilities. The key facts in the catalog include: the location of the proposed facility, the year of construction, cost priority, project description, financing schedule, prior or sunk costs, projection of future related fund requests, operating costs, and savings in operating and maintenance costs. The inventory and file of proposed projects can be updated at least once a year to ensure that decisions are based on the correct facts.

Making decisions on proposed projects is not easy and can be aided greatly if there are clear, detailed answers to the following questions:

1. What is the relationship of the proposed project to the overall development of the city?
2. How many citizens will be helped by the project, and how many citizens will be harmed or inconvenienced if the project is not constructed? Which citizens?
3. Will the proposed project replace a present worn-out service or structure or is it an additional responsibility of government?
4. Will the project add to the property value of the area, thus increasing the value of city property and receipts from property tax? How much of an increase will be realized?
5. Will the construction of the improvement add to the city's operation and maintenance budget? How much?
6. Will the project increase the efficiency of performance? How much and where? What cost savings will result? Will the project reduce the cost of performance for a particular service? How much and where?
7. Will the project provide a service required for economic growth and development of the municipality?
8. Is the estimated cost of the improvement within the city's ability to pay?

Ultimately, priorities have to be decided and judgements have to be made. Sometimes analytical techniques such as cost-benefit analysis are useful but judgment cannot be avoided. Some communities use a point system to establish priorities. One scale used is as follows:

1. urgent (highest priority);
2. essential;
3. necessary;
4. desirable;

5. acceptable;
6. deferrable (lowest priority).

Capital Budget Cycle

The budget cycle for capital budgeting is similar to the operating budget cycle. The phases are identical. A capital budget call and calendar are needed just as in an operating budget. Detailed information must be collected. Illustrations of the forms can be found by consulting the publications of the Government Finance Officers Association noted in this chapter's references.

Many governments prepare a multiyear capital improvement program each year. This helps those relying on capital decisions to understand the likely physical facilities in the near future. The program is normally funded through borrowing, grants, and the operating budget. The government formally approves the capital improvement plan and passes an ordinance or law which clearly explains what is approved and the method of financing the program.

Capital budgets are carefully reviewed. Both budget analysts and planners review the plans for possible errors and potential problems. Public hearings are commonly held, especially if revenue-sharing money is used to fund the capital budget. Careful consideration goes into deciding the best financing plan. Ultimately, the capital budget is approved by the official government policy-making unit, such as the city council (and possibly even by the electorate, if a bond issue is involved).

BONDING

Designing an Issue

Once a government has decided to borrow money, bonding is usually undertaken. Normally, competitive bidding is used to seek the lowest bidder. Prior to publishing the invitation to bid, decisions must be made on the maturity, the size of the issue, the call terms, the principal and interest return structure, the interest cost limit, and the option to reject the bids, plus a wide variety of creative financing considerations such as a put option and ZCBs. With the advent of creative capital financing, negotiated bidding is becoming more common. The complexity of this type of bonding is such that negotiations are sometimes required to get someone to accept the bond. Maturities vary in length and size. Sometimes they are 30 years, but more commonly they are 20 years or less. Traditionally, the length of the maturity is no longer than the useful life of the capital facility which is being financed. Serial bonds can be divided on an approximately equal basis but it is also possible to negotiate a deferral of payments during the first two to five years, resulting in a large final payment (called a balloon). If the issue is to appeal to the larger banking and security community, it should not be less than $1 million; $4.2 million is a normal size, but issues of more than $100 million do exist. Large issues require buyers to form syndicates, which are temporary financial partnerships to buy and sell securities. The primary buyer is called an underwriter; this can be a syndicate which will eventually sell the securities to groups and even to other syndicates. The use of syndicates is commonplace. Interestingly, their complex million-dollar agreements are often made by phone in an remarkably informal manner.

The provisions in the bond offering are important. Together with the credit standing, they largely determine the marketability of the issue. If many seek to invest in the security, then the government can get a lower interest rate. With creative capital financing, the variety of ways to structure the issue is remarkably complex. The key to the decision is to structure the issue to achieve the lowest price and other benefits for the local government.

For most bidders, the fact that there is a tax advantage for municipal bonds is significant. Exhibit 8-8 is a tax equivalency table which demonstrates that the higher a person's tax bracket, the higher the tax investment yield required in order to match a tax-free yield. For example, people filing joint returns and earning over $85,000 are in the 50 percent tax bracket; a taxable investment yielding 27 percent is equivalent to tax-free yield of 13.5 percent for them. For people filing joint returns and earning between $20,200 and $24,600, a taxable investment must return 18% in order to equal a 13.5 percent tax-free yield. This interest income is exempt from federal income taxation and is often exempt from income tax in the state of issue. If a state or local government improperly places the loaned proceeds in revenue-generating investments (e.g., only for reinvestment purposes), then the Internal Revenue Service would call the bonds arbitrage and tax the interest income from the bonds. Without such a rule and even to a certain extent with the rule, local governments would take advantage of their unique lower interest rates to invest in higher interest bearing bonds.

Other factors can also be considered before a bond is offered. The government may wish to establish an interest cost limit to protect itself from bids that are, as a group, unreasonable. Also the government may wish to add a stipulation that all bids may be rejected to further protect itself. Decisions can be made on the type of bond and whether it should be registered or not. Will the bond be sold at a public, competitive, or negotiated bidding or through private placement? When will the bond be dated? What is the best time and place of sale? What are the payment dates for principal and interest? Who will prepare the bond sale documents? Who will receive and read the bids? How will the bids be tabulated and awarded? Who will print the bonds so that the possibility of counterfeiting and theft will be minimized? How will delivery of bonds and receipts be conducted? What will be done if no bids are received? These and other matters are normally considered when an issue is developed.

Many local governments do not have the necessary expertise to handle bonding and therefore seek outside assistance. Even sophisticated local governments are often wise to hire a private financial advisor, especially for creative capital financing. Such an advisor may have added expertise in the particular market important to the local government finance officer. Some states provide assistance, but normally private advisory services are needed. The amount and degree of assistance vary with the amount and kind of funding contemplated. In moderate-sized,

EXHIBIT 8-8 Tax Equivalency Table

| TAXABLE INCOME | | | TO EQUAL A TAX-FREE YIELD OF: | | | | | |
JOINT RETURN	SINGLE RETURN	TAX BRACKET	11.00%	11.50%	12.00%	12.50%	13.00%	13.50%
			A TAXABLE INVESTMENT WOULD HAVE TO YIELD:					
$20,200–24,600		25%	14.67%	15.33%	16.00%	16.67%	17.33%	18.00%
	$15,000–18,200	27%	15.07%	15.75%	16.44%	17.12%	17.81%	18.49%
$24,600–29,900		29%	15.49%	16.19%	16.90%	17.61%	18.31%	19.01%
	$18,200–23,500	31%	15.94%	16.67%	17.39%	18.12%	18.84%	19.57%
$29,900–35,200		33%	16.42%	17.16%	17.91%	18.66%	19.40%	20.15%
	$23,500–28,800	35%	16.92%	17.69%	18.46%	19.23%	20.00%	20.77%
$35,200–45,800		39%	18.03%	18.85%	19.67%	20.49%	21.31%	22.13%
	$28,800–34,100	40%	18.33%	19.17%	20.00%	20.83%	21.67%	22.50%
$45,800–60,000	$34,100–41,500	44%	19.64%	20.54%	21.43%	22.32%	23.21%	24.11%
$60,000–85,600		49%	21.57%	22.55%	23.53%	24.51%	25.49%	26.47%
over $85,600	over $41,500	50%	22.00%	23.00%	24.00%	25.00%	26.00%	27.00%

*Taxable income is the net amount subject to federal income tax after deductions and exemptions.

Source: Merrill Lynch Asset Management Inc., 1983.

EXHIBIT 8-9 Total Marketing Cost ($5 to $10 Million Issues, Cost per $1,000)

ITEM	GENERAL OBLIGATION	REVENUE	DIFFERENCE (REVENUE-GENERAL OBLIGATION)
Legal			
Local Attorney	$1.62	$ 3.75	$2.13
Bond Counsel	2.00	2.96	.96
Bond Election	.50	.45*	−.05
Total Legal	4.12	7.16	3.04
Financial Advisor	1.44	2.63	1.19
Accountant	.97	1.05	.08
Notice	.14	.12	−.02
Prospectus	.91	1.30	.39
Printing	.23	.25	.02
Rating	.53	.78	.25
Signature	.06	.03	−.03
Other	.21	2.19	1.98
TOTAL	$8.61	$15.51	$6.90

*Mean for all revenue issues in the study.

Source: Creative Capital Financing, p. 143.

full-faith-and-credit transactions, groups such as local commercial banks, investment bankers, bond counsels, and state agencies may provide the services at no direct or minimum charge on negotiated sales. However, the services would be minimal and there might be the expectation that an advantageous relationship would be developed or protected. Often, the underwriter or potential underwriter can be helpful in suggesting approaches with a better market appeal. Exhibit 8-9 presents the costs commonly associated with obtaining bond expertise.

Purchasers of bonds need to be assured the bond itself is legal and they will not check the public record themselves. Therefore, a bond counsel is needed to certify (1) the legal existence of the government offering the bond, (2) the propriety of authorization of the bond, (3) the correctness of the procedures which have been followed in the conduct of the sale, (4) absence of litigation with respect to the validity of the bond issue, and (5) the correctness of the signatures on the bond. This assurance carries more weight if the bond counsel commands wide respect among investment bankers and investors.

Bond Prospectus, Notice of Sale, and Sale

Since the mid-1970s, a more elaborate bond prospectus has been required by investors. The prospectus is merely the information needed by investors to decide whether or not they wish to invest in the bonds. Key information in the prospectus often includes:

1. description of the bonds;
2. security for the bonds;
3. description of the government;
4. financial procedures pertinent to the issue;
5. fund revenues and disbursements;
6. explanation of the fund's budget;
7. local economic factors;
8. debt administration applicable to the issue;
9. description of the capital improvement program;
10. any contingent liabilities;
11. tax exemptions;
12. ratings;
13. certificates from necessary officials;
14. assessed valuation and tax rate;
15. tax levies and collections;
16. fund revenues and expenditures; and
17. comparative statement of financial conditions.

The GFOA "Disclosure Guidelines for Offerings of Securities by State and Local Governments" is the best guide to preparing a prospectus. It provides essential guidance and is recognized as the authoritative source. An excellent practical digest is presented in the Oregon Bond Disclosure Guidelines.

The prospectus is printed and distributed with the notice of sale. It is sent to investment bankers, a list of large investors, financial newspapers, and ratings and information agencies. The notice of sale includes:

1. the correct legal name of the issuing bond as well as the special law under which the government was organized and which gave it the authority to issue the bonds;
2. the type of bonds to be issued, the amount and purpose of the issue, the maturity schedule, and the call feature;
3. the date, time, and place of sale and the manner in which the bid is to be made;
4. limitations as to interest rate, payment dates of interest, and when and where the principal will be paid;
5. denomination and registration privileges;
6. basis for bidding;
7. amount of good faith check required;
8. bid form and basis for award;
9. name of approving attorney and statement on legality;
10. provisions made for payment of principal and interest;
11. total tax rate in the government unit and legal limits;
12. methods and place for settlement and delivery of the bonds; and
13. the right to reject any or all bids.

Some practices are fairly well accepted in the bond market. Bonds are dated as near as possible to the delivery date to avoid improper interest charges. Bonds are normally issued in $5,000 denominations except for odd amounts which should be retired the first year. Interest is paid semi-annually and bond owners often have the option of registering principal only or principal and interest. If the issue is sold on a wide market, then payments are made at large financial centers for the convenience of the bondholders. Payments must be prompt or a default occurs.

Often large issues are bought by highly competitive investment syndicates organized just for the purpose of buying the issue. The practice of these partnerships is to resell the issues as soon as possible to other investors. The syndicate members make their profit on the slight difference of what they bought and sold for each issue. Thus, municipalities selling bonds should be aware of the factors (i.e., maturity, coupon structure, points, rate limits) which permit easy syndicate reselling. If syndicates can easily resell bonds, then the municipality should be able to get a lower interest rate on its bonds.

For larger issues, a government might be wise to contract with a fiscal or paying agent. Paying agents are normally located in large financial centers, and they make the necessary principal and interest payments on the bonds. Fiscal agents have broader powers, including replacing lost or destroyed original bonds, exchanging coupons for registered bonds, canceling paid bonds and coupons, cremating canceled bonds and coupons, answering routine correspondence, and signing bonds. The advantage of having an agent at a financial center is the saving of time in the movement of credit, coupons, bonds, and checks, thus saving money.

Debt Records and Reporting

Reputation is important. The local government must develop among investors a reputation for accuracy and integrity so that full trust can be placed in its debt records, reports, and payment calendar. Surprises must be avoided. Scrupulous attention to each detail is essential. If such attention is not paid, the market automatically discounts the credit and higher interest payments result on later issues. Reports are needed by the government bond dealers, bond rating agencies, and, of course, the investors.

Essentially, the investor is interested only in the ability of the issuer to make timely payments of principal and interest. This judgment is often made on the basis of accounting data and reports. The National Committee on Government Accounting, in *Governmental Accounting, Auditing, and Financial Reporting*, has established basic standards for reporting on debt. This information cannot be segregated from the other financial reports of a government because of the interrelationship of the data and the potential significance of other financial data in understanding the government's debt and financial condition. Briefly, the investor is concerned with the balance sheet, amount of debt outstanding, status of the debt reserves, ability of the government to meet the payments, willingness of officials to use their power to service debt, and the record of the community in debt and other financial management. Also the investor is concerned with assessments, the area's economic condition, the market value of its property, the tax habits of its citizens, and any overlapping of debt with other local governments.

Timely information is important to investors. Therefore, every reasonable effort should be made to provide reports promptly and frequently.

Bond Ratings

State and local government bonds are rated, and this does reflect the likely interest rate for new issues of that jurisdiction. The fact that a government spends less per capita does not necessarily mean higher bond ratings. There is some wisdom in the adage: "Reduce your debt and increase the value of taxable property." Investors do look at such ratios, and both factors may be within the control of the government. The use of budget controls or a certificate from the Government Finance Officers Association will not lower rates. However, the use of budgets to plan and manage government does often result in lower interest rates.

The Standard and Poor's municipal bond rating process involves four broad factors: economic, debt, administrative, and fiscal. Economic factors include the economic diversity of the tax base as well as the diversity and growth of area economic opportunities. Debt factors include debt burden, debt history, trend, and type of security. Administrative factors include tax rate, levy limitations, debt limits, and other information indicating likely ability to meet debt payments. Fiscal factors include the assets and liabilities in the balance sheet as well as trends in assets and liabilities, especially pension liabilities. In the fiscal factors, comparisons are made between assets and liabilities to see if assets exceed expenditures in the present and the foreseeable future. The bond rating process does not proceed without the necessary information. Since the 1970s, more meetings on the issues, more extensive field trips, and more extensive analyses are commonly done to rate a state or municipal government. Rating decisions are based, in varying degrees, on the following:

1. likelihood of default: capacity and willingness of the obligator to observe the timely payment of interest and repayment of principal in accordance with the terms of the obligation;
2. nature of provisions of the obligation; and
3. protection afforded by, and relative position of, the obligation in the event of bankruptcy, reorganization, or other arrangement under the laws of bankruptcy and other laws affecting creditors' rights.

Ratings provide the investor and others with an informed opinion of the credit-worthiness of a particular issue. Ratings do not establish interest rates, but higher ratings normally translate into lower interest cost to the issuer. Larger investors conduct their own analyses of issues, but the Moody's and Standard and Poor's rating services provide additional guidance on credit-worthiness.

REVIEW QUESTIONS

1. What is a government debt? What are the various types and forms of debt? Why do they exist? What are the alternatives to debt and why are municipalities likely to incur debt?

2.   Compare and contrast revenue bonds, general obligation bonds, short-term borrowing, and creative financing.

3.   What criteria can be used to judge the correct level of state and local debt? Justify the criteria cited.

4.   Explain the significance of the New York City financial crisis for (a) New York City, (b) other local governments, (c) the bond market, including prospectus requirements (GFOA, federal, others).

5.   Why is the term "bankruptcy" inaccurate and misleading for municipal governments? What can be done to anticipate and remedy a financial crisis?

6.   How does the decision-making process differ in capital versus operating budgeting?

7.   Why is judgment central to any capital budget decision? What analytical questions are especially useful and why?

8.   What takes place in designing an issue? What is particularly important and why? Why are syndicates significant? Why is a prospectus important?

9.   What can a government do if it gets low bond ratings?

REFERENCES

Advisory Commission on Intergovernmental Relations. *City Financial Emergencies: The Intergovernmental Dimension*. Washington, D.C.: Government Printing Office, July 1973.

———— . *Significant Features of Fiscal Federalism*, vols. I and II. Washington, D.C.: Government Printing Office, June 1976 and March 1977.

———— . *Understanding the Market for State and Local Debt*. Washington, D.C.: Government Printing Office, May 1976.

ARONSON, J. RICHARD and ELI SCHWARTZ (eds.). *Management Policies in Local Government Finance*. Washington, D.C.: International City Management Association, Municipal Finance Officers Association, 1975.

LEVITAN, DONALD and MICHAEL J. BYRNE. "Capital Improvement Programming," in Jack Rabin and Thomas D. Lynch (eds.), *Handbook on Public Budgeting and Financial Management*. New York: Marcel Dekker, 1983.

MOAK, LENNOX L. *Administration of Local Government Debt*. Chicago: Municipal Finance Officers Association, 1970.

Municipal Finance Officers Association. "Disclosure Guidelines for Offerings of Securities by State and Local Governments." Chicago: MFOA, 1983.

National Committee on Government Accounting. *Governmental Accounting, Auditing, and Financial Reporting*. Chicago: Government Finance Officers Association, 1983.

PETERSON, JOHN E. and WESLEY C. HOUGH. *Creative Capital Financing for State and Local Governments*. Chicago: Government Finance Officers Association, 1983.

STANFIELD, ROCHELLE L. "It's a Tougher World for City Bonds," *National Journal*, 9, 34 (August 20, 1977), 1300–03.

State of Oregon. *Bond Disclosure Guidelines*. 1983.

STEISS, ALAN WALTER. *Local Government Finance*. Lexington, Mass.: Heath, 1975.

NINE
REVENUE SYSTEMS

There are two sides to every budget. One is expenditure and the other is revenue. This chapter discusses intergovernmental revenue systems, property tax, and other revenue sources. The revenue side of budgeting is explained in an intergovernmental context involving the growth of government and the current patterns in government revenue. The most controversial yet most important local tax is the property tax. This chapter explains the tax, the controversy, and the administration of the tax. The same is done for income and sales taxes. At the completion of this chapter, the reader should know:

1. the latest trend in fiscal federalism;
2. the relative tax burden in the United States;
3. a definition of property tax and the major criticisms of the tax;
4. the major suggested property tax reforms, including the *Serrano v. Priest* decision and its implication;
5. how property is assessed as well as means to test assessments;
6. the assessment cycle, application of tax rates, and foreclosures; and
7. the definition, significance, issues, and administration of both income and sales taxes.

INTERGOVERNMENTAL REVENUE SYSTEMS

Historical Background

American government is a complexity of intergovernmentally financed programs with the current pattern explainable by means of American political history. At the republic's beginning, state governments were the dominant form of government. But the federal government took on a more significant role by assuming the states' revolutionary war debt, financially assisting large transportation projects like canals, harbor improvement and railroad expansion, plus supporting education through land grants. The federal government even used land grants for social purposes such as homestead programs. In the 1930s, the federal government involved itself extensively with social programs but this time financed the programs with dollars. In the 1950s, new large grant programs, channeled through state governments, were designed primarily to help air and highway transportation. In the 1960s and 1970s, the number, variety, and type of grants greatly expanded. In the 1970s and 1980s, grant consolidation is the theme. Exhibits 9–1 and 9–2 help explain the more recent trends. Note in Exhibit 9–1 that federal grant programs grew from 132 in 1960, to 379 in 1967, to 448 in 1975, to 539 in 1981. Also note the decline to 441 in 1982 and to 409 in 1983. Exhibit 9–2 shows what activities are funded by grant programs and that 1977 was the peak year with intergovernmental transfers starting to be less significant to state and local governments.

The intergovernmental revenue story is one of increasing local dependency on transfer payments until recently. Exhibit 9–3 shows the Advisory Commission on Intergovernmental Relations means of measuring local government dependency upon state and federal government. Until 1980, dependency increased, but 1981 was a definite reversal with local dependency increasing only for special districts.

The tax burden is not constant from region to region or from state to state. Exhibit 9–4 shows (1) that more state and local taxes are collected per person in the mideast and farwest, (2) less are collected in the southeast and southwest, (3) the highest state is Alaska ($6397) which is about ten times the lowest (Arkansas $678), and (4) the national average is $1,077. Another useful way of considering tax burden is to compare state and local tax revenue to state personal income. Exhibit 9–5 shows (1) that the largest burden is in the mideast, (2) the smallest is in the southeast, (3) the largest state tax burden is Alaska (50.02 percent) and the lowest state is New Hampshire (8.68 percent), and (4) the national average is 11.29 percent with most states very close to that average. Exhibit 9–6 shows regional and state tax capacity and effort, tax diversification and equity features. Notice that some states have a larger tax capacity than others, but that capacity does not necessarily correspond to their tax effort. For example, Mississippi has a tax capacity of 69.3 and a tax effort of 96.5, but Florida has a tax capacity of 100.0 and a tax effort of 73.8. Oil producing states tend to have larger tax capacity, and higher tax effort states tend to be located in New England and the mideast.

American federal, state, and local taxes have increased in dollars but declined slightly as a percentage of the gross national product since 1970 (see Exhibit 9–7).

After World War II to 1970, there was a steady increase in the public sector but it has steadily declined from the 24.25 percent peak to a 21.95 percent level in 1982. Exhibit 9–8 shows the tax revenue by major source, level, and type of government. Note the importance of income tax to both state and federal governments with the latter very dependent on that tax source. Note also the importance of property tax to school districts and sales tax to state government. Municipalities and counties tend to have a more balanced revenue structure.

Significant New Trend

The Advisory Commission on Intergovernmental Relations uses the three Rs—the revolt of the taxpayers, reduced federal aid, and recessionary pressures with no federal bailout—to describe the reasons behind the latest trend in fiscal federalism. These three jolts came in rapid succession and created a new fiscal conservative perspective, especially for American state and local governments. Although California's Proposition 13, which rolled back property tax to 1 percent of market value, was not the first conservative tax reform, it was the most dramatic and served as the model for other states. Government growth shifted from a hefty 4.4 percent average annual increase in adjusted *per capita* expenditure to a revised 0.5 percent increase. The major state tax increases in the post-Proposition 13 era were due, not to "big spenders," but rather to severe fiscal crisis. The second R—reduced federal aid—began to occur in the second half of the Carter administration and was accelerated in the Reagan Administration. The third R—recession with no federal bailout—was the big jolt because painfully large government shortfalls severely hurt state and local government programs. Traditional federal actions in a recession, such as a national economic stimulus program, would have bailed out state and local governments, but they were not forthcoming, especially during the Reagan Administration. The effect was painful belt tightening and politically unpleasant state and local tax increases.

Since the tax revolt, state governments have followed a predictable series of actions. When unanticipated revenue shortfalls occur, the first step is belt tightening; then user charges, including the semi-user fee gas tax, are increased; the third step is increasing "sin taxes" (e.g., cigarette taxes); and finally, the general sales or individual income tax is increased. The latter step is taken when political actors see a severe revenue shortfall. Interestingly, these major state tax increases are sometimes scheduled to self-destruct in a fixed time, such as six months to a year. The three Rs have had their impact on state legislative behavior.

Exhibit 9–9 shows us the relative tax burdens borne by average and upper-income families. Note the relative significance of the progressive federal income tax and the regressive nature of social security, property tax, and sales tax, and note that local property tax is the only tax which significantly decreased from 1977 to 1980, although sales tax also dropped. The cumulative impact of the tax structure is progressive. Note also the significant tax burden jump in the "four times the average family" group from 1953 to 1977. Not surprisingly, people in this group, with their 11.2 percent tax burden increase, were strong supporters of fiscal conservatives.

EXHIBIT 9-1 Federal Grants-in-Aid in Relation to State-Local Receipts from Own Sources, Total Federal Outlays and Gross National Product, 1955–1983 (Dollar Amounts in Billions)

FISCAL YEAR[1]	FEDERAL GRANTS-IN-AID (CURRENT DOLLARS) AMOUNT	PERCENT INCREASE OR DECREASE (−)	AS A PERCENTAGE OF: STATE-LOCAL RECEIPTS FROM OWN SOURCE[2]	TOTAL FEDERAL OUTLAYS	GROSS NATIONAL PRODUCT	FEDERAL GRANTS IN: CONSTANT DOLLARS (1972 DOLLARS GNP DEFLATOR) AMOUNT	PERCENT INCREASE OR DECREASE (−)	ESTIMATED NUMBER OF FEDERAL GRANT PROGRAMS	GRANTS FOR PAYMENTS TO INDIVIDUALS AMOUNT	PERCENT OF TOTAL GRANTS
1955	$ 3.2	4.9	11.8	4.7	0.8	$ 5.3	n.a.	n.a.	$ 1.6	50.0
1956	3.7	15.6	12.3	5.3	0.9	5.9	11.3	n.a.	$ 1.7	45.9
1957	4.0	8.1	12.1	5.3	0.9	6.2	5.1	n.a.	1.8	45.0
1958	4.9	22.5	14.0	6.0	1.1	7.4	19.4	n.a.	2.1	42.9
1959	6.5	32.7	17.2	7.0	1.4	9.6	29.7	n.a.	$ 2.4	36.9
1960	7.0	7.7	16.8	7.6	1.4	10.2	6.3	132	2.5	35.7
1961	7.1	1.4	15.8	7.3	1.4	10.2	-0-	n.a.	2.9	40.8
1962	7.9	11.3	16.2	7.4	1.4	11.2	9.8	n.a.	3.2	40.5
1963	8.6	8.9	16.5	7.8	1.5	12.0	7.1	n.a.	3.5	40.7
1964	10.1	17.4	17.9	8.6	1.6	13.9	15.8	n.a.	3.8	37.6
1965	10.9	7.9	17.7	9.2	1.7	14.7	5.8	n.a.	3.9	35.8
1966	13.0	19.3	19.3	9.6	1.8	16.9	15.0	n.a.	4.5	34.6
1967	15.2	16.9	20.6	9.6	2.0	19.2	13.6	379	5.0	32.9
1968	18.6	22.4	22.4	10.4	2.2	22.5	17.2	n.a.	6.3	33.9
1969	20.3	9.1	21.6	11.0	2.2	23.4	4.0	n.a.	7.5	36.9

Year										
1970	24.0	18.2	22.9	12.2	2.5	26.2	12.0	n.a.	9.0	37.5
1971	28.1	17.1	24.1	13.3	2.7	29.3	11.8	n.a.	11.0	39.1
1972	34.4	22.4	26.1	14.8	3.1	34.4	17.4	n.a.	14.4	41.9
1973	41.8	21.5	28.5	16.9	3.3	39.5	14.8	n.a.	14.3	34.2
1974	43.4	3.8	27.3	16.1	3.1	37.7	− 4.6	n.a.	15.3	35.3
1975	49.8	14.7	29.1	15.3	3.4	39.6	5.0	448	17.4	34.9
1976	59.1	18.7	31.1	16.1	3.6	44.7	12.9	n.a.	21.0	35.5
1977	68.4	15.7	31.0	17.0	3.7	48.8	9.2	n.a.	23.9	34.9
1978	77.9	13.9	31.7	17.3	3.7	51.8	6.1	498	26.0	33.4
1979	82.9	6.4	31.3	16.8	3.5	50.7	− 2.1	n.a.	28.8	34.7
1980	91.5	10.4	31.7	15.8	3.6	51.2	1.0	n.a.	34.2	37.4
1981	94.8	3.6	29.4	14.4	3.2	48.5	− 5.3	539	40.1	42.3
1982	88.8	− 7.0	25.4	12.1	2.9	42.6	−12.2	441[3]	37.8	45.5
1983 est.	93.5	6.0	n.a.	11.6	2.9	42.9	0.7	409[4]	n.a.	n.a.
1984 est.	95.9	2.6	n.a.	11.3	2.7	41.8	− 2.6	n.a.	n.a.	n.a.

*1983 and 1984 estimates based upon OMB assumptions published in the FY 1984 *Budget*. Grant-in-aid figures from *Special Analysis H*, Table H-7; federal outlays from *Budget*, Summary Table 23; GNP and GNP deflator figures from *Budget*, Section 2, page 9. See *Special Analysis H* for explanation of differences between grant-in-aid figures published by the National Income and Product Accounts, Census and OMB.

n.a.: Not available. est: Estimated.

[1]For 1955–1976, years ending June 30; 1977–1982 years ending September 30.

[2]As defined in the national income and product accounts.

[3]Seventy-nine programs have been folded into nine block grants, and at least another twenty six-programs have not been funded as of November 1, 1981.

[4]Includes 398 categorical grants and 11 block grants.

Sources: ACIR staff computations based on U.S. Office of Management and Budget, *Budget of the United States Government*, (annual); Unpublished data from OMB Office of Financial Management; U.S. Department of Commerce, Bureau of Economic Analysis, *The National Income and Product Accounts of the United States, 1929–76, Statisical Tables; Survey of Current Business*, various issues; David B. Walker, *Toward a Functioning Federalism*, Cambridge, MA.: Winthrop Publishers, Inc., 1981, p. 79.

EXHIBIT 9-2 : Federal Aid in Relation to State-Local Own Source Revenue, 1954, 1964, and 1969 Through 1981

FISCAL YEAR	AMOUNT	AS A PERCENT OF STATE-LOCAL GENERAL REVENUE FROM OWN SOURCES	TOTAL FEDERAL AID[1]				
			EDUCATION	HIGHWAYS	PUBLIC WELFARE	HOUSING AND URBAN RENEWAL	ALL OTHER (INCLUDING REVENUE SHARING[2]
Amount (In Millions)							
1954	$ 2,967	11.4	$ 475	$ 530	$ 1,439	$ 90*	$ 433
1964	10,097	17.3	1,371	3,628	2,973	564	1,561
1969	19,421	20.4	4,960	4,314	6,358	921	2,868
1970	23,257	21.4	5,698	4,553	7,574	1,609	3,823
1971	27,121	22.8	5,907	4,738	9,766	1,611	5,099
1972	33,178	24.6	6,250	4,741	13,251	1,981	6,955
1973	41,268	27.3	6,791	4,807	12,097	2,121	15,452[2]
1974	42,854	25.8	7,496	4,555	12,837	2,391	15,575[2]
1975	49,628	27.0	8,959	4,754	14,352	2,734	18,829[2]
1976	69,057	34.4	9,254	6,243	17,225	2,820	33,515[2]
1977	73,045	32.7	10,205	6,173	19,520	2,914	34,233[2]
1978	79,172	32.1	11,602	6,197	20,051	2,969	38,353[2]
1979	85,184	31.8	11,401	7,132	23,501	6,399	36,751[2]
1980	90,836	30.4	12,889	9,457	28,494	6,093	33,903[2]
1981	94,609	28.4	12,708	9,253	34,405	6,065	32,178[2]

Annual Percent Increase or Decrease (−)

Year						
1954	—	—	—	—	—	—
1964	13.0[3]	11.2[3]	21.2[3]	7.5[3]	20.1[3]	12.9[3]
1969	14.0[4]	29.3[4]	3.5[4]	16.4[4]	10.3[4]	14.1[4]
1970	19.8	14.9	5.9	19.1	74.7	33.3
1971	16.6	3.7	8.2	28.9	0.1	33.4
1972	22.3	5.8	0.1	35.7	23.0	36.4
1973	24.4	8.7	1.4	− 8.7	7.1	122.2
1974	3.8	10.4	− 5.2	6.1	12.7	0.8
1975	15.8	19.5	4.4	11.8	14.3	20.9
1976	39.1	3.3	31.3	20.0	3.1	78.0
1977	5.8	10.3	− 1.1	13.3	3.3	2.1
1978	8.4	13.7	0.4	2.7	1.9	12.0
1979	7.6	− 1.7	15.1	17.2	115.5	−4.2
1980	6.6	13.1	32.6	21.2	− 4.8	−7.7
1981	4.2	− 1.4	− 2.2	20.7	− 0.5	−5.1

Percentage Distribution

Year						
1954	100.0	16.0	17.9	48.5	13.0	14.6
1964	100.0	13.6	35.9	29.4	5.6	15.5
1974	100.0	17.5	10.6	30.0	5.6	36.3
1979	100.0	13.4	8.4	27.6	7.5	43.1
1980	100.0	14.2	10.4	31.4	6.7	37.3
1981	100.0	13.4	9.8	36.4	6.4	34.0

*Estimate.

[1] Federal intergovernmental expenditure, as defined by U.S. Bureau of the Census. See Special Analysis H of the *U.S. Budget*, Table H-9, to reconcile Budget, Census, and NIPA figures

[2] Includes federal general revenue sharing payments of $6,636 million in 1973, $6,106 million in 1974, $6,130 million in 1975, $6,238 million in 1976, $6,758 million in 1977, $6,830 million in 1978, $6,848 million in 1979, $6,835 million in 1980 and $5,144 in 1981.

[3] Annual average increase in 1954 to 1964.

[4] Annual average increase 1964 to 1969.

Source: U.S. Bureau of the Census, *Governmental Finances in [year]*, (Tables 2 and 12 in 1980–81 edition); ACIR staff computations.

EXHIBIT 9-3   Local Government Dependency Index,* Fiscal Years 1962, 1975, 1978, 1980, and 1981

UNIT OF GOVERNMENT	1962	1975	1978	1980	1981
Federal and State Aid* Per $1 of Own Source General Revenue					
All Local Governments	$0.44	$0.73	$0.76	$0.79	$0.76
Counties	.60	.78	.80	.81	.77
Municipalities	.26	.63	.62	.56	.53
Townships	.28	.40	.41	.39	.40
School Districts	.65	.94	1.01	1.25	1.23
Special Districts	.15	.42	.44	.42	.47
Federal Aid* Per $1 of Own Source General Revenue					
All Local Governments	$0.03	$0.13	$0.18	$0.16	$0.15
Counties	.01	.13	.19	.17	.14
Municipalities	.05	.19	.26	.23	.21
Townships	.01	.09	.13	.10	.09
School Districts	.02	.03	.04	.03	.03
Special Districts	.11	.28	.34	.33	.37
State Aid* Per $1 of Own Source General Revenue					
All Local Governments	$0.41	$0.60	$0.58	$0.63	$0.61
Counties	.59	.65	.61	.64	.63
Municipalities	.21	.42	.37	.33	.32
Townships	.27	.31	.28	.29	.31
School Districts	.63	.90	.97	1.22	1.20
Special Districts	.04	.14	.10	.09	.10

*Intergovernmental revenue from state and/or federal governments. Interpretation: A figure of $.50 means that for each $1.00 of local own source revenue $.50 is received from the federal and/or state governments.

Source: ACIR staff computations based upon U.S. Bureau of the Census, *Census of Governments*, Vol. IV, 1962, and *Governmental Finances in [year]*, (Table 24 in 1980–81 edition).

The tax rebellion tended to benefit them greatly, as their 1977 to 1980 tax burden increase was held to only 0.7 percent, with actual decreases in local property taxes. However, the tax rebellion also benefited the average and the "twice the average" family.

PROPERTY TAX AND CONTROVERSY

A Simple Idea

Property tax is a simple revenue-generating idea. First, property is assessed locally so that property value is determined. Second, a tax rate is determined and applied on the basis of the property value. If the property owner fails to pay the taxes, then the owner can be fined and, as a last resort, the property can be taken by the government to pay the taxes.

EXHIBIT 9-4 Per Capita State-Local Tax Collections—Amount and Average Rate of Increase, by State and Region, Selected Years 1953-1981

STATE AND REGION	1981	1980	1975	1965	1953	ANNUAL AVERAGE PERCENT INCREASE		
						1975-81	1965-75	1953-65
Exhibit: C.P.I. (1967 = 100.0)	272.4	246.8	161.2	94.5	80.1	9.1	5.5	1.4
United States[1]	$1,077	$987	$664	$264	$132	8.4	9.7	5.9
New England	1,198*	967	658	265	138	10.5	9.5	5.6
Connecticut	1,198	1,070	697	291	141	9.4	9.1	6.2
Maine	945	858	571	233	128	8.8	9.4	5.1
Massachusetts	1,348	1,243	814	302	167	8.8	10.4	5.1
New Hampshire	795	740	525	221	128	7.2	9.0	4.7
Rhode Island	1,092	992	645	263	130	9.2	9.4	6.0
Vermont	987	900	699	278	137	5.9	9.7	6.1
Mideast[1]	1,336*	1,208	767	290	132	9.7	10.2	6.8
Delaware	1,126	1,059	727	302	100	7.6	8.3	9.6
Dist. of Col.	1,771	1,475	759	288	132	15.2	10.2	6.7
Maryland	1,178	1,104	728	261	121	8.4	8.9	6.6
New Jersey	1,229	1,137	725	269	142	9.2	10.4	5.5
New York	1,630	1,495	1,025	372	185	8.0	10.7	6.0
Pennsylvania	1,033	978	636	245	113	8.4	10.0	6.7
Great Lakes	1,040*	955	649	270	136	8.2	9.2	5.9
Illinois	1,164	1,084	730	266	135	8.1	10.6	5.8
Indiana	827	744	580	257	130	6.1	8.5	5.8
Michigan	1,153	1,075	682	290	146	9.1	8.9	5.9
Ohio	873	810	534	225	114	8.5	9.0	5.8
Wisconsin	1,147	1,061	719	310	156	8.1	8.8	5.9
Plains	978*	911	606	254	135	8.3	9.1	5.4
Iowa	1,039	967	637	276	146	8.5	7.9	5.4
Kansas	1,003	926	598	273	146	9.0	8.2	5.4
Minnesota	1,170	1,125	754	299	151	7.6	9.7	5.9
Missouri	790	759	523	223	103	7.1	8.9	6.6
Nebraska	974	963	577	220	124	9.1	10.1	4.9
North Dakota	986	847	613	248	138	8.2	9.5	5.0
South Dakota	850	789	543	241	139	7.8	8.5	4.7

EXHIBIT 9-4 *(continued)*

STATE AND REGION	1981	1980	1975	1965	1953	ANNUAL AVERAGE PERCENT INCREASE		
						1975-81	1965-75	1953-65
Southeast	824*	735	486	185	94	9.2	10.1	5.8
Alabama	739	650	415	168	75	10.1	9.5	7.0
Arkansas	678	654	405	159	79	9.0	9.8	6.0
Florida	850	758	521	233	134	8.5	8.4	4.7
Georgia	854	770	508	191	95	9.0	10.3	6.0
Kentucky	788	740	497	175	78	8.0	6.3	7.0
Louisiana	978	841	566	222	133	9.5	9.8	4.4
Mississippi	711	646	446	170	82	8.1	10.1	6.3
North Carolina	805	748	485	188	95	8.8	9.9	5.9
South Carolina	776	708	446	161	96	9.7	10.7	4.4
Tennessee	739	656	451	178	87	8.6	9.7	6.1
Virginia	946	856	563	188	90	9.0	11.6	6.3
West Virginia	837	796	533	192	87	7.8	10.7	6.8
Southwest	983*	880	551	233	122	10.1	9.0	5.5
Arizona	1,012	1,007	658	266	135	7.4	9.5	5.8
New Mexico	1,100	879	548	243	118	12.3	8.5	6.2
Oklahoma	1,010	827	482	216	132	13.1	8.4	4.2
Texas	961	806	515	207	102	11.0	9.5	6.1
Rocky Mountains	1,026*	997	595	267	143	9.5	8.3	5.3
Colorado	1,024	990	631	292	154	8.4	8.0	5.5
Idaho	808	754	528	245	137	7.3	8.0	5.0
Montana	1,101	1,000	612	265	135	10.3	8.7	5.8
Utah	912	840	506	255	126	10.3	7.1	6.1
Wyoming	1,704	1,399	697	278	163	16.1	9.6	4.5
Far West[2]	1,214*	1,028	738	314	165	8.6	8.9	5.5
California	1,260	1,172	869	361	179	6.4	9.2	6.0
Nevada	1,102	972	770	322	178	6.2	9.1	5.1
Oregon	1,106	979	635	281	148	9.7	8.5	5.5
Washington	1,037	989	676	294	156	7.4	8.7	5.4
Alaska	6,397	4,189	842	250	101[3]	40.2	12.9	5.5
Hawaii	1,393	1,278	852	298	135[3]	8.5	11.1	6.8

*Regional collections for 1953-1980 are *un*weighted averages. 1981 figures are weighted averages.
[1]Excluding Washington, D.C.
[2]Excluding Alaska and Hawaii.
[3]Estimated, based on the U.S. average change between 1953 and 1957 (the earliest year readily available).

Source: ACIR staff computations from FY 1981 data tape supplied by U.S. Bureau of the Census. For prior years see U.S. Bureau of the Census, *Governmental Finances in [year]*. See also, ACIR, *Significant Features of Fiscal Federalism*, prior years. Consumer Price Index (C.P.I.) from *Economic Report of the President*, February 1982, Table B-52.

EXHIBIT 9-5 **State and Local Tax Revenue in Relation to State Personal Income, by State and Region, Selected Years, 1953-1981.**
Tax Revenue as a Percent of Personal Income.

STATE AND REGION	1981	1980	1978	1975	1965	1953	ANNUAL AVERAGE PERCENT INCREASE OR DECREASE (−) 1978-81	1965-78	1953-65
United States[1]	11.29	11.57	12.75	12.29	10.45	7.58	−4.0	1.5	2.7
New England	11.82	12.35	13.49	12.79	9.97	7.90	−4.3	2.4	2.0
Connecticut	10.20	10.55	11.64	10.82	9.08	6.06	−4.3	1.9	3.4
Maine	11.89	12.50	13.29	12.59	10.98	8.95	−3.6	1.5	1.7
Massachusetts	13.28	13.90	15.11	14.20	10.21	8.77	−4.2	3.1	1.3
New Hampshire	8.68	9.20	10.51	10.75	9.51	8.28	−6.2	0.8	1.2
Rhode Island	11.53	11.89	12.52	11.94	10.19	7.02	−2.7	1.6	3.2
Vermont	12.58	12.73	14.48	15.46	12.72	9.62	−4.6	1.0	2.4
Mideast[1]	13.11	13.68	14.50	13.94	10.54	7.46	−3.3	2.5	2.9
Delaware	10.84	11.60	12.28	11.66	8.98	4.21	−4.1	2.4	6.5
Dist. of Col.	14.69	13.57	13.63	10.67	8.09	5.90	2.5	4.1	2.7
Maryland	11.24	12.03	13.02	12.26	9.34	6.33	−4.8	2.6	3.3
New Jersey	11.21	11.72	12.42	11.59	9.07	6.59	−3.4	2.4	2.7
New York	15.84	16.34	17.19	16.65	11.87	8.79	−2.7	2.9	2.5
Pennsylvania	10.92	11.56	12.25	11.68	9.47	6.17	−3.8	2.0	3.6
Great Lakes	10.59	10.66	11.60	11.35	9.73	6.78	−3.0	1.4	3.1
Illinois	11.05	11.25	11.80	11.73	8.89	6.37	−2.2	2.2	2.8
Indiana	9.23	8.82	10.29	11.15	10.24	7.08	−3.6	0.0	3.1
Michigan	11.57	11.50	12.67	11.66	10.67	7.31	−3.0	1.3	3.2
Ohio	9.20	9.35	9.93	9.69	8.64	5.87	−2.5	1.1	3.3
Wisconsin	12.24	12.47	14.16	13.83	12.55	8.91	−4.7	0.9	2.9
Plains	10.45	10.80	11.77	11.73	10.83	8.25	−3.9	0.6	2.3
Iowa	11.08	11.07	11.62	12.14	11.00	9.22	1.0	0.0	2.0
Kansas	10.03	10.00	11.29	10.86	11.70	8.71	−3.9	−0.3	2.5
Minnesota	12.00	12.74	14.16	13.94	12.72	9.38	−5.4	0.8	2.6
Missouri	8.77	9.30	9.94	10.35	8.74	6.14	−4.1	1.0	3.0
Nebraska	10.37	11.06	12.15	10.96	9.34	7.69	−5.1	2.0	1.6
North Dakota	11.24	10.22	11.63	10.95	11.77	11.27	−1.1	−0.1	0.4
South Dakota	10.85	10.59	11.48	11.60	12.60	10.79	−1.9	−0.7	1.3
Southeast	10.12	10.31	11.01	10.70	10.04	7.86	−2.8	0.7	2.1

279

EXHIBIT 9-5 *(continued)*

STATE AND REGION	1981	1980	1978	1975	1965	1953	ANNUAL AVERAGE PERCENT INCREASE OR DECREASE (−)		
							1978-81	1965-78	1953-65
Alabama	9.85	9.64	10.21	9.94	9.74	7.00	−1.2	0.4	2.8
Arkansas	9.32	9.87	10.18	9.90	9.77	7.92	−2.9	0.3	1.8
Florida	9.34	9.75	10.64	9.94	10.53	9.20	−4.3	0.1	1.1
Georgia	10.55	10.78	11.26	10.79	9.96	7.67	−2.1	0.9	2.2
Kentucky	10.32	10.39	11.26	11.32	9.62	6.47	−2.9	1.2	3.4
Louisiana	11.54	11.60	12.25	12.99	12.05	10.43	−2.0	−0.1	1.2
Mississippi	10.78	10.86	11.77	11.84	11.85	9.37	−2.9	0.7	2.0
North Carolina	10.29	10.62	10.93	10.58	9.97	8.25	−2.0	1.1	1.6
South Carolina	10.66	10.68	11.09	10.46	9.67	8.61	−1.3	0.8	1.0
Tennessee	9.56	9.37	10.74	10.04	9.71	7.32	−3.8	2.0	2.4
Virginia	10.05	10.25	11.05	10.67	8.55	6.09	−3.1	1.1	2.9
West Virginia	10.71	11.21	11.29	12.27	9.85	6.81	−1.7	1.1	3.1
Southwest	10.56	10.36	11.15	11.06	10.16	7.34	−1.8	0.7	2.7
Arizona	11.49	13.27	14.28	13.26	12.15	8.50	−7.0	1.3	3.0
New Mexico	14.02	12.18	13.26	13.54	12.16	8.66	1.9	0.7	2.9
Oklahoma	11.05	10.16	10.66	10.53	10.44	9.07	1.2	0.2	1.2
Texas	10.04	9.75	10.55	10.56	9.60	6.68	−1.6	0.7	3.1
Rocky Mountain	11.25	11.90	12.91	11.78	11.61	8.60	−4.5	0.8	2.5
Colorado	10.20	11.31	12.55	11.61	11.40	8.93	−6.7	0.7	2.1
Idaho	10.01	10.39	12.00	11.02	12.14	9.00	−5.9	−0.1	2.5
Montana	12.87	13.03	13.76	12.57	11.78	7.62	−2.2	1.2	3.7
Utah	11.89	12.47	12.66	11.63	11.78	8.44	−2.1	0.6	2.8
Wyoming	15.53	14.76	15.95	13.43	11.28	8.73	−0.9	2.7	2.2
Far West[2]	11.30	11.91	15.13	14.07	11.79	8.34	−9.3	1.9	2.9
California	11.49	12.17	15.80	14.59	11.98	8.41	−10.1	2.2	3.0
Nevada	10.26	10.52	13.10	13.23	10.69	7.93	−7.8	1.6	2.5
Oregon	11.85	11.41	12.80	12.13	10.94	8.24	−2.5	1.2	2.4
Washington	10.04	10.88	12.73	12.06	11.18	8.07	−7.6	1.0	2.8
Alaska[3]	50.02	36.78	17.49	21.45	8.11	5.03[4]	42.0	6.1	4.1
Hawaii	13.75	14.75	14.02	14.44	11.72	8.23[4]	−0.7	1.4	3.0

[1]Excluding the District of Columbia.
[2]Excluding Alaska and Hawaii.
[3]Because most of Alaska's revenue is derived from the taxation of oil production and the income of oil companies, the recent figures for the state of Alaska greatly overstate the actual tax burden borne by the residents of Alaska.
[4]Estimated, based on the U.S. average change between 1953 and 1957 (the earliest year readily available).

Source: ACIR staff computations from data tape for FY 1981 supplied by U.S. Bureau of the Census; U.S. Bureau of the Census, *Governmental Finances in [year]*. See also, *Significant Features of Fiscal Federalism*, prior years.

EXHIBIT 9-6 Summary of Significant Features of the 50 State-Local Revenue Systems

| State and Region | Tax Capacity & Tax Effort[1] | | 1981, All Taxes as a % of State Personal Income | 1980 State-Local Taxes as a % of Family Income[2] | Diversification,[1] 1981 (Source of State-Local General Revenue) | | | | | | State Government Percentage of State-Local Tax Revenue, (C)[4] | Equity Features, 1982[3] | |
| | 1980 RTS Tax Capacity Index | 1980 RTS Tax Effort Index | | | Taxes | | | All Other Revenue Aid | Charges and Misc. General Revenue Aid | Federal 1981 | | Food Exempt from Sales Tax (E) or Income Tax Credit Provided Programs[5] | State Financed Circuit-Breaker Property Tax Relief |
					Property	General Sales	Income						
U.S. Average	100.0	100.0	11.3%	7.4%	17.7%	13.2%	14.3%	12.6%	21.0%	21.2%	61.5%	—	
New England			11.8%		27.7%	9.5%	15.4%	10.4%	14.7%	22.4%	55.8%		
Connecticut	111.6	99.8	10.2%	7.7%	29.2%	16.4%	6.6%	14.5%	15.5%	17.9%	55.7%	E	E.H&R
Maine	80.0	111.1	11.9%	8.4%	21.7%	12.8%	11.7%	11.4%	14.4%	28.0%	63.5%	E	E.H&R
Massachusetts	96.2	134.5	13.3%	16.1%	28.2%	7.2%	21.7	7.6%	13.0%	22.3%	56.1%	E	—
New Hampshire	96.5	75.0	8.7%	6.0%	35.5%	0.0%	5.4%	15.2%	19.5%	24.5%	36.7%	NS T	—
Rhode Island	83.8	123.1	11.5%	10.8%	23.1%	9.6%	13.1%	10.0%	19.2%	25.0%	58.8%	E	E.H&R
Vermont	84.5	104.2	12.6%	7.9%	21.7%	4.6%	12.6%	13.4%	17.5%	30.3%	58.3%	E	A.H&R
Mideast			13.1%		20.4%	10.9%	20.5%	11.8%	16.6%	19.6%	54.1%		
Delaware	111.4	88.9	10.8%	7.9%	7.8%	0.0%	23.5%	20.0%	24.7%	24.0%	82.3%	NST	—
Dist. of Col.	110.8	131.2	14.5%	8.6%	11.5%	9.7%	15.8%	9.2%	7.3%	46.4%	0.0%	E	A.H&R
Maryland	99.2	108.6	11.2%	10.7%	15.2%	8.7%	22.6%	11.2%	20.4%	21.9%	59.5%	E	A.H
New Jersey	105.1	112.0	11.2%	17.3%	29.0%	9.2%	12.5%	15.0%	17.5%	16.8%	55.6%	E	—
New York	90.1	167.4	15.8%	13.9%	21.1%	12.3%	23.1%	8.6%	15.5%	19.3%	48.6%	E	A.H&R
Pennsylvania	92.6	103.8	10.9%	10.3%	16.0%	10.6%	19.2%	16.5%	16.9%	21.0%	62.0%	E	E.H&R
Great Lakes			10.6%		21.1%	12.1%	15.3%	10.1%	19.9%	21.5%	58.1%		
Illinois	107.6	102.5	11.0%	9.9%	21.4%	14.5%	13.4%	12.8%	16.0%	21.8%	55.0%	6	E.H&R
Indiana	92.2	84.2	9.2%	7.6%	21.3%	17.1%	10.7%	8.0%	22.5%	20.5%	61.9%	E	E.H&R
Michigan	97.0	115.6	11.4%	10.6%	23.0%	9.5%	16.8%	7.3%	21.7%	21.7%	57.8%	E	A.H&R
Ohio	96.8	86.7	9.2%	7.3%	19.3%	10.9%	15.1%	12.0%	21.6%	21.2%	55.6%	E	E.H
Wisconsin	94.7	116.3	12.2%	11.0%	19.8%	9.7%	20.6%	8.1%	20.3%	21.4%	67.2%	E	A.&HR

EXHIBIT 9-6 *(continued)*

| State and Region | Tax Capacity & Tax Effort[1] | | 1981, All Taxes as a % of State Personal Income | 1980 State-Local Taxes as a % of Family Income[2] | Diversification,[1] 1981 (Source of State-Local General Revenue) | | | | | | State Government Percentage of State-Local Tax Revenue (C)[4] | Equity Features, 1982[3] | |
| | 1980 RTS Tax Capacity Index | 1980 RTS Tax Effort Index | | | Taxes | | | All Other Revenue | Charges and Misc. General Aid | Federal 1981 | | Food Exempt from Sales Tax (E) or Income Tax Credit Provided Programs[5] | State Financed Circuit-Breaker Property Tax Relief |
					Property	General Sales	Income						
Plains			10.5%		18.5%	11.1%	14.5%	11.3%	23.4%	21.2%	61.3%		
Iowa	105.2	95.7	11.1%	8.3%	22.7%	10.0%	15.7%	10.4%	22.0%	19.3%	60.6%	E	E.H&R
Kansas	108.8	87.9	10.0%	5.0%	22.1%	11.7%	13.7%	9.9%	23.7%	19.0%	58.7%	—	E.H&R
Minnesota	102.2	111.1	12.0%	9.4%	15.3%	8.0%	19.8%	11.6%	24.3%	21.0%	70.8%	E	A.H&R
Missouri	93.6	83.6	8.8%	9.1%	15.8%	15.3%	13.3%	11.8%	19.4%	24.3%	55.2%	—	E.H&R
Nebraska	96.8	102.2	10.4%	6.7%	23.5%	11.7%	9.2%	10.7%	26.4%	18.5%	52.6%	C	—
North Dakota	108.3	78.8	11.2%	5.5%	13.0%	8.9%	7.1%	15.2%	36.0%	19.9%	70.1%	E	E.R[7]
South Dakota	90.2	88.2	10.9%	5.8%	21.5%	15.2%	0.3%	12.7%	22.4%	27.8%	50.7%	[8]	E.H
Southeast			10.1%		12.4%	15.1%	10.6%	15.0%	23.0%	23.8%	68.3%		
Alabama	75.7	85.2	9.8%	5.2%	5.4%	13.1%	10.2%	16.9%	30.7%	23.7%	74.7%	—	—
Arkansas	79.0	85.5	9.3%	6.5%	10.4%	12.7%	12.5%	13.7%	21.8%	29.0%	76.6%	—	E.H
Florida	100.0	73.8	9.3%	2.7%	17.1%	17.1%	2.7%	18.9%	24.3%	19.9%	64.1%	E	—
Georgia	82.0	96.2	10.6%	7.9%	13.4%	13.9%	14.3%	10.2%	24.3%	24.0%	64.7%	—	—
Kentucky	83.0	88.6	10.3%	9.2%	9.7%	11.8%	17.2%	15.3%	18.6%	27.3%	78.9%	E	—
Louisiana	109.2	77.7	11.5%	2.2%	6.4%	19.2%	5.7%	20.2%	26.4%	22.1%	68.2%	E	—
Mississippi	69.3	96.5	10.8%	4.6%	10.2%	19.5%	6.9%	11.8%	23.5%	28.3%	77.9%	—	—
North Carolina	79.5	96.9	10.3%	7.6%	13.3%	11.3%	18.9%	13.0%	19.0%	24.4%	72.4%	—	—
South Carolina	75.2	95.5	10.7%	8.8%	12.3%	13.6%	16.0%	11.7%	22.1%	24.3%	75.3%	—	—
Tennessee	79.0	84.2	9.6%	4.9%	14.8%	20.6%	3.5%	12.9%	22.4%	25.8%	57.7%	—	—
Virginia	94.8	88.3	10.0%	7.8%	16.3%	9.9%	16.9%	14.9%	19.6%	22.4%	59.9%	—	—
West Virginia	93.7	82.1	10.7%	5.2%	9.1%	19.7%	9.5%	13.2%	20.2%	28.3%	77.8%	E	E.H&R
Arizona	88.7	117.4	11.5%	5.9%	18.4%	20.9%	10.5%	9.2%	22.6%	18.4%	64.9%	E	E.H&R
New Mexico	107.1	83.1	14.0%	6.4%	6.3%	18.0%	4.1%	18.4%	33.7%	19.6%	82.3%	[9]	E.H&R

Oklahoma	116.8	71.6	11.0%	4.8%	9.2%	12.4%	11.7%	23.9%	23.3%	19.5%	73.1%	—	E.H
Texas	123.6	64.9	10.0%	5.6%	19.5%	15.1%	0.0%	23.3%	24.5%	17.6%	59.8%	E	—
Rocky Mountain			11.3%		18.6%	13.4%	10.3%	10.6%	24.9%	22.1%	56.0%		
Colorado	112.6	90.4	10.2%	5.7%	19.5%	16.8%	10.1%	8.9%	25.2%	19.6%	48.8%	E	E.H&R
Idaho	87.5	88.3	10.0%	6.5%	15.0%	9.9%	16.2%	11.2%	22.5%	25.2%	70.3%	C	E.H
Montana	112.4	92.2	12.9%	6.5%	24.8%	0.0%	11.9%	15.2%	21.6%	26.5%	53.7%	N ST	E.H&R
Utah	86.0	101.2	11.9%	8.0%	15.0%	17.2%	13.5%	7.9%	21.9%	24.6%	63.8%	—	E.H
Wyoming	196.2	74.3	15.5%	2.6%	18.3%	13.7%	0.0%	14.7%	33.7%	19.6%	58.6%	[10]	—
Far West			11.3%		14.8%	16.3%	15.7%	9.8%	21.6%	21.8%	67.9%		
California	117.0	101.8	11.5%	5.3%	14.0%	17.1%	18.1%	8.7%	20.6%	21.5%	68.7%	E	E.H&R
Nevada	154.4	59.5	10.3%	2.8%	15.9%	14.5%	0.0%	24.1%	27.0%	18.5%	58.4%	E	E.H&R
Oregon	103.1	93.3	11.8%	6.9%	20.9%	0.0%	20.5%	10.1%	26.3%	22.1%	55.2%	NST	A.H&R
Washington	102.9	93.7	10.0%	4.3%	15.3%	23.2%	0.0%	14.3%	23.7%	23.5%	72.9%	E	—
Alaska	259.7	166.2[12]	50.0%[12]	3.9%	6.2%	0.8%	16.3%	23.2%	45.0%	8.4%	90.2%	NST	A.R.
Hawaii	106.5	124.5	13.8%	8.6%	8.7%	24.4%	17.2%	9.3%	19.1%	21.2%	81.0%	[11]	A.R.

[1] Data tape supplied by U.S. Bureau of the Census (ACIR staff computations), see also *Governmental Finances in 1980-81*. For RTS figures and discussion see ACIR, *Tax Capacity of the 50 States, Supplement: 1980 Estimates*, June 1982.

[2] Estimated state-local tax burden for a family of four in 1980 with an income of $25,000 located in the largest city of each state. This figure includes (where applicable) income, property, sales and automobile taxes. For further information, see Government of the District of Columbia, *Tax Burdens in Washington, D.C. Compared with Those in the Largest City in Each State, 1980*, February 1983. Please note that these figures differ from those in the preceeding column not only because of the assumption of a family of four at the $25,000 level, but because the preceding column includes corporation and other taxes as well.

[3] Source: Commerce Clearing House, *State Tax Reporter*.

[4] NST: No state general sales tax.

[5] A.H&R: All homeowners and renters; A.R.: All renters; E.H&R: Elderly homeowners and renters; E.H.: Elderly homeowners; and E.R.: Elderly renters.

[6] Food is taxed at a reduced rate, 2 rather than 4 percent.

[7] North Dakota has a separate program which lowers the assessed value of low-income elderly homeowners by as much as $3000.

[8] A sales tax credit based on federal adjusted gross income is provided for elderly and disabled persons.

[9] An income tax credit is provided for all state-local taxes paid plus a food tax credit equal to $40 for each exemption allowed for federal income tax purposes.

[10] A sales and use tax refund is provided for low-income elderly and disabled persons.

[11] Effective January 1, 1974, a general excise tax credit replaced the consumer, educational, drug and medical, and rental tax credits.

[12] Because most of Alaska's revenue is derived from the taxation of oil production and the income of oil companies, these figures greatly overstate the actual tax burden borne by the residents of Alaska. Compare these figures to that found in the following column (column 4).

Source: ACIR staff computations and compilation.

EXHIBIT 9-7   Federal, State and Local Taxes as a Percentage of Gross National Product, Selected Years 1948-1982

ITEM	1982 (est.)	1981	1980	1978	1976	1974	1972	1970	1968	1966	1964	1956	1948
By Level of Government:													
Federal, State & Local	21.95	22.13	22.49	22.72	22.05	23.13	23.69	24.25	22.30	22.25	22.40	22.29	20.83
Federal	13.19	13.81	13.64	13.16	12.40	13.53	13.83	15.21	14.16	14.41	14.68	15.87	15.40
State & Local	8.76	8.32	8.85	9.56	9.65	9.60	9.86	9.04	8.15	7.84	7.75	6.42	5.43
State	5.30	5.10	5.43	5.59	5.50	5.45	5.38	5.00	4.38	4.07	3.93	3.26	2.74
Local	3.47	3.23	3.41	3.97	4.16	4.15	4.47	4.04	3.75	3.79	3.82	3.16	2.68
By Type of Tax, By Government:													
Federal													
Individual Income	9.73	9.72	9.51	8.68	8.10	8.74	8.52	9.42	8.28	7.68	7.90	7.83	7.85
Corporation Income	1.61	2.08	2.52	2.87	2.55	2.84	2.89	3.42	3.45	4.16	3.81	5.08	3.94
Sales, Gross Receipts and Customs	1.46	1.65	1.22	1.22	1.34	1.51	1.81	1.91	1.96	2.03	2.40	2.55	3.11
Death & Gift	.26	.23	.25	.25	.32	.37	.49	.38	.37	.42	.39	.28	.36
All Other	.13	.13	.15	.14	.09	.07	.12	.09	.10	.12	.19	.13	.14

State

Individual Income	1.48	1.39	1.47	1.44	1.32	1.25	1.17	.96	.75	.59	.55	.33	.20
Corporation Income	.46	.48	.53	.53	.45	.44	.40	.39	.30	.28	.27	.22	.24
General Sales & Gross Receipts	1.64	1.58	1.71	1.74	1.68	1.66	1.58	1.48	1.26	1.09	.99	.74	.60
Selective Sales & Gross Receipts	.90	.90	.97	1.13	1.23	1.32	1.41	1.36	1.27	1.27	1.28	1.16	1.04
Motor Vehicle & Operators Licenses	.20	.19	.21	.24	.27	.28	.30	.28	.30	.31	.31	.32	.24
Death & Gift	.08	.08	.08	.09	.09	.10	.12	.10	.11	.11	.11	.08	.07
All Other	.54	.48	.45	.42	.45	.40	.41	.42	.40	.41	.42	.41	.34

Local

Property	2.63	2.45	2.62	3.16	3.38	3.41	3.74	3.43	3.23	3.30	3.33	2.75	2.38
Sales & Gross Receipts	.46	.45	.47	.46	.44	.41	.38	.32	.23	.28	.29	.22	.16
Individual Income[1]	.18	.19	.18	.20	.19	.18	.20	.17	.13	.07	.06	.04	.02
All Other	.20	.14	.14	.14	.15	.15	.15	.12	.16	.14	.14	.16	.12

SPECIAL NOTE: These figures exclude charges and miscellaneous general revenue, utility, liquor store and insurance trust revenue. In FY 1981, the federal government trust funds received $171.2b. in social insurance taxes (Old Age, Survivors, Disability and Hospital Insurance (OASDHI), railroad retirement, unemployment insurance, federal supplementary medical insurance and employees retirement) while state and local trust funds received $53.4b. If these taxes were added in calculating the figures cited above, the federal, state and local taxes as a percentage of GNP would have been 29.78%; federal only—19.64%; state and local—10.14%. Charges and miscellaneous revenues amounted to $170.6b. for all governments in 1981—5.8% of GNP.

[1]Includes minor amounts of corporation income taxes.

Source: ACIR staff computations based on U.S. Department of Commerce, U.S. Bureau of the Census, *Governmental Finances in [year]*, Bureau of Economic Analysis, *Survey of Current Business*, [monthly].

EXHIBIT 9-8 Tax Revenue by Major Source, by Level and Type of Government Selected Years 1957-1981. Amount (in millions).

| | | | STATE AND LOCAL GOVERNMENTS | | | | | | | |
| | | | | | LOCAL GOVERNMENTS | | | | | |
FISCAL YEAR	TOTAL FEDERAL, STATE AND LOCAL	FEDERAL GOVERN-MENT	TOTAL STATE-LOCAL)	STATE GOVERN-MENTS	TOTAL	MUNICI-PALITIES	COUN-TIES	SCHOOL DISTRICTS	TOWN-SHIPS	SPECIAL DISTRICTS
Total Taxes										
1957	$98,632	$69,815	$28,817	$14,531	$14,286	$5,908	$2,790	$4,511	$794	$283
1962	123,816	82,262	41,554	20,561	20,993	7,934	4,149	7,320	1,145	445
1967	176,121	115,121	61,000	31,926	29,074	10,507	5,702	10,811	1,465	589
1972	263,342	153,733	109,609	59,870	49,739	17,009	10,076	18,939	2,765	952
1977	419,778	243,842	175,936	101,085	74,852	26,050	15,875	27,124	4,060	1,743
1979	524,446	318,932	205,514	124,908	80,606	28,762	16,958	28,226	4,762	1,898
1980	574,244	350,781	223,463	137,075	86,387	31,256	18,813	29,273	4,952	2,094
1981	650,228[1]	405,714[1]	244,514[1]	149,738	94,776	34,105	20,667	32,271	5,150	2,585
1982 est.	672,342	403,942	268,400	162,192	106,208	not available				
Property Taxes										
1957	12,864	—	12,864	479	12,385	4,297	2,613	4,448	743	283
1962	19,054	—	19,054	640	18,414	5,807	3,879	7,216	1,068	445
1967	26,047	—	26,047	862	25,186	7,351	5,253	10,634	1,359	589
1972	42,877	—	42,877	1,257	41,620	10,937	8,625	18,572	2,584	903
1977	62,527	—	62,527	2,260	60,267	15,629	12,891	26,435	3,722	1,590
1979	64,944	—	64,944	2,490	62,453	16,063	13,067	27,304	4,320	1,700
1980	68,499	—	68,499	2,892	65,607	16,859	14,300	28,140	4,459	1,849
1981	74,969	—	74,969	2,949	72,020	18,278	15,798	31,021	4,844	2,079
1982 est.	83,824	—	83,824	3,224	80,600	not available				
Sales, Gross Receipts, and Customs										
1957	20,594	11,127	9,467	8,436	1,031	934	78	3	17	—
1962	26,922	13,428	13,494	12,038	1,456	1,303	125	3	24	—

1967	36,336	15,806	20,530	18,575	1,956	1,645	257	21	33	—
1972	57,619	20,101	37,518	33,250	4,268	3,191	899	68	62	49
1977	83,821	23,180	60,641	52,362	8,278	5,798	1,973	233	140	133
1979	100,961	26,714	74,247	63,668	10,579	7,296	2,599	327	180	177
1980	111,961	32,034	79,927	67,855	12,072	8,208	3,081	373	204	205
1981	134,532	48,561	85,971	72,751	13,220	8,956	3,401	392	10	461
1982 est.	136,548	44,633	91,915	77,915	14,000	not available

Income Taxes

1957	59,525	56,787	2,738	2,547	91	181	—	7	3	—
1962	70,438	66,094	4,344	4,036	309	259	6	40	4	—
1967	103,549	95,497	8,052	7,136	916	818	16	73	9	—
1972	146,545	126,903	19,642	17,412	2,230	1,881	192	132	26	—
1977	250,037	211,617	38,420	34,666	3,754	3,099	385	197	72	—
1979	332,578	283,518	49,060	44,750	4,309	3,496	505	223	85	—
1980	364,070	308,669	55,401	50,410	4,990	4,042	576	264	109	—
1981	407,257	346,688	60,569	55,038	5,531	4,530	598	280	123	—
1982 est.	412,263	347,318	64,945	59,345	5,600	not available

All Other Taxes

1957	5,649	1,902	3,747	3,069	679	495	100	54	31	—
1962	7,402	2,740	4,662	3,847	815	565	140	60	50	—
1967	10,188	3,818	6,370	5,353	1,016	693	176	83	64	—
1972	16,301	6,729	9,572	7,951	1,621	1,001	360	167	93	—
1977	23,393	9,045	14,348	11,796	2,553	1,524	626	258	125	20
1979	25,963	8,700	17,263	13,999	3,264	1,907	786	372	178	21
1980	29,714	10,078	19,636	15,917	3,720	2,147	856	496	180	40
1981	33,470	10,465	23,005	19,000	4,005	2,341	870	578	173	45
1982 est.	39,707	11,991	27,716	21,700	6,008	not available

NOTE: Figures above exclude charges, utility, liquor store revenues as well as social insurance taxes and contributions. In 1981, the federal government trust funds received $171.2 billion in social insurance taxes and contributions (Old Age, Disability and Hospital Insurance (OASDHI), Railroad Retirement, Unemployment Insurance, Federal Supplementary Medical and Employees Retirement) while state and local government trust funds received $53.4 billion. Charges and miscellaneous general revenue amounted to $170.6 billion for all governments in 1981.

Source: ACIR staff computations based on U.S. Bureau of the Census, Governmental Finances in [year].

EXHIBIT 9-9 Comparison of Direct Tax Burdens Borne by Average and Upper-Income Families, Calendar Years 1953, 1966, 1977, and 1980 (The Steady Growth in the Federal-State-Local Tax Take)

CALENDAR YEAR	SELECTED DIRECT TAXES AS A PERCENT OF FAMILY INCOME						FAMILY INCOME (PERCENT)		
	FEDERAL PERSONAL INCOME TAX	SOCIAL SECURITY TAX 1 (OASDHI)	STATE-LOCAL TAXES			TOTAL SELECTED TAXES	TOTAL	DECREASE DUE TO DIRECT TAXES	AFTER TAX INCOME
			LOC. RES. PROP. TAX	STATE-LOC. PER. INC. TAX	STATE-LOC. GENERAL SALES TAX				
				Average Family[2] ($21,500 in 1980)					
1953	7.6	1.1	2.2	0.3	0.6	11.8	100.0	11.8	88.2
1966	9.5	3.2	3.1	1.0	1.0	17.8	100.0	17.8	82.2
1977	9.6	5.9	3.9	1.8	1.3	22.5	100.0	22.5	77.5
1980	10.1	6.1	3.2	2.2	1.1	22.7	100.0	22.7	77.3
				Twice the Average Family[3] ($43,000 in 1980)					
1953	12.8	0.5	1.8	0.9	0.5	16.5	100.0	16.5	83.5
1966	12.7	1.6	2.6	1.6	0.8	19.3	100.0	19.3	80.7
1977	14.8	3.0	3.2	2.9	0.9	24.8	100.0	24.8	75.2
1980	16.6	3.7	2.4	3.2	0.9	26.8	100.0	26.8	73.2
				Four Times the Average Family[4] ($86,000 in 1980)					
1953	16.6	0.3	1.7	1.2	0.4	20.2	100.0	20.2	79.8
1966	17.3	0.8	2.4	2.4	0.5	23.4	100.0	23.4	76.6
1977	22.6	1.5	2.6	4.0	0.7	31.4	100.0	31.4	68.6
1980	24.3	1.8	1.9	4.1	0.6	32.7	100.0	32.7	67.3

[1] Personal contributions.

[2] Estimates for average family (married couple with two dependents) earning $5,000 in 1953, $8,750 in 1966, $16,000 in 1977, and $21,500 in 1980, assuming all income from wages and salaries is earned by one spouse.

[3] Estimates for twice the average family. Family earning $10,000 in 1953, $17,500 in 1966, $32,000 in 1977, and $43,000 in 1980. Assumes that earnings include $165 (interest on state and local debt, and excludable dividends) in 1980, $125 in 1977, $50 in 1966, and $25 in 1953; also assumes the inclusion of net long-term capital gains of $1,600 in 1980, $1,200 in 1977, $625 in 1966, and $350 in 1953.

[4] Estimates for four times the average family. Family earning $20,000 in 1953, $35,000 in 1966, $64,000 in 1977, and $86,000 in 1980. Assumes that earnings include $1,515 (interest on state and local debt, and excludable dividends) in 1980, $1,100 in 1977, $525 in 1966, and $265 in 1953; also assumes the inclusion of net long-term capital gains of $9,200 in 1980, $7,300 in 1977, $3,360 in 1966, and $1,730 in 1953.

Note: In computing federal personal income tax liabilities, deductions were estimated to be 14 percent of family income for the $5,000 and $8,750 families, and 12 percent of income for the $10,000 family. Estimated itemized deductions were assumed for the remaining families. Interest on state and local debt, dividends, and nontaxable capital gains (estimated, based on IRS *Statistics of Income*) were excluded from family income for these computations.

Residential property tax estimates assume average housing values of approximately 1.8 times family income for the average family in both 1953 ($5,000) and 1966 ($8,750), 2.2 times in 1977 ($16,000), and 2.4 times in 1980 ($21,500). The ratios for the remaining family income classes are: 1.5 for $10,000 income (1953) and $17,500 income (1966); 1.8 for $32,000 income (1977); 1.9 for $43,000 income (1980); 1.4 for $20,000 income (1953) and $35,000 income (1966); 1.5 for $64,000 income (1977) and $86,000 income (1980), with average effective property tax rates of 1.35 percent in 1980, 1.75 percent in 1977, 1.70 percent in 1966, and 1.20 percent in 1953. Based on U.S. Bureau of the Census, Governments Division, various reports and *U.S. Census of Housing*; Commerce Clearing House, *State Tax Reporter*; Internal Revenue Service, *Statistics of Income, Individual Income Tax Returns*; and ACIR staff estimates.

In computing state income tax liabilities, the optional standard deduction was used for the $5,000, $8,750, and $10,000 income families, and estimated itemized deductions for the remaining families.

Estimated state-local general sales tax liabilities are based on the amounts allowed by the Internal Revenue Service as deductions in computing federal personal income taxes. The percentages shown for state-local personal income and general sales taxes are weighted averages (population) for all states, including those without a sales or income tax.

Source: ACIR staff computations.

This form of taxation is still one of the most significant revenue sources for most state and local governments. At one time, property reflected wealth; thus a real estate property tax could have been a progressive tax. Today, wealth is not reflected in real property; therefore, this form of taxation cannot be used to tax wealth uniformly and progressively. There has been a decline in the relative significance of property tax as a revenue generator because it has not provided sufficient revenue by itself. Property tax is less significant today, but it is still highly important as a revenue generator.

Property tax is placed on personal and real property. Tangible personal property includes machinery, equipment, and motor vehicles. Intangible personal property includes stocks, bonds, mortgages, and money. Real property includes land as well as improvements to the land such as buildings. Normally, property taxes are administered locally. Not all property is taxed at a universal rate. In some cases, the tax is regressive but special features can be added to minimize regressive burdens. Another interesting fact is that one person can be held responsible for taxes on both personal and real property. Also a citizen may live in overlapping local governments and thus be taxed on the same property by two common jurisdictions.

Criticisms

John Shannon of the Advisory Commission on Intergovernmental Relations pointed out that the property tax is considered to be the second most onerous tax. A 1982 poll showed that 30 percent of the nation's citizens regard property tax as the worst or least fair tax. Taxes are never popular, but property tax beat the others in nonpopularity by a margin of two to one. Why?

1. This form of taxation bears down harshly on low-income households. Lower income families must pay a higher percentage of their incomes for real estate taxes.

2. Property tax is an antihousing levy. It discourages home ownership and does not provide preferential treatment for shelter cost as commonly found in income and sales taxes. Also, as taxes increase, property tax is viewed by many as a threat to their continued home ownership. Property taxes increase as values go up, but the owner does not benefit from the "paper profit" as it is rarely converted to spendable income. This means that taxes are increased but the property remains the same.

3. The administration of property tax is difficult and often poorly done. At best, the assessment is an informed estimate, that is, a subjective judgment of market value. At worst, the assessment can be used for political or economic advantage.

4. The infrequent mass reappraisals in periods of inflation result in severe taxpayer shock and hardship. Taxes go up radically, and taxpayers may not be in economic positions to absorb sometimes doubling and tripling of tax bills. No other tax has such severe hikes.

5. Property taxes can be painful to pay. Often the property taxes are collected with the monthly mortgage payment charge. Such a "pay-as-you-go" technique is less painful for most taxpayers. Often, however, local government does not permit such practices, and payments must be made on a yearly basis, thus causing hardships.

6. Property tax does contribute to urban blight. If some houses must be foreclosed due to nonpayment of taxes, such houses are likely to be in marginal neighborhoods. The long foreclosure process will probably stimulate extreme negligence to the house, thus

harming an already weak housing market. Values will drop, and the neighborhood will deteriorate.

One very complex problem is the perennial conflict between state valuation and local assessment practices. The property tax laws of most states require that all classes of property be assessed at the same percentage of current market value. This sounds reasonable, but most state tax administrators are unable to hold county assessment at any uniform percentage of current market value. The most frequent beneficiaries—not victims—of the extralegal assessment practices are farmers and homeowners. Farmland tends to be assessed at a lower percentage of market value than residential property. Income-producing property such as a factory site tends to be assessed at a higher rate. There are examples of the company in a "company town" benefiting, but that is not the common pattern.

There is a natural reluctance on the part of state officials to raise the assessments of all classes of property to the state valuation standard. Such reforms are politically grim to those officials. Local rate makers should cut back tax rates if the state hikes local assessment; thus each taxpayer would pay about the same tax amount. However, local governments are pressed for added revenue so by not lowering the tax rate they can generate more income while placing the tax hike blame on the state. Another problem for state leaders is creation of a uniform tax policy, which means that they will be repealing the popular "little assessment break" given farmers and homeowners. Both headaches are political liabilities which state officials do not wish to bear. Tax reform designed to bring the law and practice into reasonable alignment does require heroic action. Thus such reforms—when they do occur—take place normally because of court rather than legislative or administrative action.

Property Tax Reforms

Given the number of criticisms of property taxes, no one should be surprised to find an active reform movement involving property tax. Few argue that the tax should be eliminated because it does generate large quantities of tax revenue. Many do argue for the less radical reforms designed to improve the process.

Some obvious improvements are to have better assessors and to use better assessment techniques. Better pay would attract more qualified people. Persons hired should be given added training. Also, selection of assessors should be on the basis of professional merit, not ability to win local elections. Assessment can be improved by using cadastral maps and parcel information files. The work of assessment lends itself to data processing; thus, much routine work can be done by computers. Another technique is to use building permit data to alert assessors to important changes. Another useful device is to enact a real property transfer tax act which includes a provision requiring that the assessor be automatically notified of changes in market value. Statistical techniques like multiple regression analysis can be useful to identify market data which best indicate rapid changes in market value. Other reforms are to use professional consulting firms, especially for major reassessments.

Another reform involves government reorganization. Assessment districts often can be consolidated. This would lead to some economies of scale. It also would permit more specialization, better job development for assessors, and the use of sophisticated equipment which could not be justified in small operations.

A reform addressed to correcting the regressive character of property tax is called a circuit breaker. Circuit breakers are normally designed to aid the families with the lowest incomes or the elderly. The details of circuit breakers vary from state to state. A typical circuit breaker in the mid-1970s covered only the aged, aided renters as well as homeowners, limited benefits to households with incomes below $5,000 with no asset test, and imposed a maximum total relief of $500 or less.

More radical reforms are advocated. One is the site value approach which exempts reproducible capital from the property tax base. Proponents argue that there would be no tax loss but taxing would be done in a different way. They say taxing the building as improved property tends to slow down renewal while taxing only land does the opposite. Thus, urban areas would be improved. These debates will continue as long as there are legitimate criticisms of the property tax.

The most notable property tax reform was California Proposition 13, in 1978, which was copied in Idaho, Nevada, and Massachusetts. This reform radically cut California's property tax back to 1 percent of the market value and moved property assessment back to the 1975–76 rolls. In addition, it provided for a 2 percent growth rate annually. California's property tax rate moved from a 2.21 percent average effective tax rate to a 0.98 percent rate with that single reform. Exhibit 9–10 shows the change in the average effective property tax rates. The U.S. average is 1.26 percent, with 12 states near the 1 percent rate, 5 states at over 2 percent, and 10 at less than 0.9 percent. Reducing property tax receipts does not mean a uniform decrease in state and local government services because some services rely more heavily on property tax than others. Exhibit 9–11 shows that state government is not affected directly, but that school districts and townships which rely heavily on property tax will be hurt the most when major cutbacks occur.

Serrano v. Priest

A particularly significant reform is shifting the property tax to the state level. Reformers point out that this would solve many of the problems most commonly cited.

In 1971, the State of California Supreme Court ruled in *Serrano v. Priest* that the relationship between a district's property tax wealth per pupil and its educational expenditure must be broken. In other words, the property tax may be administered locally, but the funds must go into a state-wide pool. The level of spending for a child's education may not be a function of wealth other than the wealth of the state as a whole.

This decision has remarkable property tax implications. At least in education, there is no longer such a thing as a rich or poor district. The Serrano decision, strictly applied, would invalidate many existing patterns of real property school

EXHIBIT 9-10 Average Effective Property Tax Rates, Existing Single Family Homes with FHA Insured Mortgages, by State and Region, Selected Years 1958–1981[1]

STATE AND REGION	1981	1980	1977	1975[2]	1971	1966	1958
United States	1.26	1.28	1.67	1.89	1.98	1.70	1.34
New England							
Connecticut	1.53	1.55	2.17	1.94	2.38	2.01	1.44
Maine	1.42	1.25[3]	1.65	1.86	2.43	2.17	1.58
Massachusetts	2.43	2.51	3.50	3.26	3.13	2.76	2.21
New Hampshire	n.a.	1.73[4]	n.a.	(2.38)	3.14	2.38	1.81
Rhode Island	n.a.	1.93	n.a.	2.27	2.21	1.96	1.67
Vermont	n.a.	1.60[5]	n.a.	(2.21)	2.53	2.27	1.63
Mideast							
Delaware	0.79	0.85	0.88	0.92	1.26	1.14	0.71
District of Columbia	1.22	1.30	n.a.	1.78	1.80	1.37	1.08
Maryland	1.25	1.61	1.69	2.01	2.24	2.05	1.47
New Jersey	2.53	2.60	3.31	3.15	3.01	2.57	1.77
New York	2.75	2.75	2.89	2.56	2.72	2.40	2.09
Pennsylvania	1.50	1.57	1.85	1.71	2.16	1.88	1.50
Great Lakes							
Illinois	1.47	1.50	1.90	2.21	2.15	1.96	1.35
Indiana	1.13	1.19	1.66	1.64	1.96	1.64	0.84
Michigan	2.74	2.54	2.63	2.38	2.02	1.81	1.45
Ohio	1.07	1.08	1.26	1.29	1.47	1.44	1.07
Wisconsin	1.75	1.67	2.22	2.63	3.01	2.31	1.82
Plains							
Iowa	1.75	1.48	1.76	2.20	2.63	2.12	1.34
Kansas	0.93	0.94	1.37	1.55	2.17	1.96	1.65
Minnesota	0.79	0.93	1.39	1.58	2.05	2.14	1.57
Missouri	0.95	1.00	1.59	1.85	1.79	1.64	1.12
Nebraska	2.31	2.37	2.48	2.50	3.15	2.67	1.90
North Dakota	1.01	1.00	1.26	1.53	2.08	1.81	1.54
South Dakota	1.69	1.70	1.79	2.14	2.71	2.64	2.01
Southeast							
Alabama	0.38	0.56	0.74	0.75	0.85	0.66	0.56
Arkansas	1.42	1.53	1.49	1.41	1.14	1.09	0.84
Florida	0.92	1.02	1.13	1.18	1.41	1.09	0.76
Georgia	1.21	1.24	1.27	1.33	1.44	1.30	0.84
Kentucky	1.14	1.19	1.25	1.23	1.27	1.03	0.93
Louisiana	0.28	0.26	0.61	0.64	0.56	0.43	0.52
Mississippi	0.86	0.93	1.10	1.12	0.96	0.93	0.66
North Carolina	1.07	0.95	1.35	1.51	1.58	1.31	0.90
South Carolina	0.84	0.81	0.82	1.07	0.94	0.60	0.48
Tennessee	1.42	1.27	1.40	1.31	1.53	1.37	0.97
Virginia	1.39	1.26	1.21	1.32	1.32	1.13	0.90
West Virginia	0.37	0.43	n.a.	0.78	0.69	0.71	0.56

EXHIBIT 9-10 *(continued)*

STATE AND REGION	1981	1980	1977	1975[2]	1971	1966	1958
Southwest							
Arizona	0.74	1.16	1.72	1.54	1.65	2.41	2.14
New Mexico	1.14	1.12	1.65	1.56	1.70	1.30	0.93
Oklahoma	0.82	0.91	0.95	1.27	1.35	1.11	0.86
Texas	1.68	1.57	1.84	2.06	1.91	1.62	1.36
Rocky Mountain							
Colorado	1.01	1.05	1.80	1.99	2.45	2.20	1.72
Idaho	0.94	0.96	1.46	1.86	1.72	1.23	1.14
Montana	1.08	1.11	1.31	1.60	2.19	1.70	1.32
Utah	1.03	1.02	1.03	1.20	1.49	1.52	1.05
Wyoming	0.47	0.50	0.87	1.12	1.38	1.34	1.17
Far West							
California	1.04	0.98	2.21	2.08	2.48	2.03	1.50
Nevada	1.13	1.22	1.71	1.53	1.48	1.47	1.06
Oregon	1.56	1.72	2.25	2.18	2.33	1.98	1.55
Washington	0.95	1.06	1.75	1.86	1.62	1.14	0.92
Alaska	n.a.	1.35	n.a.	1.73	1.61	1.42	1.12
Hawaii	0.36	0.42	n.a.	(0.95)	0.92	0.81	0.62

Note: These effective rates are for existing FHA insured mortgages only, which represent small and varying percentages (by state) of total single-family homes. These rates may or may not be representative of the rates applicable to all homes in a particular state. The U.S. average tax rate for 1981 (1.26) indicates that, on average, the property tax on a home with a market value of $100,000 would be $1,260.

n.a.—Data not available.

[1]Effective tax rate is the percentage that the tax liability represents of the market or true value of the house.

[2]Figures in parentheses are for 1974; data for 1975 not available.

[3]Fourth quarter of 1977 increased to 1980 on the basis of the U.S. average percentage change.

[4]ACIR staff estimates based on 1974 (latest year readily available) increased to 1980 on the basis of the U.S. average percentage change (75%) and the 1977 Census of Governments, "Taxable Property Values and Assessment/Sales Price Ratios" (25%).

[5]ACIR staff estimates based on 1974 (latest year readily available) increased to 1980 on the basis of the U.S. average percentage change.

Source: Computed by ACIR staff from data contained in U.S. Department of Housing and Urban Development, Housing-FHA, Management Information Systems Division, Single Family Insured Branch, *Data for States and Selected Areas on Characteristics of FHA Operations Under Section 203(b)*, various years.

financing. The decision does not void real estate property tax, but does require a major design constraint on the tax.

In 1973, the U.S. Supreme Court in *San Antonio Independent School District v. Rodriguez* did not extend the Serrano decision to the national level. In a five-to-four opinion, the court ruled that education is not one of the funadmental rights; thus, it is not covered under the equal protection clause of the Constitution. Interestingly, the lawyers for Rodriguez could have argued discrimination and equal opportunity and the court decision might have been otherwise. However, the court ruling meant that the Serrano decision did not apply on a national level.

More states are following the California reasoning, normally by court ruling. Some call this a Robin Hood approach as the state serves to equalize the tax among the local districts. The Serrano decision continues to be influential and property tax is being revised around the country due to that decision.

ASSESSMENT AND TAXATION

Taxable Property and Assessment

Real estate property normally is defined to include the land, structures, and fixtures. The key test is "Is the item fixed?" (For example, the item nailed to the wall is "fixed.") If the answer to the test is yes, it is considered part of the real property for tax purposes. Repairs are not considered to add *per se* to the property value, but improvements do. Here the test is: "Is the change an adddition or alteration, as opposed to a restoration to a previous condition?" Both tests are difficult to apply and much controversy arises out of using them. One common problem is how to handle mobile homes because, as the name implies, they are not fixed to the property. Most states supplement the test of being fixed by using the length of time the mobile home is on the property or other actions taken to indicate fixture such as removing wheels.

The first step in property taxation is to determine the tax base. An inventory must be taken. This is normally done using owner declarations, surveys, and building permits. Care must be taken to record properly all relevant details, especially improvements to the property.

The assessment process is complex. It must be accurate and uniform or charges of unfairness can be made resulting in possible court action. Normally, assessment is based on a uniform fraction of market value or on full market value. Classes of property (e.g., farms, vacant land, one-family residences, multiple residences) are taxed at different rates. Sometimes tax exemptions exist, such as homestead, elderly, sovereignty (e.g., Indian tribe or foreign embassy), or meritorious service (e.g., religious, charitable, educational, or veterans).

The assessment is normally made on market price. Whenever possible, the test used is the market price for the property. That is defined as the price at which a willing seller will sell and a willing buyer will buy where the seller is not forced to sell and buyer is not forced to buy. If the property was recently sold, then that price would probably constitute market price. Normally, the assessor does not find such a situation, and judgments are based on sales information. A sales ratio, that is, the ratio between price and assessed value, is developed based on sales reports. If the assessment is accurate, the ratio would be one for full market value assessment. Statistical measures, such as central tendency and dispersion, are applied to the sales ratios. This helps the assessor isolate current assessed value inaccuracies as well as determine the quality of assessment. These ratios can then be used to de-

EXHIBIT 9-11 Tax Revenue by Major Source, by Level and Type of Government Selected Years 1957-1982 Percentage Distribution, by Type of Tax

FISCAL YEAR	TOTAL FEDERAL, STATE AND LOCAL	FEDERAL GOVERNMENT	STATE AND LOCAL GOVERNMENTS		LOCAL GOVERNMENTS					
			TOTAL STATE-LOCAL)	STATE GOVERNMENTS	TOTAL	MUNICI-PALITIES	COUN-TIES	SCHOOL DISTRICTS	TOWN-SHIPS	SPECIAL DISTRICTS
Total Taxes										
1957	100.0	100.0	100.0	100.0	100.0	100.0	100.0	100.0	100.0	100.0
1967	100.0	100.0	100.0	100.0	100.0	100.0	100.0	100.0	100.0	100.0
1977	100.0	100.0	100.0	100.0	100.0	100.0	100.0	100.0	100.0	100.0
1982	100.0	100.0	100.0	100.0	100.0	100.0	100.0	100.0	100.0	100.0
Property Taxes										
1957	13.0	—	44.6	3.3	86.7	72.7	93.7	98.6	93.6	100.0
1967	14.8	—	42.7	2.7	86.6	70.0	92.1	98.4	92.8	100.0
1977	14.9	—	35.5	2.2	80.5	60.0	81.2	97.5	91.7	91.2
1982 est.	12.5	—	31.2	2.1	75.9	—————————— not available ——————————				

Sales, Gross Receipts, and Customs										
1957	20.9	15.9	32.9	58.1	7.2	15.8	2.8	0.1	2.1	—
1967	20.6	13.7	33.7	58.2	6.7	15.7	4.5	0.2	2.3	—
1977	20.0	9.5	34.5	51.8	11.1	22.3	12.4	0.9	3.4	7.6
1982 est.	20.3	11.0	34.2	48.0	13.2	not available				
Income Taxes										
1957	60.4	81.3	9.5	17.5	1.3	3.1	—	0.2	0.4	—
1967	58.8	83.0	13.2	22.4	3.2	7.8	0.3	0.7	0.6	—
1977	59.6	86.8	21.8	34.3	5.0	11.9	2.4	0.7	1.8	—
1982 est.	61.3	86.0	24.2	36.6	5.3	not available				
All Other Taxes										
1957	5.7	2.7	13.0	21.1	4.8	8.4	3.6	1.2	3.9	—
1967	5.8	3.3	10.4	16.8	3.5	6.6	3.1	0.8	4.4	—
1977	5.6	3.7	8.2	11.7	3.4	5.9	3.9	1.0	3.1	1.1
1982 est.	5.9	3.0	10.3	13.4	5.7	not available				

*Less than 0.5 percent.

Source: ACIR staff computations based on U.S. Bureau of the Census, Governmental Finances in [year], see previous tables.

velop a percentage factor to adjust improper assessments. A more sophisticated approach is multiple regression analysis, which identifies variables which reflect market value. This approach could be used to find property value indicators and use them to update assessments. Another approach is to analyze market data to select independent variables which help to predict or estimate sales prices accurately, or identify comparable properties to determine property value.

In some situations, other market approaches must be used in making an assessment. One is the cost or replacement cost approach. This approach is a particularly useful means of valuating large numbers of buildings. The stress is on how much it would cost to replace the building at the time of assessment. Data can be gathered from builders and others to determine reproduction cost of the building. Then age and condition can be determined to recognize the depreciation factors. Next, land value is estimated. Finally, the replacement cost minus depreciation is compared against the recent sale price of similar property.

A third approach is the income approach, and it is seldom used as the sole basis for assessment. It is particularly useful where the market for the property is imperfect (e.g., no willing buyer). Net income for the property is first calculated and then divided by the current discount rate to arrive at an estimated property value. This value should be validated by using the income approach on similar property which can be assessed by the market approach. The results should be comparable.

Assessments should be done frequently enough so that the assessment is comparable with the market price. In many assessing jurisdictions—which are sometimes not the same as taxing jurisdictions—the practice is to have extremely infrequent reassessments. This leads to the "welcome stranger distortion." People who move into an area are assessed automatically at the market price when their house is bought. The residents who do not sell their homes are assessed at the lower past assessment. Thus newcomers pay higher property taxes for comparable property.

A hardship sometimes caused by reassessment involves circuit breakers. As inflation occurs, an owner can move from nearly zero property taxes to significant taxes because the property exceeds the relief level. However, the circuit breaker can be carefully worded to provide a gradual increase in property taxes rather than a harsh drastic increase.

So-called tax havens do exist. Let us say a family owns an expensive, even highly assessed home. Normally, this would mean high property taxes. If that home is in a tax district which has a great deal of industry, then the tax rate may be low on residential property because enough revenue to run the government is generated from the industrial property tax owners. This would be a tax haven for the residential property owners. Taxes paid depend on both the assessment and the tax rate.

A state requires that a uniform property tax assessment exist throughout the state, but the practical problem is that there are many local assessing jursidictions. One means to achieve the desired objective is for a state board of equalization to convert each local assessment into a uniform statewide assessment. This conversion process can be done by multiplying the local assessment by a ratio or rate much like

EXHIBIT 9-12 State Equalization Rate Determination

Step 1:	The assessed value of the property is established by using the local government assessment rolls.
Step 2:	The market value of all property is established. This is done by examining sales information. An estimate for all the property is based on the sales information.
Step 3:	The ratios are determined for all classes of property based on the assessed and market values.
Step 4:	Each of the classes are accumulated, and the weighted average ratio for all classes is computed. The computation appears as follows:

ASSESSED VALUATION	MARKET VALUE	RATIOS	WEIGHTED AVERAGE	WEIGHTED RATIO
A Class	Am Class	A:Am	A:M_T	A:M_T
B Class	Bm Class	B:Bm	B:M_T	B:M_T
C Class	Cm Class	C:Cm	C:M_T	C:M_T
etc.	etc.	etc.	etc.	etc.
	M_T			

Source: Thomas A. Dorsey, *Understanding the Real Property Tax* (Syracuse, N.Y.: Syracuse Governmental Research Bureau), 1974.

the one used in the sales ratio assessment approach. The state equalization rate is the ratio of assessed value of real property to market value. Exhibit 9–12 explains how a state determines the equalization rate.

The equalization rate serves as a measure of assessment quality. If the market value of a house is $40,000 and the equalization rate is 50 percent, then the assessment should be about $20,000. If it is not, then the house is either under- or overassessed.

Testing Assessments

The assessment process is often highly controversial. People do not want to pay any more taxes than necessary, especially if the tax is increased as a result of a recent tax reassessment. Taxpayer "rebellions" occur when a large number of property owners protest increased reassessments. Considering the subjective nature of assessment, mistakes can easily be made and differences of opinion can make a difference in the tax due. Individual taxpayer complaints and appeals are common. This section discusses several tests which can be applied to test the assessment process.[1] There are three key questions:

1. Has the assessor apportioned the property tax burden among owners on the basis of the value of their property?

[1]This section draws heavily from Arnold H. Raphaelson, "Property Assessment and Tax Administration," in *Management Policies in Local Government Finance*, ed. J. Richard Aronson and Eli Schwartz (Washington, D.C.: International City Management Association, 1975).

2. Does the assessor tend to favor or to discriminate against certain types of property?
3. Are the higher-priced properties underassessed?

The test for apportioning the tax burden on the basis of value is the coefficient of dispersion for the district. The coefficient reflects how closely the assessment values are to each other relative to market value. The steps for calculation are as follows:

1. Determine the assessment ratio for each of a sample of properties sold. Let us say there are three parcels. Each is sold for $10,000 and assessed separately at $5,000, $6,000, and $7,000. The separate assessment ratios are:

   50%   60%   70%

2. Determine the average of these assessment ratios for the sample of transactions. Average (or median) assessment ratio:

   60%

3. Compute the average deviation of the separate assessment ratios from the average or median assessment ratio. Average deviation:

   $$(10\% + 0\% + 10\%) \div 3 = 6.6\%$$

4. Relate the average deviation to the median or average assessment ratio. Coefficient of disperson:

   $$6.6\% \div 60\% = 0.11 \text{ or } 11\%$$

Note: Margin of 10% expected given imperfection in data.

In the above explanation, the test tells us the assessor has *not* apportioned the property tax burden among the owners on the basis of their property's value. The coefficient of dispersion was 11 percent, which is 1 percent over the excusable margin. The problem is probably not significant, but a problem does exist.

The test for determining if the assessor is discriminating against some types of property is made by substituting above each category the average assessment ratio for each coefficient of dispersion category assessment ratio. This relates the average category assessment ratio to the overall ratio, thus relating the shares of the property tax burden of the different categories. The calculations are similar to the ones cited previously. For example:

1. The assessment ratios for each category are:

   40%   60%   80%

2. Average of median assessment ratio:

    60%

3. Average deviation:

    $(20\% + 0\% + 20\%) \div 3 = 13.3\%$

4. Coefficient of dispersion:

    $13.3\% \div 60\% = 0.22$ or 22%

The coefficient of dispersion indicates definite discrimination.

The test to determine if higher priced properties are underassessed is done by calculating the price-related differential. It is a measure of the relative accuracy of higher and lower priced property assessments. The steps for calculation are as follows:

1. Calculate the aggregate assessment-sales ratio, which is weighted by the values of the parcels in the sample. Let us say the following example exists:

SALE PRICE	ASSESSED VALUE	ASSESSMENT RATIO
$100,000	$20,000	20%
10,000	4,000	40%
10,000	4,000	40%
10,000	4,000	40%
$130,000	$32,000	140%

The aggregate assessment-sales ratio is:

$(\$32,000 \div \$130,000) = 0.246$ or 24.6%

2. Calculate the average of the assessment ratios of the separate parcels. The average assessment ratio of properties is:

    $140 \div 4 = 0.350$ or 35%

3. Divide the mean of the assessment ratios by the aggregate assessment-sales ratio to determine the price-related differential. The price-related differential is:

    $35.0 \div 24.6 = 1.42$ or 142%

The deviation from 100 percent is the key concern in this analysis. If the calculations result in about 100 percent, then there is no under- or overassessment. If the calculations result in more than 100 percent, then there is underassessment of higher priced properties. If the calculations result in less than 100 percent, then there is underassessment of lower priced properties. In the above example, 142 percent is significantly more than 100 percent; therefore, there is underassessment of the $100,000 property.

There are three types of improper assessment situations: illegal assessment, inequitable assessment, and overvaluation. Illegal assessment is when some specific legal rule or law is violated in the assessment process. Inequity is when assessed value exceeds the uniform percentage for the class of property. Overvaluation is when assessment exceeds the actual market value. The following illustrates the concepts:

	HOUSE A	HOUSE B	HOUSE C
Current market value	$20,000	$20,000	$20,000
Equalization rate	.50	.50	.50
Calculated assessed value	10,000	10,000	10,000
Actual assessed value	25,000	10,000	15,000
	over-valuation	equitable assessment	inequitable assessment

The assessor can expect complaints from the owners of both Houses A and C.

Assessment Cycle, Taxation, and Foreclosure

The assessment cycle is built upon an assessment calendar much like the budget calendar. By the taxable-status day, the assessor must determine the value of the property. By the tentative completion date, the assessment role is considered complete and legal copies are filed. By the grievance day, formal petitions for change of assessment to the review board must be filed. The final completion day is the beginning of court reviews of review board decisions. Eventually, the state or local legislative body must certify the assessment. The final step is that the assessment roll becomes the tax roll. All this must be done each year.

The state or local government now must calculate how much revenue it needs and the tax rate needed to generate that amount of revenue. The government computes estimated expenditures and subtracts other revenue. The remainder must be generated by the so-called tax of last resort—the property tax. The needed revenue is divided by the assessed valuation, which is converted into a rate per thousand assessed value. The tax rate is determined by the tax base and the amount of money needed to run the government.

The process does have its constraints. Often a law establishes a maximum tax rate. Certainly there are economic constraints because high rates discourage commerce and discourage people from living in an area. There are also political constraints because high tax rates can lead to taxpayer rebellions which can force some officials out of office.

The yield from property tax is due both to the tax rate and to the assessed value. The tax yield can increase if the assessed value goes up or the tax rate is increased. If the local government is at the maximum tax rate, then pressures increase for reassessment, which is an often neglected task. If a community has a growing tax base, then it has the advantage of getting a greater yield without necessarily increasing the tax rate or reassessing the established property. However, if a community has a shrinking tax base, then it has the unfortunate prospect of reaching its tax rate limit and reassessing its property as much as possible. This tends to discourage commerce and to encourage greater flight from the community.

Taxes are collected in a variety of ways. Some governments demand a yearly or possibly a quarterly payment directly to the government. Most people must borrow money from a bank to buy a home, and they have monthly mortgage payments to make to the bank. Often the bank will also collect the property taxes as a part of the monthly payment. The tax amount goes into an escrow account until payment is due to the government. If the government does not receive payment, there is an extra interest charge or penalty amount added on to the already delinquent tax obligation.

If no payment is made, then a long, complex foreclosure begins. The process varies from state to state, but the following illustrates a typical situation. First, a tax lien is imposed which includes the interest and the penalties. Tax liens are in the form of tax certificates. They are negotiable securities and can be sold as they represent a debt which must be liquidated before clear title can be conveyed. The property serves as the security for the debt.

The whole process is designed to give the taxpayers a fair opportunity to save their property. Public notice on major foreclosure actions on the property in question must be given, but often individual notice is not required. At the sale, certificates on the title are given and the owner has one year to redeem or to lose the property. If it is not redeemed, then title is conveyed to the owner of the tax certificate unless there is actual occupancy of the property or the property is also subject to a mortgage. If those conditions exist, the tax certificate owner can foreclose. The process involves years. Often the property in question is neglected during this period. Its value goes down, and it becomes an eyesore to the neighborhood.

OTHER REVENUE SOURCES

Income Tax

Income tax is thought of as a federal tax, but it is also a revenue source for state and local government. For example, in 1982 $412,263 million in income tax was collected in the United States, of which $64,945 million was state and local income tax revenue. About 14 percent or $5,600 million was local income tax revenue. At the federal level, income tax is collected from both corporations and individuals, with the latter being much more significant. The federal tax is collected on all types of income, but there are many complex exceptions which are beyond the scope of this text. The state income taxes are normally related closely to the federal tax, with some specific changes mandated by each state's legislature. Local income taxes are normally flat-rate taxes on wages and salaries.

Like the property tax, the income tax is not without its issues. The complexity of the federal tax and the related "tax loopholes" are now common issues. At the state and local level, taxation of nonresidents and taxation of nonlabor income are frequent subjects of controversy. Most agree that taxation should be a means to redistribute revenue among classes and among localities, but disagreement exists on how much should be redistributed and which localities should receive the benefit. One particular concern to state and local governments is that the tax can produce an out-migration of individuals and businesses to areas where taxes are lower.

The details of income taxation administration vary, but the major features are rates, base, withholding, administrative staff and equipment, revenue potential and implementation. Rates can provide the progressive feature of the tax because higher income persons are taxed at a higher rate. Federal and state income taxes have progressive rates, but most local income taxes are done on a flat rate. The base is that to which the rate is applied in order to arrive at the tax. At the local level, it is simply the wages and salaries earned. At the federal level, the base is difficult to calculate, but it is the net taxable income after various adjustments are made. The withholding is a key administrative feature of this tax because it makes tax payment less painful to the average taxpayer. Employers are required to deduct specific amounts from each employee's paycheck for taxes. Thus, an amount is set aside for the yearly taxes. The income tax is difficult to administer and qualified staff plus sophisticated equipment, such as electronic data processing, are needed. The revenue potential is quite good for this tax, and sophisticated revenue estimating procedures are often important, as explained in an earlier chapter. Tax administration involves maintaining a bookkeeping and audit staff and reporting forms, the continuing surveillance of tax collections, and prosecution of tax evasion and fraud cases.

Sales Tax

The sales tax is primarily a state tax, but some local governments use it. Out of $136,548 million collected in 1982, $77,915 went to the state level, $14,000 to the local level, and none to the federal level. A sales tax applies to goods and services normally levied at the retail stores and expressed in percentage terms. Sales tax can be general (i.e., broadly applicable) or selective (i.e., limited to a few items). The use of this tax increased as a result of the need for greater revenue than the income or property tax alone could provide. It has proven to be a highly successful tax.

The policy issues related to sales tax include jurisdictional liability, loss of business, and compliance. Should sales tax liability for a particular transaction be established at the *place of delivery* or at the *location of the vendor*? The *place of delivery* answer would result in added tax revenue but also added administrative headaches. One way to deal with the problem is the use tax. It is a tax levied in lieu of the sales tax on an item purchased outside the sales tax jurisdiction but still used and enjoyed in that jurisdiction. In practice, use taxes are poorly enforced and the *location of the vendor* is the most practical jurisdictional liability test to apply. A community does lose retail business if its sales tax is higher than that of adjacent areas. The best policy is to have sales tax uniformity throughout a county or metropolitan area. Compliance problems always exist with contractors, itinerant sellers, installation workers, and multiple operations having locations in different cities.

Three other policy issues are regressivity, overlapping governments, and allocation. Sales tax applies mostly to the consumers and the poor must consume all of their resources. Therefore, the sales tax will affect the poor more. Sales taxes are regressive. One attempt to lessen regressivity is to exempt food and similar vitals from the tax. Often more than one government unit covers an area and each imposes sales tax. Thus there is an overlapping of local sales taxes. A potential sales tax policy conflict exists and certainly confusion for the retailers collecting the tax exists. Another issue is allocation because of the lack of correlation between sales tax base and revenue needs. Areas with concentrations of retail stores, such as shopping centers, will benefit greatly from the tax, but the greater tax needs may be in the poorer neighborhoods with fewer stores. If the tax is statewide and placed in a general fund, then this is not a significant problem. However, there are many local governments which collect sales taxes themselves.

These issues are implicit in state and local sales tax. Approaches can be taken to mitigate the problems, but the problems do remain and must be weighed when decisions are made about how to administer this tax.

There are four steps in administration of the sales tax. First, a list of vendors must be prepared and updated. Second, return forms explaining the tax collected by vendors must be prepared. Third, the returns or collections are mailed, with stress placed on speed. Return lists must be compared with the vendor list so that delinquents can be isolated. Sometimes court action is necessary to get the returns. The fourth step is to have trained auditors examine a sample of vendor accounts and records. This is essential to maintain successful retail sales tax administration. Each step requires expertise and careful attention to detail.

Other Taxes

There is a large variety of other taxes and government revenue sources, each with its unique and administrative difficulties. User charges exist for some government services, much as in private industry. Tolls, fees, and license fees are charged. Transfer taxes and other legal transaction charges exist. Special assessments and utility service taxes are also common.

REVIEW QUESTIONS

1. What are the major trends in intergovernmental revenue systems? Explain the implications of those trends.
2. Why is the property tax considered to be an onerous tax? Explain why achieving a uniform, full-market-value property tax is extremely difficult.

3. What are the most easily adopted property tax reforms, and why is it difficult to achieve those reforms? Why is *Serrano v. Priest* an important case?

4. Explain why judgment is important in applying the key tests associated with property tax. Explain the various approaches to assessment and why it is a difficult judgment to make.

5. What are equalization rates in real property tax? How are they applied? What aspects of the assessment process should be tested, and how is this done? How is the tax rate determined?

6. How are property taxes collected, and what happens if taxes are not paid?

7. Compare and contrast the issues involving income and sales taxes. Compare and contrast income and sales tax administration.

REFERENCES

Advisory Commission on Intergovernmental Relations. *Significant Features of Fiscal Federalism, 1981–82*. Washington, D.C.: Government Printing Office, April 1983.
——— . *Changing Public Attitudes on Governments and Taxes*. Washington, D.C.: Government Printing Office, 1982.
ARONSON, J. RICHARD and ELI SCHWARTZ (eds.). *Management Policies in Local Government Finance*. Washington, D.C.: International City Management Association, Municipal Finance Officers Association, 1975.
ARRON, HENRY J. *Who Pays the Property Tax*. Washington, D.C.: Brookings Institution, 1975.
BLECHMON, BARRY E., EDWARD M. GRAMLICK and ROBERT W. HARTMAN. *Setting National Priorities: The 1976 Budget*. Washington, D.C.: Brookings Institution, 1976.
BLINDER, ALAN S. et al. *The Economics of Public Finance*. Washington, D.C.: Brookings Institution, 1974.
BREAK, GEORGE F. *Agenda for Local Tax Reform*. Berkeley: University of California, Institute of Governmental Studies, 1970.
DORSEY, THOMAS A. *Understanding the Real Property Tax*. Syracuse, N.Y.: Syracuse Governmental Research Bureau, 1974.
DUNCOMBE, SYDNEY and THOMAS D. LYNCH. "Taxpayer Revolt," in Thomas D. Lynch (ed.), *Contemporary Public Budgeting*. New Brunswick, N.J.: Transaction Books, 1981.
ECKER-RACZ, L. L. *The Politics and Economics of State-Local Finance*. Englewood Cliffs, N.J.: Prentice-Hall, 1970.
MAXWELL, JAMES and J. RICHARD ARONSON. *Financing State and Local Governments*. Washington, D.C.: Brookings Institution, 1977.
PETERSON, GEORGE E. (ed.). *Property Tax Reform*. Washington, D.C.: Urban Institute, 1973.

TEN
INTERNAL SERVICE
FUNCTIONS

This chapter covers three important financial management topics: (1) property management, (2) risk management, and (3) pension funds. The subjects are important and useful for a person working in budgeting. At the conclusion of this chapter, the reader should know:

1. the steps in a systematic preliminary review of property management;
2. what purchasing is and why a specialist in purchasing is useful to a government;
3. what competitive bidding is and its disadvantages;
4. the importance of standardization and specifications;
5. the usefulness of preventative group replacement, computing maintenance and equipment cost in purchasing decisions, and cooperative intergovernmental arrangements;
6. the usefulness of central stores and the challenge of inventory management;
7. the significance of property control;
8. the potential applications of bar technology;
9. what risk management is and why it is an important concern;
10. what exposure identification is and how one goes about risk evaluation;
11. what risk control is and its significance;
12. what self-insurance is and when it is appropriate;
13. what insurance is, how it is selected, and some general standards applicable to it;
14. the elements of administration related to proper risk management;
15. the significance of retirement plans to public budgeting;

16.   the significance of pensions to budgets; and
17.   policy issues relevant to public pension funds.

PROPERTY MANAGEMENT

Preliminary Review

A government may own extensive and valuable property which needs to be managed. In a systematic preliminary review of property management, the first step is to inventory the property describing location, identifying its use, recording its value, and identifying persons responsible for the property. The second step is to determine if up-to-date and comprehensive regulations exist which ensure proper management, including a property accounting system and adequate frequency and scope of internal audits. Auditing should complement property management and a preliminary review should discern whether audits cover property management practices and whether audit findings are seriously considered. In addition, employees using the system are often the best source of ideas for improvement, and a preliminary review should check to see whether their opinons are effectively sought and used. One last review concern should be risk associated with the property. This subject will be covered later on in the chapter.

A sound system ensures that no one individual or small group controls all aspects of property management transactions. Certain specific duties, such as purchasing, receiving, accounting for, paying for, and disposing of property, should be divided among different people to minimize the possibility of pilferage or misuse of property. Duties and responsibilities should be identified and documented so that each employee clearly knows his or her role. If separation of key functions is impossible, then management reviews and internal controls should be more frequent. In addition, personnel need to be adequately trained in their responsibilites, including care and protection of property, proper and safe practices, and the ethical implications of their jobs.

The following is a more detailed list of the duties which should be separated whenever possible.

1.   requesting purchases;
2.   authorizing purchases;
3.   purchasing;
4.   receiving and inspecting property;
5.   maintaining physical custody of property or inventories;
6.   maintaining property ledgers or detailed inventory records;
7.   maintaining financial accounting records for property or inventories;
8.   conducting physical inventories;
9.   reconciling physical inventory counts with property book balances;
10.   performing surveys for shortages, losses, thefts, or damage;
11.   authorizing transfers or disposition of property;

12. reconciling property records with accounting records;
13. making payments for purchases; and
14. performing reviews and audits.

Purchasing

In an organization, goods and services must be acquired. This activity is called purchasing. Materials, supplies, and equipment must be procured which best suit the job to be done by the operating unit. Ideally, the correct quantity should be ordered and in the hands of the operator when the units are needed. This proper timing of orders should also anticipate potential emergency shortage situations. The goods, services (including technical services), or equipment should be purchased at the lowest possible price. Unneeded inventory must be disposed of appropriately.

A central purchasing agent should be in charge of the procurement. Purchasing requires a knowledge of supply sources, pricing, business practices, market conditions, and appropriate laws, ordinances, and regulations. The procurement system should be devised to insure that discounts are taken, quality is tested, items are properly received and stored, and deliveries are prompt. Expertise is needed in dealing with salespersons, contractors, and people in the government seeking goods and services to get their jobs done. In other words, procurement is a separate administrative specialty and often can best be done by a central purchasing agent.

In spite of the obvious advantages, there are serious problems in properly conducting purchasing operations. As a result of political pressure, contracts are sometimes awarded to favorite persons or groups. Because of the enormous amounts of money involved, corruption is always a threat. Another problem is that procurement approaches (discussed later) do not lend themselves to undisputedly proper purchases of services, especially if high levels of talent are being acquired. Also, the process can be so involved that quick purchases are simply not possible. In other words, procurement is not an easy administrative undertaking.

Procurement

Centralized and sometimes cooperative approaches to procurement are often taken. Centralization and cooperation lead to sufficient activity to justify hiring a specialist purchasing agent. A specialist can take the time to better monitor delivery services, develop a list of qualified vendors, and improve purchased items through standardization, use of standard specifications, better inspections, and testing. Responsibility for procurement can be more easily established in problem cases. Also greater fiscal control over expenditures for materials, supplies, and equipment can be achieved. These benefits are not automatic. Often central purchasing can mean friction between the ordering departments and the purchasing department as well as other problems if the purchasing department is inefficient, corrupt, or lacks sufficient budget authority.

In most governments, the law requires most purchases to be made with competitive bidding in order to minimize cost and to avoid corruption. Advertising for many bids and maintaining up-to-date lists of suppliers are essential if the spirit of the law is to be kept. The opportunity to bid should be unrestricted in most circumstances. The invitation or request for bids should involve related items and specify the conditions of delivery. The sealed bids should be opened publicly and awards to other than the lowest bidder must be clearly explained in terms of the previously stated criteria. Awards must be in accordance with the stated specifications. Care should be taken to discourage and, if necessary, to prosecute seller collusion.

Competitive bidding has its disadvantages. It is inflexible and takes a great deal of time to process. It does not lend itself to small purchases, emergency buying, or contracts for professional services. If only one or even a few bids are received, then the government must be able to refuse the bid, or the process may result in higher prices rather than lower ones. In such circumstances, negotiated bidding may be a better purchasing process.

Standardization and specification are important procurement activities. Standardization of purchased items can lead to reducing the number and kinds of items purchased, thus reducing cost through quantity buying. Exceptions to standardization exist, especially with highly specialized and technical goods. However, standardization is often desirable as it leads to price savings, quality improvements, and lower administrative costs. A procurement specification is a product or material description upon which bids are solicited. An adequate specification must be accurate and complete, but not overspecific. It must describe the methods of inspection and testing; state special requirements such as packing; conform, if possible, to national standards; and be internally consistent and simply stated. Good specification should place all bidders on an equal basis, minimize disputes, and avoid expensive brand-name buying. Both standardization and specification require enormous work and a highly qualified staff. If they serve no practical purpose in a given context, they should be avoided as they should serve to increase, not lower, efficiency.

Goods should be inspected and tested. Were the goods delivered on time and in good condition? Were the goods received those that were ordered? Are the goods of the quality ordered? Inspection and testing answer these vital questions. Not all items need be inspected, but a random sample should be taken.

Another purchasing department responsibility is disposal of property. If possible, reassignment of items should be made. However, the time comes when an item such as an automobile should be traded, sold at auction, or sold as surplus. The objective should be to save the government money by using items as much as possible and recovering any value for the goods after they have ceased being useful to the government.

Selected Purchasing Challenges

One purchasing challenge is deciding if particular items should be replaced as a group or individually. A preventative maintenance program can sometimes result in overall savings by replacing all items in a given category (e.g., light bulbs) at one time rather than individually. Group replacement can be cheaper owing to efficiency in scheduling labor and quantity price discounts. If this is to be done, then a replacement cycle must be established so that buying and labor scheduling can be properly coordinated. Also, some research is needed to decide the expected life of the item and the best replacement time.

Another challenge is including maintenance cost with the equipment cost so that total cost can be computed. The maintenance cost can be estimated by the supplier or the government. In fact, the contract with the supplier can include a proviso declaring the maximum maintenance cost and guaranteeing that any excessive maintenance cost would be reimbursed by the seller. Exhibit 10-1 is an illustration cited in chapter 14 of *Management Policies in Local Government Finance*.

EXHIBIT 10-1   Total-Cost Purchasing or Least-Cost Purchasing

Three suppliers bid as follows on heavy equipment:

Supplier	Purchase Price	Total Five-Year Guaranteed Maintenance Cost	Repurchase Price
A	$23,000	$11,000	$ 2,000
B	30,000	5,000	15,000
C	26,000	12,000	10,000

Supplier C has specified a five-year guarantee of $800 times the age of the machine each year. Suppliers A and B have agreed to apportion their guarantees evenly over the five years (i.e., $2,200 per annum for A and $1,000 per annum for B).

The formula to calculate total cost is as follows:

$$K = P + \left[\sum_{i=1}^{5} R_i \left(\frac{1}{1.2}\right)^i \right] - T \left(\frac{1}{1.2}\right)$$

where

K = net present value R_i = maintenance cost in year i

P = purchase price T = repurchase price

Using a 20 percent discount, the formula results in the following:

Supplier	Purchase Price +	Present Value of Maintenance Cost −	Present Value of Repurchased Price =	Net Present Value
A	$23,000	$6,579	$ 804	$28,775
B	30,000	2,991	6,029	26,962
C	26,000	6,318	4,019	28,299

The least expensive total-cost bid is B.[1]

A third purchasing challenge is maintaining cooperative intergovernmental arrangements. Such arrangements can mean cost savings, but they should be undertaken with a clear understanding of all the factors involved. A basis for cost sharing must be negotiated. The level of service should be the same; or, if reduced, then this must be accepted. Labor disputes can sometimes arise when jobs are eliminated. Also the parties must understand who controls the planning, specifications, and service availability. Cooperative arrangements are normally difficult to apply because of disagreements over uniform items, the need for detailed records, and the allocation of shared costs. Beside cost-savings advantages, cooperative programs lead to a better sharing of ideas and greater personnel growth opportunities. Some important services that can be contracted or shared include street lighting, garbage disposal, sanitation services, health services, tax assessment and collection, water supply, law enforcement, and street and highway maintenance.

Central Stores and Inventory

Central warehousing, including tanks and storage yards, can foster significant savings since it makes possible quantity buying at the right time and price. Central stores permit better use of lead time to stock for emergencies and to allow the management of uneven requirements for goods. The disadvantage of central stores is the administrative cost of operation. Thus, warehousing should be minimized. Problems to avoid include:

1. overstocking, especially if the goods can become obsolete;
2. a nonrestrictive inventory, not limited to substantial demand items;
3. failure to balance stocking cost against value of having the item in stock when needed; and
4. failure to consider the full range of cost elements.

The critical challenge of inventory is to calculate and to achieve the optimum amount of commodities so that necessary goods are available but storage costs are minimized. If supplies were available instantly and if purchase unit price did not vary by such factors as size of purchase, there would be no need for inventory. However, inventory is needed to reduce the likelihood of being out of needed goods and to obtain lower prices through bulk purchase and by taking advantage of fluctuations in market price. Those "savings" must be balanced against storage costs. This calculation is much like the decisions on investing idle cash discussed in an earlier chapter.

Safety stock must be determined. There are various ways to determine that level of stock, but they all should recognize the various inventory costs:

[1]A. Wayne Corcoran, "Financial Management," in *Management Policies in Local Government Finance*, ed. J. Richard Aronson and Eli Schwartz (Washington, D.C.: International City Management Association, 1975).

1. ordering cost—preparing specifications, obtaining competitive bids, negotiating, receiving items;
2. incremental cost—unique extra costs due to specific order;
3. carrying cost—deterioration, obsolescence, storing, issuing, theft, handling, interest, and insurance;
4. shortage cost—associated with disappointing a client, legal settlements, lost labor costs, other costs due to delay or failure to provide service.

The solution for optimal safety stock is to keep the total of holding costs and expected shortage costs minimal. These calculations assume sound estimates, but once those costs are determined, the actual calculation for optimal safety stock is relatively simple, especially with a computer. Rules of thumb can be developed in terms of days of normal use. Ideally, these rules of thumb should be checked against the more sophisticated calculations.

Another calculation involves ordering cost. For this, the economic ordering quantity (EOQ) model is used. The ordering costs must be weighed against the holding costs which arise on account of the size of the order. The calculation is similar to the optimal safety stock determination. The optimum ordering quantity is reached when the total of the two types of costs are at a minimum. The following EOQ model is used:

$$Q = \sqrt{2C_0D \div C_H}$$

where

Q = the optimum (i.e., most economic) quantity to order
C_O = the cost of ordering per order
C_H = the cost of holding per unit per time period
D = the quantity of units used or demanded in each time period

An example is as follows:

D = 110 cubic yards of gravel used per day
C_O = $20.00 per order (ordering costs)
C_H = $0.02 per yard per day (holding costs)

$$Q = \sqrt{2(20)110 \div .02} = 469 \text{ yards}^2$$

Again, most analysts develop simpler rules of thumb. However, the results of those casual estimates should be tested against the more sophisticated approach discussed here.

Total desirable inventory is calculated by adding the EOQ and safety stock solution. A more accurate solution would use a simultaneous solution, but that higher degree of accuracy is not normally warranted.

[2]This explanation and example are from Corcoran, "Financial Management."

The calculations described above use quantifiable costs, but often important government or social costs cannot be reduced to numbers. This should be understood when applying the techniques.

Property Control

A property control officer is needed to ensure that personal property and the equipment of government is being efficiently managed. No operational control is necessary, but procedures must be devised and practices must be monitored to ensure efficient management. This type of control should be applied only to cases in which poor use of items can easily mean inefficiency or corruption.

Records control fixes actual responsibility for the care of an item. Periodic reports are needed on the condition of the item. Records help with insurance loss claims, preventative maintenance decisions, and reordering. Records should use identifying numbers, acquisition purchase orders, transfers, and repair and disposal orders.

An option to owning goods is leasing. This is an alternative which may be the best economic investment. The calculations to determine this are similar to the ones involving present value discussed in an earlier chapter.

Bar-Code Technology

In the early 1960s, supermarkets and their suppliers began using bar codes to identify items for automatic check-out and inventory control. Since then, bar codes and other machine-readable symbols (see Exhibit 10-2) have been used on material components, finished goods, shipping containers, warehouse bins, bills of lading, and other distribution documentation. Optical scanners are increasingly common in factories, private warehouses, and government agencies. Scanners convert the symbols into an acceptable computer input.

The hardware consists of the optical code reader and bar-coded labels. The reader is a mini-computer which records, stores, and transmits coded data to the main computer. The reader often uses a lightpen to focus a light beam on the bar-coded surfaces to sense reflections. The reader may also have a cathode-ray tube (CRT) to display the data being scanned in its proper place on the record being updated. It may be on-line—interfaced directly with a large computer—or off-line, with interface devices used on occasion to transmit stored data. For inventory and property control, the portable, hand-held models are most widely used. Bar-code labels must be readable and durable, and must adhere properly to the labeled items.

Great productivity gains in property management can result from bar-code technology. If faster and more accurate data entry is important, then this technology can lead to increased operational effectiveness. The following are some of the more common bar-code applications:

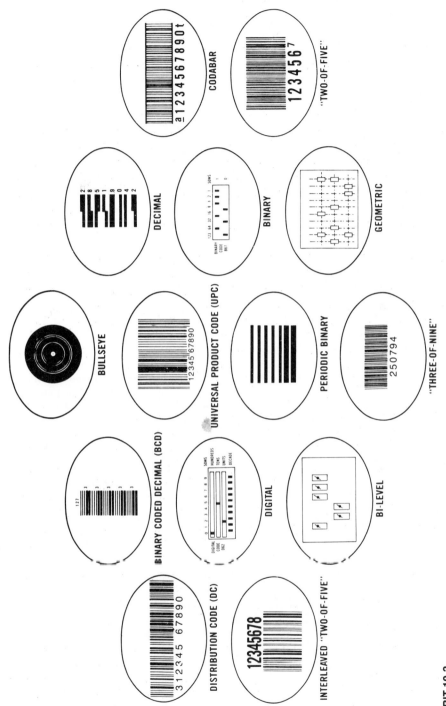

CODABAR

a 1 2 3 4 5 6 7 8 9 0 t

"TWO-OF-FIVE"

1 2 3 4 5 6 7

DECIMAL

BINARY

GEOMETRIC

BULLSEYE

UNIVERSAL PRODUCT CODE (UPC)

1 2 3 4 5 6 7 8 9 0

PERIODIC BINARY

"THREE-OF-NINE"

250794

BINARY CODED DECIMAL (BCD)

DIGITAL

BI-LEVEL

DISTRIBUTION CODE (DC)

3 1 2 3 4 5 6 7 8 9 0

INTERLEAVED "TWO-OF-FIVE"

12345678

EXHIBIT 10-2

1. forms management;
2. document sorting;
3. tracking and locating work in progress;
4. production control;
5. order processing and automatic billing;
6. quality control inspection;
7. distribution or warehouse control;
8. mail operations, including sorting and tracking;
9. motor vehicle accountability and maintenance;
10. productivity measurement;
11. "job shops" for billing purposes;
12. libraries/central files;
13. security in controlling access to restricted areas; and
14. shipping and receiving control.

RISK MANAGEMENT

A Practical Necessity

Forbes magazine reported the following true account:

> On a clear, dry night in 1974, 26-year-old Thomas J. Garchar cruised down a straightaway on Broward County's (Fla.) University Drive and smashed his car headlong into a 560-pound decorative limestone boulder lying on the road's median. Paralyzed from the neck down as a result of the accident, Garchar sued the retirement town of Tamarac (population: 31,000), essentially on the grounds that Tamarac's city fathers knew that the boulder was there, but had not removed it.
>
> In court Garchar admitted to having been up 18 hours straight and to having downed three drinks just prior to the accident. Yet last November, a local jury found Tamarac guilty of negligence and awarded Garchar and his wife $4.7 million in damages. (Broward County, responsible for placing the boulder on the median, settled out of court for another $1.15 million.) The town is appealing the case, and $1 million of the judgment is covered by liability insurance, but meanwhile Tamarac faces the prospect of raising taxes to pay the award."[3]

In *Governmental Finance* the following case was cited.[4] A 23-year-old patrol officer was hired. He was in generally good health when hired, but after 18 months he suffered a lifting injury to his lower back. This led to two months' lost work time, surgery, and two more months of operative recovery. The officer returned to work but was extremely bothered by back pain resulting from work activities. This led to more lost time, medical bills, and physical therapy. After two-and-a-half years' service, he stopped working because of his back problem and was retired one year later on a disability pension at age 26. The cost was:

[3]Lawrence Minard, "The Premiums of City Life," *Forbes*, 119, 6 (March 15, 1977), 96.
[4]Edward G. Lengyel, "Counting Risk: The Safety Factor," *Government Finances*, 6, 33 (May 1977), 47.

Medical expenses for disc surgery	$ 6,300
Lost time compensation costs	5,500
Ongoing medical expenses	4,000
Retirement benefit (two-thirds average monthly salary which was $620 with projected mortality of 50 years)	372,000
Cost to hire and train replacement patrol officer	2,000
Estimated partial disability settlement by compensation carrier	15,000
Other hidden costs estimated	2,000
Total Cost	$406,800

Both public and private concerns are subject to significant risks which could be costly to the government. Risk management is merely deciding how best to deal with those risks and to manage the problem accordingly. The above cases dramatically point out that risk is a significant consideration in good financial management. Insurance is one way to deal with risk, and the costs of insurance are rising dramatically. The League of California Cities in 1975 surveyed municipal liability insurance premiums and discovered a one-year increase of 96 percent as well as many nonrenewals of insurance. In other words, risks are significant and the traditional solution—insurance—is becoming more expensive and harder to acquire.

The risks or liabilities for government include civil damages, breach of contract, dishonesty protection, worker's compensation, activity interruption, and even health protection. What losses can take place? Property can be damaged. People can be hurt. Property can be stolen. People can get sick. Each represents a loss which can cost a government significant sums of money.

The most serious loss exposure concerns third-party liabilities. In the first case cited above, the town of Tamarac has been held liable for not removing a traffic safety hazard. This resulted in a large damage award. Similar awards can occur if a public employee is involved in an accident. Suits can be brought for environmental pollution. For example, the town of Hopewell, Virginia, was sued in the mid-1970s for either actively or passively condoning the contamination of the James River by a small firm connected with Allied Chemical Company. New loss exposures are being defined in the courts today: Jail inmates have sued Dutchess County, New York, for providing inadequate medical treatment. The City of Los Angeles was sued by property owners near the airport because aircraft noise reduced their property value. The potential cost to state and local government is high.

Exposure Identification and Risk Evaluation

The first step in risk management is the identification of government resources and the losses that are possible. What kind of damages to people and property could take place? What type of damage can result if the government's responsibility is not met? What happens if someone is in an accident, is sick, or is dishonest? This step requires an inventory of the government's resources and a careful evaluation of responsibilities and potential damages. This evaluation can be facilitated by a knowledge of the types of risk liabilities governments commonly experience and the types of claims currently found in the courts. This step must be done on a continuing basis by using checklists, questionnaires, interviews with employees, physical inspections, and a careful monitoring of the contemporary risk management literature.

Part of exposure identification must be a full understanding of the tort doctrine of government immunity. This doctrine gave government immunity from many civil tort actions, such as negligence. However, this doctrine has been reconsidered since the 1940s, and governments are increasingly vulnerable. This means, for example, that governments can be sued for not maintaining property to prevent injuries. Care must be taken in these areas by governments, or costly judgments can occur. An awareness of state law is necessary in order to understand the status of the doctrine of government immunity in each particular state.

Information is the key to exposure identification. Accurate and timely data on costs must be available so that costs can be identified with specific departments and activities. Financial statements, especially involving capital projects, help identify property exposures and areas of new activity not analyzed for risks. Another useful source of data is analyses of operations. By following through the process, the risk manager can identify services that could be disrupted, potential hazards in procedures, health dangers, and equipment safety concerns. In looking over such data, the manager is particularly concerned with the likely frequency and severity of the exposure potential. Other concerns include neat storage of goods and equipment, proximity of storage to fire sources, freedom of movement so that people can escape from dangerous situations and proper officials can have easy access to them, and special handling of flammable liquids.

Exhibit 10-3 is a useful risk and insurance checklist. This checklist can aid in a systematic review of the exposures facing a government unit.

The measurement of potential losses is not easily accomplished. A complete inventory of property is needed, including distance from building location to hazards; proximity to highway, air, or rail traffic; available fire protection, including quality indicators such as water pressure; and a description of the surrounding property. The inventory should also include the construction details, specifics of safety protections used, and building and equipment replacement costs. In measuring liability exposure, an evaluation of the laws covering government immunity, a review of the current history of local claim awards, and a review of all contract terms are essential. In measuring fidelity exposure, careful examination must be made of cash receipts, opportunities to convert assets to cash, and potential for dealings between high officials and vendors or grantees. Periodic outside audits are essential. Risk managers must review (1) the audits, (2) accounting reports which show balances, (3) purchasing procedures, (4) electronic data processing concerning money, (5) the location and volume of cash, and (6) cash internal control procedures. Losses must be weighed in terms of exposure and severity.

EXHIBIT 10-3 Risk and Insurance Checklist

I. Real Property
   A. Buildings owned
     1. Nature, use and location
     2. Value replacement and actual cash value
     3. Rental value of space used
     4. Income from space rented to others
     5. Laws and ordinances for demolition and for replacement standards
   B. Buildings rented from others
     1. Nature, use and location
     2. Value of improvements and betterments made by tenant
     3. Total rent paid by tenant
     4. Rental income derived from subletting space to others
     5. Value of the lease (is the lease favorable?)
     6. Type of insurance clauses and hold harmless agreements in the lease
   C. All buildings and other real property (includes A and B above)
     1. Alterations and additions in progress or contemplated
     2. Boilers and pressure vessels in operation
     3. Power machinery in operation (switchboards, motors, engines, generators, etc.)
     4. Cold storage vaults and other special provisions for maintaining controlled temperature or humidity
     5. Electric or neon signs
     6. Plate or ornamental glass
     7. Elevators and escalators
     8. Possible fire department service charges
     9. Fire and other protection (sprinklers, alarms, watchmen)

II. Personal Property
   A. Stock, including packaging materials (each location)
     1. Peak value and low values (month by month)
     2. Susceptibility to crime loss
     3. Values dependent on parts difficult to replace
     4. Values susceptible to damage by lack of heat or cold
   B. Furniture and fixtures attached to the building
     1. Those permanently attached to the building
     2. Unattached furniture, fixtures, machinery, office equipment
     3. Supplies and prepaid expense items
   C. Personal Property belonging to others
   D. Personal property in the custody of others
   E. Coins and currency (maximum amounts)
     1. Payroll cash (when)
     2. Other cash
     3. Cash in custody of each bank messenger
     4. Cash in custody of each truck driver or collector
     5. Cash kept in safes overnight
     6. Liability limit or armored car carrier
   F. Incoming checks (maximum amounts)
     1. On premises
     2. In safes overnight
     3. In custody of each bank messenger
     4. In custody of each truck driver or collector

G. Bank accounts (locations, amounts, uses)
H. Securities (maximum amounts)
   1. In safes
   2. In custody of each bank messenger
   3. In safe deposit vaults
   4. At other locations (specify)
I. Especially valuable property (maximum amounts) (e.g., precious stones, fine arts, antiques, rare metals, isotopes, radium)
   1. In safes
   2. Elsewhere on premises
   3. In custody of each truck driver
   4. In safe deposit vault
   5. At other locations or in transit (specify)
J. Valuable papers, documents, records
   1. Kind
   2. Where kept
   3. Value
   4. Protection afforded
K. Accounts receivable
   1. Maximum and minimum values
   2. Where account records are kept
   3. How protected
L. Automobiles, airplanes, boats, trains, buses (owned or used)
   1. Ownership
     a) Owned
     b) Non-owned
   2. Value and extent of concentration in one place at one time

III. Operations
A. Central operations: principal services
   1. Nature of all services regularly provided
   2. Sources of materials and supplies used
   3. Flow of goods, steps or processes in provision of services: any bottlenecks
   4. Extent, nature, and location of goods on installment or similar credit arrangements
   5. Installation, demonstration, or servicing away from premises
   6. Quality control
B. Service for employees
   1. Operation of a hospital, infirmary, or first-aid station
   2. Operation of a restaurant for employees
   3. Sponsorship of employee athletic teams
C. Operation of a medical facility or other service in which a malpractice hazard exists
D. Operation of a restaurant for the general public
E. Work let out under contract
F. Advertising signs, vending machines, booths, etc., owned or operated away from the premises
G. Sponsorship of outside athletic team
H. Liability assumed under contract
   1. Sidetrack agreements
   2. Leases
   3. Hold harmless agreements
   4. Purchase orders
   5. Elevator or escalator maintenance agreements
   6. Easements
   7. Service agreements (for or by the entity)
   8. Other contracts
   9. Warranties

I. Shipments (values shipped annually and the maximum value of any one shipment, both incoming and outgoing)
   1. Own trucks
   2. Truckmen
   3. Rail
   4. Railway express
   5. Air
   6. Parcel post prepaid and C.O.D.
   7. Registered mail
   8. Inland or coastal water
   9. Foreign
   10. Marine cargo
J. "Time element" exposures
   1. Payroll: key persons; "ordinary" payroll
   2. Cost of merchandise
   3. Cost of heat, light, and power
   4. Trend of revenue for current year; estimate for next year
   5. Maximum time required to replace facilities subject to damage
   6. Percentage of revenue that would be affected by a business interruption loss
   7. The availability and probable cost of substitute facilities to reduce loss of revenue in case of damage to present facilities
   8. Extra expense to maintain operations following loss
   9. If plans are interdependent, the percentage of revenue affected by a stoppage at each such plant or location, assuming damage at only one location
   10. Extent to which operations are dependent on outside sources of heat, light, or power

IV. Personnel
   A. Home-state employees
      1. Duties
      2. Use of automobiles
      3. Estimated annual payroll
   B. Employees in other states
      1. Residence state and states traveled
      2. Duties
      3. Use of automobiles
      4. Estimated annual payroll
   C. Employees annual payroll
   D. Employees required to use or travel in aircraft
   E. Classification of employees according to duties
   F. Key individuals (individuals whose loss might seriously affect operations)

V. Principal Property Hazards (Probable Maximum Loss)
   A. Fire
   B. Earthquake
   C. Flood
   D. Other

VI. Data Processing Machines
   A. Owned or leased
   B. Protection
   C. Lease to others?
   D. Disaster plan
   E. Analysis of extra expense costs

Source: Gerald M. Surfus, "Identifying and Evaluating Potential Risk," *Government Finances*, 6, 28 (May 1977), 28-29.

Given the difficulty of gathering information and other aspects of risk management, previous government practice, not surprisingly, was to buy insurance and transfer the risk. This permitted the government officials to forget about the risk and pay attention to other, more pressing problems. Today, government cannot afford to handle risk in that manner because:

1. premiums are expensive and increasing in price;
2. some forms of coverage do not exist;
3. government immunity is shrinking;
4. damage awards are radically increasing beyond maximum insurance award limits;
5. preventative and safety programs can dramatically reduce exposure risks;
6. self-insurance is often a cheaper alternative than insurance; and
7. knowledge of insurance and exposure risks can translate into better insurance coverage at less cost.

Risk Control

Risk control is the reduction of risk or loss through careful procedures and practices in security, personnel safety, fire prevention, auto safety, product safety, environmental protection, and emergency planning. For the most part, state and local governments do not perform adequate risk control. In 1975, the National Safety Council said the national average lost time personnel rate was 13.1 (lost time accidents per million man hours worked). Some claim that organizations with a lost time injury rate of more than 41 can be accused of inaction bordering on criminal negligence. The chemical, aerospace, and automotive industries all rated less than 4. Federal civil employees rated 6.5. The rate for municipalities was 41.3. Police, refuse, and fire rates were 54.8, 98.7, and 149 respectively. In 1975, 1 out of 14 municipal employees, 1 out of 10 police employees, 1 out of 6 refuse handlers, and 1 out of 4 fire fighters were involved in a lost time accident. This is a record of inaction and inadequate attention to safety. However, the problem is being recognized as a result of social, economic, and legal pressures. Sound risk control programs include:

1. *Security*—preventative techniques and procedures to combat theft, burglary, and vandalism;
2. *Personnel safety*—meeting occupational safety and health standards, setting work safety standards, monitoring work environment and record keeping on accidents, maintaining safety training and safety committees;
3. *Fleet safety*—systematic review of driving records and implementation of stringent defensive driving courses;
4. *Property conservation*—regular inspection by fire, electrical, police, and other officials to identify and to correct hazards to physical property;
5. *Environmental protection*—procedures to dispose of solid, liquid, and gaseous wastes in accordance with state and federal standards;

6. *Emergency preparedness*—plans for and practice in dealing with a wide variety of emergencies, such as bomb threats, national disasters including fires and floods, and nuclear war; and

7. *Contract liability*—procedures to review likely contracts so that the government will not assume liability for others, as well as care to get contractors for public authorities to sign stiff hold-harmless agreements with evidence of adequate insurance.

Over the years the following safety beliefs have proven to be helpful: (1) Unsafe acts and conditions lead to accidents and injuries; (2) reducing the frequency of injury will also lessen the severity of injury; (3) safety means education, engineering, and enforcement. The key person for safety is the first line supervisor. Post-injury investigations are essential to identify and remove unsafe acts and conditions. Safety programs translate to actively caring about safety and implementing the proper remedies. Safety plans should reflect those beliefs in most instances.

Risk control costs money, as does insurance. A public authority can approach decisions on risk control and insurance on the basis of lowest cost to the government. Exhibit 10-4 illustrates how the cost can be charted. The cost of risk control is calculated and related to the likely cost of insurance and self-insurance. The solution is the lowest joint risk control and insurance cost. Obviously, human compassion

EXHIBIT 10-4 Risk Control Plus Insurance

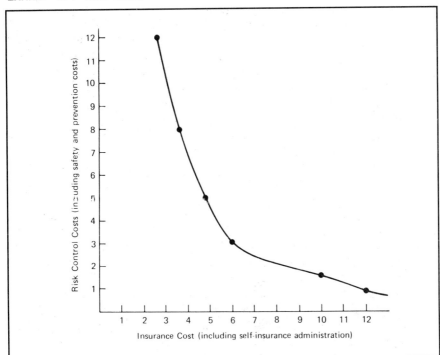

must be considered, and those values dictate that higher sums of money be spent for risk control than our economic analysis suggests. However, the chart does help us see the relationship between safety and insurance costs.

Risk Funding and Self-Insurance

Risk funding is providing for sufficient funds to meet loss situations, if they occur, by the most effective use of internal and external financial resources. A public body can retain the risk and pay losses through extraordinary means or the regular budget. Another option is to transfer the risk through a pooling of insurance. The self-insurance or partial self-insurance option is often desirable because it is the most economical approach for a public body. Even the insurance industry is encouraging the use of high deductibles—that is, partial self-insurance—today.

Insurance is merely the pooling of risks plus charge for administering that pooling. Insurance companies will generally collect from $1.50 to $2.00 in premiums for every dollar spent in claims. Some governments are larger than insurance companies and are in a better position to fund the potential losses than are the companies. A guideline to help decide the proper risk retention amount is that a government body should be willing to accept up to one-tenth of one percent of its operating budget in uninsured losses arising out of a single occurrence, or up to one percent of the operating budget as the aggregate of all such self-insured losses in a single fiscal year.

The following corollary objectives exist in risk funding: (1) Sufficient funds must be provided to meet the worst possible loss event. Some use a "maximum foreseeable loss" criterion and others also use a "maximum probable loss" estimate for the loss. (2) The management of risk funding should include proper use of idle cash reserves. (3) The maximum stability of risk funding should be maintained over time. (4) Administration should be both as efficient and as effective as possible.

Governments are in much better position to absorb losses than most private concerns. They can use the following special factors:

1. federal disaster assistance (Public Law 93-288);
2. funded reserves or an insurance company created especially for that purpose;
3. spreading judgments over, say, a 10-year period;
4. bond issues;
5. special tax levies; and
6. citizen or group donations.

Another type of self-insurance option is pooling on a local, regional, or state basis. For example, the cities in Contra Costa County, California, have pooled together their liability and property risks. Pools for workers' compensation claims have been set up in Alabama, Texas, and Maine. This alternative does work well; and as the liability insurance marketplace deteriorates, this joint action may become the only practical alternative. The biggest problem with pooling is the challenge of reaching administrative consensus on such matters as the cost allocation system. The accompanying chart is a useful guideline on risk retention.

TYPE OF RISK	RETENTION POLICY
Low frequency and low severity	This risk should be retained due to the low exposure.
High frequency and low severity	Normally, this risk should be retained as self-insurance.
High frequency and high severity	Handling this risk depends on the size of the government and insurance marketplace. Worker's compensation is a typical exposure of this type.
Low frequency and high severity	This risk cannot normally be absorbed; risk transfer by insurance is wise. An alternative is partial self-insurance. This can reduce insurance and total risk costs. Property and liability exposures are prime examples of this type.

Partial self-insurance can be practiced by selecting high deductibles and special insurance plans which permit a sharing of risk with the insurance company. The decisions on this subject should weigh premium credits and administrative savings. Do not risk a lot for a little. A deductible should result in savings commensurate with the risk which is retained. However, the government should set the deductible at the level it can afford based on its own financial ability and not on the saving generated in any one year. An annual aggregate deductible should be used rather than a single occurrence deductible because this provides greater budgeting certitude. The following list addresses common practices by type of insurance:

1. *Fire insurance*—high deductibles are often used. Normally the deductible should be on a "per occurrence" basis and not on a "per loss" basis because a single windstorm represents one occurrence but many losses. Also an aggregate deductible should be used.

2. *Workers' compensation*—most private bodies—and, increasingly, public bodies—use self-insurance for catastrophic loss (e.g., over $100,000 on a per occurrence basis).

3. *Public liability*—the use of insurance above set limits is critical, but such insurance is getting increasingly more difficult to obtain. The following are two examples of coverage used in the state of California:
   a. In the mid-1970s, the county of Orange went from a per loss self-insurance of $25,000 to $500,000 on any liability loss.
   b. The city of San Diego increased its liability self-insurance retention from $500,000 to $5 million.

The planning process for self-insurance takes about six months. The first month is spent gathering data, especially on premiums and losses, as discussed earlier. In the second month, the maximum amount which can be retained should be determined. In the third month, the insurance bidding process should begin. In the fourth month, the bids should be reviewed or costs negotiated. In the fifth month, the contracts should be awarded.

A true self-insurance program means that the government performs all the various functions which would have been handled by an insurance carrier. These functions include accounting for premiums, a safety and loss control service, adjusting services, legal services, and funding for losses. A fund from which losses will be paid up to the retained limit must be established. Such funds are accumulated on a gradual basis, and the idle funds are invested. Also, the department incurring the loss should be charged back a predetermined amount of each loss. This serves to encourage department heads to be sensitive to their risks and the importance of risk control.

Insurance

Many public authorities require bidding for insurance. There is some controversy associated with bidding. Advocates point out that open competitive bidding gives every company a fair opportunity to receive the contract, and the process leads to the best price for the government. Those against the process point to several problems. Yearly bidding discourages long-term company-to-client relationships, thus negating a potential advantage and adding to the cost of overhead in the insurance industry. Increasingly fewer companies are willing to bid; thus artificially high bids do exist. If individual negotiations occur instead, they might result in lower bids. An alternative approach is limited competitive bidding, in which stress is placed upon selecting qualified agents or brokers. Two or three are selected and asked to submit firm quotations. The contract is awarded on the basis of those bids.

The forms of insurance include property insurance, crime coverage, liability coverage, and employee benefits. Property insurance includes both fire, "all risk" contracts on buildings, contents, and property, and other coverages. Crime coverages include employee dishonesty, faithful performance bonds, and protection against burglary, robbery, and theft. Liability coverages include all forms of public liability insurance, automobile insurance, and workers' compensation. Umbrella protection is essential and should include the governing body, all boards, commissions, elected officials, and employees, and even volunteers. Employee benefits are often subject to labor-management negotiations, but they can include health insurance, major medical insurance, long-term disability income insurance, accident insurance, group life insurance, and pension plans.

A few general standards apply to all insurance contracts. The named insured group should be consistent on all policies. Property limits should be updated to actual cash or replacement value. All insurance contracts should have a 60-day written notice of cancellation, nonrenewal, or material reduction. Retention and participation in risk should be carefully spelled out in the contract. Proper notification of loss should begin after the risk manager is aware of the loss and payments on losses should be to the governmental body. Normally, all the contracts, or as many as possible, should expire at the end of the fiscal year. Cash flow arrangements should be made to the advantage of the government's idle cash plans.

Some general suggestions on content can be made. Coverage should be very broad on account of the variety of risk exposures found in government. Large maximum limits should be used. For example, in the mid-1970s, a limit of $5 million was appropriate for small governments and $10 to $20 million or more for larger entities. Umbrella coverage is getting more difficult to obtain so some risks must be insured separately, such as airport, aircraft, and bus line liability.

Administration

A risk management program requires continuous direction and careful attention. For larger governments, a full-time risk manager is essential and an additional safety staff would be wise. For smaller governments, this activity can be part of the budget office responsibilities. For both large and small governments, outside assistance can be quite valuable at times owing to the complex nature of this subject.

A formal risk management policy should be developed which sets out important understandings. The policy must have active top legislative and executive support. The policy should establish the goals of the program as well as define authority and responsibility in this area. The necessary types of interdepartmental coordination should be spelled out. Guidelines on risk retention should be stated in the context of the risk management philosophy of loss reduction and prevention. Insurance purchasing should be centralized. A model policy statement is presented in Exhibit 10-5.

Two keys to risk management are communication and cooperation. Risk identification depends on getting the necessary information for the governing body, the legal staff, the program units, the personnel department, purchasing, and others. A government has outstanding in-house expertise which must be tapped. The expertise includes the fire department, police, inspection units, attorney's office, finance, personnel, and others. Each can be quite helpful. For example, the fire department can help devise a fire loss prevention effort, and the finance office can help devise the best means to deal with idle cash resulting from the risk management program.

The risk managers should report annually on their program to top management. The report should point out major changes in the program, the outline of new

EXHIBIT 10-5   Risk Management Policy

1. The function of risk management has as its purpose:
   a.   Protecting the municipality from catastrophic losses
   b.   Minimizing the total cost of accidental loss to the municipality
2. Risk management is to place the greatest emphasis on reduction rather than reimbursement of loss, through professional attention to loss control techniques, motivational incentives, prompt claims payments, and other loss prevention measures.
3. All insurance shall be purchased through the city risk management department.
4. Subject to the risk manager's discretion, the amount of insurance purchased shall provide protection whenever a single accidental loss would result in property loss in excess of $50,000 per incident or liability judgment that would potentially exceed $50,000 per incident. Lesser amounts may be retained if financially feasible.

Source: "Risk Management in Local Government," *Government Finances,* 6, 2 (May 1977), 44

program departures in the future, and comparisons to programs with similar government units. The loss prevention program should be presented and total cost savings stated. The report should also contain an analysis of claims paid, reserves, and administrative and legal costs.

In conclusion, the risk manager should have responsibility for:

1. aiding units in analyzing risks, including accidental losses;
2. advising and adjusting major losses for all units on loss prevention, safety, and self-insurance levels;
3. allocating insurance and risk costs to the units;
4. maintaining records of losses, loss costs, premiums, and related costs;
5. reviewing all new contracts for hold-harmless requirements;
6. purchasing insurance; and
7. coordinating all activities involving risk.

PENSION FUNDS

Budget Concerns

Pensions are budget concerns. Salaries and wages constitute a significant portion of government expenses—especially for local governments—and half of the related fringe benefits are pensions and social security payments. Such costs vary, but some governments pay as much as 42 percent of salaries and wages for fringe benefits. In the court-determined contractual relationship between governments and their employees, such expenses represent a mandatory liability and an appropriation due former employees. Pensions thus have first or near-first demand on government revenue. Normally, governments establish special pension funds to which both the employer and the employee make payments in each pay period. Pension fund liability is usually covered wholly or partially from the pension fund, which receives its revenue from employer and employee payments plus investment income. There are approximately 6,000 public pension plans in the United States, with 90 percent of all employees belonging to the 100 largest plans. Pension assets exceed $135 billion and have a growth rate over 12 percent a year.

Like risk management, the key to pension funds is to spread liability among many people. With pension funds, the liability is the future pension benefits which will be received by each former employee from retirement until death. Thus, the future costs of the pension benefit payments and associated administrative expenses must equal the combined employee and employer fringe benefit payments, investment income from the fund, and any general fund subsidy. Many systems do have a partial or full subsidy. If the pension benefit outlays are financed by existing member pension payments, a "pay-as-you-go" system exists. If the pension fund income is calculated to cover future likely pension outlays without present or future general fund subsidy, then the system is actuarially sound. The latter type of system is not always present, even though the municipal finance investment community, in judging credit-worthiness, prefers and sometimes demands that pension plans be completely funded. However, fully funded pension funds are more costly in the budget year, whereas a pay-as-you-go strategy will meet immediate pension expenses and be less expensive in the BY. There is a strong temptation to use the less expensive approach and let future legislatures or city councils find the money to meet the future expenses. In summary, the case for a fully funded pension plan is as follows:

1. good fiscal management means knowing what programs cost;
2. it adds security to the pension obligation;
3. it protects employers from overgenerous benefit arguments in labor-management negotiations because the future pension burden on the budget is more easily understood; and
4. the financial community, in determining government credit-worthiness, is increasingly demanding fully funded pension plans.

Both private and public pensions are so common today that their recent origin is surprising. The first public pension program was started in 1857 to cover the New York City police force. However, it was not until the turn of the century that pension systems became widely adopted in either the public or the private sector. Today, pension plans are fragmented, with one city sometimes maintaining many separate plans for police, fire, sanitation, general administration, and other employee groups. Because the Tenth Amendment to the Constitution preserves the rights of states, there has been little federal regulatory oversight; but at the state level one finds increasing state oversight concern, even to the extent of having a state-administered pension fund in which both state and local employees participate.

Pension policy is often a concern of labor-management negotiations. Union negotiators often use a tactic called "leapfrogging," which means establishing higher benefits for one union and then demanding comparable features for another union. For example, the firefighters' union would argue for added benefits and any success would be used by the police union in their negotiations. In the public sector, unlike the private sector, legislative policy makers are usually involved in setting pension policy. Thus, unions can and do lobby legislators for pension policy changes, in addition to negotiating for them. Rarely are pension policies major political issues because they require specialized skills and knowledge, have long-term implications, and have low visibility. In addition, pension systems have no general authoritative standards and system growth has been haphazard. These conditions are ideal for negotiated settlements which can have expensive hidden long-term budget implications.

Policy Issues

Pension fund policy can be viewed in terms of benefits, investments, and administration. Benefit policy involves questions of how much money employees can collect and of when they can collect it. Investment policy is concerned with questions of who controls the investments, limitations on investment, and investment performance. Administration policy is concerned with the potential for pension fund abuse, collection of employee contributions, and state centralization.

The major concern of those who deal with pension funds is the benefit package. The four major benefit policy issues are wage replacement, who pays contributions to the fund, indexing, and double coverage. Not surprisingly, employees would like retirement benefits to replace their wages, but that is costly. Exhibit 10-6 is an illustration of one common method of calculating retirement benefits. Normally, an average of the last three or five years is used to calculate retirement benefits. One government used the last day of regular employment and found that this produced an artificially high amount because overtime was added to the already high last salary day.

EXHIBIT 10-6   Sample Calculations of Retirement Benefits

Step 1. Creditable Service and Percentage Value

	% VALUE PER YEAR OF SERVICE	TOTAL YEARS OF SERVICE	TOTAL % VALUE PER PLAN
Retirement up to Age 62 or 30 Years	1.60%	× _____	= _____
Retirement at Age 63 or 31 Years	1.63%	× 25	= 40.75
Retirement at Age 64 or 32 Years	1.65%	× _____	= _____
Retirement at Age 65 or 33 Years or more	1.68%	× _____	= _____
Total Years		25	

Step 2. Average Final Compensation (AFC)

Mr. Smith worked 25 years under the sytem and retired at age 63. In this step we list his five highest fiscal year salaries and divide their total by five.

$11,257.00
12,851.00
13,201.00
13,706.00
13,904.00

Total $64,919.00

$64,919.00 ÷ 5 = $12,983.80 = Average Final Compensation (AFC)

Step 3. Monthly Benefit Calculation

Average final compensation (step 2)	$12,983.80
Total % value per plan (step 1)	×.4075

$ 5,290.90 Annual benefit
$5,290.90 ÷ 12 = $440.91 Monthly benefit

The second concern of those who deal with pension funds is who contributes; employees prefer that all costs be paid by the employer. The third concern is inflation, which can particularly hurt retired employees living on a fixed pension. The solution is to link the benefits to a cost-of-living index such as the Consumer Price Index. Not surprisingly, indexing is popular with employees, but it becomes very expensive in subsequent years. The fourth concern is double coverage, which normally results from an overlap with Social Security benefits—an employer option for state and local governments.

Three other pension issues not illustrated by Exhibit 10-6 are vesting, portable systems, and disability/survivor protection. What if you are fired just before retirement? Will you collect any retirement benefits? The answer depends on whether or not you are vested—i.e., whether you have worked the number of years required before an employee can collect any money at retirement. Vesting varies from system to system. Normally 3 to 5 years is used, but some systems use 10 years. What if you are vested in one government pension plan but take a new job with another government? Can your new government contribute to your old pension plan? Normally, the answer is no, but some states have combined state and local systems which do permit some portability. What if you become disabled? Do you receive retirement benefits (or does your spouse, in the event of your death)? Again, provisions vary. For example, if your disability was incurred while you were at work, benefits are computed in the manner described in Exhibit 10-6. If the disability was incurred outside the workplace, you may still be eligible, but other requirements must be met, such as 10 years of service. Survivor benefits are also common. For example, under one plan, if an employee dies in the line of duty, his or her spouse receives a monthly benefit of half the regular monthly salary until the spouse's remarriage or death. If an employee dies elsewhere, the spouse receives benefits calculated under the policy in force at the time of death.

Investment policy debates center on who controls the investments, on what investment limitations should exist, and finally on the adequacy of the investment performance. Government pension funds are rarely controlled by unions, as sometimes occurs in the private sector. Recently, the dispute over control has centered on the issue of decentralized versus centralized state systems. The advantages of a centralized state system include uniform benefits, greater decision-making expertise, greater cost effectiveness, and potentially higher yields, given the advantage of size. Nevertheless, many local governments prefer to retain control over investments. This is especially true if the portfolio managers are concerned about making investments that will benefit the local community. Advocates of this policy stress that such investments achieve both important public policy goals and employees' economic security. One example is the use of pension funds for local mortgage projects. In the case of New York City, pension funds controlled by unions were used to buy city bonds when no other investors could be found.

State governments place some restrictions and limitations upon pension fund investments. The 11 major types of investment restrictions are as follows:

1. maximum percentage of fund assets that can be invested in *common stock*;
2. maximum percentage of fund assets that can be invested in the securities of any *one company*;
3. maximum percentage of fund assets that can be invested in securities of any *one industry*;
4. maximum percentage of fund assets that can be invested in *real estate mortgages*;
5. maximum percentage of fund assets that can be invested in *real estate equities*;
6. maximum percentage of assets that can be held in *cash reserves*;
7. minimum *size* of company in which investments can be made;
8. minimum total *rate of return* for income to be earned on investments;
9. minimum *quality of bonds* in which the fund can invest;
10. maximum *price/earning ratio* on common stocks in which the fund can invest; and
11. minimum number of consecutive years of *dividends paid* on common stock (divided-payment record).

The adequacy of investment performance is an important matter to budget officials because a stronger performance means a decrease in employer and employee contributions. In general, managers of public pension plans are cautious investors who prefer fixed income obligations rather than equity securities (e.g., common stock). In a survey conducted by the Municipal Finance Officers Association in 1980, public pensions did better than private pensions, but that fact was attributed to the relatively greater use of equity securities by the private pension funds during a period of declining stock prices. One interesting finding was that public pensions outperformed private pensions in the rate of return of equities. Private pensions, however, outperformed public pensions on bond portfolios. Probably, public and private pension plans perform at about the same level. Exhibit 10-7 shows the assets of state and local retirement systems by type of investment. Note the growth in cor-

EXHIBIT 10-7   Assets of State and Local Retirement Systems by Type of Investment: 1950–79 (billion of dollars)

	1950	1960	1970	1975	1979
Deposits & Currency	$0.1	$ 0.2	$ 0.6	$ 1.7	$ 4.0
Corporate Equity	*	0.6	10.0	25.8	37.8
U.S. Governments:	2.5	5.9	6.6	6.8	30.3
short-term	0.1¹	0.3	0.8	0.5 ⎱	
long-term	2.4	5.4	4.3	1.7 ⎰	14.5
agencies	0.0	0.2	1.5	4.6	15.8
State & Local	1.5	4.4	2.0	2.5	3.9
Corporate Bonds	0.6	7.1	35.0	60.9	87.1
Mortgages	0.1	1.5	5.9	8.2	9.4
TOTAL	$4.9	$19.7	$60.3	$106.0	$172.5

*less than $50 million
¹Estimated on basis of distribution of U.S. Government obligations in 1951.
Note: Items may not sum to totals because of rounding.

Source: Board of Governors of the Federal Reserve System, *Flow of Funds Accounts 1946–1978* (December 1979) and *Flow of Funds Accounts 4th Quarter 1970* (February 1980).

porate equity and bonds. Short-term and long-term U.S. government securities dropped in the early 1970s but experienced new growth from 1975 to 1979, when plan managers were trying to preserve liquidity while waiting for markets to change during that recessionary period.

Administrative policy disputes center on the largely unregulated and unknown status of pension funds. Controversy about disclosure practices has arisen because there is disagreement over what information should be made known, in what form it should be given, who should make it known, and who should receive it. Pension information can be expensive to prepare, but the expense must be balanced against the importance of acquiring data, especially for actuarial analysis. The frequency and quality of the latter are critical to the accuracy and value of pension plan financial disclosures. They inform employees and government policy makers of the relative soundness of the pension funds. With the recessionary pressures on state and local governments in the early 1980s, concern grew that governments might not be able to meet future pension liabilities, that governments might be diverting pension funds to other areas such as the general operating fund, and that pension funds might not be properly invested. Unfortunately, the shortage of adequate data only increased fears. Not surprisingly, some have argued for federal regulations, but the Advisory Commission on Intergovernmental Relations (ACIR) has taken a position against federal regulation of public pension systems. Exhibit 10-8 presents the ACIR argument.

Public pensions are significant activities and they significantly affect government budgets.

EXHIBIT 10-8   Advisory Commission on Intergovernmental Relations: Reasons for the Commission's Recommendation Against Federal Regulation

---

In recommending against federal regulation of state and local pension systems, the Commission rested its case upon five major arguments.

- Our federal system with its emphasis on state sovereignty requires that states have full responsibility for determining all basic components of their public employees' compensation, and that of the local employees within the states.
- The unique and diverse nature of state and local retirement systems requires the kind of adaptation and fine tuning that only state and local government control and regulation can provide.
- State and local governments have made significant progress during the past few years in putting their own retirement systems in order.
- There is no convincing evidence that the federal government has any compelling "national interest" in regulating state and local public pension systems.
- Even mild or limited forms of federal regulations are undesirable given the tendency for federal regulatory agencies and the courts to take a friendly piece of legislation and turn it into an unfriendly set of regulations.

Source: ACIR, *State and Local Pension Systems,* December 1980, p. 54.

REVIEW QUESTIONS

1. Explain what should take place in a preliminary review of property management. Explain also the challenge of procurement, including the difficulty of using a competitive bidding process.
2. Explain the administrative implications of bar-code technology on government property management.
3. Explain the relationship between risk control and insurance. Explain what factors should be weighed in deciding how much risk should be retained.
4. What type of knowledge and skill is needed for exposure identification and risk evaluation? What types of continuous direction and careful attention connote excellent risk management?
5. The proper funding of public pensions has budgetary implications. What are the concept behind pension funds, the policy issues related to pensions, and the budgetary implications of pension funds?

REFERENCES

Advisory Commission on Intergovernmental Relations. *State and Local Pension Systems.* Washington, D.C.: Advisory Commission on Intergovernmental Relations, December 1980.

Government Finance Officers Association. *Guidelines for the Preparation of a Public Employee Retirement System Comprehensive Annual Financial Report.* Chicago: Government Finance Officers Association, May 1980.

———. "Pension Training Seminar," *Resources in Review,* 2, 1 (September/October 1979), 6–7.

———. "Public Employee Retirement," Number 3 in *Elements of Financial Management.* Washington, D.C.: Government Finance Officers Association, Government Finance Research Center, 1981.

CORCORAN, A. WAYNE. "Financial Management," in J. Richard Aronson and Eli Schwartz (eds.), *Management Policies in Local Government Finance.* Washington, D.C.: International City Management Association, 1975.

HILDRETH, W. BARTLEY and GERALD J. MILLER. "Risk Management and Pension Systems," in Jack Rabin and Thomas D. Lynch (eds.), *Handbook on Public Budgeting and Financial Management.* New York: Marcel Dekker, 1983.

International City Management Association. *Municipal Finance Administration.* 6th ed. Chicago: International City Management Association, 1962.

MOAK, LENNOX L. and ALBERT M. HILLHOUSE. *Local Government Finance.* Chicago: Municipal Finance Officers Association, 1975.

———. "Risk Management in Local Government," *Government Finances,* 6, 2 (May 1977).

PETERSON, JOHN E. *A Summary of State and Local Government Public Employee Retirement System Investment Practices and Policies.* Washington, D.C.: Government Finance Officers Association, Government Finance Research Center, December 1980.

———. *State and Local Pension Fund Investment Performance.* Washington, D.C.: Government Finance Officers Association, Government Finance Research Center, December 1980.

ROSS, NESTOR R. and JOSEPH S. GERBER. *Governmental Risk Management Manual.* Tucson, Ariz.: Risk Management Publishing Company, 1977.

U.S. Joint Financial Management Improvement Program. *Bar Code Technology: A Means to Improve Operational Efficiency and Internal Control.* Washington, D.C.: U.S. Joint Financial Management Improvement Program, May 1982.

———— . *Property Management Evaluation Guide for Federal Agencies.* Washington, D.C.: U.S. Joint Financial Management Improvement Program, March 1982.

GLOSSARY

Ability to Pay   The principle that the tax burden should be distributed proportionally among taxpayers, according to the size of their income. It is based on the assumption that as a person's income increases the person can and should contribute a larger percentage of his or her income to support government activities.

Accounting System   The total structure of records and procedures that record, classify, and report information on the financial position and operations of a government unit or any of its funds, balanced account groups, and organizational components.

Accounts Payable   Amounts owed to others for goods and services received and assets acquired.

Accounts Receivable   Amounts due from others for goods furnished and services rendered. Such amounts include reimbursements earned and refunds receivable. (*See also* Accounts Payable.)

Accrual Basis of Accounting   The basis of accounting under which revenues are recorded when earned and expenditures are recorded when goods are received and services performed, even though receipt of the revenue or payment of the expenditure may take place, in whole or part, in another accounting period.

Accrued Expenditures   Liabilities incurred during a given period that reflect the need to pay for (a) services performed by employees, contractors, other government accounts, vendors, carriers, grantees, lessors, and other payees; (b) goods and other tangible property received; and (c) amounts owed under programs for which no current service or performance is required (such as annuities, insurance claims, other benefit payments, and some cash grants, but excluding the repayment of debt, which is considered neither an obligation nor an expenditure). Expenditures accrue regardless of when cash payments are made, whether invoices have been rendered, or, in some cases, whether goods or other tangible property have been physically delivered.

Agency Generally, any department, independent commission, board, bureau, office, or other establishment of the government, including independent regulatory commissions and boards.

Allocations The amount of obligational authority from one agency, bureau, or account that is set aside in a transfer appropriation account to carry out the purposes of the parent appropriation or fund.

Allotment An authorization by the head (or other authorized employee) of an agency to his or her subordinates to incur obligations within a specified amount.

Annual Budget Revenues and expenditures presented for one fiscal year period.

Anti-Deficiency Act of 1906 Legislation enacted by Congress (a) to prevent the incurring of obligations or the making of expenditures (outlays) in excess of amounts available in appropriations or funds; (b) to fix responsibility within an agency for the creation of any obligation or the making of any expenditure in excess of an apportionment or reapportionment or in excess of other subdivisions established pursuant to 31 U.S.C. 665(g); and (c) to assist in bringing about the most effective and economical use of appropriations and funds.

Apportionment The distribution by the Central Budget Office of amounts available for obligation, including budgetary reserves established pursuant to law, in appropriations or fund accounts. In an apportionment, amounts available for obligation are divided among specific time periods (usually quarters), activities, projects, objects, or a combination thereof. The amounts so apportioned limit the amount of obligations that may be incurred.

Appropriation A legislative authorization that permits government agencies to incur obligations and to make payments out of the treasury for specified purposes. An appropriation usually follows enactment of authorizing legislation. An appropriation act is the most common means of providing budget authority, but in some cases the authorizing legislation itself provides the budget authority. (*See also* Backdoor Authority.) Appropriations do not represent cash actually set aside in the treasury for purposes specified in the appropriation act; they represent limitations of amounts that agencies may obligate during the period of time specified in the relevant appropriation act. Several types of appropriations are not counted as budget authority, since they do not provide authority to incur additional obligations. Examples of these include: (a) appropriations to liquidate contract authority—Congressional action to provide funds to pay obligations incurred against contract authority; (b) appropriations to reduce outstanding debt—Congressional action to provide funds for debt retirement; and (c) appropriations for refunds of receipts.

Appropriation Act A statute that generally provides authorization for agencies to incur obligations and to make payments out of the treasury for specified purposes. An appropriation act, the most common means of providing budget authority, generally follows enactment of authorizing legislation unless the authorizing legislation itself provides the budget authority.

Appropriation Limitation A statutory restriction in appropriation acts that establishes the maximum or minimum amount that may be obligated or expended for specified purposes.

Arbitrage Bonds The exemption from income tax of government bonds as long as state and local governments do not use the funds from the bonds for investment rather than for the prescribed public purpose.

Asset Any item of economic value owned by a government unit. The item may be tangible (that is, physical and actual) or intangible (that is, a right to ownership, expressed in terms of cost or some other value).

Audit   An investigation of the accuracy and correct operation of an agency's accounting system, including validation of inventories and existing equipment, documentation of proper legal authority to carry out agency activities, adequacy of controls on fraud, waste, and mismanagement, and the effectiveness of the agency's programs.

Authorizing Committee   A standing legislative committee with jurisdiction over the subject matter of those laws, or parts of laws, that set up or continue the legal operations of programs or agencies. An authorizing committee also has jurisdiction in those instances in which backdoor authority is provided through substantive legislation.

Authorizing Legislation   Substantive legislation that sets up or continues the legal operation of a program or agency, either indefinitely or for a specific period of time, or that sanctions a particular type of obligation or expenditure within a program. Authorizing legislation is normally a prerequisite for an appropriation. It may place a limit on the amount of budget authority to be included in appropriation acts or it may authorize the appropriation of "such sums as may be necessary." In some instances, authorizing legislation may provide authority to incur debts or to mandate payment to particular persons or political subdivisions of the country.

Automatic Stabilizer   A mechanism having a countercyclical effect that automatically moderates changes in incomes and outputs in the economy without specific decisions to change government policy. Unemployment insurance and the income tax are among the most important of the automatic stabilizers used in the United States. Also known as a built-in stabilizer.

Backdoor Authority   Budget authority provided in legislation outside the normal appropriations process (that is, through appropriations committees). The most common forms of backdoor authority are authority to borrow (also called borrowing authority or authority to spend debt receipts) and contract authority. In other cases (for example, interest on the public debt), a permanent appropriation is provided that becomes available without any current action by Congress. Section 401 of the Congressional Budget and Impoundment Control Act of 1974 (31 U.S.C. 1351) specifies certain limits on the use of backdoor authority.

Balance of Payments   A statistical record of economic transactions between one country—for example, the United States—and the rest of the world. Balance of payments accounts normally distinguish among transactions involving goods, services, short-term capital, and long-term capital.

Balance Sheet   An accounting statement designed to balance total assets, total liabilities, and fund balance.

Balanced Budget   A budget in which receipts are equal to outlays.

Benefit-Cost Analysis   *See* Cost-Benefit Analysis.

Block Grant   *See* Grant.

Bond   A written promise to pay a specified sum of money (called the face value or principal amount) at a specified date or dates (called the maturity dates) together with periodic interest at a specified rate.

Bond Maturity   A set period of time at the end of which the principal on a bond is completely paid. The length of the maturity normally is not longer than the useful life of the facility that is being financed.

Bond Prospectus   The formal statement of information used by bond sellers to help investors decide whether or not they wish to invest in the bonds.

Borrowing Authority   Authority to spend debt receipts; statutory authority that permits an agency to incur obligations and to make payments for specified purposes out of borrowed monies. (*See also* Debt.)

Budget   A plan for the accomplishment, within a definite time period, of programs related to established objectives and goals, setting forth estimates of the resources required and the resources available (usually in comparison with one or more past periods) and showing future requirements. Also, a request for funds to run the government.

Budget and Accounting Act of 1921 Federal legislation that provided for an executive budget for the national government and for an independent audit of government accounts.

Budget and Accounting and Procedures Act of 1950 Federal legislation that gave the president authority to prescribe the contents and arrangement of the budget, to simplify its presentation, to broaden appropriations, and to mandate progress toward performance budgeting.

Budget Authority Authority provided by law to enter into obligations that will result in immediate or future outlays of government funds; it does not include authority to insure or guarantee the repayment of indebtedness incurred by another person or government. The basic forms of budget authority are appropriations, borrowing authority, and contract authority. Budget authority may be classified by the period of availability (one-year, multiple-year, no-year), by the timing of legislative action (current or permanent), or by the manner of determining the amount available (definite or indefinite).

Budget Call An announcement distributed by the budget office to all government departments and agencies, instructing them to prepare the budget and providing guidance on proper procedures to use. Much of the guidance is standardized and published in official bulletins and circulars.

Budget Execution System A set of procedures that gives direction to ongoing agency activities and allows for continuous and current reviews to determine if planned objectives are being met. One approach is to link an operating budget with management-by-objectives.

Budget-Wise Model An approach to budgeting in which all government decisions are perceived to be politically motivated, to the exclusion of all other factors. A person following this model stresses the futility of trying to make decisions on the basis of anything but political expediency and insists that a budget staff can do nothing but react to political events as they unfold.

Budget Year (BY) The fiscal year for which the budget is being considered; the fiscal year following the current year.

Built-in Stabilizer *See* Automatic Stabilizer.

Business Cycles The recurrent phases of expansion and contraction in overall business activity, evidenced by fluctuations in measures of aggregate economic activity, notably real gross national product. Both the duration and the magnitude of individual cycles vary greatly.

Call Provision The right of the borrower to buy back bonds at set prices regardless of the current market rate.

Capital In economic theory, one of the three major factors of production (the others being land and labor). Capital can refer either to physical capital, such as plant and equipment, or to the financial resources required to purchase physical capital.

Capital Budget A budget that deals with large expenditures for capital items normally financed by borrowing. Usually, capital items have long-range returns and useful life spans, are relatively expensive, and have physical presence (for example, buildings, roads, and sewage systems).

Cash Basis of Accounting The basis of accounting whereby revenues are recorded when received and expenditures (outlays) are recorded when paid, without regard to the accounting period in which the transactions occurred.

Categorical Grant *See* GRANT.

Circuit Breaker A reform recommendation for property taxation that would reduce the regressive nature of the tax. Circuit breakers often provide for tax exemptions to families at the lowest income level or to elderly people on fixed incomes to relieve them of paying some of their property taxes.

Clientele Group The people who are perceived to be affected by an agency's programs and who take an active interest in its policies and actions.

Comprehensive Budget   All revenues and expenditures included in the budget.

Congressional Budget and Impoundment Control Act of 1974   Federal legislation that was one of several reforms directed toward strengthening the legislative branch. It created the new Senate and House Budget Committees and the new Congressional Budget Office, required a current services budget, and required various reforms in the presidential budget and in presidential impoundment powers. It created a unified Congressional budget approach. (*See also* First Concurrent Resolution of the Budget *and* Second Concurrent Resolution of the Budget.)

Congressional Budget Office (CBO)   Federal office responsible for presenting the Congress with reasonable and viable forecasts of aggregate levels of spending and revenue. The office also makes cost estimates for proposed legislation reported to the floor and provides cost projections for all existing legislation.

Consolidated Decision Package   Package prepared at high organizational and program levels that summarizes and supplements information contained in decision packages received from subordinate units in an agency using zero base budgeting.

Constant Dollar   A dollar value adjusted for changes in prices. Constant dollars are derived by dividing current dollar amounts by an appropriate price index, a process generally known as deflating. The result is a constant dollar series as it would presumably exist if prices and transactions were the same in all subsequent years as in the base year. Any changes in such a series would reflect only changes in the real volume of goods and services. Constant dollar figures are commonly used for computing the gross national product and its components and for estimating total budget outlays.

Consumer Price Index (CPI)   Either of two measures of change in the price of a fixed "market basket" of goods and services customarily purchased by urban consumers. CPI-U is based on a market basket determined by expenditure patterns of *all urban households,* while the market basket for CPI-W is determined by expensive patterns of *urban-wage-earner and clerical-worker families.* The level of the CPI shows the relative cost of purchasing the specified market basket compared to the cost in a designated base year, while the current rate of change in the CPI measures how fast prices are currently rising or falling. Current rates of change can be expressed as either monthly or annual rates. Although the consumer price index is often called the "cost-of-living index," it measures only price changes, which constitute just one of several important factors affecting living costs. Both CPI-U and CPI-W are published monthly by the U.S. Bureau of Labor Statistics.

Contingent Liability   An existing condition, situation, or set of circumstances involving uncertainty about a possible loss to an agency that will ultimately be resolved when one or more events either occur or fail to occur. Contingent liabilities include such items as loan guarantees and bank deposit insurance.

Continuing Resolution   If a decision has not been reached on appropriations prior to the beginning of the new current year, then Congress can pass a resolution that says that the government can continue to obligate and spend at last year's budget levels or the lowest level passed by a chamber of Congress. The wording is usually framed to permit spending at the lowest amount the legislature is likely to pass.

Contract Authority   Statutory authority that permits obligations to be incurred in advance of appropriations or in anticipation of receipts to be credited to a revolving fund or other account. Contract authority is unfunded and must subsequently be funded by an appropriation to liquidate obligations incurred under the contract authority, or by the collection and use of receipts.

Cost Accounting Standard   A statement promulgated by the Cost Accounting Standards Board that becomes effective unless disapproved by Congress. These statements are intended to achieve uniform and consistent standards in the cost accounting practices followed by defense contractors.

Cost-Based Budgeting An approach to budgeting that is based on the costs to be incurred—that is, on the resources that will be consumed in carrying out a program, regardless of when the funds to acquire the resources were obligated or paid, and regardless of the source of funds (i.e., the appropriation). For example, inventory items become costs when they are withdrawn from inventory, and the cost of buildings is distributed over time, through periodic depreciation charges, rather than in a lump sum when the buildings are acquired.

Cost-Benefit Analysis An analytical technique that compares the economic and social costs and benefits of proposed programs or policy actions. All losses and gains experienced by society are included and measured in dollar terms. The net benefits created by an action are calculated by subtracting the losses incurred by some sectors of society from the gains that accrue to others. Alternative actions are compared to determine which ones yield the greatest net benefits, or ratio of benefits to costs.

Cost-Effectiveness Analysis An analytical technique used to choose the most efficient method for achieving a program or policy goal. The costs of alternatives are measured by their requisite estimated dollar expenditures. Effectiveness is defined by the degree of goal attainment, and may also (but not necessarily) be measured in dollars. A comparison is made between either the net effectiveness (effectiveness minus costs) or the cost-effectiveness ratios of the various alternatives. The most cost-effective method may involve one or more alternatives.

Countercyclical Action Action aimed at smoothing out swings in economic activity. Countercyclical actions may take the form of monetary and fiscal policy (such as countercyclical revenue sharing or jobs programs). Automatic (built-in) stabilizers have a countercyclical effect without necessitating changes in government policy.

Crosswalk Any procedure for expressing the relationship between different classifications of budgetary data, such as between appropriation accounts and government programs.

Current Dollar The dollar value of a good or service in terms of prices current at the time the good or service was sold. This is in contrast to the value of the good or service in constant dollars.

Current Services Budget An executive budget projection that alerts the Congress—especially the Congressional Budget Office, the budget committees, and the appropriation committees—to anticipate specific revenue, expenditure, and debt levels, assuming that current policy is unchanged. It also provides a base line of comparison to the presidential budget.

Current Year The fiscal year in progress.

Debt A government credit obligation.

Decision Package In zero base budgeting, a brief justification document containing the information managers need in order to judge program or activity levels and resource requirements. Each decision package presents a level of request for a decision unit, stating the costs and performance associated with that level. Separate decision packages are prepared for incremental spending levels.

1. *Minimum Level.* Associated with performance below which it is not feasible for the decision unit to continue because no constructive contribution could be made toward fulfilling the unit's objectives.

2. *Intermediate Level.* Performance between the minimum and current levels. There may be more than one intermediate level.

3. *Current Level.* Performance that would be reflected if activities for the budget year were carried on at current year service or output levels without major policy changes. This level permits internal realignments of activities within existing statutory authorizations.

4. *Enhancement Level.* Level at which increased output or service is consistent with major objectives and at which sufficient benefits are expected to warrant the serious review of higher authorities. A series of decision packages is prepared for each decision unit. Cumulatively, the packages represent the total budget request for that unit.

Decision Package Set   A set of documents used in zero base budgeting, consisting of the decision unit overview and the decision packages for the decision unit.

Decision Unit   In zero base budgeting, that part or component of the basic program or organizational entity for which budget requests are prepared and for which managers make significant decisions on the amount of spending and the scope or quality of work to be performed.

Decision Unit Overview   In zero base budgeting, that part of the decision package set that provides information necessary to evaluate and make budget decisions on each of the decision packages; eliminates repetition of the same information in each package.

Default Risk   The possibility that a borrower will fail to pay the principal or interest on a loan. All other factors being constant, the greater the possibility that the borrower will fail to meet the obligation, the greater the premium or market yield on the security.

Deferral of Budget Authority   Any action or inaction by an officer or employee of the government that temporarily withholds, delays, or effectively precludes the obligation or expenditure of budget authority, including authority to obligate by contract in advance of appropriations as specifically authorized by law.

Deficiency Apportionment   A distribution by the U.S. Office of Management and Budget of available budgetary resources for the fiscal year that anticipates the need for supplemental budget authority. Such apportionments may only be made under certain specified conditions provided for under the Anti-Deficiency Act, 31 U.S.C. 665(e).

Deficiency Appropriation   An appropriation made to an expired account to cover obligations that have been incurred in excess of available funds.

Deficit Financing   A situation in which the federal government's excess of outlays over receipts for a given period is financed primarily by borrowing from the public.

Definite Authority   Authority that is stated as covering a specific sum at the time the authority is granted. This includes authority stated as ''not to exceed'' a specified amount.

Deflation   A decrease in the general price level, usually accompanied by declining levels of output, increasing unemployment, and a contraction of the supply of money and credit.

Deobligation   A downward adjustment of previously recorded obligations. This may be attributable to the cancellation of a project or contract, to price revisions, or to corrections of estimates previously recorded as obligations.

Depreciation   The systematic and rational allocation of the costs of equipment and buildings (having a life of more than one year) over their useful lives. To match costs with related revenues in measuring income or determining the costs of carrying out program activities, depreciation reflects the use of the asset(s) during specific operating periods.

Devaluation   In a system of fixed exchange rates, the lowering of the value of a nation's currency in relation to gold, or to the currency of other countries, when this value is set by government intervention in the exchange market. (In a system of flexible exchange rates, if the value of the currency falls, it is referred to as depreciation; if the value of the currency rises, it is referred to as appreciation.)

Direct Loan   A disbursement of funds (not in exchange for goods or services) that is contracted to be repaid with or without interest.

Discounting to Present Value   A method of adjusting dollar values in order to compare dollars expected to be received or spent in the future with dollars received or spent today.

Discount Rate   The interest rate that a commercial bank pays when it borrows from a Federal Reserve bank. The discount rate is one of the three tools of monetary policy used by the Federal Reserve System. The Federal Reserve customarily raises or lowers the discount rate to restrain or ease its money and credit policies.

Disposable Personal Income   Personal income less personal taxes and nontax payments to the federal government. It is the income available to persons for consumption or saving.

Earmarked Revenue   Funds from a specific course to be spent only for a designated activity (for example, gasoline taxes that can be spent only for highway construction and maintenance).

Economic Growth   An increase in a nation's productive capacity leading to an increase in the production of goods and services. Economic growth is usually measured by the annual rate of increase in real gross national product (as measured in constant dollars).

Economic Indicator   Statistics that have a systematic relationship to the business cycle. Each indicator is classified as leading, coincident, or lagging, depending on whether the indicator generally changes direction in advance of, at the same time as, or subsequent to changes in the overall economy. Although no one indicator or set of indicators is a wholly satisfactory predictor of the business cycle, taken as a whole they are valuable tools for identifying and analyzing changes in business cycles.

Economic Ordering Quantity   A means to determine total desirable inventory. The cost of ordering must be weighed against the cost of holding a sizable quantity of goods.

Electronic Funds Transfer System   A communication system that provides the capability for automatic receipts of funds, as well as for computer assisted generation of fund transfers among the treasury, the Federal Reserve banks, member banks, and other institutions. Processing of checks takes an instant rather than several days, thus virtually eliminating the float.

Employment Act of 1946   Federal legislation that called for economic planning and for a budget policy directed toward achieving maximum national employment and production.

Employment Rate   In economic statistics, the total number of people who, during a specific week, did any work for pay or profit, or who worked for fifteen hours or more without pay on a farm or in a business operated by a member of the person's family. Also included are those who neither worked nor looked for work but who had a job or business from which they were temporarily absent during the week.

Entitlement   Benefits mandated by law to be paid to any person or unit of government that meets the eligibility requirements established by such law. Authorizations for entitlements constitute a binding obligation on the part of the government, and eligible recipients have legal recourse if the obligation is not fulfilled. Budget authority for such payments is not necessarily provided in advance; thus, entitlement legislation requires the subsequent enactment of appropriations unless the existing appropriation is permanent. Examples of entitlement programs are Social Security benefits and veterans' compensation or pensions.

Expenditure   Payment of an obligation.

External Audit   An investigation carried out by separate independent agencies that examine accounts, check on the accuracy of recorded transactions and inventories, make on-site reviews of stocks, verify physical existence of equipment, and review operating procedures and regulations.

Federal Reserve System (Fed)   The central banking system of the United States, which operates to control the economy's supply of money and credit.

First Concurrent Resolution on the Budget   The annual resolution, containing governmentwide budget targets of receipts, budget authority, and outlays, that guides Congress in its subsequent consideration of appropriations and revenue measures. It is required to be adopted by both houses of Congress no later than May 15, pursuant to the Congressional Budget and Impoundment Control Act of 1974 (P.L. 93–344, 31 U.S.C. 1324).

Fiscal Policy   Collectively, all federal government policies on taxes, spending, and debt management; intended to promote the nation's macroeconomic goals, particularly with respect to employment, gross national product, price level stability, and equilibrium in balance of payments. The budget process is a major vehicle for determining and implementing federal fiscal policy. The other major component of federal macroeconomic policy is monetary policy.

Fiscal Year (FY)   Any yearly accounting period, without regard to its relationship to the calendar year. The fiscal year of the federal government begins on October 1 and ends on September 30. (Prior to fiscal year 1977, the Federal fiscal year began on July 1 and ended on June 30.) The fiscal year is designated by the calendar year in which it ends; for example, fiscal year 1980 for the Federal government is the year beginning October 1, 1979, and ending September 30, 1980. (*See also* Budget Year; Current Year; Prior Year.)

Fixed Costs   Those costs in any project or program that remain constant regardless of the increase or decrease in units produced.

Float   The difference between the total amount of checks drawn on a bank account by the government and the amount shown for that account on the bank's books.

Formula Grant   *See* Grant.

Full Employment Budget   The estimated receipts, outlays, and surplus or deficit that would occur if the U.S. economy were continually operating at full capacity.

Full-Faith-and-Credit Debt   A long-term debt in which the credit (including the implied power of taxation) is unconditionally pledged by the government.

Full Funding   Provision of budgetary resources to cover the total cost of a program or project at the time it is undertaken. (The alternative is incremental funding, in which budget authority is provided or recorded for only a portion of total estimated obligations expected to be incurred during a single fiscal year.) Full funding is generally discussed in terms of multi-year programs, whether or not obligations for the entire program are made in the first year.

Functional Classification   A system of classifying budget resources by function so that budget authority and outlays of budget and off-budget entities, loan guarantees, and tax expenditures can be related in terms of the needs being addressed. Budget accounts are generally placed in the single budget function that best reflects its major end purpose (for example, national defense or health), regardless of the agency administering the program. A function may be divided into two or more subfunctions, depending upon the complexity of the need addressed by that function.

Fund Accounting   The legal requirement for agencies to establish separate accounts for separate programs—that is, to segregate revenues and other resources, together with all related liabilities, obligations, and reserves, for the purpose of carrying on specific activities or attaining certain objectives in accordance with special regulations, restrictions, or limitations. The aim is to control the handling of money to ensure that it will be spent only for the purpose intended. Fund accounting, in a broad sense, is required by the government to demonstrate agency compliance with requirements of existing legislation for which funds have been appropriated or otherwise authorized.

General Accounting Office (GAO)   The Congressional audit agency for the federal government. This agency reports directly to Congress. GAO investigates fraud, waste, and mismanagement. Its audits focus upon delegation of responsibility, policy direction and program evaluation, budget and accounting practices, and the adequacy of internal controls, including internal auditing.

GNP Gap The difference between the economy's output of goods and services and its potential output at full employment—that is, the difference between actual GNP (gross national product) and potential GNP.

Government Corporation Act of 1945 Federal legislation that directed the General Accounting Office to audit public corporations in terms of their performance rather than merely in terms of the legality and propriety of their expenditures.

Grant A transfer of funds from the federal government to another unit of government. The two major forms of federal grants are block and categorical.

1. *Block grants*. These are given primarily to general-purpose government units in accordance with a statutory formula. Such grants can be used for a variety of activities within a broad functional area. Examples of federal block grant programs are the Omnibus Crime Control and Safe Streets Act of 1968, the Comprehensive Employment and Training Act of 1973, the Housing and Community Development Act of 1974, and the 1974 amendments to the Social Security Act of 1935 (Title XX).

2. *Categorical grants*. These can be used only for specific programs and are usually limited to narrowly defined activities. Categorical grants consist of formula, project, and formula-project grants. Formula grants allocate federal funds to states or their subdivisions in accordance with a distribution formula prescribed by law or administrative regulation. Project grants provide federal funding for fixed or known periods for specific projects or for the delivery of specific services or products.

Grant-in-Aid For budget purposes, a grant-in-aid consists of a budget outlay by the federal government to support state or local programs of government service to the public. Grants-in-aid do not include purchases from state or local governments or assistance awards to other classes of recipients (e.g., outlays for research or support of federal prisoners).

Gross National Product (GNP) The gross national product is the total productive activity in a country during a certain period of time. It is the sum of personal consumption plus gross private domestic investment plus government purchases of goods and services plus net exports of goods and services.

Identification Code An eleven-digit code assigned to each appropriation or fund account in *The Budget of the United States Government* that identifies (a) the agency, (b) the account, (c) the timing of the transmittal to Congress, (d) the type of fund, and (e) the account's functional classification. Such codes are common in budget systems.

Impoundment Any action or inaction by an officer or employee of the U.S. government that precludes the obligation or expenditure of budget authority provided by Congress.

Impoundment Resolution A resolution by either the House of Representatives or the Senate that expresses disapproval of the president's proposed deferral of budget authority as set forth in a special message transmitted by the president, as required under Sec. 1013(a) of the Impoundment Control Act of 1974, P.L. 93-344, 31 U.S.C. 1403.

Income Tax Revenue source used at all levels of government, but principally at the federal level. The tax is levied on the income of both corporations and individuals. It can be graduated or a flat percentage.

Incremental Budgeting An approach to budgeting that focuses on the budget request, with emphasis on increases from the current year. Analysts of such a budget normally want information on all activities being planned in the budget year, but most of their attention will be on the program changes from the current year.

Incremental Funding The provision or recording of budgetary resources for a program or project based on obligations estimated to be incurred within a fiscal year when such budgetary resources will cover only a portion of the obligations to be incurred in completing the program or project as planned. (The alternative is full funding, in which budgetary resources are provided or recorded for the total estimated obligations of a program or project in the initial year of funding.)

Indefinite Authority Budget authority for which a specific sum is not stated but which is determined by other factors, such as the receipts from a certain source or obligations incurred. Borrowing authority that is limited to a specified amount that may become outstanding at any time—i.e., revolving debt authority—is considered to be indefinite budget authority.

Indirect Cost Any cost incurred for common objectives that therefore cannot be charged directly to any single cost objective. Indirect costs are allocated to the various classes of work in proportion to the benefit to each class. Indirect cost is also referred to as overhead or burden cost.

Inflation A persistent rise in the general price level that results in a decline in the purchasing power of money.

Input In a systems model, the resources used by a system to accomplish its work.

Internal Audit An investigation of legality, effectiveness, and efficiency within the agency.

Internal Control The plan of organization and all of the coordinating methods and measures adopted within a federal agency to safeguard the agency's assets, check the accuracy and reliability of its accounting data, promote operational efficiency, and encourage adherence to prescribed managerial policies.

Issue Assessment A written presentation that identifies and describes the major features of a significant issue facing the government. The assessment is only a few pages long, but it clearly sets forth the ingredients that would be considered in preparing a study of a major issue.

Journal A chronological listing of transactions, setting forth the date and dollar amount of each transaction and a brief explanation.

Legal Reserve Requirement One of the three tools used by the Federal Reserve to promote for economic stabilization. The Fed can tighten the money supply by requiring a greater reserve to be maintained, thus shrinking the amount available for loans. The converse normally increases the money supply.

Liability Amount owed for items received, services rendered, expenses incurred, assets acquired, or construction performed (regardless of whether invoices have been received); also, amounts received but as yet unearned.

Lien A claim on property arising from failure of the owner to make timely payment of a previous claim.

Line-Item Budget A budget format that presents the exact amount planned to be spent for every separate good or service to be purchased.

Macroeconomics The branch of economics concerned with aggregate economic analysis. Macroeconomics includes the study of the general price level, national output and income, and national employment.

Management by Objectives (MBO) A technique for establishing specific objectives for agencies; it requires regular periodic reports on the agency's progress toward achieving those objectives.

Method of Averages A technique of forecasting revenue by averaging the revenue generated over the last three to five years. It assumes the existence of a growth trend in the tax receipts and the economy.

Microeconomics The branch of economics concerned with the analysis of individual economic units, markets, or industries. Microeconomics includes the study of the prices of individual commodities, individual incomes, and the employment practices of individual firms. (*See also* Macroeconomics.)

Miller-Orr Model A method of determining a government's proposed fund cash balance that focuses on the upper dollar limit needed for cash purposes. When the cash balance touches the upper boundary, then a predetermined amount of securities are automatically purchased. When the cash balance touches zero or an amount slightly above zero, then a predetermined amount of securities are sold, thus increasing the cash balance.

Monetary Policy Collectively, those policies affecting the money supply, interest rates, and credit availability that are intended to promote national macroeconomic goals, particularly with respect to employment, gross national product, price level stability, and equilibrium in balance of payments. Monetary policy is directed primarily by the Board of Governors of the Federal Reserve System and by the Federal Open Market Committee. Monetary policy works by influencing the cost and availability of bank reserves. This is accomplished through (a) open-market operations (the purchase and sale of securities, primarily government securities), (b) changes in the ratio of reserves to deposits that commercial banks are required to maintain, and (c) changes in the discount rate.

Money Supply The amount of money in the economy. The supply is divided into categories. M1-A consists of currency (coin and paper notes) plus demand deposits at commercial banks, foreign banks, official institutions, and the U.S. government. M1-B consists of M1-A plus other verifiable deposits, including negotiable orders of withdrawal and automatic transfers from savings accounts at commercial banks and thrift institutions, credit unions' shared draft accounts, and demand deposits at mutual savings banks. M-2 consists of M1-B plus savings and small denomination time deposits at all depository institutions, overnight repurchase agreements at commercial banks, Eurodollars held overnight by U.S. residents other than Caribbean branches of member banks, and money market mutual fund shares. M-3 consists of M-2 plus large denomination time deposits at all depository institutions and term repurchase agreements at commercial banks and savings and loan associations.

Monthly Treasury Statement (MTS) A summary statement prepared from agency accounting reports and issued by the Treasury Department. The MTS presents the receipts, outlays, and resulting budget surplus or deficit for the month and the fiscal year to date.

Mortgage Bond A type of bond that uses property to secure the debt obligation without transferring the title.

Muckrakers Journalists and book writers who document abuses and advocate reform; in the United States, their heyday was in the early twentieth century. As a result of their efforts, many government budgeting reforms were successfully enacted, especially at the municipal level.

Multi-Year Authority Budget authority that is available for a specified period of time in excess of one fiscal year. This authority generally takes the form of two-year, three-year, or some other yearly period of availability, but may cover periods that do not coincide with the start or end of a fiscal year. For example, the authority may be available from July 1 of one year through September 30 of the following fiscal year (fifteen months). This type of multi-year authority is sometimes referred to as forward funding.

Multi-Year Budget Planning A budget-planning process designed to make sure that the long-range consequences of budget decisions are identified and reflected in the budget totals.

National Income Accounts Accounts prepared and published quarterly and annually by the U.S. Department of Commerce, providing a detailed statistical description of aggregate economic activity within the American economy. These accounts depict in dollar terms the composition and use of the nation's output and the distribution of national income to different recipients. The accounts make it possible to trace trends and fluctuations in economic activity.

Net National Product (NNP) The net market value of finished goods and services produced by labor and property supplied by the residents of the United States. Net national product equals gross national product less capital consumption allowances, which are estimates of the value of the capital goods "used up" in producing the gross national product.

Nonguaranteed Debt   A long-term debt payable from earnings of revenue-producing activities, from special assessments, or from specific nonproperty taxes. The government does not guarantee its assets and earnings in support of the debt. Also known as moral debt.

No-Year Authority   Budget authority that remains available for obligation for an indefinite period of time, usually until the objectives for which the authority was made available are attained.

Object Classification   A uniform classification identifying the transactions of the government by the nature of the goods or services purchased (such as personnel compensation, supplies and materials, and equipment), without regard to the agency involved or the purpose of the programs for which they are used. Data category titles arranged by object classification are provided in an object classification schedule.

Obligational Authority   The sum of (a) budget authority provided for a given fiscal year, (b) balances of amounts brought forward from prior years that remain available for obligation, and (c) amounts authorized to be credited to a specific fund or account during that year, including transfers between funds or accounts.

Obligations Incurred   Amounts of orders placed, contracts awarded, services received, and similar transactions during a given period that will require payments during the same or a future period. Such amounts will include outlays for which obligations had not been previously recorded and will reflect adjustments for differences between obligations previously recorded and actual outlays to liquidate those obligations.

Off-Budget Federal Entities   Certain federally owned and controlled entities whose transactions (e.g., budget authority or outlays) have been excluded from budget totals by law. The fiscal activities of these entities are therefore not reflected in either budget authority or budget outlay totals. However, the outlays of off-budget federal entities are added to the budget deficit to derive the total government deficit that has to be financed by borrowing from the public or by other means.

Off-Budget Outlays   Outlays of off-budget federal entities whose transactions have been excluded from the budget totals by law, even though these outlays are part of total government spending.

One-Year Authority   Budget authority that is available for obligation only during a specified fiscal year and that expires at the end of that time. Also known as annual authority.

Open-Ended Expenditure Forecasting   An approach to estimating future expenditures, based either on detailed work plans that often take months to prepare or on quick judgments involving a few minutes' preparation.

Open-Market Operations   The purchase and sale in the open market of various securities, chiefly marketable federal government securities, by the Federal Reserve System for the purpose of implementing Federal Reserve monetary policy. Open-market operations, one of the most flexible instruments of monetary policy, affects the reserves of member banks and thus the supply of money and the availability and cost of credit.

Operating Budget   The current year budget that guides agencies' everyday activities.

Outcome   In the systems model used in this book, a benefit to individuals and society resulting from an agency program.

Outlay   The liquidation of an obligation, usually by the issuance of a check or the disbursement of cash, but also by the maturing of interest coupons (in the case of some bonds), by the issuance of bonds or notes, or by increases in the redemption value of bonds outstanding. Outlays during a fiscal year may be for payment of obligations incurred in a prior year (prior year outlays) or in the same year. Outlays therefore derive partly from unexpended balances of prior year budget authority and partly from budget authority provided for the year in which the money is spent.

Output   In the systems model used in this book, the specific products and services produced by a government unit.

Overhead Cost *See* Indirect Cost.

Oversight Committee   The legislative committee charged with general oversight of the operation of an agency or program. In most cases, but not all, the oversight committee for an agency is also the authorizing committee for that agency's programs.

Performance Budgeting   A budget format that presents government program input and output, thus allowing easy verification of the program's economy and efficiency.

Personal Income   In the national income accounts, income received by persons (i.e., individuals, nonprofit institutions, private uninsured welfare funds, and private trust funds) from all sources. These sources include production transfer payments from government and business and government interest, which is treated as a transfer payment. Personal income is the sum of wage and salary disbursements, other income from labor, proprietary income, rental income, dividends, personal interest income, and transfer payments, less personal contributions for social insurance.

Planning-Programming-Budgeting (PPB)   An attempt in the federal government and some state and local governments to bring more analysis into the budgeting process. It is not itself an analytical technique, but it stresses the use of analytical tools in deciding budget issues related to specific government programs.

Policy Letter   Document used in government to convey executive guidance and budget ceilings to the lower levels of the executive branch.

Potential Gross National Product   An estimate of how much the economy could produce with full utilization of its productive resources and existing technology.

Prime Rate   The rate of interest charged by commercial banks for short-term loans to their most creditworthy customers.

Prior Year   The fiscal year immediately preceding the current year.

Process Analysis   An analytical approach that seeks to determine if an agency's existing process makes effective use of resources and to identify idle or partly used resources.

Producer Price Index   A set of indicators that measure average changes in the prices received in all stages of processing by producers of commodities in the manufacturing, agriculture, forestry, fishing, mining, gas and electricity, and public utilities industries. Producer price indexes can be organized either by commodity or by stage of processing (finished goods, intermediate materials, or crude materials). Stage-of-processing indexes are more useful for analyzing general price trends. Formerly known as wholesale price index.

Productivity   A measure of efficiency, usually expressed as the ratio of the quantity of output to the quantity of input used in the production of that output. Usually it focuses on output per man-hour of change or on changes in cost per unit of output.

Program and Financial Plan (PFP)   A set of summary budget tables, categorized by major programs and activities. In the federal government, the PFP includes both obligations and disbursements. For some state and local governments, obligations alone or expenditures alone are sufficient. The information in a PFP covers the prior year, current year, budget year, and budget year plus five additional years. The PFP should reflect any policy changes; it is particularly useful prior to a budget call to forecast possible agency requests.

Program Budget   A budget format in which the budget material is arranged in such a way as to aid the executive and legislature to understand the broader policy implications of their decisions.

Project Grant *See* Grant.

Property Tax   A revenue source for local and some state governments. Property (such as real estate) is normally assessed by the local government; then a tax rate is determined and applied on the basis of property value.

Quality Indicator   A measurement of characteristics, duration, content, extent, or degree used in evaluating outputs and outcomes.

Ratio Indicator   A measurement of the quantity of government service or product in relation to some larger entity such as population or area size.

Rational Decision-Making Model   An approach to budgeting that emphasizes (a) setting goals and objectives; (b) defining the alternatives; (c) analyzing the alternatives in terms of the established goals and objectives; and (d) selecting the best option.

Reactive Budget Decision Model   An approach to budgeting that is based on a stimulus-response pattern. Those who take this approach consider budgeting merely as a task to be done as defined in the job description. They act in response to the requirements of the budget calendar and the request, but give little thought to shaping events or making a difference.

Recession   A decline in overall business activity that is pervasive, substantial, and of at least several months' duration. Historically, recessions have been identified by a decline in gross national product for at least two consecutive quarters.

Registered Bonds   Type of bond that provides more protection to the bond holder because its ownership is registered on the books of the issuing government or its paying agent.

Reimbursement   A repayment for commodities sold or services furnished, either to the public or to another government account, that are authorized by law to be credited directly to specific appropriation and fund accounts. These amounts are deducted from the total obligations incurred (and outlays) in determining net obligations (and outlays) for such accounts.

Reprogramming   Utilization of funds in an appropriation account for purposes other than those contemplated at the time of appropriation.

Repurchase Agreement   An innovation of government security dealers who recognize the selling potential of securities tailored to specific short time periods. Dealers agree to repurchase a security at a specific future date, thus increasing the number of transactions and the resulting total fees from those transactions.

Research and Development   Research is systematic, intensive study directed toward fuller scientific knowledge or understanding of the subject studied. Development is the systematic use of the knowledge and understanding gained from research, directed toward the production of useful products or services.

Rescission   the consequence of executive and legislative action that cancels budget authority previously provided by Congress before the time when the authority would otherwise have lapsed (i.e., when appropriated funds would have ceased to be available for obligation). The Congressional Budget and Impoundment Control Act of 1974 (P.L. 93–344; 31 U.S.C. 1402) specifies that whenever the president determines that all or part of any budget authority will not be needed to carry out the full objectives or scope of programs for which the authority was provided, the president will propose to Congress that the funds be rescinded. Likewise, if all or part of any budget authority limited to a fiscal year—that is, annual appropriations, or budget authority of a multi-year appropriation in the last year of availability—is to be reserved from obligation for the entire fiscal year, a rescission will be proposed. Budget authority may also be proposed for rescission for reasons of fiscal policy or other reasons. Generally, an amount proposed for rescission is withheld for up to forty-five legislative days while the proposal is considered by Congress. All funds for rescission, including those withheld, must be reported to Congress in a special message. If both houses have not completed action on the rescission proposed by the president withing forty-five calendar days of continuous session, any funds withheld must be made available for obligation.

Rescission Bill   A bill or joint resolution that cancels, in whole or in part, budget authority previously granted by Congress. Rescissions proposed by the president must be transmitted in a special message to Congress. Under Sec. 1012 of the Congressional Budget and Impoundment Control Act of 1974 (P.L. 93–344), unless both houses of Congress complete action on a rescission bill within forty-five days of continuous session after receipt of the proposal, the budget authority must be made restored. (*See also* Rescission.)

Reserve Requirement   The percentage of deposit liabilities that U.S. commercial banks are required to hold as a reserve either at their Federal Reserve bank, as cash in their vaults, or as directed by state banking authorities. The reserve requirement is one of the three tools of monetary policy. Federal Reserve authorities can control the lending capacity of the banks (thus influencing the money supply) by varying the ratio of reserves to deposits that commercial banks are required to maintain.

Revenue Forecasting   Any of several systematic approaches used by governments to estimate the levels of revenue they can anticipate in future years.

Revenue Shaping   The distribution, by formula, of federal funds to state and local governments, with few or no limits on the purposes for which the funds may be used and few restrictions on the procedures that must be followed in spending the funds.

Risk Control   The reduction of risk or loss through careful procedures and practices in security, personnel safety, fire prevention, auto safety, product safety, environmental protection, and emergency resources.

Risk Funding   The provision of sufficient funds to meet loss situations, if they occur, through the most effective use of internal and external financial resources.

Rule of Penultimate Year   A technique for forecasting that calls for the forecaster to use the last completed year as a basis for estimating future revenue. This technique assumes growth in the economy and in related revenue sources.

Safety Stock   The level of inventory that should be maintained for effective operations.

Scorekeeping   A procedure for tracking the status of Congressional budgetary actions. Examples of scorekeeping documents are up-to-date tabulations and reports on Congressional actions affecting budget authority, receipts, outlays, surplus or deficit, and the public debt limit, as well as outlay and receipt estimates and reestimates. Scorekeeping data published by the Congressional Budget Office include, but are not limited to, status reports on the effects of Congressional actions (and, in the case of scorekeeping reports prepared for the Senate Budget Committee, the budget effects of potential Congressional actions), and comparisons of these actions to targets and ceilings set by Congress in the budget resolutions.

Second Concurrent Resolution on the Budget   The annual resolution adopted by Congress that contains budget ceilings classified by function for budget authority and outlays and a floor for budget receipts. This resolution may retain or revise the levels set earlier in the year in the first concurrent resolution, and may include directives to the appropriations committees and to other committees with jurisdiction over budget authority or entitlement authority. The second resolution may also direct the appropriations committees to recommend changes in budget receipts or in the statutory limit on public debt. Changes recommended by various committees pursuant to the second budget resolution are reported in a reconciliation bill (or resolution, in some cases) on which Congress must complete action by September 25, a few days before the new fiscal year commences on October 1.

Serial Bond   The most common type of bond. It matures periodically (normally, every year).

Spending Authority   The collective designation for appropriations, borrowing authority, contract authority, and entitlement authority for which the budget authority is not provided in advance by appropriation acts. The latter three authorities are also commonly referred to as backdoor authority.

Stagflation   The simultaneous existence of high unemployment and high inflation.

Substantive Law   Statutory public law other than appropriation law; sometimes referred to as basic law. Substantive law usually authorizes, in broad general terms, the executive branch to carry out a program of work. Annual determination of the amount of work to be done is usually thereafter embodied in appropriation law.

Supplemental Appropriation   An act appropriating funds in addition to those in an annual appropriation act. Supplemental appropriations provide additional budget authority beyond the original estimates for programs or activities (including new programs authorized after the date of the original appropriation act) in cases where the need for funds is too urgent to be postponed until enactment of the next regular appropriation bill. Supplemental appropriations sometimes include items not appropriated in the regular bills for lack of timely authorizations.

Sunset Legislation   Laws requiring the automatic expiration of government programs unless positive action is taken to renew them every few years by the legislature. In many cases, the sunset provisions permit the program to remain on the law books after the legal authorization for funds expires.

Tax Anticipation Note   Borrowing by a local government against future anticipated tax revenue.

Tax Certificate   A form of tax lien on property owned by a delinquent taxpayer. Tax certificates are negotiable securities and can be sold, as they represent a debt which must be liquidated before a clear title to the property can be given. At the sale of the property, certificates on the title are presented and the owner normally has one year to redeem them. If they are not redeemed, the property goes to the holder of the certificates.

Tax Credit   Any special provision of law that results in a dollar-for-dollar reduction in tax liabilities that would otherwise be due. In some cases, tax credits may be carried forward or backward from one tax year to another; other tax credits lapse if not used in the year earned. Tax credits may result in a reduction of tax collections or an increase in the value of tax refunds.

Term Bond   A bond that matures at one time. A sinking fund is normally used to accumulate the necessary funds over time.

Transaction   A financial decision, such as obligating money, deciding on disbursement, or setting aside funds for a purpose.

Transfer Payments   Money moved from one government to another or to private persons. They often serve as automatic stabilizers built into the economy. These payments normally rise substantially during periods of recession and fall during periods of prosperity. For example, the unemployed receive unemployment compensation; in recessionary times they may eventually receive welfare and food stamps as well.

Treasury Bills   The shortest-term federal security. The maturity dates of treasury bills normally vary from three to twelve months. They are sold at a discount from face value, instead of carrying a specific rate of interest.

Trend-Line Approach   A forecasting technique that develops and extends an agency's trend line of expenditures or revenue from the past into the desired forecast period.

Unemployment Rate   In economic statistics, the total number of people who, during a specific week, had no employment but were available for work and who sought employment within the past four weeks, were laid off from their jobs, or were waiting to report a new job within thirty days; expressed as a percentage of the civilian labor force. (*See also* Employment Rate.)

Unemployment Rate, Insured   The number of insured unemployed i.e., those persons who are eligible to receive unemployment compensation benefits—expressed as a percentage of covered employment.

Volume Indicators   The quantity of a government unit's service or products, such as the number of graduates from a university.

Voucher   A document that confirms the fact that a financial transaction has taken place.

Wages and Salaries   Monetary remuneration of employees, including the compensation, commissions, tips, bonuses, and receipts in kind that represent income to the recipients.

Warrant   A banking service in which a draft is paid through a bank with the express permission of the government. It is used to slow and control disbursements. When a warrant is presented for payment, the bank will not pay until the warrant is accepted by the government.

Wholesale Price Index   *See* Producer Price Index.

Wise Budget Model   An approach to budgeting whose proponents recognize that politics is extremely important and sometimes of overriding importance. They also believe that, while analysis has its limitations, it can often greatly help in decision-making situations.

Zero Base Budgeting (ZBB)   An approach to public budgeting in which each budget year's activities are judged anew, with no reference to the policy precedents or dollar amounts of past years.

INDEX

Accelerated Cost Recovery Schedules (ACRS), 246
Accountability
  auditing and, 196–97
  as main purpose of budget system, 3
  MIS and, 216
  systems model and, 132–33
Accountant's perspective, 4
Accounting, 224–38
  basic governmental, 228–29
  budget execution and, 206
  financial administration, 227–29
  fundamentals, 224–27
  reports and analyses, 229–38
  system design, 229
Accounts payable, 226
Accrual method of accounting, 227
ACRS, 246
ACTION, Budget Division of, 78–79
Adaptive filtering, 148
Adjustments, current year, 208
Administration
  controls on expenditures of, 209–14
  financial, 227–29
  pension fund, 333
  risk management, 327–38
Administrative reservation, 209, 214
Adoption, legislative, 118–23
Advisory Commission on Intergovernmental Relations, 333
Agency, 78–86
  as advocate, 93–95
  budget behavior, 83–86: Budget Office, 78–81; preparing for hearings, 91–93
  budget cycle and, 124–25, 128
  call, 108–10
  cultivation of active clientele, 77–78
  influence patterns, 73–75
  objectives, 75–76
  review process for, 110–18, 129
  securities, 223
Agenda for budget, 67–68
Allotments, 12, 208–9, 212–14
"Allowance" letter, 105
Alternative choice models, 158
American Institute of Certified Public Accountants (AICPA), 198
American Municipal Bond Assurance Corporation (AMBAC), 250
American Revolution, budgeting issues in, 36
Analysis, 131–62
  accounting, 229–38
  auditing, 163, 196–201
  benefit-cost concept, 156–61
  budget examination, 163, 172–87: automation and, 185–87; code of ethics in, 173–74; detailed, 184–85; of effectiveness and efficiency, 182–83; of emphases and change, 179–81; forecasting and, 183–84; information sources for, 172; responsiveness in, 181–82; of services performed, 174–75
  causal, 144–45
  crosswalks, 140–42, 205

  elementary, 138–40
  expenditure forecasting, 145–49
  factors influencing results of, 168–70
  performance time, 190–91
  in PPB, 47–48
  process, 187–95
  productivity, 149–56
  program, 56, 163, 164–71
  program evaluation, 163, 195–96
  revenue forecasting, 143–45
  theoretical foundation, 132–38: application difficulties, 135–37; data measure constraints, 137–38
  time series, 143–44, 147–48
  unit cost, 144, 182
"Anniversary put," 252
Annual Report on budget options, 56
Anticipation notes, 244, 245
Anticlientele groups, 77
Anti-deficiency Act, 85, 204
Appropriation, 12–13
  expense and, ledger, 231–34
  structure, 141
  transfer of, 208
Aronson, J.R., 229
Assets, 235. *See also* Accounting
Auditing
  analysis, 163, 196–201
  evaluation and, 10, 13–14
  in federal budget cycle, 129
  property management and, 308
  self-audit, 150–51
Audits of State and Local Governmental Units, 198
Authorizations, 12–13, 205–6, 233
Automation, preparation by, 185–87
Autoregressive moving averages, 148
Averages, moving, 147, 148

Backdoor spending, 58–60, 95, 176
Balanced budgets, format design and, 104–5
Balance sheet, 235–37
Bankruptcy, 258–59
Bank services, commercial, 220
Bar-code technology, 314–16
Bargaining approach to expenditure forecasting, 146
Beame, A., 4
Beard, C., 38
Behavior, budget, 72–100
  agency, 83–86: budget office, 78–81; preparing for hearings, 91–93
  budget officers, 79–85, 88–89
  cultivation of active clientele, 77–78
  decision-making models and, 86–87
  demonstrating results, 90–91
  institutional roles, 73–77
  strategies, 89, 93–100
Benefit(s)
  classification of, 159
  -cost concept, 156–61
  employee, 326, 328–33
Bidding, 214, 261, 309–10, 326
Bills, treasury, 223, 224

Bolling, R., 62
Bond, bonding, 261–67
  anticipation notes (BANs), 244, 245
  authority, 13
  counsel, 264
  ratings, 267
  types of, 243–53, 257, 261, 262
Box-Jenkins method, 148
Bricklin, D., 186
Briefing information, 111
Brookings Institution, 38
Brownlow committee, 40
Buck, A.E., 38
Budget
  agenda, 67–68
  behavior. See Behavior, budget
  building the, 105–10
  calendar, 106–7, 188
  call, 106–10
  concepts, 208–9, 214
  cycle. See Cycle, budget
  emphasis, 179–81
  estimates, 14, 55–56, 112, 159
  examination. See under Analysis
  execution system, 204–7
  format, 102–5
  message, 111–12
  milestones, 113
  officer, 79–85, 88–89, 103
  purposes, 3, 45
  realities, 7–9
  reviewers, 83, 88, 93–95, 172
  summary, 112
  timetable, 57–58, 113–15
  -wise person, 87
  year (BY), 6–7
Budget and Accounting Act of 1921, 39–40
Budget and Accounting and Procedures Act of 1950, 41
Budgeting
  approaches to, 41–46
  economy's influence on, 22–25
  in 1800s, 37
Bureau of the Budget, 39–40

Caiden, N., 65
Calendar, budget, 106–7, 188
California Proposition 13, 292
Call, budget, 106–10
Call provision, 222
Capital budgeting, 259–61
Capital facilities planning, 260–61
Capital financing, 246–59
  creative, 247–49, 261, 262
  in 1980s, 246–47, 248
  nontraditional, 249–50
  tests and limits of, 253–579
Capitalism, 15–16
Carter, J. E., 30, 50
Carter administration, 271
Cash
  flow problem, 218
  internal control, 215–16
  management, 218–24
  method of accounting, 227
Categorizations in budgets, 179–80
Causal analysis, 144–45
Cautions, strategy, 99–100
Central Bank, 25–26
Central stores, 312–14
Certificates of deposit (CDs), 223–24
Certificates of indebtedness, 243
Chang, S., 145
Checklist
  for review of performance reports, 176–77
  risk and insurance, 318–21
Checks, internal control of, 215–16
Chief executive, role in program analysis, 171

Choate, P., 246
Circuit breakers, 292, 298
Classification Act of 1949, 41
Clearance process, legislative, 53
Clientele, 73–78
Code of ethics, 173–74
Coefficient of dispersion, 300–301
Colonial America, budgeting in, 36–37
Commercial bank services, 220
Competitive bidding, 214, 261, 309–10, 326
Computers
  automation with, 185–87
  bar-code technology, 314–16
Conduct, professional, 173–74
Conflict, intra-legislative, 94–95
Congressional Budget and Impoundment Control Act of 1947, 53–62
Congressional Budget Office (CBO), 54–59, 114
Congressional budget process, 126–27
Congressional budget timetable, 113–15
Consensus forecasting, 183
Consistency, determining, 142
Contingent liability, 244
Contract authority, 13
Control
  cash internal, 215–16
  designing, 204–8
  expenditure, 209–15
  of federal budget, 128
  importance of, 3
  MIS and, 216
  of payables, 220–21
  property, 314
  reform stressing, 45–46
  risk, 322–24
Cooptation, 195
Cost
  analysis, marginal, 139–40
  -benefit concept, 156–61
  -effectiveness analysis, 157
  estimates, 55–56
  maintenance, 311
  opportunity, 4, 160
Counsel, bond, 264
Counterstrategies, 98
Coverage. See Insurance
Credit, 250
Crime coverage, 326
Crosswalks, 141–42, 205
Current program expenses, 185
Current Services Budget, 57, 114
Current year (CY), 6–7, 208
Cutters' strategies, 97–98
Cycle, budget, 10–14
  assessment, 302
  capital, 261
  federal, 124–29
  local government, 14
  nature of, 10–11
  phases of, 7, 11–14

Data measures, 134–38
Deadlines, 83, 113
Debt
  classifications of, 243–44
  defined, 242
  early developments in concept, 245–46
  records, 266–67
  service, 255
  short-term, 244–45, 256
Debt administration, 241–68
  bonding, 261–67
  capital budgeting and, 259–61
  capital financing, 246–59
  creative, 247–49, 261, 262
  in 1980s, 246–47, 248
  nontraditional, 249–59
  tests and limits of, 253–57

Decision-making
  current federal budget, 66
  format design and, 103–4
  models, 18–22, 44–46, 86–87
Deductibles, 325
Default risk, 224, 226
Deficit spending, 29
Demand responsive programs, 175
Democracy, 15–16
Design
  of accounting system, 229
  of bond issue, 261–64
  of control, 204–8
Detailed budget examination, 184–85
Detailed revenue and expenditure estimates, 112–13
Differential, price-related, 301–2
Disability/survivor protection, 331
"Disclosure Guidelines for Offerings of Securities by
    State and Local Governments," 265
Discounting, 26, 140, 159–60
Dispersion, coefficient of, 300–301
Document, executive budget, 111–13
Double-entry system, 228
Duncombe, S., 2, 3–4

Econometric forecasting, 145, 148–49
Economic Ordering Quality, 218, 219
Economic Ordering Quantity model, 313
Economic Recovery Tax Act of 1981, 246
Economy
  economist's perspective, 4–5
  influence of government action on, 28
  influence on budgeting of, 22–25
  stagflation, 31
Effectiveness and efficiency, program, 182–83
Emergencies, government financial, 258–59
Emphasis of budget, 179–81
Employee benefits, 326, 328–33
Encumbrance, 214, 226, 233
England, early budgeting influence of, 35–36
Enrichment, job, 150
Entitlement programs, 30
Envelope budgeting, 52
Equalization rate, state, 298–99
Estimates, budgetary, 14, 55–56, 112, 159. See also
    Forecasting
Ethics, code of, 173–74
Evaluation
  auditing and, 10, 13–14
  program, 195–96
  risk, 317–22
Evolution of reform, 38–46
Examination, budget, See under Analytical processes
Execution system, budget, 204–7
Executive
  branch, economic policy mechanism in, 25
  budget document, 111–13
  budget hearings, 110–11
  focus, 46–53
  influence patterns, 73–75
  policy message, 108
  role of, 76
Expenditure(s)
  in accounting, 226
  controls, 209–15
  estimates, 112
  federal, 17
  forecasting, 145–49
  local government, 17–18
Expense ledger, appropriation and, 231–34
Exponential smoothing, 147–48
Exposure identification, risk, 317–22
External audits, 198
Externalities, 160

Facilities planning, capital, 260–61
Feasibility of program analysis, 165
Federal budget
  cycle, 124–29
  expenditures, 17

grants-in-aid, 270–76
process, 59, 65–66
Federal Electronic Funds Transfer System, 220
Federal income tax, 38–39, 303–4
Federalism, 17–18
Federalist Paper No. 10, 15
Federal Reserve System, 25–27
Federal Tax Act (1982) (TEFRA), 246
Filtering, adaptive, 148
Financial administration, 227–29
Financial reports, 229–38
Financing. See Capital financing; Operating budget
Fiscal analysis, 56
Fiscal policy, 27–32
Fiscal year, 6
Float, playing the, 220
Flow charting, process analysis and, 188
Ford, G., 61–62
Forecasting
  budget examination of, 183–84
  consensus, 183
  econometric, 145, 148–49
  expenditure, 146–49
  identifying errors in, 231–34
  program financial schedule, 105–6
  revenue, 143–45
Foreclosure, 303
Format, budget, 102–5
Frankston, R., 186
Fraud, 214–15
Full Employment Act of 1946, 41
"Full-faith-and-credit" debt, 244
Fund, funding
  balance change, 234–35
  concept, 227–28
  no-year, 12–13
  pension, 242, 328–33
  risk, 324–26
  sinking, 243
  transfer, 95

Gallatin, A., 37
General Accounting Office (GAO), 40, 128, 129,
    198–200
"General Ledger and Budgeting Accounting Program,"
    237–38
General obligation debt, 247–49
Gimmicks, 84
Governmental Accounting, Auditing and Financial
    Reporting, 266
Government Corporations Act of 1945, 41
Government Finance Officers Association, 103
Gramm-Latta I, 63
Grant(s)
  in accounting, 226–27
  anticipation notes (GANs), 244
  -in-aid, federal, 270–76
  programs, 185
Great Depression, 23–25
Gross National Product (GNP), 28, 29, 270–73,
    284–85
Gubernatorial policy, 3
Guidance, budget, 108
Guilick, L., 38

Hamilton, A., 37, 40
Hatry, H.P., 168
Hearings
  executive budget, 110–11
  legislative, 115
  preparing for, 91–93, 110
High-risk strategy, 96–97
Hills, C.A., 62
Hitch, C., 47
Honesty, reputation for, 194–95
Hoover Commission, 41, 44, 47
House Appropriations Committee, 37
How Effective Are Your Community Services, 196
Hyperinflation, 22, 23

Ideal-rational model, 21
Ideology, 14–16
IFMS, 217–18
Immunity, tort doctrine of government, 318
Impact theory, program, 133–35
Implementation
  of federal budget, 128
  of PPB, 48
Impoundment, 12, 60–62
Improved program, 181–82
Income approach to property assessment, 298
Incomes taxes, 38–39, 297, 303–4. *See also* Revenue
  systems
Incremental model of decision-making, 18–19, 21,
  44–46
Industrial revenue bonds, 247
Inflation, 30–32, 56
Information sources for budget examination, 172
Institutional roles, 73–77
Instrumentation, 196
Insurance
  bond, 250–51
  risk management and, 317–23, 326–37
  self-, 324–26
Integrated financial management systems (IFMS),
  217–18
Interest rates, investments and, 222
Intergovernmental revenue systems, 270–76
Internal audits, 198
Internal control, cash, 215–16
Internal service functions, 307–35
  pension funds, 328–33
  property management, 308–16
  risk management, 316–28: administration, 327–28;
    control, 322–24; exposure identification and
    evaluation, 317–22; funding and self-insurance,
    324–26; insurance, 317–23, 326–37
Interpersonnel skills, 193–94
Intra-legislative conflict, 94–95
Inventory, 226, 312–14
Investments, 221–23, 331–33
Investment Tax Credit (ITC), 30, 246

Jasper, H., 54
Jefferson, T., 37, 40
Job enrichment, 150
Johnson, L.B., 30, 47
Journal, defined, 227
Judgment, 243–44
Justification, program impact theory and, 134

Klay, W.E., 143

Labor-management negotiations, 329
Laffer, A.B., 31
Laffer curve, 31
Lease
  agreements, 252–55
  -cost purchasing, 311
  rental bond, 245
Ledgers, 227, 231–34
Legislation, sunset, 65
Legislative branch, economic policy mechanism in, 25
Legislative clearance process, 53
Legislative reform. *See under* Reforms
Legislature
  adoption by, 118–23
  budget consideration in, 115–18
  influence patterns, 73–75
  role of, 76
Lehan, E.A., 102, 253
Letter of credit, 250
Leverage lease, 253
Liabilities
  in accounting, 235
  contingent, 244
  coverage, 326
  pension, 244, 328
  third-party, 317
Lien, 243

Line-item budgeting, 41–44
Line-item format, 102
Line-item vetoes, 12
Line manager, 191–95
Line of credit, 250
"Loan-to-lender" financing, 251
Lobbying, 15, 77
Local government
  authorization and appropriation distinction, 13
  budget cycles, 14
  current budgetary situation, 66–70
  debt. *See* Debt administration
  dependency index, 276
  expenditures, 17–18
  influence patterns in, 75
Losses, potential, 318
Lost time accident, 322
Lotus 1-2-3 program, 187
Lynn, J.T., 62

Macroeconomic policy. *See* Fiscal policy
Maier, H., 4
Maintenance cost, 311
Maintenance program, 310
Management
  budget as instrument of, 3
  as budget purpose, 45
  cash, 218–24
  determining consistency of, 142
  format design and, 105
  operating budget and, 207
  process analysis and, 192–93
  property, 308–16
  reform stressing, 46
  risk. *See under* Risk
Management by objectives (MBO), 13, 49–50, 141–42,
  205
Management information systems (MIS), 216–18
Manager, line, 191–95
Marginal cost analysis, 139–40
Marketable securities, 221–24
Market price, property, 295
Massachusetts Welfare Model, 148
MBO, 13, 49–50, 141–42, 205
McNamara, R., 47
Message
  budget, 111–12
  executive policy, 108
Microcomputers, 186
Milestones, budget, 113
Miller, G., 103
Miller-Orr Model, 218–20
"Minimum level of service," 188
Mini-municipal bonds, 253
MIS, 216–18
Models
  alternative choice, 158
  decision-making, 18–22, 44–46, 86–87
Modifications to budget, 117
Monetary policy, 25–27
Moral debt, 244
Mortgage bonds, 243
Moving averages, 147, 148
Multiple regression, 153
Municipal Bond Insurance Association (MBIA), 250
Municipal bonds, 246–47, 249, 253, 261, 262
Municipal Finance Officers Association, 103
Municipalities. *See also* Local government
  budget reform, 37–38
  debt administration, 256–57
  financial emergencies, 257–58
Murray, K., 257

National Capital Area Chapter of American Society for
  Public Administration, 66, 68–69
National Council of Governmental Accounting
  (NCGA), 198
National Municipal League, 38
National Safety Council, 322
Negotiable certificates of deposit (CD), 223–24

Negotiated bidding, 261
Negotiations, labor-management, 329
New programs, 96, 98–99, 181–82
New York Bureau of Municipal Research, 38, 47
New York City financial crisis, 257–58
Nixon, R., 30, 53–54, 60–61
Nixon administration, 49–50, 73–74, 75
Nonperformance option, 136–37
Nonreactive measures, 138
Norms, accounting, 225–27
Notes, 223, 224, 243–45
Notice of sale, bond, 265
No-year funds, 12–13

Object classification budget, 38
Obligations in accounting, 225–26
O'Neill, T.P., 63
Open Market Committee, 26
Operating budgets, 203–24
    capital vs., 259–60
    cash management and investments, 218–24
    concepts and reports, 208–18
    defining, 6
    designing control in, 204–8
    MBO and, 13
Operating lease, 253
Opportunity cost, 4, 160
Ordinances, 118–23
Organizational size, process analysis and, 188–91
Original issue discount bond, 252
Output data measures, 134–36

Parliament vs. King in England, 35–36
Payables. See also Expenditures
    accounts, 226
    controlling, 220–21
Pension funds, 242, 328–33
Performance
    budgeting, 44, 102, 103
    reports, 176–77
    standards, 206
    time analysis, 190–91
Personal property, 290
Personnel, 176–77, 178
Peterson, J., 145
Phillips curve, 24, 30
Pitfalls, 170
Planning
    budget as instrument of, 3–4
    as budget purpose, 45
    in capital budgeting, 259–61
    MIS and, 216
    phase in budget cycle, 10, 11
    PPB, 46–49
    reform stressing, 46
"Playing the float," 220
Policy, 10–13
    analysis by CBO, 56
    execution, 10, 12–13
    fiscal, 27–32
    formulation, 10, 11–12
    gubernatorial, 3
    letter, 106
    message, executive, 108
    pension fund, 329–33
    risk management, 327
Politics
    choice of commercial bank and, 220
    politician's perspective, 4
    realities of, 9–10
    sensitive subjects in, 184
Portability of pension plan, 331
Portfolio, 224
Post-audits, 197
Potential losses, 318
PPB (planning-programming-budgeting), 46–49
Pre-audits, 197, 206
Present value, discounting to, 140
Presidential budget, 114, 124–25

Preventative maintenance program, 310
Price-related differential, 301–2
Prior years (PY), 6–7
Private opportunity costs, 160
Process analysis, 187–95
Procurement, 309–10
Productivity analysis, 149–56
Professional conduct, 173–74
Program and financial plans (PFP), 180–81
Program Evaluation and Review Technique (PERT), 183
Program(s)
    analysis, 56, 163, 164–71
    budgeting, 44
    defining, 187–88
    demand responsive, 175
    demonstrating results, 90–91, 170–71
    effectiveness and efficiency, 182–83
    entitlement, 30
    evaluation, 163, 195–96
    financial schedule, 105–6
    format, 102
    goals, 196
    grant and trust, 185
    impact theory, 133–35
    improved, 181–82
    inputs and outputs, 176–79
    new, 96, 98–99, 181–82
    nonperformance option, 136–37
    structure, 141
Property
    insurance, 326
    management, 308–16
    tax, 276–303: assessment of, 295–303; criticism of, 290–91; determining rate of, 302–3; reforms, 291–92; Serrano v. Priest, 292–95; as simple idea, 276–90
Prospectus, bond, 264–65
Public budgeting, 1–34
    budget realities and, 9–10
    decision-making models of, 18–22, 44–46, 86–87
    federalism and, 17–18
    fiscal policy and, 27–32
    ideology and, 14–16
    monetary policy and, 25–27
    operational definition of, 6–7
    perspectives on, 2–6
Public relations, 3
Purchasing, 309–12
Put option, 252
PY, 6–7
Pyhrr, P.A., 50

Qualitative revenue forecasting, 143

Ratings, bond, 267
Rational model of decision-making, 19, 21, 22, 45, 46, 86–87
Reactive budget person, 87
Reagan, R., 31, 52–53, 62–63
Real property, 290
Reconciliation, 57–58, 62–64
Records. See Accounting; Reports
Red tape/fraud dilemma, 214–15
Reforms, 35–71
    evolution of modern, 38–46
    executive focus on, 46–52
    historical, 35–38
    legislative focus on, 52–70: backdoor spending, 58–60, 95, 176; impoundment, 12, 60–62; motivations, 52–54; state and local challenges, 66–70; sunset legislation, 65; united Congressional reform, 54–58
    property tax, 291–92
Regression analysis, 145, 152–53, 191
Reinterpretation, 10
Relationships, defining, 138–39
Replacement cost approach, 298
Replacement purchasing, 310–11

Reports
  debt, 266–67
  as expenditure control, 214
  financial, 229–38
  operating budget, 208–18
  performance, 176–77
  risk management, 327–38
Repurchase agreement (REPO), 223, 224
Reputation, 88–89, 194–95
Reservation, administrative 209, 214
Reserves, 26, 235
Responsibility, fixing, 204, 205–6
Responsiveness of budget examiner, 181–82
Results, program, 90–91, 170–71
Retirement benefits, 330–31
Revenue
  anticipation notes (RANs), 244
  bond, 245, 247, 248, 257
  estimates, 14, 112
  forecasting, 143–45
  statement of, 230
Revenue Act of 1964, 30
Revenue systems, 269–305
  income tax, 38–39, 197, 303–4
  intergovernmental, 270–76
  property tax and controversy, 276–202: assessment,
    295–303; criticisms, 290–91; determining rate
    of, 302–3; reforms, 291–92; *Serrano* v. *Priest,*
    292–95; as simple idea, 276–90
  sales tax, 297, 304–5
Review. *See also* Analysis
  agency, 110–18, 129
  PERT, 183
  preliminary, of property management, 308–9
Reviewers, budget, 83, 88, 93–95, 172
Risk
  in benefit-cost analysis, 160
  default, 224, 226
  management, 316–28; administration of, 327–28;
    control, 322–24; exposure identification and
    evaluation, 317–22; funding and self-insurance,
    324–26; insurance, 317–23, 326–37
  in spenders' strategies, 96–97
Roosevelt, F.D., 24–25, 40

Safe-harbor lease, 253
Safety, risk control for, 322–23
Sale, bond, 265–66
Sale-leaseback, 253, 254–55
Sales ratios, 295–98
Sales tax, 297, 304–5
San Antonio Independent School District v. *Rodriguez,*
  294–95
Satisficing model of decision-making, 19, 21
Schedule, program financial, 105–6
School financing, property tax and, 292–95
Schwartz, E., 229
Securities, marketable, 221–24
Self-audit, 150–51
Self insurance, 324–26
Sensitive subjects, politically, 184
Serial bonds, 243, 261
Serrano v. *Priest,* 292–95
Service
  internal. *See* Internal service functions
  minimum level of, 188
  performed, budget examination of, 174–75
  units, 136
Shannon, J., 290
Short-term debt, 244–45, 256
Simple regression analysis, 152–53
Simplification, work, 150
Sinking fund, 243
Skills, interpersonnel, 193–94
Sleight-of-hand techniques, 95–96, 176
Smith, L., 54
Smoothing, exponential, 147–48
"Social contract" political thought, 38
Socialism, 16

Special obligation bond, 246
Specification, procurement, 310
Spenders' strategies, 95–97, 98
Spending. *See also* Expenditures
  backdoor, 58–60, 95, 176
  deficit, 29
Staff analysis, 189
Staff units, 136
"Stages of problem solving" model, 19–22
Stagflation economy, 31
Standard and Poor's, 256, 267
Standardization, 310
Standards
  auditing, 198–200
  performance, 206
Standards for Audit of Governmental Organizations,
  Programs, Activities and Functions, 198
State equalization rate, 298–99
State government
  authorization and appropriation distinction, 13
  current budgetary situation, 66–70
  debt. *See* Debt administration
  influence patterns in, 75
  power over local governments, 17
State income taxes, 304
Statement of revenue, 230
Statistical analysis, 139
Stock, safety, 312–13. *See also* Purchasing
Strategies, 89, 93–100
Summary of budget, 112
Sunset legislation, 65
Systems model, 132–33, 135–38

Taboos of hearings, 93
Taft, W.H., 39
Target base budgeting (TBB), 52
Tax(es). *See also* Revenue systems
  advantage for municipal bonds, 261, 262
  anticipation notes (TANs), 244, 245
  base, 295
  burden, 270–71, 288–89
  equivalency table, 262
  -exempt bonds, 247
  -exempt commerical paper (TECP), 251–52
  status, investment yields and, 223
Technology. *See* Computers
TEFRA, 246
Tender option, 252
Tennessee accounting system, 237–38
Term bonds, 243
Third-party liabilities, 317
Time series analysis, 143–44, 147–48
Timetable, budget, 57–58, 113–15
Tinbergen, J., 145
Tort doctrine of government immunity, 318
Total-cost purchasing, 311
Transactions, recording. *See* Accounting
Transfer
  of appropriations, 208
  fund, 95
  payments, 29–30, 270–76
Travel Expense Act of 1949, 41
Treasury bills, 223, 224
Treasury notes, 223, 224
Trend analysis, 143–44, 147
Trust programs, 185
Turn-downs, 89

U.S. Constitution, shaping of, 36–37
U.S. Department of Agriculture, 50
U.S. Department of Transportation, 74
U.S. Maritime Administration, 73–74, 75
U.S. Office of Management and Budget (OMB), 47,
  53, 73–74, 75, 124–25, 128, 129, 204
U.S. Treasury obligations, 223
Underwriter, 261–62, 264
Unemployment, 22–23, 30–32
Unfunded pension liability, 244
Unit cost analysis, 146, 182
Use tax, 304–5

Vagueness, 6
Variable rate securities, 252
Vesting, 331
Vetoes, line-item, 12
VisiCalc program, 186
Voucher, defined, 227

Warehousing, 312–14
Warrants, 243, 253
Watergate crisis, 54

Wildavsky, A., 19, 21, 22, 104
Windfalls, 170
"Window put," 252
Wise budget person, 87
Withholding of income tax, 304
Workpapers, audit, 199–201
Work simplification, 150

Zero-base budgeting, 46, 50–52
Zero-coupon bonds (ZCBs), 249, 250